Iowa ▪ Kansas ▪ Nebraska ▪ North Dakota ▪ South Dakota

PRAIRIE LANDS
Gardener's Guide

Published by Cool Springs Press, a Division of Thomas Nelson, Inc., P. O. Box 141000, Nashville, Tennessee, 37214.

Barash, Cathy Wilkinson.
   Prairie lands gardener's guide / Cathy Wilkinson Barash.
       p. cm.
   Includes bibliographical references (p.   ).
   ISBN 1-59186-069-5 (pbk.)
   1. Prairie gardening. 2. Prairie plants. 3. Native plants for cultivation. I. Title.
SB434.3.B37 2004
635.9'5178--dc22

                              2003021654

First Printing 2004
Printed in the United States of America
10 9 8 7 6 5 4 3 2 1

Managing Editor: Ramona D. Wilkes
Horticulture Editor: Ruth Rogers Clausen
Copyeditor: Sally Graham
Production Design: S.E. Anderson
Cover Designer: Sheri Ferguson Kimbrough

On the cover: Sunflower (*Helianthus annuus*), photographed by Rob Cardillo

Visit the Thomas Nelson website at www.ThomasNelson.com

Iowa ▪ Kansas ▪ Nebraska ▪ North Dakota ▪ South Dakota

PRAIRIE LANDS
Gardener's Guide

Cathy Wilkinson Barash

COOL
SPRINGS
PRESS

Nashville, Tennessee
A Division of Thomas Nelson, Inc.
www.ThomasNelson.com

Dedication

I dedicate this book to my mother and father, May and Fritz Wilkinson, who instilled in me from a very young age the love of gardening, a respect for all life, the appreciation of the beauty that surrounds me, and the pleasure that comes from enjoying the fruits of the harvest—both ornamental and edible. I only wish they were here to see the gardener and person I am now and will continue to become.

To my uncle, Ted Key, who at 91 still shares his love of gardening, thanks for having "cow padding" as part of our annual pre-prandial Thanksgiving tradition.

Acknowledgments

There are so many people who have helped me—not only on this book in particular, but also on the life-long road of gardening that led to it. Thank you all. The Garden Writers Association (GWA)—as a group and individual members—are always supportive, knowledgeable, and helpful. The network continues to awe me. Thanks in particular to Doug Jimerson, who encouraged my move from Long Island to Des Moines nearly seven years ago. Although prepared for the winters, no one warned me about the summers—and I had thought Long Island was hot and humid! My gratitude goes out to my fellow gardeners in the Prairie Lands states—professional and amateur—who have taught me by example or by other means, how to adapt and garden in this region and introduced me to a whole new world of plants. For fairness, the listing is alphabetical: Janine Adams, James Baggett, Jamie Beyers, David Cavagnaro, David Clem, Teva Dawson, Cindy Haynes, Nancy Itani, Rosemary Kautzsky, Dave Kvitne, Alan and Helene MacGruder, Elvin McDonald, Michael McKinley, Darrell Mertz, Luke Miller, Kathy and Raymond New, Steve Nordmeyer, Marilyn Rogers, Glen and Katherine Siebert, Ton Stam, Todd Steadman, Andy Sullivan, Kristin Bean Sullivan, Karen Weir-Jimerson, and Deb Wiley. And even my non-gardening landlords, Joe and Sarah Hlad, who really had no idea what I meant when I said I wanted to tear up the front lawn and put in a garden, which is exactly what I did—not a blade of non-ornamental grass in sight.

Special thanks to Felder Rushing who stepped in at the last moment to help a friend in need. Without him, I could not have finished this book.

My deep gratitude to Hank McBride at Cool Springs Press for giving me the opportunity to write this book and in the process learn so much about this amazing area of the country. And last, but far from least, I am truly grateful for having Ramona Wilkes as my editor for this project. Her compassion, understanding, gentle nudging, and guidance (and of course great editing) have been incomparable.

Table of Contents

Featured Plants *for the Prairie Lands*

Welcome to Gardening
in the Prairie Lands

Not being a native to the Prairie Lands States, I believe I have a different perspective on gardening here than someone who grew up in this region. I had no idea how spoiled I was living most of my life on Long Island, where the weather is buffered by the warmth of the Gulf Stream (and there is that huge ocean on one side of the island, and the Sound that separates it from Connecticut on the other). I can count on one hand the times the thermometer dipped below zero. I gardened in comparably tropical Zone 7 (with microclimates of Zone 8), in fairly well-drained, rich, acid soil—the soil the glaciers had moved in the last Ice Age from New England.

The Unique Prairie Lands

Moving to Iowa more than six years ago, I had 55 large cartons filled with potted-up outdoor plants accompanied by my furniture in the moving van—in August. No guarantees on their being alive upon arrival, according to the movers. Nevertheless, if you are a gardener, you know how hard it is to leave behind that part of yourself, especially if you have been gardening in the same place for 18 years. It rained (one of those nice light continual rains) for two days before moving day. How the movers even lifted my cat's personal planter—a half whiskey barrel planted with catmint, chives, and dianthus—I'll never know. But because of the gentle and complete soaking from the rain, the plants not only survived the trip but 10 days in storage until they were finally unloaded in my new back yard.

Needless to say, my priority was getting things out of boxes and into the ground. My plan included getting plants through moving and transplant shock, established in their new home, and then worrying more about placement the next spring. I am the first to admit that I did not do the basic research I should have. Yet, for me, learning by trial and error leaves a more indelible impression on my brain than reading something on the Internet or in a book.

Alas, back then there were no regional gardening books; in fact, many books had a Northeast bias. That is another reason I was so excited to do this book and share my experiences with other gardeners.

Weather

When I moved here, I was warned about the winters, hearing stories of a month with no sun, days on end when the high is in the minus twenties. What no one warned me about was the summers and how

A Colorful Mixture of Annuals and Perennials

unbearably hot and humid (yet dry) they can be. Nor did they mention the wind. These are the basic elements you have to deal with when creating a great garden in the Prairie Lands. Yes, it can be challenging, but so rewarding when it all works. All you need to do is drive around and see the splendid and varied gardens that people have successfully created. And, I'll bet that those charming small front yard gardens on farms are not molly-coddled. Either it grows or it doesn't. Many of my Zone 7 plants did not make it through the first mild winter.

Fortunately, one of the gardening tenets I grew up with was not to bemoan a dead plant. Unless it is diseased, it goes on the compost pile and will become food to nurture the soil for future plants. That was good, because by the next summer, I had a lot of compost in the works.

Understanding Hardiness Zones

After many years of studying and recording winter temperatures (mostly though agricultural colleges and Cooperative Extension records), the USDA (United States Department of Agriculture) came up with a remarkable tool for farmers and gardeners alike—the USDA Hardiness Zone Map. The original map listed 10 zones, each with a low winter temperature range 10 degrees to the next zone. In full color, you could look at the map and see you lived in Zone 4, for example, and know that the average minimum temperature would be between minus 30 and minus 20 degrees Fahrenheit. Zone 3 was 10 degrees chillier—between minus 30 to minus 40, while Zone 5 seemed almost balmy at minus 10 to minus 20.

The plant growers caught on, as did books about plants, so much less trial and error was necessary. (Remember my axiom – a dead plant is merely new compost in the making). In the 1990s, the map was revised. In general, the demarcations were the same, with the northern half of both Iowa and Nebraska a Zone 4, with the southern sections Zone 5. However, they divided each Zone in half, calling them A and B, with the increments between each of these only 5 degrees.

As this book goes to press, they are working on revising the Hardiness Zone Map once again. It is expanding to 15 Zones (adding warmer ones, which may affect those of you who are snowbirds and garden in the South in winter) and removing the A & B. What was remarkable to me when I first gazed upon a rough draft of the map was that most of Iowa and Nebraska were solid Zone 5, with only small patches of Zone 4 dotted in the northern regions. Are there any non-believers in global warming now? In addition, this map is reflective of changes within a little more than a decade!

In moving to Iowa I have saved thousands of dollars on plants. Now as I look through the plant catalogues, when it's -10 degrees Fahrenheit, instead of dreaming over the pictures or reading the captivating descriptions I head right to the heart of the matter—the hardiness zone of the plant. Although my choices are more limited for Zone 5, I am discovering wonderful new plants all the time, and falling madly in love with them. And yes, some of my prized plants from New York still thrive, but they are interspersed with a vast majority of newly discovered gems. My precious 'Scentsation' lilac lasts weeks longer here in the cooler spring. As spring starts later, the season is compressed with wonderful combinations blooming together here that would not exist in the rush of eastern spring.

Learn by Doing

One of the best ways to learn what will grow well is to visit friends and neighbors to see what's in their yards. If you're a novice, and you admire some perennials they have a lot of, offer to help divide them when the time comes; no doubt you'll be rewarded by a division or two for your own garden.

Ask questions. Gardeners are the friendliest people, usually willing to share their knowledge. How can anyone resist when you walk up to them as they are working in their garden and you complement the garden and the plants? Ask specific questions about plants that pique your interest. Carry a pocket-sized notebook to take down notes. Not only will they be impressed, you'll remember and do what they suggest. This method had definitely worked for me. Looking for a place to live, I was directed to one street in the historic Sherman Hill area of Des Moines and saw a wonderful front-yard garden in the making. Thinking it might be the duplex I was seeking, I got out of my car, introduced myself and started chatting with the man (it didn't hurt that I was a newly arrived executive garden book editor for a large local publisher). I would never have done that in New York—just go up to a stranger in a strange place and start talking—even about gardening. He knew of a duplex for rent nearby, and now, after two moves, I live two houses up the block from him and his partner.

Over the ensuing six-plus years, we have shared gardening triumphs and woes. When I ran out of space (and for a brief time lived in an apartment with no garden—alas!), or I received some new plants, invariably much of the plant material found its way into his garden. Then when I moved and my neighbor was revamping his garden, many of my former babies came back to me. Gardening takes you full circle—and lets you meet the most interesting folks.

Ask the Experts

When seeking advice, although they are fewer and farther between here than in other areas of the country, visit your nearest botanical garden or arboretum. Plan to make a day of it. Bring along a camera to take some snaps to refresh your memory later. And by all means go with someone else—to share the beauty, and help see different things you may not notice.

The Cooperative Extension Service in your county (despite budget cuts) offers lots of free information, pamphlets, and guidance. They may also offer soil testing and a lab where you can bring in samples of plant problems. The Extension Service is generally the local authority on what you can successfully grow within your hardiness zone. In addition, many offer Master Gardener courses where you can gain a broad base of plant knowledge in exchange (sometimes in addition to a fee) for serving the community for a certain number of hours (doing tasks, answering phones, etc).

The term Master Gardener, I feel, gives others a feeling of inferiority in the field. No Master Gardener is all-knowing. Even someone who has gardened all his or her life with no formal training is constantly learning. So, have fun with gardening and get growing!

Microclimates

Although you can look on a map or call your Cooperative Extension Service to find out your hardiness zone, that is not the sole determination of what will grow well in your garden. You have probably already discovered that you have some areas that are warmer than others—against or near a south-facing wall, protected by a piece of hardscape or large stones. Then there are the cooler areas—the north-facing side of the house, exposed and open areas, and, often, low-lying spaces. These are microclimates.

Use the microclimates to your advantage. For example, if a plant is questionably hardy in your Zone site it in one of the warmer spaces. Conversely, if you live in Kansas, and the plant you want to grow is hardy to a colder Zone, place it where it will be kept cooler by shade and breezes. When considering the microclimate, take into account the soil type and drainage before you plant. For a plant to survive is one thing, but you want your plants to thrive!

The Dirt on Soil

The soil in this region is generally on the alkaline side, with a pH of about 7.5. (The pH is the relative measure of acidity and alkalinity, with a pH of 7 being neutral.) My plants and I were used to more acid soil in the 5.5 to 6.0 range. It varies here from rich loam to clay, with some rocky and even sandy areas. In general though, the soil is rich.

The first time I drove though the countryside in late fall, after the corn and soybeans were harvested, I saw what I thought was the remains of a huge fire—the blackest soil I had ever seen. I was informed that what I was seeing was the actual soil—rich and dark as can be. Much of it was the result of being the bed of a great inland sea millions of years ago. Even today, many farmers have to tile the land, creating a drainage system, as the water level can be high.

Wherever you live, the first and most important thing to do is determine the general type of soil you have. Some people use the words soil and dirt interchangeably. To me, soil is what is in the garden—the nourishing medium we put our plants in. Soil is a living substance with a variety of biological, chemical, and physical forces constantly at work. You may be surprised to learn that soil is comprised of five major components: air, living organisms (microscopic bacteria, fungi, earthworms and insects), humus (organic material in varying states of decay), water, and inorganic particles of minerals and rocks.

To my way of thinking, dirt is the result of a day in the garden—it's what's smeared on my face and ground in under my nails, it's in every corrugation of my sneakers, leaving muddy tracks on the carpet. And, of course, it is on my clothing, especially the back of my pants where it is so easy to wipe my hands, or on the sides of my waist, denoting my pose of great concentration. Whatever you want to call it—dirt or soil—you'll want to know what you're starting with.

You can have major analyses done of your soil, or you can perform a simple test right in the garden that well get you off to a good start. Gently squeeze a small amount of soil in your hand and then rub it between your fingers. Sandy soil is comprised of the largest particles, does not stay together when squeezed, and is

Herb Garden with Yarrow, Allium, Thyme, and Roses

The Blooms of the Tuliptree

gritty to the touch. Sandy soil is easy to work and drains very well, however, the water draining through removes most of the nutrients. Clay (sometimes called heavy soil) absorbs and holds a tremendous amount of moisture. Its particles are so fine that it holds its shape when compressed, not letting air or moisture move through it. Silt is midway in size between sand and clay, with a smooth texture. Silt can be squeezed together but does not remain compacted, especially when it is dry.

The ideal garden soil is loam, which is a mixture of the three types. When you rub it between your fingers, it breaks up into smaller particles. It holds moisture well and encourages the biological activity necessary for healthy, living soil.

Once you know what you have, it's time to make a decision. Work with the soil you have, and plant things that thrive in that environment, or amend the soil to make it ideal. Or, you could do a little of each, making your all-over landscape more varied. For example, in a very clayey area make a water garden, and in a sandy area grow succulents and prickly pear cactus (*Opuntia humifusa*),which is extremely hardy.

Feed the Soil, Not the Plants

Like most ideals, we often have to work to achieve them. That goes for soil, as well. It is the major source of food and water for any plant. Taking the time to choose the proper location (and knowing what your plant requires) is well worth it. The highest quality, most expensive plant, if grown in the wrong soil conditions will likely die. Conversely, a so-so plant put in ideal growing conditions will, with some TLC, probably thrive. For a majority of plants, the qualities that will help it flourish are good drainage, plenty of humus, and an abundance of nutrients available to the plant.

I am a strong believer in composting—it sure saves hauling heavy garbage bags and cuts down on the landfills. I am constantly using compost to mix into my soil, which is on the clayey side. Good compost is full of all those wonderful microorganisms that help get the nutrients from the soil to the plant through the plant's rootlets. Some gardeners call compost black gold—it's certainly pulls its weight.

I add compost to the soil when planting (unless the plant prefers less fertile soil). Also, each spring I spread a layer of compost around my plants, and it in turn feeds the soil. I do not use compost as mulch, as birds flying overhead can drop seeds that will germinate easily in such fertile ground. I cover the compost with an organic mulch, such as wood chips, shredded bark, grass clippings (no more than $3/4$ inch thick at a time), or shredded leaves. Each spring I renew the mulch, much of which has broken down into compost on its own. If you continue this simple process, you will have healthy soil, which then grows healthy plants, which in turn are less susceptible to pests and diseases.

Planting

If you want only one or two plants of a particular variety, you are better off buying plants locally. They are available in a range of sizes—based on the container. A 4- or 6-cell pack is the smallest. Each cell is about 1-inch square. You can find individual young plants in 3-, 4-, 6-inch pots or larger. Many full-sized plants are also available in a variety of containers, especially hanging baskets. Obviously, the larger the container, the higher the price. However, if you want instant gratification and need to fill in a hole in the garden, by all means go for the larger pot.

Choose the best plant. When selecting plants, look at the bottom of the container for roots coming out through the holes. Avoid these, as they are probably rootbound and likely to be stressed. Although it is tempting to buy a plant in full bloom, look for plants with buds and lots of leaves. While purchasing the plants, get a container of transplant/starting solution—invaluable when planting or transplanting. It consists mainly of vitamins in solution that stimulates root growth. I use it whenever I am planting or transplanting and have found that it can bring new life to rescued plants that look pitiful (such as those in the sale bin at the end of the season).

The ideal time to plant or transplant is on a cloudy day or late in the afternoon when bright sunlight won't stress the plant. When you are ready to plant, mix up a batch of transplant solution in a bucket or container deep enough so you can set the plant in it to soak up solution. The amount of solution to make depends on how many plants you are putting in the ground. Allow for at least $1^1/2$ cups per small plant, 3 cups for 6-inch pots and larger.

Dig a hole the size and depth of the container. Remove any flowers and buds from the plant. At this time, you want to stimulate root growth; flowers will take away energy from the roots. Dip the container in the transplant for about one minute. Gently remove the plant from its pot. If it is rootbound (little visible soil, roots wrapped around each other or coming out of the bottom of the pot, take these steps to loosen the roots so they can grow:

    1. Rip (or cut off) the bottom $1/2$-inch of roots and soil.

2. With both hands on the bottom of the plant, gently pull outwards to make a small separation in the middle of the root system.

3. If there are roots that wind around the bottom, gently tease them loose.

4. Cut off any overly long roots.

5. Set the plant in the hole so that soil level from the pot is even with the soil level of the surrounding soil. You may need to add or take out soil.

6. Gently firm the plant and surrounding soil with your hands.

7. Water the soil with 1 cup of transplant solution.

When you have a larger container that is rootbound, skip steps one and two. Instead, work your fingers around the plant to loosen roots. If it is a large plant and very potbound (if you move it and no loose soil comes off the plant), use a knife to make four $1/2$-inch deep slashes down the side of the root mass. Then proceed to Step 3 and follow the steps to the end.

The Beauty of Mulch

Mulch is almost as valuable as compost. It keeps the soil temperature more constant, helps retain water, and most of all it keeps weeds out. A proper mulch application will be at least three inches thick and kept at least an inch away from the stem of the plant so as not to introduce any creatures to the plant. In my travels through the Prairie Lands states, I have been surprised at how few gardeners use mulch. Perhaps that is from farm lineage, where the idea of mulching great fields would be outlandish. Yet, I constantly hear people complaining about weeds. Mulch solves that problem almost completely. Yes, there are a few noxious weeds that may grow up through the mulch, but very few. In addition, if you plan your garden so there are not large bare spots between plants, weed seeds will not have the space or light to germinate.

As previously mentioned, I generally choose an organic mulch that can break down over time. However, there are exceptions. Many herbs are of Mediterranean origin and don't tolerate wet soil; some of the perennials as well. They benefit from a mulch that will let water pass through it quickly, such as sand, turkey grit, gravel, pebbles, river rock—it depends on the size of the plant as your aesthetic taste. The most unique mulch I've seen was potshards—bits of broken terra cotta planting pots surrounding a large shrub. Not only was it unusual to look at, it kept critters away—and people as well.

Plants for the Prairie Lands

The plants I have included in this book are suited to our tough and variable climate. Unless otherwise noted, they are hardy to Zone 3. Especially in the perennials section, native plants abound in this book. Moreover, they are the easiest to grow, needing the least care. Very few need special attention. The icons for light indicate how much sun a plant needs—full sun is more than 6 hours a day (including midday);

part sun is 4 to 6 (including midday), part shade is 4 hours or less of dappled or direct sun—morning or afternoon. Shade is less than 3 hours of sun. However, you cannot grow plants in complete darkness.

Look at plants for a clue that you may be doing something wrong. A plant that is leaning toward the sunlight needs to be moved to where it gets more light. Sun lovers will have more vivid colors with more light. Conversely, some shade-lovers will wilt in the heat of the day, and colors may fade.

When, Where, and How to Plant provides you with the information to select the right site for the plant. However, depending on your conditions, you may find that the plant is happier moved to a drier or moister, richer or poorer soil site. Do not be too quick to give up on a plant. The mere act of putting it in the ground shocks the plant by moving it from its old environment to a new one. It is best to plant on a cloudy or overcast day. Planting in the mid to late afternoon lessens transplant shock. I have found that the use of transplant solution has made me a more successful gardener. This simply requires soaking the potted plant in solution for a few minutes prior to planting, watering the hole with the solution, and giving it a good drink of the solution once the plant is in the ground.

Follow Your Vision

As I have been writing, I have had visions of my great-great-grandmother crossing the Prairie Lands in a covered wagon a hundred and fifty or so years ago. I can't help but wonder what her view was—grasses and perennials taller than she was. And the remarkable thing is I know that on her journey she either dug

some roots, took cuttings, or more likely collected seed. The evidence was in my grandmother's garden— the plants were so unique that few people in southern California in the 1940s, 50s, and 60s were at all familiar with them. The vision of my grandmother's garden flashes through my mind and I can see the plants as vividly as if it were yesterday. The property was sold long ago. I think my aunt may have a few of the plants still. Yet, here am I, starting it all over again, relearning what my ancestor did so many years ago. And so the tradition of gardening continues.

Purple Coneflowers

How to Use the *Prairie Lands Gardener's Guide*

Each entry in this guide provides you with information about a plant's particular characteristics, its habits and its basic requirements for vigorous growth, as well as my personal experience and knowledge of it. I have tried to include the information you need to help you realize each plant's potential. Only when a plant performs at its best can one appreciate it fully. You will find such pertinent information as mature height and spread, bloom period and seasonal colors (if any), sun and soil preferences, planting tips, water requirements, fertilizing needs, pruning and care, and pest information. Each section is clearly marked for easy reference.

Sun Preferences

For quick reference, I have included symbols representing the range of sunlight suitable for each plant. "Full Sun" means a site receiving at least 6 hours of direct sun daily. "Part Sun" means a site that receives at least 4 to 6 hours of direct sun daily. "Part Shade" means a site that receives about 4 or less hours of direct or dappled sun daily. "Shade" means a site that gets dappled light or less than 3 hours of sun. Some plants grow successfully in more than one range of sun, which will be indicated by more than one sun symbol.

Full Sun **Part Sun** **Part Shade** **Shade**

Additional Benefits

Many plants offer benefits that further enhance their appeal. The following symbols indicate some of the more notable additional benefits:

 Attracts Butterflies, Caterpillars, or Moths

Attracts Hummingbirds

 Produces Edible Parts

 Has Fragrance

Produces Food for Birds and Wildlife

Drought Resistant

Suitable for Cut Flowers or Arrangements

Long Bloom Period

Native to North America

Supports Bees

Provides Shelter for Birds

Colorful Fall Foliage and/or Winter Interest

Companion Planting and Design

In this section, I provide suggestions for companion plantings and different ways to showcase your plants. This is where many people find the most enjoyment from gardening.

I Also Recommend

This section describes those specific species, cultivars, or varieties that I have found to be particularly noteworthy. Give them a try—many times I mentioned favorite plants I just couldn't bear to leave out of the book.

USDA Cold Hardiness Zones

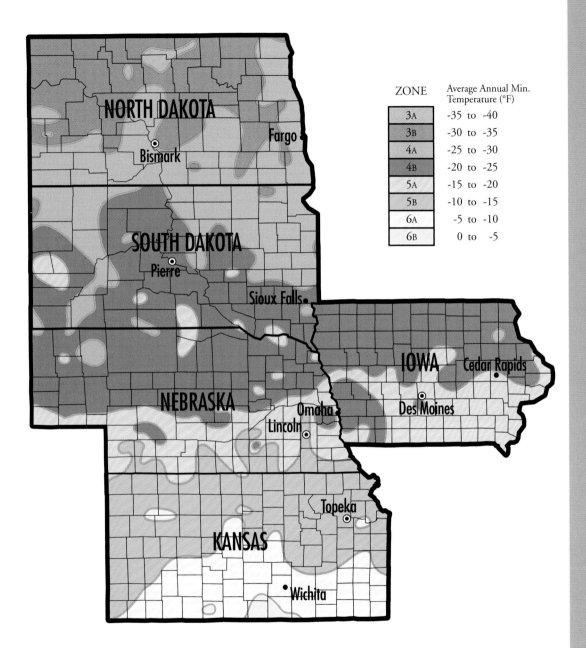

ZONE	Average Annual Min. Temperature (°F)
3A	-35 to -40
3B	-30 to -35
4A	-25 to -30
4B	-20 to -25
5A	-15 to -20
5B	-10 to -15
6A	-5 to -10
6B	0 to -5

Hardiness Zones

Cold-hardiness zone designations were developed by the United States Department of Agriculture (USDA) to indicate the minimum average temperature for an area. A zone assigned to an individual plant indicates the lowest temperature at which the plant can be expected to survive over the winter. Unless noted otherwise, plants in this book are hardy to Zone 3.

Annuals & Biennials
for the Prairie Lands

Although perennials are great and will grow and bloom each year, their bloom period is generally short—sometimes only a week or two, while others may last a month or more.

Annuals and biennials, interspersed among perennials and shrubs or just planted on their own, provide long-lasting color in the garden throughout the summer.

In the Prairie Lands, annuals are exactly what their name says—plants that live one year. You plant annuals in spring (timing depends on the plant), they bloom (many are already in bloom when you buy them), set seed (if you don't deadhead them), and die in autumn, usually with the first frost. For those of you who are snowbirds and travel to warm climates for the winter, you will notice that, in areas with no frost, most annuals will just keep growing. (Indeed, in those climates they are perennial and may not even go through a period of dormancy.)

Some annuals, such as spring-planted pansies, are not heat tolerant and will die in summer. Fall-planted pansies, however, are extremely cold tolerant and will last through the winter, often blooming when the snow melts, and continue to bloom through spring. They are also surprisingly heat-tolerant and may last through the summer, to die in fall. However, these are exceptions to the usual behavior of annuals.

Pansies

After planting, do not mulch for two weeks. Then use two inches of organic matter (compost, well-rotted manure, or leaf mold) around the plant. Keep the mulch one inch away from the stem of the plants. Otherwise, you might smother the stem and introduce insects or disease. Do not mulch seeded beds. Wait until the plants are thinned to their proper spacing and have at least four sets of leaves.

There are some annuals that self-sow, which means that their seeds drop to the ground and germinate the following year. They give the impression of being perennial when, in fact, these annuals were not deadheaded and were allowed to set seed and thus returned.

By definition, biennials grown from seed put out leaves the first year and often die back in fall. The roots, however, do not die. Often the leaves remain, looking rather tattered by spring. It

Globe Amaranth

is not until their second year that they send out flowers. Once the flowers set seed (reproduction is what a plant's entire life cycle is all about), the plant dies.

Biennials can be a bit confusing. They are sometimes mistaken for annuals and sometimes for perennials. Generally, when you purchase a biennial plant—a hollyhock or foxglove, for example—at a nursery, garden center, or home store, it is already in its second year and is either in bloom or about to bloom. It will bloom in the garden, go to seed, and die.

Here is where the magic of Mother Nature steps in, especially with hollyhocks and foxgloves. Try letting the seedheads remain on the plant. Some of the seeds will fall on the ground near the original plant and germinate that season; therefore, next year, they will be in their second year and bloom. Since the new plants are in the same general location as the original plant, an erroneous assumption may be made that the plant is perennial when in truth it is a biennial.

The self-sowers, or self-seeders, as they may be called, are my favorites among both annuals and biennials. Once you plant them, you will continue to have long-lasting bloom for years to come with virtually no effort. With some plants, such as perilla, datura, four-o'clocks, and the amaranths, this can almost work too well since they are very prolific and can easily overrun a garden within a few years. However, if you are like me and love these plants, you will quickly learn to recognize the seedlings and pull them out when they are young.

Below is a list of self-sowing annuals and biennials that you could try. Those with asterisks (*) are included as plant selections in this chapter.

Self-Sowing Annuals & Biennials

Common Name	Botanical Name	Type
*Bachelor's button	*Centaurea cyanus*	Annual
Black-eyed Susan	*Rudbeckia hirta*	Annual
Calendula	*Calendula officinalis*	Annual
*Cleome	*Cleome hasslerana*	Annual
*Cosmos	*Cosmos bipinnatus*	Annual
Dame's rocket	*Hesperis matronalis*	Biennial
*Flowering tobacco	*Nicotiana alata* and *N. sylvestris*	Annual
Foxglove	*Digitalis* spp.	Biennial
Golden coreopsis (tickseed)	*Coreopsis tinctoria*	Annual
Golden marguerite	*Anthemis* spp.	Biennial
*Johnny jump-up	*Viola tricolor*	Annual
Money plant	*Lunaria annua*	Biennial
Rose moss	*Portulaca grandiflora*	Annual
*Sweet William	*Dianthus barbatus*	Biennial

If the plants are cultivated hybrids and they self-sow, it is quite possible that the resulting plants will not be the same as the original ones. I enjoy letting these plants go to seed and watching the variations that pop up the following year. If you want the same plant from seed, you need to grow species plants (those that occur in nature) or open-pollinated heirloom seeds. Heirloom seeds, which have been passed down from generation to generation, were often part of the few belongings immigrants brought to America. They are still being kept in families, and they are now available from several mail-order sources, including Seed Savers Exchange and mail-order plant sources. (See resources in the back of this book). Their names alone make them tempting to grow—Grandpa Ott's morning glory, 'Mortgage Lifter' tomato, and more.

Space limits me from writing more about the many beautiful and colorful annuals and biennials for Prairie Lands' gardens. To really explore the tremendous range of these plants, visit friends' and family members' gardens, go to a local botanic garden, and, of course, take a trip to nurseries, garden centers, and home stores. You will be amazed at the diversity and range of plants that can enliven your garden all year long.

Find Inspiration at Botanic Gardens

Bachelor's Button
Centaurea cyanus

When you grow bachelor's button, dark sky-blue, daisy-like flowers are borne atop multibranched stems, providing eye-catching bloom in summer. Although you may read that it prefers cool weather, in partial shade (afternoon sun) it thrives from late June through August. Even mowers cannot defeat it, as it will rise up to bloom again, often continuing through the summer. Grown organically in the garden, the petals are edible, with a slightly bitter flavor. Toss them with red tomatoes, fresh mozzarella cheese, and a light dressing of olive oil and white balsamic vinegar for a patriotic Fourth of July salad. I particularly like them planted in drifts, mixed with other medium height flowers which lend support, yet they can sway with the breeze.

Other Common Name
Cornflower

Bloom Period and Seasonal Color
Annual: Deep sky blue from late spring to midsummer and sometimes later.

Mature Height and Spread
8 to 32 in. × 6 in.

When, Where, and How to Plant
Bachelor's button is one of the few annuals you can sow in early fall to bloom next spring. I have equal success sowing it atop the snow in late winter as I do with annual poppies. Most people sow the seeds directly in the ground where they will be growing as soon as the soil temperature is at least 55 degrees Fahrenheit. Put about 1/2 inch of soil over them. Tamp the soil down firmly and water the area gently to avoid washing away the seeds. For a head start, sow the seeds indoors in early spring in peat pots. Bachelor's button does not like to have its roots disturbed, so you can plant the peat pot directly into the ground without disturbing the roots.

Growing Tips
For the first two weeks after sowing the seed, you may have to water several times a day to prevent the soil from drying out. Once the plant is several inches tall, it will need water daily or every other day. As the soil heats up and the days become longer, the sun is brighter, and with the probability of wind, you may have to go back to a daily watering regimen. Water the soil in the root area monthly using compost tea or other liquid fertilizer. Avoid wetting the leaves, as wet leaves are more susceptible to downy mildew.

Care and Maintenance
To prolong the bloom time, deadhead—cut off spent blooms—down to the next lower branching stems. With high humidity, bachelor's button is prone to powdery mildew or downy mildew. Treat with baking soda solution (see page 233). Never spray if the temperature is above 80 degrees Fahrenheit.

Companion Planting and Design
Bachelor's button is perfect for a naturalistic, meadow-type garden of poppies (*Papaver* spp.), mallows (*Malva* spp.), tickseed (*Coreopsis* spp.), and tall annuals like zinnias (*Zinnia elegans*) and cosmos (*Cosmos bipinnatus*). My "meadow" is only 3 feet by 6 feet and it's beautiful all summer.

I Also Recommend
The Florence series with multi-branched, compact plants and numerous pink, cherry-red, and white flowers.

Blanket Flower
Gaillardia pulchella

When, Where, and How to Plant

Start seeds in peat pots. Pre-moisten some seed-starting mix, fill the pot within 1/2 inch of the top, and add three seeds. Barely cover the seeds with mix and press lightly. Cover loosely with plastic wrap to retain moisture. Vent them daily. Place the pots in a warm place. Mist daily to keep the soil evenly moist. Once the seeds germinate, remove the plastic. Move pots to a sunny window or under grow lights. When you see two sets of leaves, thin to one plant per pot, keeping the strongest plant. Cut off the stems of the other plants. Blanket flower prefers fertile, well-drained soil and must be grown in full sun. Plant the peat pots out in the garden, spacing them about 8 to 12 inches apart, after all danger of frost has passed. Gently tear off the top edge of the peat pot and set it so the soil in the pot is level with the ground. You can also sow the seed directly in the ground after the last frost date.

Growing Tips

Keep the plants evenly moist after planting. Once established, they are quite drought tolerant. If leaves droop, water them and they will perk right up. Foliar feed monthly.

Care and Maintenance

Cut off flowers after they fade to encourage new blooms. Cut the flower down to the next lowest branch without removing any other flower buds. Blanket flower may be prone to downy mildew. Treat with a baking soda solution (see page 233). Never spray if the temperature is above 80 degrees Fahrenheit.

Companion Planting and Design

Blanket flower is ideal in a meadow setting with ox-eye (*Heliopsis* spp.), tickseed (*Coreopsis* spp.), and feather reed grass (*Calamagrostis* × *acutiflora*). It is equally at home in a mixed flowerbed with zinnias (*Zinnia elegans*), asters (*Aster* spp.), and goldenrod (*Solidago* spp.)

I Also Recommend

The bushy plants of the Plume series have double flowers, an almost round head, and grow only 12 inches tall. 'Red Plume' is brilliant brick red.

There are both annual and perennial blanket flowers. Both are native to the Prairie Lands. If you visit a native or restored prairie in summer, blanket flower will be among the brightest, most vivid flowers you will see. The flowerhead is daisy-like with a single circle of bright, red flowers tipped with sunny yellow. The slightly jagged-edged petals surround dark purple disk florets (as the white petals of a daisy surround a center of yellow disk florets) for an impressive flower that is about 2 inches across. Natural variations occur, so you may see solid red or solid yellow blooms that are the species and not a special cultivated variety. I love their cheery colors radiating in my garden from June until frost, even brightening my spirits during the dog days of August.

Other Common Name
Indian Blanket

Bloom Period and Seasonal Color
Annual: Red-banded yellow, yellow, or red from summer to frost.

Mature Height and Spread
18 to 24 in. × 12 to 15 in.

Cleome

Cleome hassleriana

To me, cleome is a plant that shows Mother Nature's sense of humor. It is quite unusual looking, with descriptions ranging from clouds of blooms to flowers arranged on long racemes, opening from top to bottom. Rather gangly and growing up to 6 feet tall (but doesn't need staking), it comes into its glory when the flowers near the top of the plant start to unroll—another unusual trait. As more blooms are exposed, notice the long protruding stamens, reminiscent of cat whiskers. Along the stem are the long narrow seedpods, which easily open, making it easily self-sowing. Cleome is a long-lasting cut flower for dramatic arrangements. It's equally at home at the back of a border, center of an island bed, or in a cottage garden.

Other Common Name
Spider Flower

Bloom Period and Seasonal Color
Annual: Pink, white, or purple from summer to frost.

Mature Height and Spread
4 to 5 ft. × 15 to 18 in.

When, Where, and How to Plant

If you are counting on self-sown cleome, be patient. It germinates in late spring, so wait until late June to clean and mulch the area. Plants are readily available; choose ones in larger pots. They are sturdier and usually not rootbound. Plant or sow seeds outside two to three weeks after the last frost date. Allow 1 to 3 feet between plants. Cleome prefers light, fertile, very well-drained soil (add sand to loam) and full sun. It tolerates part sun.

Growing Tips

Keep plants and seeds well watered until they are established. After that, they are somewhat drought tolerant, but water them deeply after a week with no rain. Cleome doesn't require feeding, but I foliar feed once in midsummer (on that rare day when the temperature is less than 80 degrees Fahrenheit).

Care and Maintenance

To prevent self-seeding, cut the long seedpods forming along the stem. If you want to save the seed, wait until the pod dries. Carefully cut it off; it easily spills seeds. Alternatively, just let Mother Nature take her own course. If aphids, small caterpillars, whitefly, or spider mites are a problem, spray the plant with insecticidal soap weekly. Allow ample room between plants to lessen stress, which makes them susceptible to pests and diseases.

Companion Planting and Design

Create a beautiful purple garden with cleome mixed with any of these plants: 'Blue Vein' petunia (*Petunia* × *hybrida* 'Blue Vein), 'Lavender Lace' cuphea (*Cuphea rosea* 'Lavender Lace'), English lavender (*Lavandula angustifolia*), and Brazilian vervain (*Verbena bonariensis*).

I Also Recommend

Not all cleome are fragrant, but I like dual-purpose plants—scented and pretty. 'Helen Campbell' is the exception, but she is so courtly with her pure white flowers that she stays in my gardens anyway. The Color Fountains strain grows 4 feet tall, is nicely scented, and is crowned with clusters of white, rose-violet, or pink flowers. 'Pink Queen' is free flowering, perfumed, and one of the longest lasting of all the cleomes. Its pink flowers keep their color and do not fade.

Coleus

Solenostemon scutellarioides

When, Where, and How to Plant

Coleus is the plant equivalent of comfort food—one of the first plants children grow successfully. It grows easily from cuttings. Snip a 4- to 6-inch stem. Remove all but the top two to four leaves. Place as many cuttings as you want, even from different plants, in a glass with enough room-temperature water so the stem is underwater and the leaves above. Place it in a semi-sunny spot and wait for roots to grow. Once rooted, plant cuttings in pots (indoor or outdoor container gardening) or in the garden in rich, well-drained soil after the last frost date. Some coleus love shade while others prefer sun. (See page 15 for more on planting.)

Growing Tips

Coleus grows best in rich, lightly moist, well-drained, humusy soil. Do not grow a shade-loving coleus in full sun; it will burn out. Sun lovers can grow in shade but will have muted tones. Foliar feed twice a month with of a solution of kelp or fish emulsion. Keep the soil very lightly moist. Do not let it dry out.

Care and Maintenance

Many new varieties are self-branching and do not need the top set of leaves pinched out to produce a bushy plant. At the end of the season, take cuttings to overwinter indoors. Coleus is susceptible to mealybug. It is difficult to control, so isolate any new plant for a week. If a plant is infested, dispose of it.

Companion Planting and Design

I grew 'Kiwi Fern' with toothache plant (*Spilanthes* spp.), with its mustardy eyeball-looking flowerhead, and *Lysimachia* 'Firecracker'—all complementary earth tones. Coleus pairs well with canna, adding color at ground level. I have seen an extreme 10-foot design that was pinwheel-shaped with five contrasting coleus.

I Also Recommend

'The Line' has chartreuse leaves and burgundy veins. 'Saturn' has otherworldly maroon leaves, a bright green central splash, and smaller satellite spots. 'India Frills' resembles the diminutive Ducksfoot series' footprint: dark red leaves, edged green, spotted vivid yellow and green.

Coleus was all the rage back in Victorian times, with dozens upon dozens of named varieties. It was used in great formal gardens, as a bedding plant, and as a houseplant. As with many fads, its popularity waned, and it is remembered by many of us as the unremarkable, common pale pink, cream, and green houseplant in grandmother's parlor. Over the past ten years, coleus has made a huge resurgence, especially with the development of the Sun series that thrives in full sun. Today, there are hundreds of varieties, with leaves that vary from the 1/2-inch 'Ducksfoot' to the 6-inch bright green 'Japanese Giant'. 'Kiwi Fern' is my favorite for its unusual coloration—deep burgundy edged in green with an intermittent spot of yellow and red—and its narrow, deeply scalloped leaves.

Bloom Period and Seasonal Color

Annual: Blue flowers in summer, but grown for colorful leaves.

Mature Height and Spread

8 to 24 in. × 6 to 30 in.

Cosmos
Cosmos bipinnatus

With fernlike foliage that appears a month or so before the flowers, cosmos (an annual) makes itself known relatively early in the season. From dwarfs to giants, the yellow-centered, daisy-like flower deserves space in the garden. I plant one or two tall, old-fashioned, single pink cosmos near the front of the garden. Like a veil, you can look through it and still see the rest of the garden. For mass plantings, consider the middle or back of the garden, depending on the height. Today's cosmos is a far cry from the pink or white ones of my childhood. Whether you grow cosmos that is bicolor pink and white, or carmine, or white with a picotee edge, it adds a country charm all its own.

Bloom Period and Seasonal Color
Annual: White, pink, bicolor, or carmine from summer through fall.

Mature Height and Spread
1 to 5 ft. × 12 to 18 in.

When, Where, and How to Plant
Sow cosmos seeds directly in the garden in well-drained, slightly acidic, average to poor soil in late spring, after the last frost. Get a head start by planting the seeds indoors in peat pots four to six weeks before the last frost date. (Follow seed planting instructions described on page 25.) Most nurseries and garden centers carry cosmos in 2- or 4-inch pots or cell packs. Whether you sow the seed directly in the ground or plant out transplants, allow 1 to 3 feet between them.

Growing Tips
Until the seeds sprout and have several leaves, do not let the soil dry out. When transplanting from pots, use a planting solution (readily available in garden centers, nurseries, home stores, and even grocery stores) to stimulate root production and growth. Do not fertilize cosmos; it does not need it, and it may become disease or insect prone. Since it is drought tolerant, it does not need a lot of watering. If you have an automatic sprinkler system, make sure to plant it out of range of the regular watering cycle.

Care and Maintenance
To prolong the bloom time, deadhead any spent flowers. As cosmos is susceptible to leaf spot and anthracnose (two fungal diseases), avoid overwatering the plant. Allowing for ample air circulation around the plant also helps prevent any fungal problems.

Companion Planting and Design
To me, cosmos and cleome (*Cleome hassleriana*) make perfect partners. The heights and colors are similar, and the large blousy cleome blossoms enhance the dainty air of the cosmos. Cosmos also pairs well with *Verbena bonariensis*, also in the same height and color range. Plant the verbena in front of the cosmos, even in large numbers, and you can still see through the tall stems to the cosmos.

I Also Recommend
'Sonata', with its diminutive stature, growing 12 to 16 inches tall is perfect for the front of the border. The white variety is spectacular with deep colored *Dahlia* spp. Also available in magenta and pink, it is an ideal container plant.

Datura

Datura meteloides

When, Where, and How to Plant

As the species readily self-sows; after the first year, you will have plenty of plants. To grow datura from seed, sow seeds indoors (follow seed planting instructions described on page 25). six to eight weeks before the last frost date. Datura thrives in rich, humusy, well-drained, alkaline soil and full sun but will also grow in poorer soil and part shade. Transplant into the garden two or three weeks after last frost date. It is an excellent container plant. Wear disposable gloves when handling the plant—all parts are toxic.

Growing Tips

Although you do not need to fertilize, your plant will be more impressive if foliar fed every three weeks. Do not allow the soil to dry out—wilting leaves are a signal to water immediately.

Care and Maintenance

Remove the faded flowers and the golf ball-sized, spiky seedheads to promote more blooms. Near the end of the season, allow one or two seedheads to ripen and drop seeds for next year's fragrant delight. If grown in a container, it needs to be brought indoors for the winter. Cut it back by one-third. If the there is ample light and warmth, it will continue to grow. Otherwise, let it go dormant by placing it in a cool dark place, watering lightly once a month. Keep an eye on the plant for any sign of mealybugs or spider mites. For spider mites, spray with an insecticidal soap. Use a swab dipped in rubbing alcohol to wipe off the cottony mealybugs. To avoid spreading, throw out the swab after each use.

Companion Planting and Design

When planting, consider how large the plant grows and do not put anything within 2 to 3 feet. The Wave™ series of petunias (*Petunia* × *hybrida* The Wave™), which spreads to form a lovely carpet of pink, white, or lilac, is beautiful surrounding datura. Add some height by planting datura in front of a morning glory (*Ipomoea tricolor*).

I Also Recommend

'Evening Fragrance' has 8-inch-long, white flowers with a soft lavender picotee. Its leaves are slate blue.

Every garden needs at least one datura to herald the night. The upfacing, large (5- to 8-inch), trumpet-shaped white flowers open as the sun goes down, filling the air with their sweet perfume, attracting pollinators like the exotic luna and sphinx moths. Although the blooms generally only last a single night, more are produced as the plant grows so that at full maturity it may be 5 feet wide and tall with dozens of blooms. If the day is cloudy or rainy, the flowers will remain open but scentless. What is a boon to most gardeners (but a bane to a few) is that datura readily self-sows and will come back year after year. Beware: All parts of the plant are poisonous.

Other Common Names

Angel's Trumpet, Moonflower

Bloom Period and Seasonal Color

Annual: White from midsummer to frost.

Mature Height and Spread

3 to 5 ft. × 3 to 5 ft.

Flowering Tobacco
Nicotiana alata

Much hybridizing has been done with flowering tobacco, but to me (and my sense of smell) the species is the best. It is one of the stars of an evening garden. The narrow tubular flowers flare at the end to form a five-petaled star. Although the flowers droop somewhat during the day, they perk up at night. Their sweet scent perfumes the garden and attracts their pollinators, including the magnificent luna moth and sphinx moth. In summer, the central stem quickly grows 4 feet or higher with secondary stems as long as 2 feet. The overall effect is like a giant candelabra with white flowers in graceful sprays. An added bonus is that flowering tobacco self-seeds, so you can enjoy it year after year.

Bloom Period and Seasonal Color
Annual: White from midsummer to frost.

Mature Height and Spread
4 to 5 ft. × 12 to 16 in.

When, Where, and How to Plant
The nicotianas readily available at nurseries and garden centers are usually the smaller hybrids, which are rarely fragrant. For the true, old-fashioned flowering tobacco, start the seed indoors in late winter or early spring. (Follow seed planting instructions described on page 25.) In the garden, it will grow best in rich, lightly moist, well-drained soil. In all my years of gardening, I have found it will grow in all but very clayey soils. It prefers sun but will do fine in partial shade. Transplant outdoors several weeks after the last frost date. Space the plants at least 12 to 15 inches apart.

Growing Tips
Unless the plant is in a protected location, it is a good idea to stake it so that the tall stem does not break in high winds or heavy rain. Put in the stake and pound it at least 12 inches into the ground. I use 6-foot, green, plastic-covered metal stakes and spray paint them bright colors for interest before the plant shoots up. Unpainted, the stake blends into the garden. The choice is yours. To avoid damaging tender roots, install the stake before you put the plant in. Water regularly. Foliar feed with a solution of kelp or fish emulsion every three to four weeks.

Care and Maintenance
As with most plants, deadheading helps produce new flowers. Instead of removing each individual flower when it has finished blooming, I wait until the spray of flowers has passed its prime.

Companion Planting and Design
One of the best combinations I have ever seen was flowering tobacco planted among ornamental grasses (various species of *Miscanthus*). The grasses help support the flowering tobacco, and in the evening the sweet scent is a delightful surprise. For those who like the look of the smaller and more colorful nicotianas, such as the Nikki or Domino series, plant them in front of the taller species, and you will have both color (red, pink, chartreuse) and scent.

I Also Recommend
Grow the species or *Nicotiana sylvestris*, which is very similar.

Four O'Clock
Mirabilis jalapa

When, Where, and How to Plant

Four o'clock self-sows, but may not come true the following year. If you enjoy varied, fragrant volunteers, just plant it once. In subsequent years, plants will sprout from mature seeds that dropped on the ground during the growing season. Plants are sometimes available in nurseries but are more readily available as seeds. It is easy to grow. Start the seed indoors six to eight weeks before the last frost (follow seed planting instructions described on page 25). or sow directly in the garden when you plant tomatoes. That is also the time to transplant seedlings outdoors. Four o'clock likes ordinary garden soil and full sun or partial shade.

Growing Tips

Although four o'clock is relatively drought tolerant, do not ignore it completely. Give it a good drink of water at least every seven to ten days. Foliar feed monthly by spraying the leaves with a dilution of liquid seaweed fertilizer (follow package instructions).

Care and Maintenance

Four o'clock is about as close as you can get to a care-free plant. It is self-cleaning. The spent flowers, which bloom for a single night, fall off the plants, so no deadheading is needed. However, if you do not want to save seed or let it fall where it may, you might want to cut off the sepals of the spent flowers. Best of all, it thrives in the high humidity prevalent in summer in the Prairie Lands states. Despite its name, I have always found that it opens much later than four o'clock—often at dusk. For me it has never been synchronized to my clock. Four o'clock is relatively pest and disease free.

Companion Planting and Design

Four o'clock is divine paired with night-blooming daylilies (*Hemerocallis* spp.) or day-blooming varieties that close after the four o'clock opens. For vibrant daytime color, plant 'Peppermint Stick' zinnia (*Zinnia elegans* 'Peppermint Stick') and any of the myriad coleus (*Solenostemon scutellarioides*) that suits your fancy.

I Also Recommend

'Jingles' has multi-colored flowers—solid and striped—in hues of cerise to yellow on one plant.

More of us have less time to spend enjoying our gardens, so plants that are fragrant and bloom in the evening are important in today's gardens. Evening is often the only time when we can truly relax—especially when we cannot see the weeds. Four-o'clock needs to be incorporated into an evening garden for its scent and especially its color—white, yellow, cerise, and candy-cane—which most night bloomers lack. The plant is bushy, bearing sweet little 1- to 2-inch trumpets that open in late afternoon—thus their common name. In fact, it is not the time that triggers the flowers to open but the concurrent temperature drop. Sit quietly after dusk to see the magnificent luna and sphinx moths that drink its nectar.

Other Common Name
Marvel of Peru

Bloom Period and Seasonal Color
Annual: Cerise, yellow, white, or pink and white from midsummer to frost.

Mature Height and Spread
2 to 3 ft. × 2 to 3 ft. or more

Globe Amaranth

Gomphrena haageana

Globe amaranth is a wonderful multipurpose flower. With its 1-inch clover-like blossoms, it is a great addition to any garden—in a sunny border, formal garden, mixed bed, or cutting garden. Globe amaranth is well named since it resembles a field of tall strawberries when planted en masse. With its bright color, it pops out even on a dreary day. The cultivar 'Strawberry Fields' is a long-lasting cut flower and is one of the best flowers for air-drying for dried flower arrangements. Its color is unique among the different globe amaranths and is a real eye-catcher in the garden. It thrives in the hot summers of the Prairie Lands states, holds up to the high humidity, and is fairly drought tolerant. It also is an excellent container plant.

Bloom Period and Seasonal Color
Annual: Red, purple, white, or pink from summer to frost.

Mature Height and Spread
2 to 3 ft. × 12 to 15 in.

When, Where, and How to Plant
Small plants are available at some nurseries, garden centers, and home stores. Sow seeds directly in the garden 1/4-inch deep once the soil has warmed. Globe amaranths grow best in well-drained, fertile, garden soil in full sun. Or start the seeds inside (follow seed planting instructions described on page 25). eight to ten weeks before the last frost date. Seed can take three weeks to germinate, so be patient. Outdoors, plant or thin so plants are 18 inches apart. With our hot summers, add a 2- to 3-inch layer of organic mulch around the plant—keeping the mulch an inch away from the stem—to keep the soil cool.

Growing Tips
Although globe amaranth is fairly drought tolerant, it requires regular watering until it is established. Because I cut it for bouquets and to dry, I do not foliar feed. Instead, I put 1 cup of well-rotted manure around the base of the plant and water it in. Alternatively, use an all-purpose or high-phosphorus fertilizer, following package instructions. In drought conditions, water every ten to fourteen days.

Care and Maintenance
If you plan on cutting globe amaranth for use as dried flowers, cut the stem at least 6 inches long before the flower opens. The stems become brittle, so reinforce them with florist's wire. Cut a 10-inch length and bend one end to form a small hook. Push the straight end through the center of the flower and along the stem until the hook portion is down in the center of the flower. Tie a bunch (eight to twelve) of stems together at the base and hang them upside-down in a dark, warm, dry space for several weeks. In damp summers, spray weekly with insecticidal soap to prevent mold or mildew.

Companion Planting and Design
Outstanding companions are purple fountain grass (*Pennisetum setaceum* 'Purpureum') and 'Perestroika' kale for a superb contrast of texture, form, and color.

I Also Recommend
'Lavender Lady' has bright lavender blooms. 'White' bears large 1 1/2-inch balls of pure white.

Hollyhock
Alcea rosea

When, Where, and How to Plant

Traditionally, hollyhock is a pass-along plant—seeds of non-hybrid varieties are collected and passed along to friends and family. I have a pale apricot, double hollyhock that came from seeds a friend gave me eight years ago. She collected seed from her mother's garden, which came from her grandmother. My seeds have passed through four generations and more than seventy-five years. Since hollyhock self-sows, I will always have this beautiful plant. When I moved, I brought some seeds with me and sowed them in my new garden. Hollyhock grows best in good to rich, well-drained soil in full sun. You can buy second-year plants (which will bloom that year). If you get pass-along seeds or buy seeds, plant them 1/2-inch deep in midsummer, and they will bloom the following year. If you are growing a tall variety in an exposed area, stake the plant to prevent it breaking in strong winds. (See page 15 for more on planting.)

Growing Tips

Keep the soil evenly moist after sowing seed or setting out a plant. Once you see several sets of leaves, cut down on the watering but do not let the soil dry out. Foliar feed once every two to three weeks during the growing season.

Care and Maintenance

Be sure to label the plant so you don't pull it up accidentally during fall cleanup when it goes dormant. Hollyhock is prone to rust and both bacterial and fungal leaf spots. Although the leaves may be somewhat unsightly up close, the diseases don't affect the flowers. Slugs are more of a problem, feasting on new young leaves in spring. Sprinkle diatomaceous earth in a 1-inch-wide circle around the base of the plant to deter slugs. Repeat after heavy rains.

Companion Planting and Design

The cottagey look of hollyhock is accentuated by foxgloves (*Digitalis* spp.), delphiniums (*Delphinium* spp.), and valerian (*Centranthus ruber*).

I Also Recommend

Chater's Double strain has large double flowers in both bright and pale colors, usually purchased as a mix. 'Nigra' is eye-catching with nearly black petals accentuated by a yellow throat.

Standing proud and tall at 5 to 8 feet with single or double flowers spaced around the stem, hollyhock is a standard for any informal garden, especially cottage-style gardens. The lowest flowers on the stem open first. Over a period of several weeks or more (depending on the weather), the flowers above burst into bloom in succession. Although the entire stalk is not in bloom at one time, it continues to provide color and a strong vertical accent from early to midsummer. Hollyhock is biennial yet is often mistaken for a perennial since it comes back and blooms year after year. The lower flowers have already set seed while the upper ones are blooming. The ripe seeds drop, germinate in summer, put out leaves, and bloom the following year.

Bloom Period and Seasonal Color

Biennial: A rainbow of hues—red, pink, white, yellow, apricot, carmine, deep maroon, lavender-blue, and purple—from early to midsummer.

Mature Height and Spread

3 to 8 ft. × 1 to 2 ft.

Impatiens
Impatiens walleriana

Impatiens is the quintessential flowering annual for shady spaces. Since it is easy to grow and readily available, most gardeners rely on it to instantly brighten any dark area—under a tree, in a shady bed or border. A single plant quickly grows into a mound of flowers 8 to 24 inches high, depending on the variety, and they are impressive planted en masse. Impatiens make excellent container plants, especially in open hanging baskets (also planted outside). Much hybridizing has been done with impatiens in the last decade, so there are myriad choices: flower colors, single color or bicolor, from bright to subdued, single or double (resembling miniature roses) blooms, and leaves of different hues. With new varieties arriving on the market each year, impatiens is the choice for shade.

Other Common Name
Busy Lizzie

Bloom Period and Seasonal Color
Annual: Pink, red, orange, magenta, white, or bicolors from summer to frost.

Mature height and spread
8 to 24 in. × 1 to 2 ft.

When, Where, and How to Plant
You can find plants everywhere in cell packs of four or six plants (the smallest plants) and in pots ranging from 3 inches to fully grown hanging baskets and containers. Always avoid those with roots growing through the bottom of the pot since they are root-bound. Impatiens prefers rich, well-drained soil in part sun to full shade. Mix a quart of transplant starter solution in a bucket, following the package instructions. Set the cell pack or container in the solution for about minute. Dig a hole the size of the container and pour in a cup of transplant solution. Remove the plant from its container. If it is rootbound, tear off the bottom $1/2$-inch of roots. Slightly tease apart the roots on the side. Place it in the hole at the same depth it was growing in the container. Add more soil if necessary. Tamp the soil gently. Water with another cup of transplant solution. Pinch off any flowers to encourage root growth.

Growing Tips
Impatiens grows best when kept lightly moist. In containers, it may require water twice a day. Lining a container with a disposable diaper ("skin side" facing up) can help hold water and release it slowly during the day. Foliar feed monthly. Never spray when the temperature is over 80 degrees Fahrenheit.

Care and Maintenance
For a full, bushy plant, pinch back the stems to the next set of leaves. Some impatiens are self-cleaning, dropping spent flowers; others benefit from deadheading. Take cuttings of favorite plants in late summer and grow them in pots indoors through the winter. Pests, apart from slugs, are rare.

Companion Planting and Design
The many hues of impatiens are enchanting with colorful caladiums (*Caladium bicolor*). They enliven any hosta planting. For color impact, encircle a tree with impatiens.

I Also Recommend
The Super Elfin series is flatter, growing only 10 inches tall in a range of colors including red, orange, pink, and violet. 'Fiesta™ Deep Orange' with its deep green leaves seems to flaunt its rich, scarlet-orange double flowers.

Impatiens 'Jungle Gold'

Impatiens auricoma 'Jungle Gold'

When, Where, and How to Plant

'Jungle Gold' is a great container plant, adding pizzazz to any shady spot. Even large containers can be moved after they are planted. As this is such a new plant, it may be at home centers before ideal planting time (a week after the last frost date). Buy it anyway, replant it in a pot one inch larger than it is sold in, and keep it indoors in a north or west window. Once all danger of frost has passed, repot it in your container of choice. Fill your container to within an inch of the top with lightly moistened potting mix (use a wheelbarrow or tarp to wet large amounts of soil). Look for a good-quality potting mix that contains slow-release fertilizer and moisture-retainer since 'Jungle Gold' is a hungry, thirsty plant. Gently remove the plant from its pot and loosen any roots if they have wound around themselves. Plant it at its original depth. Water well with a transplant starter solution.

Growing Tips

The larger the pot, the less danger there is of 'Jungle Gold' drying out during a hot summer day. I did not use a water-grabber with my potting mix, so I watered in the morning and late afternoon when the temperatures soar over 90 degrees Fahrenheit. Foliar feed every three weeks.

Care and Maintenance

'Jungle Gold' is self-cleaning—dropping its spent flowers. Deadheading is unnecessary, and slugs are usually the only pest.

Companion Planting and Design

The more plants and the bigger the container, the greater the impact. For large containers, I prefer to use faux materials or plastic since they are lightweight. They simulate the look of stone, terracotta, poured concrete, and even lead. 'Jungle Gold' is outstanding alone in a large container (12-inch or more). I grew it in a window box with 'Peek a Boo' *Spilanthes* (doll's eyes or toothache plant) in front. It was also a knockout with coleus 'Sherbet' (eye-catching peach and green leaves) surrounding it, spilling over the edge of the pot.

'Jungle Gold', new for 2004, is a different species from the common impatiens. Its flower resembles a wide-open snapdragon or a tiny orchid. It is three-dimensional, while most impatiens (except doubles) are flat. The blossom is a lovely mellow yellow, with red-orange striations in the throat and soft peach on the reverse of some flowers—often when immature. Very floriferous, the blooms stand out above the dark green leaves. It is best suited as a container plant for shade. I grew one in the garden, which was less than a third of the size of the container-grown plants. During a neighborhood tour, people came onto my porch to see this eye-catcher up close; it was so unusual and beautiful. No one guessed it was an impatiens.

Bloom Period and Seasonal Color

Annual: Buttery yellow from summer to frost.

Mature Height and Spread

15 to 18 in. × 15 to 18 in.

Johnny Jump-up
Viola tricolor

Johnny jump-up is one of the cutest flowers to grow. Looking at its five-petaled 1-inch flower with its coloration of purple, white, and yellow, resembling a face, always makes me smile. It is a prolific seeder and will pop up in unexpected places in the garden from year to year—hence its name. Its long season of bloom makes it attractive from early spring well into the summer (especially in more shaded areas). The flowers (grown organically) are edible with a slightly wintergreen flavor. Pick the entire flower (including the green sepals that hold it together) and pop it in your mouth. Johnny jump-up is a pretty addition to salads and makes an elegant, easy hors d'oeuvre when placed atop a cracker spread with cream cheese.

Other Common Name
Heartsease

Bloom Period and Seasonal Color
Annual: Purple with white and yellow from mid-spring through summer.

Mature Height and Spread
3 to 5 in. × 3 to 6 in.

When, Where, and How to Plant
Johnny jump-up is readily available in cell packs. If you don't want to buy it, some of your friends or neighbors may have extra. If they allow you to take some, bring a large pot filled with potting mix lightly moistened with transplant solution. Place the plants in the pot; it doesn't matter if they are right next to each other, as you will be transplanting them soon. If you purchased the plants in pots, gently remove the plant from its container and loosen any roots if they have wound around themselves. (See page 15 for more about planting.) Johnny jump-up will grow in full sun to partial shade in most types of well-drained soil except clay. In partial shade, where it remains cooler, it will last longer into the summer. Water it in with transplant solution. Remove the first set of flowers on the plant to encourage root growth.

Growing Tips
When you purchase Johnny jump-up in cell packs, it is often rootbound. To avoid this problem, learn the habits of your local nursery or garden center and visit them the day they receive delivery of new plants. Foliar feed once a week and water regularly. Keep the soil lightly moist until the plants are established

Care and Maintenance
Water every ten to fourteen days. Do not fertilize. Deadhead early flowers as they fade. As it gets later in the season, leave the flowers to set seed. Pests are not a problem.

Companion Planting and Design
Johnny jump-up is lovely paired with its larger cousin, the pansy (*Viola × wittrockiana*). It is colorful in rock gardens and good in containers. Include it in a kitchen or vegetable garden as a pretty, tasty accent.

I Also Recommend
'Bowles' Black' is closer to true black than any other touted flower. Its small central golden eye makes it stand out. You can fool your friends because, when you eat it, your tongue will turn black—only from the color. It is as edible as other Johnny jump-ups and makes an unusually dark syrup.

Love-Lies-Bleeding
Amaranthus caudatus

When, Where, and How to Plant
Although you may find potted plants at nurseries, love-lies-bleeding is generally grown from seed. There are more varieties as seed. You can start the seeds indoors (see page 25) in peat pots six to eight weeks before the last frost date for a jump-start on the season. Since this plant grows quickly, it is easier to sow the seeds by placing them 1/2-inch deep directly in the garden. A sheltered location is ideal to keep the wind from battering the plants around. Love-lies-bleeding thrives in rich, well-drained soil in full sun. Add some organic matter (well-rotted manure or leaf mold) to the soil before sowing the seeds. Keep the soil evenly moist until after the seeds germinate.

Growing Tips
This plant needs regular feeding and watering in order to keep producing its magnificent blooms. It cannot tolerate drought. Water early in the day so the leaves are not damp at night. Foliar feed every two weeks with a half-strength solution of liquid kelp or fish emulsion, following package directions.

Care and Maintenance
Although it is susceptible to aphids and some fungal diseases, keeping the plants well fed and well watered can often thwart these problems.

Companion Planting and Design
So beautiful in a cottage garden, consider placing love-lies-bleeding against a white picket fence. This provides support and sets off the vivid color. In a cottage setting, it consorts well with sweet William (*Dianthus barbatus*), hollyhocks (*Alcea rosea* 'Chater's Double White'), and old-fashioned roses (*Rosa* 'Gertrude Jekyll'). It also makes an outstanding container plant, thereby limiting seed scattering.

I Also Recommend
Long, blood-red tassels are the hallmark of 'Love Lies Bleeding' cultivar. Plant Pony Tails Mixed strain for a lovely combination of tassels in hues of red and green. Ideal for a container, middle of a border, or a smaller garden, red-stemmed 'Pygmy Torch' grows only 2 feet tall. It is unique for its upright spires of flowers, rather than the traditional trailing panicles that are the hallmarks of *Amaranthus caudatus*. Most other species of *Amaranthus* have upright blooms.

Love-lies-bleeding is a striking plant and not for those who are faint of heart. Tall (3 to 5 feet high) with green, red, or purple stems, its light green leaves are a foil for the main attraction—the flowers. Tiny fuchsia-pink flowers are borne on 18- to 24-inch long, cascading, chenille-textured panicles that sway gently with the breeze. As the flowers mature, the brightly colored seeds attract songbirds. While feasting, birds inadvertently spread the seed around the garden, so it self-sows readily. An historic plant, it is included in period gardens including Old Sturbridge Village in Massachusetts. An excellent cut flower, it is stunning in a large arrangement. Love-lies-bleeding dries well. Cut it just as the flowers open and hang it upside-down in a warm dry place for several weeks.

Other Common Names
Tassel Flower; Velvet Flower

Bloom Period and Seasonal Color
Annual: Bright fuchsia-pink summer to early autumn.

Mature Height and Spread
3 to 5 ft. × 18 to 30 in.

Mexican Sunflower
Tithonia rotundifolia

Mexican sunflower, with its bushy form, handsome dark green leaves, 3-inch, brilliant-orange daisy flowers, and impressive size (growing to 6 feet tall), is the perfect plant to bridge the seasons. From late summer to frost it veritably glows in the garden. As the days grow shorter and start to cool down, its color makes me feel like it is still midsummer. The blossoms, which resemble single dahlias, are frequented by bees and butterflies. Several times, I have seen hummingbirds visit, but that is not documented in common literature. Mexican sunflower is long lasting as a cut flower. Because of its size, a few plants are usually enough for a garden. Although it isn't touted as a self-seeder, I have had it return several years in my gardens.

Bloom Period and Seasonal Color
Annual: Vivid orange from late summer to frost.

Mature Height and Spread
2¹/₂ to 6 ft. × 12 to 15 in.

When, Where, and How to Plant
The species is available as plants at many garden centers, nurseries, and home stores. Since there are several varieties of Mexican sunflower available only as seed, you may want to try one of them. Start the seeds indoors about four to six weeks before the last frost date. (Follow seed planting instructions described on page 25.) Mexican sunflower grows best in moderately rich, well-drained soil in full sun. Choose a space that is sheltered from the wind. Transplant it outdoors at the same time you would plant tomatoes (at least two weeks after all danger of frost has passed and soil temperature is above 60 degrees Fahrenheit). You can sow seeds directly in the garden at the same time. Young seedlings and transplants are temperature sensitive and will turn yellow when they are exposed to cold. Keep the plants well watered until they are established.

Growing Tips
I suggest staking them since the extra support keeps them upright no matter what. Once established, Mexican sunflowers require water only during dry spells. Foliar feed once a month.

Care and Maintenance
Slugs feast on new young foliage. Protect transplants and seedlings by pouring a 1-inch-wide circle of garden-grade diatomaceous earth around the base of the plant. This scratches the soft underbellies of slugs and snails, keeping them at a distance. In periods of heavy rain, renew the circle. Deadhead all spent flowers to prolong the bloom and to make the plant even bushier.

Companion Planting and Design
Mexican sunflower makes a brilliant show with the golden yellow petals of black-eyed Susans (*Rudbeckia fulgida* 'Goldsturm') and the vivid red of montbretia (*Crocosmia* 'Lucifer'). Mix and match it with any of the myriad sunflowers (*Helianthus* spp.).

I Also Recommend
'Torch' is the most outstanding variety color-wise, with dramatic red to red-orange flowers. 'Gold Finger' is somewhat smaller in stature (3 to 3¹/₂ feet tall) but is bushier (allow 30 inches between plants) with larger leaves, so the flowers don't appear as prominent as on the species or 'Torch'.

Nasturtium

Tropaeolum majus Alaska hybrids

When, Where, and How to Plant

Today, Alaska hybrids are found in some nurseries, garden centers, and home stores. However, the seed is readily available and easy to grow. Although you can start the seeds indoors four to six weeks before the last frost date (follow seed planting instructions described on page 25), it is easy to sow the large seeds outdoors 1 inch deep, two weeks after this date. Nasturtium thrives in poor to sandy, well-drained soil in full sun. Alaska hybrids and other nasturtiums are fairly drought tolerant; they thrive in containers.

Growing Tips

Do not feed nasturtium or grow it in good soil. The result will be large leaves but no flowers. Water it regularly until the plant is established, then only once a week or when the leaves start to wilt. Avoid pesticides if you will be eating any plant parts.

Care and Maintenance

If you don't keep up with eating the flowers, dead-head them. Nasturtium is susceptible to black aphids. I have found that if I intersperse nasturtium throughout my garden, these insects are not a problem. When I grow a passel of beans, I plant a row of nasturtiums nearby to attract the aphids away from the beans. Do not eat aphid-infested flowers, leaves, or stems.

Companion Planting and Design

Nasturtium was a staple in Victorian gardens. It consorts well with rose moss (*Portulaca grandiflora*), love-in-a-mist (*Nigella damascena*), lavender (*Lavandula* spp.), and thyme (*Thymus* spp.). These are all plants that thrive in the same type of soil.

I Also Recommend

Other delectable varieties include: 'Empress of India'—a Victorian heirloom with deep purplish-green leaves and velvety red, double flowers. 'Peach Melba'—beautifully bicolored creamy yellow flowers marked with peachy orange at the centers. 'Climbing Moonlight'—a vining variety, which quickly covers a trellis or arbor, or hides an unsightly chain link fence with soft primrose yellow blossoms. 'Whirlybird'—upward-facing single to semi-double flowers in shades of red, pink, yellow, and orange with a sweet flavor that is perfectly balanced with the spiciness.

Alaska is one of the most beautiful strains of nasturtium with its handsomely round, variegated leaves (light green accented with creamy white splotches and dots) that set off the delectable flowers that may be cream, yellow, orange, or mahogany. The plant has a nice bushy shape. The leaves have the same peppery flavor as the flowers, making a savory addition to a salad. Pop an entire flower in your mouth. As you chew on it, you first get a sweet sensation from the nectar, and then the peppery flavor comes through. For a show-stopping yet simple hors d'oeuvre mix chopped nasturtium petals and leaves into whipped cream cheese. Stuff individual flowers with the mixture or put on a cracker. Nasturtium is great grown in containers and in the garden.

Bloom Period and Seasonal Color

Annual: Cream, yellow, mahogany, or orange from summer to frost.

Mature Height and Spread

8 to 12 in. × 15 to 18 in.

Pansy
Viola × wittrockiana

Pansies have five petals and gives the appearance of a face. 'Antique Shades' is my favorite pansy because of its semi-muted, delicate colors of pale magenta to lilac blending into white. Its flower is 2 to 3 inches across, borne on stems above attractive, rippled-edged elliptical, dark green leaves. Pansy flowers are edible (grown organically) with a slight wintergreen taste. You can eat the entire flower, including the green sepals that hold it together. Pansies make a flavorful and pretty addition to fruit salads. Place one on top of any hors d'oeuvre to dress it up. Warning: Eating more than ten pansies a day has a diuretic effect. Plant pansies for early color in windowboxes, containers, and anywhere in the garden.

Bloom Period and Seasonal Color
Annual: Single, double, or tricolor flowers in hues of red, purple, white, yellow, maroon, blue, and pink from spring to early summer and fall to spring.

Mature Height and Spread
6 to 9 in. × 9 to 12 in.

When, Where, and How to Plant
Pansies are easily found very early in the season and in the fall. As they are tolerant of light frosts, you can plant pansies as soon as they are available—provided the ground has thawed. Since they are an edible flower, I rinse the soil from the plant, cut off any blossoms, and then plant them using transplant solution. Pansies prefer slightly moist, fertile, well-drained soil and grow in full sun, part sun, or part shade. Plant pansies in late summer or early fall (six to eight weeks before your first frost date in fall), or as soon as the ground thaws in spring. (See page 15 for more on planting.)

Growing Tips
Keep pansies lightly moist. Since I eat the flowers, I do not foliar feed them but instead add a layer of compost around the plants monthly. I recommend making compost tea and watering with that every two weeks. Several varieties have been bred for fall planting in the North, including the Icicle™ series. I have been growing fall pansies for more than a dozen years, and they will keep going through the winter. During January thaw, you may even get a flower or two. The pansies perk right back up as soon as the snow melts.

Care and Maintenance
If you are not eating all the flowers, deadhead any spent blossoms to prolong blooming. I have seen aphids but only in public gardens where they are grown in mass plantings. They shouldn't be a problem in your home garden.

Companion Planting and Design
In spring, pansies are beautiful with pink daffodils, such as *Narcissus* 'Mrs. R. O. Backhouse', blue Siberian squill (*Scilla siberica* 'Spring Beauty'), and Dutch hyacinths (*Hyacinthus orientalis*). In fall, it is stunning with New England asters (*Aster novae-angliae* 'Purple Dome').

I Also Recommend
'Jolly Joker' has marvelous coloring—deep purple and bright orange. Majestic Giant series has huge 4-inch flowers with the typical dark blotch or face and a range of colors including blue, red, purple, white, and yellow.

Shirley Poppy
Papaver rhoeas

When, Where, and How to Plant

Like other poppies, Shirley poppy may self-sow. It grows well in cool, well-drained soil in full sun. It is very easy to grow from seed. Save seed from ripe pods or buy seed and sow it in winter or early spring (see page 24 for more seed planting information). In winter, it gives me great joy to go out in February and sprinkle the seeds on top of the snow, knowing they will work their way down to the soil and germinate in early spring. The gardening season is short in the Prairie Lands states, and this gives me the feeling that spring is around the corner—even if it is not.

Growing Tips

Usually spring rains and the damp soil from winter provide ample moisture. However, if there has been a dry season, especially if you sow the seeds in spring, keep the soil lightly moist until the plants are up and have at least four leaves. After that, water weekly or more often if the temperatures soar. It does not need feeding.

Care and Maintenance

To promote longer bloom, cut off spent flowers down to where its stem attaches. When it finishes blooming, remove the plant. Pests and disease are rare.

Companion Planting and Design

Shirley poppies are beautiful in my meadow-like planting with pink, white, or blue bachelor's buttons (*Centaurea cyanus*), white wild indigo (*Baptisia leucantha*), blue love-in-a-mist (*Nigella damascena*), pinkish mallow (*Lavatera trimestris*), and little bluestem grass (*Schizachyrium scoparium*). They are excellent flowers for a cottage garden.

I Also Recommend

The Shirley series, which grows to 2 feet tall, blooms in hues of red, salmon, pink, white, and crimson. Some are bicolored. This series produces both single and double flowers. 'Rev. Wilkes' is a cultivar in the Shirley series with single or semi-double flowers of red, pink, or white. Some blooms are picotee or bicolored. 'Mother of Pearl' is subtler in its coloration—dove gray, lilac-blue, peachy pink, and soft pink. 'The Clown' is a charmer and quite unusual with an almost saw-toothed red-edged, white flower.

The sight of a field of Shirley poppies in bloom on a sunny day, with the light illuminating the translucent red petals dancing on the slightest breeze, is breathtaking. But you don't need a field for that effect. Even among other plants, its luminescence makes a single flower stand out from any others growing around it. The single, bowl-shaped flowers, up to 3 inches across, may have black markings at the center. The blooms are borne singly atop light green, downy stems. Shirley poppies are beautiful as cut flowers but are not long lasting. Although I have seen them grown in deep window boxes, they are best suited for the garden. Veterans on Memorial and Veterans Days wear a silk boutonniere version.

Other Common Names
Corn Poppy, Flanders Poppy

Bloom Period and Seasonal Color
Annual: Hues of red, pink, white, or crimson in single or bicolors from early to midsummer.

Mature height and spread
30 to 36 in. × 8 to 12 in.

Sunflower

Helianthus annuus

Many of us got our first taste of gardening when we were small children growing sunflowers. We planted a small sunflower seed in late spring and watched it grow daily, until it towered over our heads and kept on growing. We saw the flowerhead (ray florets surrounding disk florets) appear, grow, and set seed. We left the seeds for the birds and squirrels or cut down flowerheads to dry for our own munching. That magic—that a seed less than an inch long can grow into a 15-foot mammoth plant in a couple of months—stays with us forever. Today there are numerous hybrids—from edging plants 2 feet tall to our childhood giants—in single and bicolors in a range of colors.

Bloom Period and Seasonal Color
Annual: Yellow with brown center in summer to frost.

Mature Height and Spread
16 in. to 15 ft. × 1 to 2 ft.

When, Where, and How to Plant
Sunflowers need rich, moist, neutral to alkaline, well-drained soil. After all danger of frost has passed, plant seeds 1 inch deep in full sun. Spacing depends on variety, and can be determined with seed packet information. Water sunflowers well at planting.

Growing Tips
Once the plant is established, it tolerates dry soil. However, if the leaves start to droop, water immediately. Foliar feeding is difficult on the tall varieties. Instead, water with compost tea bimonthly.

Care and Maintenance
Tall types may need staking in exposed areas. If you plan to eat the seeds, cover the flower with bird netting. Cut it down when the seeds are well formed and full sized. Put it in a warm, dry space with good air circulation. Powdery mildew on the leaves can be treated by weekly spraying with baking soda solution (see page 233)—or just accept it.

Companion Planting and Design
A great combination of colors, shapes, and textures is produced by 'Kid Stuff' sunflower, planted with Gloriosa daisy (*Rudbeckia hirta* var. *pulcherrima*), and creeping zinnia (*Santvitalia procumbens*). To make a sunflower house with a child, plant a 6- to 8-foot rectangle of tall sunflowers—the house—spaced 12 inches apart. Leave an open space for the "door." Run strings from the sunflowers on one side of the house to those on the other. Plant blue morning glories (*Ipomoea tricolor* 'Heavenly Blue') at the base of the sunflowers on the two sides. This will create a shelter of sunflowers with a sky blue roof of morning glories.

I Also Recommend
Musicbox strain is a diminutive 28 inches tall with numerous 4- to 5-inch flowers with ray florets in a range of colors and bicolors from creamy yellow to deep red surrounding a black center. 'Sunzilla' is excellent for eating, growing up to 14 feet tall with lots of golden flowers. Eighteen inch high 'Teddy Bear' blooms resemble 5-inch chrysanthemums with double, golden-yellow ray flowers.

Sweet William

Dianthus barbatus

When, Where, and How to Plant

Sweet William is a self-sowing biennial often grown as an annual. It's available potted for spring planting and will bloom that year. It thrives in rich, well-drained, slightly alkaline soil in full sun. It's an excellent container plant; I mix in several cupfuls of compost with the potting mix before planting. Self-sown, it may not come true to color; however, I enjoy these surprises. In the garden it seems perennial because the seeds that form this summer will germinate, set leaves, go dormant for the winter, and then bloom the following spring and summer. When sowing from purchased seed, sow the seeds in late spring or early summer in a rich, well-drained seedbed. Cover with 1/2 inch of soil. Gently water. Keep lightly moist. In fall, transplant into their flowering site for next year.

Growing Tips

Water regularly throughout the growing season. Foliar feed every two weeks until the plant begins to bloom.

Care and Maintenance

As a flower cluster fades, cut it back to the next set of branches, and you will often be rewarded with a second or third flush of bloom. Unless you are trying to save seeds, remove the plant from the garden once it has finished flowering. Prevent fungus by spraying weekly with baking soda solution (page 233).

Companion Planting and Design

Sweet William is striking in a large container with dusty miller (*Senecio cineraria*), 'Pretty in Pink' double petunia (*Petunia* × *hybrida* 'Pretty in Pink'), and 'Blackie' sweet potato vine (*Ipomoea batatas* 'Blackie'). It is a lovely cottage garden, grown with valerian (*Centranthus ruber*) and delphiniums (*Delphinium* spp.).

I Also Recommend

'Amazon Neon' is one of the largest-flowered (with clusters 4 to 7 inches across), longest-blooming sweet Williams, with zingy magenta or cherry rose blooms. Unlike other dianthus, seeds sown in late spring flower in three months. It is extra long lasting as a cut flower. 'French Frills' boasts a 3- to 4-inch nosegay of blossoms in four colors—pink, white, red, and magenta.

Sweet William is cousin to carnations, with a similar, clove-sweet scent. Its delicate flowers come in hues of white, pink, crimson, and purple, blended or banded, often with a white center. They are densely clustered, creating the illusion of a 3- to 4-inch tussie-mussie. The petals are flat, with edges that look like they have been cut with miniature pinking shears. If grown organically, the colored portion of the flowers are edible, with a sweet clove-like flavor. Pull a petal and remove the bitter portion—the long perpendicular part that attaches it to the sepal. The flowers make delicious jelly, scrumptious shortbread, and a flavoring for sugar. Butterflies flock to the blooms in late summer. Sweet William is an excellent, long-lasting cut flower for colorful arrangements.

Bloom Period and Seasonal Color

Biennial: Single or bicolor purple, red, pink, cherry, or white from late spring through summer.

Mature Height and Spread

4 to 28 in. × 10 to 15 in.

Wave™ Petunia

Petunia × hybrida Wave™ series

When it first arrived on the scene, the Wave™ series practically revolutionized the way people grew petunias. Unlike those we have grown for years, which required constant deadheading and got leggy without severe pruning, The Wave™ is virtually maintenance free. With little attention except watering and fertilizing, a single plant can spread up to 3 feet, making The Wave™ ideal for large containers, gracefully cascading over the side—almost to the ground. It is equally at home in the garden and makes a super bedding plant. The large size of the flowers is impressive—2 to 3 inches across. The range of hues is broad enough to fit most any color scheme. Most important, it thrives in our hot humid summers.

Other Common Name
Spreading Petunia

Bloom Period and Seasonal Color
Annual: Lilac, pink, purple, blue, or salmon from summer to frost.

Mature Height and Spread
8 to 24 in. × 2 to 3 ft. or more

When, Where, and How to Plant

The Wave™ and its relatives are readily available as plants. Petunia grows best in moderately fertile (rich soil grows leaves not flowers) to poor soil in full sun protected from the wind. Plant after the danger of frost has passed. It comes in relatively large pots and is unlikely to be rootbound; check the bottom of the pot to be sure. Plant at the same depth as it was in the pot. Remember, it spreads, so allow at least 2 feet between plants. (See page 15 for more about planting.) When planting in a container, use at least an 18-inch pot for a single plant. I grow them in 24- to 36-inch pots singly or combined with other plants. If you combine them with those plants, choose those that are taller and plant the petunias closer to the edge of the pot. When planting in a hanging basket, line it with a disposable diaper (skin side up) to help retain moisture.

Growing Tips

Keep well watered, and foliar feed every two weeks.

Care and Maintenance

Dead flowers often fall off by themselves, unless there is a lot of rain and they remain wet and stick to the plant. New flowers may cover up those that are spent. You do not need to prune out the dead flowers; they readily pull out from the sepals. You may need to cut the plant back to keep it within a confined area. Pests are rare.

Companion Planting and Design

With the range of colors and combinations in both plants, any of the taller coleus (*Solenostemon scutellarioides*) grows beautifully with The Wave™. It also pairs well with impatiens (*Impatiens walleriana*).

I Also Recommend

Distinguished by semi-double blooms, Ride The Wave™ also spreads vigorously. The Easy Wave™ series blooms earlier than The Wave™ in cherry, shell pink, and white. Double Wave™ petunias have exquisite flowers in shades of lavender, pink, purple, white, and rose. 'Blue Vein' is outstanding with double, deep lavender blossoms highlighted by darker lavender veins.

Zinnia

Zinnia elegans

When, Where, and How to Plant

Although zinnia is available as a potted plant, seeds have more varieties. Plant seeds in rich, well-drained, moist soil in full sun, 1/4-inch deep, 9 inches apart. Keep well watered until they are established. (Follow seed planting instructions on page 24.) Avoid wetting the leaves. Zinnia is versatile—equally at home in a container, cutting garden, cottage garden, mixed border, or as a bedding plant.

Growing Tips

Zinnia requires regular watering. Avoid wetting the leaves. A soaker hose or drip irrigation system is ideal. Foliar feed once a month.

Care and Maintenance

Pinch back early flowers to the next lower stem for a bushier plant. Deadheading faded flowers encourages more blooms. Zinnia is susceptible to powdery mildew. To discourage this, allow ample air circulation between plants. Water early in the day at ground level to keep the leaves dry. Feed regularly, as a healthy plant is less susceptible to pests and diseases. To fight mildew, spray the tops and bottoms of the leaves (only when temperatures are below 80 degrees Fahrenheit) weekly with a baking soda solution. (See page 231.) When cutting flowers for bouquets, avoid cutting off more than one set of side stems.

Companion Planting and Design

Zinnia works well in a container alone or in combination with other plants. I dazzled the neighborhood with a yellow embossed, Art Deco wastebasket with drainage holes drilled in the bottom planted with 'Swizzle' zinnia and a 'Purple Wave'™ petunia. Another suggestion is to interplant mildew-resistant 'Pinwheel' zinnias with curly parsley (*Petroselinum crispum*).

I Also Recommend

'Swizzle', a new introduction, is a bicolor of scarlet and yellow in circular bands around the fully double, 3-inch-wide flowers. It grows about 20 inches tall. Profusion Mixed strain grows 15 inches high with a mix of colors—white, cherry, orange, and red-orange. Unlike most zinnias, it is self-cleaning, dropping its flowers, so deadheading is unnecessary.

Zinnia is a must-have plant for any garden. It recalls childhood memories at my grandmother's and parent's gardens, watching the bees searching for pollen. Flowers range through almost every color of the rainbow. Some zinnias are single with prominent yellow stamens; others are fully double, resembling dahlias. With hybrid varieties in all heights, there's a zinnia for the edge, front, middle, or back of the garden. Zinnia is unsurpassed as a cut flower. As a child, we always had a juice glass in the bathroom with fresh zinnias. I had the responsibility and honor of checking to see how fresh the flowers were each day, cutting 1/4 inch off each stem and putting them in fresh water or discarding them and cutting new zinnias for simple beauty.

Bloom Period and Seasonal Color

Annual: Hues of red, pink, yellow, cream, white, and bicolors from summer to frost.

Mature Height and Spread

6 to 40 in. × 8 to 15 in.

Bulbs *for the Prairie Lands*

Bulbs have a specialized food storage organ that allows them to have a long period of dormancy and come back yearly. Think of it, you see crocus start blooming in early spring, the flowers die back, the leaves remain for a while, they die down, and then the plant disappears until the following spring.

I use the term bulb loosely, encompassing true bulbs, tubers, corms, tuber-corms, and rhizomes. It is helpful to understand the difference between them. A true bulb is a modified, enlarged bud with a fore-shortened stem and the beginnings of leaves, which grow extremely tightly along the stem forming a dense, somewhat spherical mass. Look under the skin of true bulbs (very obvious with lilies) and you see some-what scaly leaves swollen with stored food. Cut a daffodil, or tulip in half, and the structure is evident.

In a tuber (or tuberous root), the food storage mechanism is a swollen root, which grows just beneath the surface of the soil. Buds develop around the base of the old stem, becoming new plants. New fibrous roots form in this area, feeding the plant during the growing season. Winter aconite is a tuber.

A corm is a swollen, vertical, solid stem with the bud for leaves and flowers at the top. Buds on the sides (lateral buds) form cormels (offsets). Although a corm is an annual, using its food to grow leaves and flowers, it develops a new replacement corm from each lateral bud. When purchasing corms, look for ones with many lateral buds. Without lateral buds, the corm dies after one season. Gladiolus, Dutch iris, and crocus are corms.

Ring of Crocus

Another form of a modified stem is a rhizome—like a horizontal corm. It may sit on the soil or be just under soil level. Leaves, stems, and flowers grow from the upper portion (apex), and the bottom produces roots. Cannas and agapanthus have rhizomes, as do some iris.

A combination category is a tuber-corm, including tuberous begonias and cyclamen. Disk- or top-shaped, it has one or more buds on the upper portion and annual roots on the bottom. Like a tuber, it is perennial, growing in size each year.

Tiger lilies, which grow from bulbs, produce bulbils along the stem just above each leaf. Bulbils store food, drop to the ground, and germinate like seeds. It takes several years for a bulbil to produce a flowering plant.

Bulbs are categorized as hardy or tender. Most spring-blooming bulbs (crocus, daffodils, tulips, glory-of-the-snow, and snowdrops) are hardy—needing a period of cold to induce bloom. Once planted, they remain in the ground for years. Tender bulbs—summer-blooming bulbs, such as dahlias, calla lilies, cannas, peacock orchids, and gladiolas—cannot survive our winter cold and must be dug up in the fall.

Bulbs are low-maintenance plants. The key to success is to let the leaves die back on their own. There is a great temptation, especially with spring-blooming bulbs such as daffodils and tulips with long leaves, to cut down the foliage. Some people braid the leaves or tie them back with rubber bands to disguise their maturation (turning yellow or brown), but it is best to leave them alone. Leaves play an important role in a bulb's life cycle. Through photosynthesis, they replenish the bulb's food stores. Remove the leaves too early and the odds of the bulb returning the following year are not good.

Planting

Most bulbs need sun and rich, well-drained soil—exceptions are noted in the individual plant listings. As a rule, they do not need fertilizer or so-called boosters added to their planting hole. If they do need fertilizer, feeding is more important during the active growing and flowering season. Unless otherwise noted, the bulbs included here are hardy to Zone 3.

Soil Preparation

Before planting, perform a perk test: Dig a ten-inch hole, fill it with water, and wait. If the water hasn't drained into the soil within an hour, you can often solve the problem by digging six inches deeper and amending the soil with builder's sand and organic matter (compost, well-rotted manure, or leaf mold). Add six inches of the amended soil back into the hole and see if that helps. If not, you can install drains, assuming there is a place to send the water, but that can be time-consuming and costly. A raised bed is the easiest solution. Depending on your physical needs, you might want to make a raised bed two feet or higher, with a broad edge so you can sit and garden. Design the bed to be as long as you like, but make the width so that the middle is easily reached from either side. In the Prairie Lands states, a raised bed has an advantage besides good drainage—the soil warms up earlier in the spring so you can start enjoying your flowers before your neighbors can.

Rules of Thumb for Planting

Depth: Plant the bulb two to three times as deep as its height. For example, plant a one-inch crocus in a hole two to three inches deep. A three-inch lily would go down six to nine inches. *Spacing:* Allow three times the width of the bulb between each bulb—from center to center. Therefore, one-inch-wide crocus would actually have two inches of soil between them; the other inch is half the diameter of each bulb. Three-inch-wide lilies have six inches of soil between the bulbs—the measurement is from the center of one bulb to the center of the next.

Support

Some of the taller bulbs (over four feet), such as dahlias and lilies, blow over or break from strong winds or heavy rains. There are many different materials you can use for support—green plastic-coated metal stakes, wood stakes, bamboo, metal rods, PVC pipe, long dowels (waterproof or paint to keep them from rotting), and even tomato cages for dahlias. Choose a support that is at least twelve inches longer than the mature height of the plant. The extra length goes in the ground for stability. The longer the support, the deeper it should be. If you the stake the bulb after it is growing, you risk piercing it. "Plant" the support with the bulb. I paint the support bright colors (there is even spray paint for plastic) to add interest until the foliage covers them. If you plant lilies and their supports in autumn, use the support for attaching holiday decorations. I attach the dried bloom of a giant allium (sprayed life-like purple) to give life to the winter garden. Once the plant is up and growing, use twine or a piece of old pantyhose to loosely attach the stem to the stake. *Do not use twist-ties* as the wire core can damage the stem as it grows. Make a loose figure-eight around the stem and the support, and tie it to the support. As the plant grows, tie it every six to eight inches.

Spring-blooming Bulbs

Spring-blooming bulbs put on such a great show, relieving the darkness and drabness of winter. When planting, think big. Bulbs have the most impact in natural-looking clusters, drifts, or swaths. For large bulbs, such as hyacinths or tulips, plant groups of five, seven, or more. Planting in odd numbers is one of the tenets of gardening. Small bulbs like crocus or snowdrops show off best in groups of fifteen, twenty-five, or more.

Interplant spring-blooming bulbs with each other. You can plant them individually, but I prefer to dig a large hole to the depth of the largest bulb. Place the large bulbs first; feel free to put those of the

Stunning Color with Massed Tulips

same size in groups at the same level within the hole (such as hyacinths, lilies, and large daffodils). *Do not plant them in soldierly rows.* Place plant markers in with the bulbs that are tall enough to reach above soil level. Cover the bulbs with an inch or two of soil and then add a layer of the next largest bulbs (tulips and species daffodils) with markers. Add more soil and plant smaller bulbs (such as crocus and snowdrops) so that each bulb is at its proper depth. If you start out with large lilies, you may have four layers of bulbs. Try not to put one layer right on top of the bulbs below. In spring, the result will be a riot of color and continuous bloom. In addition, subsequent blooms and leaves hide the ripening foliage of the earlier ones. I often include several daylilies—even though they are perennials and not bulbs—as they continue the bloom season and hide the foliage of the later bulbs.

In late summer and autumn, squirrels and other critters look upon newly planted bulbs as haute cuisine. One of the best deterrents is to lay chicken wire over the planting and pin it down. That also keeps cats from inadvertently digging. Be sure to remove it in late winter before you anticipate any bulbs sticking their heads up through the snow. Unless otherwise mentioned in the individual entry, there are no other pest or disease problems.

Summer-blooming Bulbs

Summer-blooming bulbs are planted in late spring, generally after all danger of frost has passed. (Any exceptions are noted in the individual plant listing.) They begin to grow as soon as you plant them, and pest deterrents are not necessary. Include summer blooming bulbs in perennial beds, mixed borders, and other plantings. They are more easily incorporated into existing plantings than spring bloomers. As they do not tolerate the cold, they need to be dug up and stored for the winter, generally after the first frost. Drying and storage vary from plant to plant, but all summer-bloomers need to be kept in a place where the temperature is between 40 and 50 degrees Fahrenheit.

Asiatic Lily
Lilium 'Connecticut King'

In addition to species lilies (dozens that are Nature's creations and the hybrids thereof), there are two main categories under which the majority of other hybrid lilies fall—Asiatic and Oriental lilies. Asiatic lilies bloom in summer, with their 3- to 6-inch-wide, six-petaled flowers in clusters. They have no scent, but their beauty makes up for any lack of fragrance. The flowers may be up-facing, outfacing, or pendant. 'Connecticut King' is a reliable, favorite Asiatic lily. Its up-facing, yellow 4- to 5-inch, cuplike blooms set the garden aglow at any time of day. A group of flowers blooms at once, making an instant bouquet for cutting and arranging indoors, or left on the plant. The flowers are long lasting, indoors and out, and hold up well in the rain.

Bloom Period and Seasonal Color
Yellow in summer.

Mature Height and Spread
2 to 3 ft. × 18 to 24 in.

When, Where, and How to Plant
Asiatic lilies, unlike most summer-blooming bulbs, are available to plant both in fall and spring. Choose the largest, weightiest, and most solid bulbs. Avoid bulbs with soft spots or signs of mold or mildew. Asiatic lilies grow best in rich, loamy, very well-drained soil and full to part sun. In fall, plant them immediately so that the roots establish before winter. If moles, voles, or mice are a problem, roll the bulb in sulfur before planting. Space 8 to 15 inches apart. Plant with the bottom of the bulb 3 times as deep as its height. Fill the hole with soil and firm down gently with your hands. Water well. (See page 47 for more planting information.)

Growing Tips
Fertilize at the beginning of the growing season with Bulb Booster™ or any well-balanced liquid or granular fertilizer, such as 5-5-5, (following package instructions). If there is no rain, water deeply once a week until it begins to flower. Once blooming is over, decrease watering so the bulb can ripen.

Care and Maintenance
If it's growing in an exposed, windy area, stake the bulb when planting (see page 48 regarding staking). If you are cutting the flowers for an arrangement, you may want to cut off the anthers because the pollen drops off and can stain material. Remove spent blooms. Enjoy the green foliage for an extended period. Mulch with 3 inches of organic matter in winter.

Companion Planting and Design
'Connecticut King' is handsome in the ground or in a container combined with yellow evening primrose (*Oenothera biennis*) and trailing greater periwinkle (*Vinca major*). Mix several different Asiatic lily varieties together for a riot of color.

I Also Recommend
Other Asiatic lilies include: 'Montreux' (30 to 36 inches)—medium pink with brown-speckled center; 'Enchantment' (2 to 3 feet)—deep orange, cuplike petals; 'Tiger Babies' (36 to 42 inches)—pendant flowers with recurved petals—salmon peach with brownish pink undersides; and 'Sterling Star' (3 to 4 feet)—short clusters of large, up-facing, off-white flowers with a flush of cream and brown speckling.

Autumn Crocus
Colchicum autumnale

When, Where, and How to Plant

Choose the largest, firmest bulbs. Avoid ones that have sprouted. Autumn crocus prefers deep, fertile, well-drained soil and full sun. As soon as the bulb arrives, plant it with the top four inches below the soil surface. Cluster seven or more bulbs 2 to 3 inches apart for an impressive show. Water well. They will bloom within several weeks (see page 47 for more on planting.) To prove their magical quality, place one or two on a sunny windowsill. Watch them send up their goblet-shaped, 2- to 3-inch, lavender-pink flowers. Their show will be fleeting, however, from lack of water.

Growing Tips

Keep the plant lightly moist while in bloom. Allow the soil to dry when it goes dormant. Add a 3-inch layer of organic mulch after the ground freezes. Remove mulch in spring. Foliar feed with liquid kelp or fish emulsion (following package directions) when the leaves appear.

Care and Maintenance

Since it goes dormant until spring and again when the leaves fade, it is important to mark where autumn crocus is. Otherwise, you may inadvertently dig into the area when planting something in later spring or summer, ruining the bulbs before they rebloom in late summer. A small metal marker withstands the test of time; blue jays steal plastic labels, using them in their nests.

Companion Planting and Design

For a sense of a Monet painting, interplant autumn crocus in a sea of periwinkle (*Vinca minor*). It is gorgeous planted with any coleus (*Solenostemon scutellarioides*) with pink in its leaves.

I Also Recommend

'Waterlily' is the showiest cultivar, with large blossoms reminiscent of water lilies on Monet's pond. 'Alboplenum' (white meadow saffron) is very striking with large, white, double blossoms that are not knocked down by heavy rains, as are many of the species. *Colchicum atropurpureum* is an interesting species. One bulb can produce as many as twelve flowers, adding a large splash of deep rosy lilac. Unlike the more common autumn crocus, this one sends ups its leaves after the flowers fade in autumn.

This well known and showiest of the fall-blooming bulbs is often advertised as a "magic bulb" that will bloom right on the windowsill, without a pot or water—and it will. Autumn crocus is a misnomer. Not a crocus at all, although it resembles one, it is a member of the lily family. In late summer, each bulb produces two to six, showy, goblet-shaped, leafless blossoms. The flowers can last for several weeks with ample water and cool temperatures. A grouping of bulbs will give an impressive show. The leaves come up in the spring, big and bold, deep green, and growing up to 6 inches high. After about six weeks, the leaves disappear and the plant goes dormant, disappearing from sight until it blooms.

Other Common Names
Meadow Saffron, Magic Lily

Bloom Period and Seasonal Color
Lavender-pink in late summer to early fall.

Mature Height and Spread
4 to 6 in. × 4 to 6 in.

Zone
5

Caladium
Caladium bicolor

Caladiums are showy with multi-colored (muted or bold), 6- to 8-inch, heart-shaped leaves. Grown for their foliage (I have never seen a bloom), they are prized as plants for livening up any shady area. To me, they are the Dolly Partons of shade plants—big, bold, and beautiful. They are as far from shrinking violets as you can go in the plant world. Color combinations may be simple—the leaf one color with the veins highlighted another—or complex with splashes, dots, edgings, and other permutations of color mixes in shades of red, pink, green, and white. Caladiums make great container plants. Although the tubers are usually dug up and brought in for winter storage, you can keep them growing indoors in a container.

Other Common Name
Fancy-leaf Caladium

Bloom Period and Seasonal Color
Seldom blooms in the garden; bi- and tricolor foliage mixed with shades of white, green, pink, red, and burgundy from summer to frost.

Mature Height and Spread
18 to 24 in. × 18 to 24 in.

When, Where, and How to Plant
Eight to ten weeks before the last frost date, start caladiums indoors in 6-inch pots filled with lightly moistened potting soil or milled sphagnum moss. Cover with 2 inches of soil. Keep it between 80 to 85 degrees Fahrenheit (try a heating mat) and lightly moist. If you plan to grow it in a container outdoors, start it in that pot. Caladium thrives in rich, slightly acid, humus-rich, moist, well-drained soil in part to full shade. Transplant outdoors once the soil has reached at least 60 degrees Fahrenheit. Allow 8 to 10 inches between plants. Water well with transplant solution (see page 47 for more on planting).

Growing Tips
Water well. Never let the soil dry out. Spray leaves frequently during hot, dry weather. Foliar feed monthly with a solution of kelp or fish emulsion (following package instructions).

Care and Maintenance
Cut off faded leaves to the ground. After the first frost, carefully dig the tubers. Place them on a screen in a warm, dry, airy place for about a week to dry. Store the tubers on a shallow tray in a warm, dry place. If you grew the caladiums in a pot, the leaves begin to droop in autumn. Bring the pots inside and water very sparingly until the leaves shrivel and fall off. Store the pots in a warm place—about 70 degrees Fahrenheit. As caladiums are susceptible to tuber rot, check them in the spring before replanting—they should be firm. Otherwise, destroy them.

Companion Planting and Design
Caladium is magnificent in hanging baskets. In moss-lined baskets, plant one on the top and poke several plants into the soil so the outside of the basket is radiant with leaves. In the garden, combine it with hosta (*Hosta* spp.) to enliven a shady spot with their vivid colors. Mix and match caladium with impatiens (*Impatiens walleriana*) for fun color echoes.

I Also Recommend
'Miss Muffett' has creamy leaves with strokes of pale green and bright fuchsia spots. 'White Christmas' is pure white with bold green veins. 'Florida Cardinal' is a bold cardinal red, edged in deep green.

Canna
Canna × generalis

When, Where, and How to Plant

Canna is easiest to start from a potted plant. Consider it an investment in the future. The following spring, make cuttings from the rhizome for more plants. Canna thrives in rich soil in full sun. It can tolerate very moist soil—growing at the edge of ponds. Plant it at the same time as tomatoes; space 18 inches apart. Water well with transplant solution.

Growing Tips

Keep well watered. Foliar feed monthly.

Care and Maintenance

Deadhead to prolong bloom. After frost blackens the leaves, cut off the stems and leaves, and lift the rhizomes. Overwinter rhizomes in barely moist peat moss in a cool (above freezing) place. In spring, pot rhizomes (cut them so there are one or two buds per piece) 2 inches deep in 6-inch pots. Water well. Set on a sunny windowsill until planting time. There is an old variety with deep purplish green leaves and red flowers growing in neglected gardens and farms—with no attention. I have asked folks what the variety is and they reply, "Canna lilies. They've been here as long as I remember. They just come up each year; I don't do a thing to them." If you see these plants, ask for one or two since they are particularly tough. One came up in my garden unbidden and grows unattended. Fungal leaf spot can be a problem; cut off and destroy any suspect leaves.

Companion Planting and Design

Create a tropical look by growing canna with calla lily (*Zantedeschia aethiopica*), summer hyacinth (*Galtonia candicans*), elephant's ear (*Alocasia* spp.), and 'Burgundy Stem' taro (*Colocasia esculenta* 'Burgundy Stem').

I Also Recommend

'Tropicanna' has leaves striated with the colors of a tropical sunset. Plant it where the sun shines through its leaves in early morning or late afternoon like stained glass. 'Mr. President' ('President') is stately with blue-green leaves and scarlet blossoms. 'Wyoming' has deep brownish-purple leaves with dark purple veins highlighted with 4-inch frilled orange flowers. 'Bengal Tiger' ('Pretoria') has dramatic 6-foot, maroon-edged, yellow- and green-striped leaves with bright orange blooms.

Canna, which like coleus and other tropical plants that were held in great esteem in Victorian times, is also enjoying a resurgence of popularity in gardens everywhere. Canna is favored for its large, lush leaves that accentuate the tropical look (called the "banana-canna craze" by some) enjoyed by many northern gardeners. In fact, some people cut the flower off before it even blooms, preferring just the foliage. Yet, the flower is a colorful accent atop a plant that ranges from 2 to 6 feet tall. With modern hybridizing, leaves range from varying shades of green to a plethora of variegations—some subtle, some bold. From the colors of a tropical sunset to green and white stripes, there is at least one canna for every garden.

Other Common Names

Canna Lily, Indian Shot Plant

Bloom Period and Seasonal Color

Whitish, yellow, orange, or red in summer.

Mature Height and Spread

2½ to 8 ft. × 1½ to 3 ft.

Crocus
Crocus spp.

Although it may not be the first bulb to peek through the snow in late winter, it is the first to show color—a true harbinger of spring. There are many species and cultivars of crocus (some fragrant), from the earliest snow crocus (Crocus tommasinianus and C. chrysanthus) to the best known—Dutch or giant crocus (C. vernus)—and even some fall-blooming species. The colors of crocus can be so pure—white, yellow, purple, lilac—bold or muted and even gorgeous bicolors. Some crocus are one color on the inside of the petal that you see when they are wide open in daytime and another for nighttime viewing. Crocus is meant to be planted by the dozens or hundreds in curving swaths and naturalistic groupings.

Bloom Period and Seasonal Color
Hues of yellow, white, purple, blue, mauve—single and bicolor—from late winter to early spring; and late summer to early fall.

Mature Height and Spread
1/2 to 6 in. × 1 to 6 in.

Zone
4

When, Where, and How to Plant
Plant the corms soon after you get them in late summer. Crocus thrives in full sun in humus-rich, lightly moist, well-drained soil, but it tolerates most well-drained soils. Plant it 3 to 4 inches deep and 3 inches apart. Water well. (See page 47 for more planting information.)

Growing Tips
Keep the soil lightly moist after planting and during spring growth, watering weekly with compost tea during the growing period. After that, do not water; allow them to dry.

Care and Maintenance
Let the leaves remain until they yellow or brown. With crocus planted in the lawn, let the grass grow up to 3 inches high (the current recommended height). Fertilizing the lawn *only* in fall will be adequate. Spring lawn fertilization increases leaf growth at the expense of root growth; if you apply fertilizer in spring, your lawn could be 6 inches high before the crocus ripens! Crocus naturalizes readily.

Companion Planting and Design
Crocus is beautiful planted in a lawn, giving early color in a sea of green. Use crocus in borders or as edging. It's a sight to behold them naturalized in the lawn, in a deciduous woodland, on a slope, or beneath a single deciduous tree. Plant snow crocus and Dutch crocus together for a succession of bloom. Mix and match colors.

I Also Recommend
Snow crocus (1/2- to 1-inch high, scented) include: 'Advance'—lemon yellow inside, purplish outside; 'Ruby Giant'—deep velvety purple with contrasting orange stigma; and 'Lady Killer'—white blooms with bold purple streak on outside of petal. Dutch (giant) crocus (4 to 6 inches high) includes: 'King of the Striped'—beautifully striped purple and white; 'Golden Yellow'—outstanding deep sunny yellow; and 'Jeanne d'Arc'—pure snow white with prominent orange stigmas. Fall bloomers (plant 3 to 4 inches deep in well-drained soil in mid to late summer) include: *Crocus goulimyi*—one to three fragrant lilac-colored flowers per corm simultaneously with narrow green leaves; and the true saffron crocus (*Crocus sativus*)—the orange-red stigma is the costly culinary saffron thread.

Daffodil
Narcissus spp.

When, Where, and How to Plant
When buying bulbs, you get what you pay for. Great bargains are often small bulbs—too immature to flower immediately. However, with patience and a large area, they are worth it. Otherwise, choose the largest size possible. If you are hand picking them, choose firm, solid bulbs with smaller bulbs growing off the sides. The side bulbs may bloom the first year, if not, then the second. The main bulb can produce numerous flowering stems. Daffodils grow best with full sun in average to rich, well-drained soil that is moist in spring. Plant it three times its depth, with at least 3 inches of soil covering it. Water well. (See page 47 for more planting information.)

Growing Tips
Keep lightly moist after planting and during spring growth. Water weekly with compost tea during the growing period. After that, do not water. Fungal infections can be avoided by inspecting the bulb before planting—discard any with soft, greenish-blue, or black areas.

Care and Maintenance
Remove the flower stem or deadhead it when the blooms fade so the plant's energy goes to the bulb. Let the leaves remain until they yellow or brown. Do not braid or tie them back. If the bulbs don't bloom but have healthy leaves, it is time for dividing. Dig up the clump and gently tease the bulbs and roots apart. Replant at their original depth, spaced two to three times the width of the bulb (center to center). Water well with transplant solution.

Companion Planting and Design
Daffodils highlight blue grape hyacinths (*Muscari armeniacum*). Interplant early, small yellow daffodils like 'Wee Bee' and 'Small Talk' with blue Siberian squill (*Scilla siberica*) and starry blue and white glory-of-the-snow (*Chionodoxa luciliae*). Grow with tulips (*Tulipa* spp.)

I Also Recommend
'Cheerfulness' (16 inches, midseason bloom) has fragrant clusters of double white blooms. 'Actea' (18 inches, late season bloom) has fragrant, broad white petals with a short, red-edged yellow cup. 'Jack Snipe' (8 inches, early bloom) has recurved white petals with a short lemon-yellow cup.

Daffodils are the essence of springtime in hues of yellow. Although there are white and bicolored—sometimes accented with pink or orange—and even scented daffodils, daffodils bring to mind the vision of sunny yellow, large trumpeted daffodils, such as the classic 'King Alfred'. The hundreds of daffodils have been classified into twelve divisions. The main divisions are based on the relative length of the trumpet (cup) to the petal and whether it has a single or double flower. From the earliest species daffodil that grows through the snow (Narcissus asturiensis) to the last that blooms with the peonies (often called pheasant's eye daffodil, Narcissus poeticus 'Actea'), there are myriad daffodils to grace any part of your garden. Most naturalize—three to five bulbs becoming a foot-wide cluster in a few years.

Other Common Names
Narcissus, Jonquil

Bloom Period and Seasonal Color
Yellow, white, and bicolor with pink or orange, from early to late spring.

Mature Height and Spread
4 to 20 in. × 2 to 8 in.

Gladiolus
Gladiolus spp.

The elegant stalks of gladiolus shoot from 12 to 40 inches tall, with flowers opening in succession up the stem, clasped by swordlike leaves. Gladioli are classified by the size of the flower—from miniatures less than 2 1/2 inches wide to giants 5 1/2 inches across. Flower spikes range to 3 feet tall with as many as twenty-seven buds—ten open at a time—and are long-lasting cut flowers. Blooms are borne in either a formal style—side by side so that when they are open there appears to be no space in between— or less formal with one flower above another, stepladder fashion, so you see the stem. The range of colors, variations, and combinations is not seen in any other flower.

Other Common Name
Gladiola

Bloom Period and Seasonal Color
Single, bi- and tri-colored in every color of the rainbow in summer.

Mature Height and Spread
12 to 42 in. × 8 to 16 in.

When, Where, and How to Plant
Gladiolus is only available as a corm. It prefers fertile, well-drained soil in sheltered full sun. Dig a 6- to 8-inch hole, depending on the size of the corm. Add 1 inch of organic material (compost, well-rotted manure, or leaf mold). Top with 1 inch of builder's sand to ensure good drainage. Place the corms, spacing them 6 inches apart. Fill in with soil and water well. To extend the period of bloom, plant some corms every two weeks until ninety days before the first frost. (See page 47 for more on planting.)

Growing Tips
Once the flower spikes reach one-third of their height, apply a high potash fertilizer (following package instructions). Water every ten days until they finish blooming.

Care and Maintenance
Gladiolus is a superb cut flower, lasting at least a week indoors. Pull out faded blooms, cut 1/2-inch off the stem, and change the water daily. Gladiolus is only hardy to Zone 7—not in our zones. Either grow it as an annual and let it die or dig the corm and store it for the winter. When the leaves start to wither, lift the corms. Cut the stem close to the corm, roll the corm in sulfur, and place it on a screen in a well-ventilated area for several days to dry. Separate the new corms from the old, discarding the old ones and any that show signs of rot. Store in a cool, dry area.

Companion Planting and Design
Many people grow gladiolus in rows—sensible in a cutting garden. In a mixed border or perennial garden, try groupings of them intermingled with other plantings. Grow gladiolus among perennials, annuals, or shrubs. It is lovely with canna (*Canna × generalis*) and calla lily (*Zantedeschia aethiopica*), which emphasizes their verticality.

I Also Recommend
'Moon Mirage' (24- to 32-inch spike) produces twenty-six buds with ten open at once and has ruffled 5 1/2-inch canary yellow flowers with darker lips. 'Pink Lady' (34-inch spike) produces twenty-five to twenty-seven buds with eight or nine open in deep rose pink with a white throat.

Glory-of-the-Snow
Chionodoxa lucillea

When, Where, and How to Plant
Small, early spring bulbs tend to dry out if you don't plant them within a few weeks of receiving them. Keep them cool and dry until planting. Glory-of-the-snow needs full sun. Think full sun for when it is up and blooming but not at planting time. You can remember this by keeping in mind it may be shady under a deciduous tree or shrub when you are planting in fall, but it will be sunny when the early bulbs bloom because the tree will not have leafed out. Glory-of-the-snow grows in any type of soil as long as it is well drained. Plant the bulbs 3 inches deep and 3 inches apart. Water well. (See page 47 for more on planting.)

Growing Tips
Keep the soil lightly moist during the growing season. Add a 2-inch layer of mulch (compost, leaf mold, or well-rotted manure) after the ground freezes to protect the bulbs from heaving during winter thaws. It also breaks down, providing all the nutrition the bulbs need.

Care and Maintenance
Don't be disappointed if the first year's bloom is not as spectacular as you hoped. Leave the bulbs in place. Since they self-seed freely, you'll soon have a starry carpet.

Companion Planting and Design
Cut some flowers for a lovely mini-bouquet. I put six or eight stems in an antique cut-glass saltshaker. They give me a bit of the outdoors when I'm stuck at my computer. Glory-of-the-snow is magnificent in a low section of a rock garden. Mass them either alone or combined with Siberian squill (*Scilla siberica*) or grape hyacinth (*Muscari armeniacum*) for a blue carpet under forsythia (*Forsythia* spp.), dwarf purpleleaf sand cherry (*Prunus × cistena* 'Crimson Dwarf'), or star magnolia (*Magnolia stellata*). Add a few early daffodils such as *Narcissus* 'Jack Snipe' or 'Téte-à-Téte'. Mass early bulbs under deciduous trees where it is often difficult to get grass to grow.

I Also Recommend
'Pink Giant' has large (¹/₂-inch) pale pink flowers with white centers.

Glory-of-the-snow adds a touch of magic to my early spring garden. Looking at it always makes me smile. Its star-shaped flowers face upward—bright blue with an almost iridescent white center. Since it sets seed with abandon and hybridizes freely, the size of the white center is quite variable. I found a single clump of pure white flowers growing on our hillside. Every year I meant to mark them to propagate but, alas, I never remembered. A single small bulb sends up several flower stems. It is very hardy, commencing to bloom before the crocuses have finished. Although you might not consider it a cut flower, a group of eight to twelve flowers is charming in a small container, such as an antique inkwell or saltshaker.

Bloom Period and Seasonal Color
Deep sky blue with white centers in early spring.

Mature Height and Spread
2 to 4 in. × 1 to 2 in.

Grape Hyacinth
Muscari armeniacum

Grape hyacinth is aptly named. Growing only 6 to 8 inches high, it resembles a miniature hyacinth or a tiny bunch of grapes—depending on your point of view. Look closely at the florets, which are rounded and gathered at the bottom with contrasting white, like the white elastic on old-fashioned 1890s ladies' bloomers. Take a whiff of the flowers; they have a delightful light grapey aroma. It multiplies well and can provide an effective spring groundcover under deciduous trees. It sends up its handsome, strap-like leaves in autumn, within weeks of planting, that last through winter. The leaves will die back after the flowers finish blooming. Plant in a raised bed or deep windowbox where you can appreciate the delightful scent.

Bloom Period and Seasonal Color
Bright blue with white in spring.

Mature Height and Spread
6 to 8 in. × 3 to 4 in.

When, Where, and How to Plant
Whether you purchase grape hyacinth bulbs at a nursery, garden center, home store, or through a mail-order nursery, get them early (by mid August) and plant them within the next two weeks. They need time to develop a strong root system and send up their leaves before the weather turns cold. Grape hyacinths grow best in rich, lightly moist, well-drained, but somewhat sandy, soil in full sun. Plant the bulbs 3 to 4 inches deep, allowing 3 to 4 inches between each bulb. Like other small bulbs, they have the most impact when planted in large numbers. Water them well. (See page 47 for more on planting.)

Growing Tips
Keep the soil lightly moist until the ground freezes. Fertilization is not necessary.

Care and Maintenance
Grape hyacinths need little attention and increase rapidly. If the planting becomes congested, dig it up in summer or fall when the plants are dormant. Gently tease the bulbs and roots apart. Replant at the original depth and spacing. You will have plenty to start a new area or share with friends.

Companion Planting and Design
Grape hyacinths are beautiful with tulips of all colors, yet are most outstanding in front of red tulips such as 'Red Emperor' (*Tulipa* 'Red Emperor'). Create a patriotic mix by adding some white tulips (*Tulipa* 'Purissima' or 'Spring Green') or white hyacinths (*Hyacinthus orientalis* 'White Pearl').

I Also Recommend
'Blue Spike' with its larger, densely bunched, double flowers resembles a miniature lilac. 'Fantasy Creation' is one of the most unique bulbs, changing colors over a span of six to eight weeks. The flowers are fascinating to watch as they go from heavenly blue when they first open, gradually change to a handsome bluish-green, and finally in late spring become totally green. They deserve a special space in the garden where you can watch them day-to-day. 'Mount Hood' is also special, resembling the typical grape hyacinth, but the sky blue florets go only part way up the stem. The top is white, like a snow-capped mountain peak.

Hyacinth
Hyacinthus orientalis

When, Where, and How to Plant

Hyacinth bulbs are available in late summer. Choose large, firm, weighty bulbs. Reject any with soft spots or skin discoloration. Hyacinths thrive in average to fertile, well-drained soil in full to part sun. In our region, planting them deeper—6 to 8 inches—allows us to grow them successfully. Space 3 inches apart. Water well (see page 47 for more on planting). You can buy hyacinths in bloom, but it is easy, more economical, and fun to force them into bloom yourself. For a group of hyacinths, use a shallow 12-inch pot (bulb pan), or for one bulb use a 4-inch pot. Fill the container to within an inch of the rim with lightly moistened potting soil, then plant the bulbs close together, but not touching, with the tips just above soil level. Refrigerate, and don't allow the soil to dry out. After eight to twelve weeks, when the stem is 1 inch high, gradually—over a week—introduce it to warmth and brighter light. Put the container on a sunny windowsill; keep the soil lightly moist. Within a few weeks, the hyacinths will bloom. If you are trying to get it to bloom by a certain date, slow it down by keeping it cool. Warmer temperatures accelerate blooming but the flowers will fade faster.

Growing Tips

Keep the soil lightly moist until the ground freezes to allow for strong root growth. Feeding is not necessary.

Care and Maintenance

When forced hyacinths finish blooming, plant them outdoors when the ground thaws. They will bloom the following spring. Some hyacinths are magnificent the first year but subsequently have fewer florets. You can move them to a less prominent area.

Companion Planting and Design

Hyacinths are magnificent with pansies (*Viola × wittrockiana*) in all their hues.

I Also Recommend

'Delft Blue' has soft violet to flushed purple flowers and is the king of hyacinths. 'Carnegie' has beautiful pure white blooms. 'Gypsy Queen' was a sensation when first introduced with its salmon-orange flowers. 'City of Haarlem' has soft primrose-yellow blooms. 'Queen of the Pinks' produces deep pink flowers.

For me, the scent of hyacinth conjures up childhood memories of Easter morning—the Easter basket, jellybeans, and especially the coveted chocolate bunny. Hyacinths were not necessarily blooming outdoors at Easter, but we always had a large pot of 'Delft Blue' hyacinths that we had forced into bloom. We kept them on a sunny windowsill in the coolest room—the living room—and the flowers lasted nearly a month. By then, hyacinths were bursting into bloom outdoors. A hyacinth spike is composed of numerous of closely packed, 1-inch florets around the stem in hues of carmine, pink, purple, blue, white, yellow, and orange—both single and double. They are great show-offs in the garden; their sweet perfume leads you to them.

Other Common Name
Garden Hyacinth

Bloom Period and Seasonal Color
Shades of white, pink, yellow, purple, blue, and orange in mid-spring.

Mature Height and Spread
8 to 12 in. × 3 to 4 in.

Zone
5

Magic Lily
Lycoris squamagera

Magic lily is one of many names for this unique bulb. It is one of the few bulbs, besides autumn crocus, that blooms one season and leafs out another. In mid- to late summer (but it seems like overnight), the 24-inch flower stalks appear, topped with 4-inch umbels of fragrant, lilac-pink florets that radiate in all directions, looking very much like a bouquet of miniature lilies. They are beautiful and deceivingly delicate-looking as they stand up to summer storms. As a bonus, they attract butterflies and hummingbirds. The flowers last for several weeks. After the flowers die down, the leaves appear—rarely in autumn, usually in spring. Leaves are deep green and straplike. They can be forced and grown indoors like amaryllis.

Other Common Names
Naked Lady, Hardy Amaryllis, Resurrection Lily

Bloom Period and Seasonal Color
Rosy lilac in mid- to late summer.

Mature Height and Spread
18 to 28 in. × 8 to 14 in.

Zone
5

When, Where, and How to Plant
Magic lilies are available as bulbs, more readily found through mail-order merchants than at garden centers. They are occasionally sold as *Amaryllis hallii*. As soon as the bulbs arrive in mid- to late summer, get them in the ground. Magic lilies prefer fertile, well-drained soil and full sun. Plant them 4 to 6 inches deep and 8 inches apart. They are impressive in groupings of seven or more. (See page 47 for more on planting.) Water well. You can force the bulbs and grow them inside. Choose a deep pot that is 1 to 2 inches wider than the bulb (for a single planting) or a 12-inch pot for multiple bulbs. Fill the pot with a lightly moistened mix of equal parts garden soil, perlite, and compost. Plant the bulb so that the tip is just above soil level. Put it in an area that gets full sun such as a south-facing window. The flowers will soon appear, followed by the leaves. During this growth period, keep watering so that the soil remains lightly moist. Once the leaves die back, cut the watering down to once a month and keep the plant in a warm place.

Growing Tips
After planting, keep the soil lightly moist until the first hard frost hits. Water frequently during its growth cycle; however, when it goes dormant, let it go dry.

Care and Maintenance
Once the ground is frozen, mulch with 3 to 4 inches of organic matter (compost, leaf mold, or well-rotted manure). Remove mulch in spring after the last frost. Once planted, magic lilies do not transplant well.

Companion Planting and Design
Magic lilies are most enchanting when they suddenly appear in the lawn. Mark their space so that they are not accidentally mown down. Include them in a foundation planting or in a perennial bed where they will not be disturbed. Surround them with autumn crocus (*Colchicum autumnale*), which bloom after the lilies fade.

I Also Recommend
Grow only the species.

Oriental Lily
Lilium 'Casa Blanca'

When, Where, and How to Plant

'Casa Blanca' is so popular that potted plants (with one plant or groups of three to five) are available at nurseries, garden centers, and even supermarkets. Take one home, put it—pot and all—in a cachepot or decorative containers, and place it in a sunny spot outside. Alternatively, dig a hole and plant the potted lily in the garden. If you want the lily to come back next year, it should be planted in the ground. Place the pot in transplant solution for several minutes. Carefully unpot the plant; if it is full grown, get assistance to avoid breaking the stem. Loosen the roots and plant it. Water with 2 cups of transplant solution. Or, instead of paying for a grown plant, purchase bulbs in spring or fall. Oriental lilies need full sun and rich, well-drained soil. Plant bulbs as soon as you get them—the depth three times their height, spaced three times their width apart. Water in well. If they are in an unprotected area, add a stake for support. (See pages 47 through 48 for more planting information.)

Growing Tips

Keep soil lightly moist. Water weekly when there is no rain. Feed at the beginning of the growing season by watering weekly with compost tea. After flowering, decrease watering and allow the bulbs to slowly dry.

Care and Maintenance

Lilies can be host to many pests and diseases. However, if it is not disfiguring or diminishing the plant, natural enemies will often control a problem. If needed, use insecticidal soap for aphids or small caterpillars. Viruses may be transmitted from plant to plant. To be safe, dig up and destroy any infected plants. The ultimate enemy is the lily beetle, which can quickly decimate a plant. Currently there is no treatment.

Companion Planting and Design

No white garden is complete without 'Casa Blanca'. Grow with *Phlox* 'David' and moonflowers (*Ipomoea alba*).

I Also Recommend

'Imperial Gold' (6 feet) has white petals with a central golden yellow stripe. 'Star Gazer' (3 to 5 feet) is crimson red with darker spots.

Oriental lilies are flowers of mystique—you can sense them at a distance by their sweet scent that perfumes the air during the day and even more in the evening. They are the essence of a romantic evening outdoors. Large and blousy, bigger and more fully open than the earlier blooming Asiatic lilies (bowl rather than cup shape), the flowers are borne in clusters or sprays—an instant bouquet for cutting. Gardeners eagerly await their appearance each year. 'Casa Blanca', with its pure white petals and contrasting red-orange anthers, is one of the most popular. The tips of the petals curve back, adding to its exotic look. Like other lilies, it is an excellent cut flower. Remove the anthers since the pollen drops and stains.

Bloom Period and Seasonal Color
White in mid- to late summer.

Mature Height and Spread
$3^1/2$ to 4 ft. × 18 to 24 in.

Zone
4

Peacock Orchid

Gladiolus callianthus

The peacock orchid is an elegant, night-fragrant, summer bloomer—a must-have for any evening garden. Watch as it lures lovely luna and sphinx moths. It has gone through a number of botanical name changes (formerly Acidanthera bicolor *and* Acidanthera murieliae *and is now officially* Gladiolus callianthus). *A peacock orchid by any name is a wondrous sight—day or night. It sends up a fan of sword-shaped leaves and a single stem, bearing six to eight flowers that open in succession from lowest to topmost. The flower is beautiful—like a wide-open gladiolus with white petals and a deep purple center that makes it even more alluring. Not hardy, it is an inexpensive corm; so many gardeners grow it as an annual rather than dig it up.*

Other Common Name
Abyssinian Gladiolus

Bloom Period and Seasonal Color
White with purple throat in mid- to late summer.

Mature Height and Spread
28 to 36 in. × 2 to 5 in.

When, Where, and How to Plant
Peacock orchid is only available as a corm, not as a potted plant. It prefers full sun and rich, slightly moist, well-drained soil—even clayey soils. Plant it in clusters or groupings of seven or more corms, spaced 4 to 6 inches apart. Incorporate several clusters throughout the garden. Staggering the planting of several groupings every two weeks for six to eight weeks will extend the bloom season. Water well. (See page 47 for more planting information.)

Growing Tips
Keep the soil lightly moist during the growing season. No fertilizer is necessary.

Care and Maintenance
Cut the flower stems for fragrant flower arrangements. Since the flowers open from the lower part of the stem up, pull off any faded flower, cut ¼ of an inch off the bottom of the stem, and change the water daily. The cut stem can last for a week or more. Outdoors, it is more weather-dependant; in very hot weather the flowers open quickly, but when it is cooler, they can last several weeks. If you want to lift the corms and overwinter them, treat them like gladioli. When the leaves start to wither, lift the corms. Cut the stem close to the corm, roll it in sulfur, and place it on a screen to dry. Separate the new corms from the old, discarding the old ones and any that show signs of rot, discoloration, or soft spots. Store in a dry area at about 60 degrees Fahrenheit. When time is more valuable than money (peacock orchid is one the lowest-priced bulbs), just let the plants die and buy new corms next year.

Companion Planting and Design
The possibilities of using peacock orchids in an evening garden are almost limitless. A word of caution when placing fragrant plants in the garden (especially night-fragrant blooms): Allow ample space (at least 10 to 15 feet) between different plants, as the scents can clash with each other. Combine them with white dahlias (*Dahlia* spp.), gladiolus (*Gladiolus* spp.), and fuchsia (*Fuchsia* 'Annabel').

I Also Recommend
There is only the species.

Rubrum Lily

Lilium speciosum var. *rubrum*

When, Where, and How to Plant

Rubrum lilies prefer moist, acidic soil in partial shade—ideal for woodlands with dappled shade. Like 'Casa Blanca' lilies, they are so popular that they are available—even blooming—in containers in summer. Plant the containers or start from bulbs available in spring and fall. Mix peat moss into the soil to acidify and help retain water. (See pages 47 through 48 for complete directions.) Water well.

Growing Tips

Keep the soil consistently, but lightly, moist. Do not fertilize.

Care and Maintenance

Rubrum lilies are susceptible to botrytis and gray mold, which if caught in early stage can be treated by weekly spraying (top and bottoms of leaves) with a solution of 1 gallon of water, 3 tablespoons of baking soda, several drops of Ivory® liquid dish soap, and several drops of vegetable oil. Rubrum lilies are a favorite of deer, rabbits, voles, and groundhogs. Unless you are fenced in, deer will forage much of the garden. A "fence" of hardware cloth or small-holed metal fencing sunk a foot into the ground and 2 feet above the ground keeps rabbits and voles away and may deter groundhogs. The biggest threat—yet smallest—is the lily beetle, which is quickly becoming the scourge of all lilies. As yet, there are no known treatments and no known natural enemies of the lily beetle.

Companion Planting and Design

Some of the best plant combinations are serendipitous. One misty morning, I was drawn into my friend's garden by the sheer size and brilliance of bright pinks and reds. Approaching, I saw it was a simple combination of three plants: hollyhock (*Alcea rosea* 'Chater's Double Pink'), beebalm (*Monarda didyma* 'Cambridge Scarlet' and 'Croftway Pink'), and rubrum lilies. A landscaper, he had "tossed" some leftover plants in what was to be a compost heap; they all seeded or took root, making a splendid midsummer display.

I Also Recommend

Turk's cap lily (*Lilium superbum*) is 5 to 8 feet tall, with sprays of red-orange, spotted blooms with very reflexed petals. It grows in the same conditions as rubrum lilies.

Rubrum lily is one of the most popular species lilies—and for good reason. It can grow from 3 to 5 feet tall, making a dramatic statement in any garden, even at the edge of a woodland. Nodding sprays of ten to twelve flowers, each 4- to 5-inches across, top the plant. Highly fragrant blooms with deep pink to crimson, slightly recurved petals fading to white with raised deeper pink markings reveal long, brown-tipped stamens. Its purplish-brown stems make it even more outstanding in the garden. It is an excellent cut flower—long lasting, filling the room with its sweet perfume. Since the pollen can drop off the flower and stain fabric, some people choose to cut off the stamens before bringing flowers inside.

Bloom Period and Seasonal Color

Crimson to pink, fading to white in summer.

Mature Height and Spread

3 to 5^1/$_2$ ft. × 2 to 2^1/$_2$ ft.

Siberian Squill
Scilla siberica

Siberian squill is one of the easiest bulbs to grow. Its bright blue, nodding bells push right up through the thawing ground and are not bothered by late snows. It makes quite an impact when planted in large groupings of 50, 100, 250, or more. Like many of the other early bulbs, you wouldn't necessarily consider it as a cut flower, but cut seven or more stems for darling mini- bouquets. The flowers grow in small loose spikes in groups of four or five, opening from bottom to top. Look closely in spring; the pollen is blue. Beekeepers always know when it is in flower as the bees come home with blue legs. If you get close, you can detect a slight honey-like scent.

Other Common Names
Spring Squill

Bloom Period and Seasonal Color
Bright blue in early spring.

Mature Height and Spread
2 to 4 in. × 1 to 2 in.

When, Where, and How to Plant
Siberian squill is only available as bulbs. As soon as you get the bulbs in late summer or early fall, plant them. Using a spade, dig up the soil 5 inches deep (an ample hole to accommodate the swath of bulbs), putting the soil in a wheelbarrow or tarp. Add a cupful of bone meal for each cubic foot of soil dug (measurements are not critical) and mix them together. Put a 1-inch layer of the soil mix in the hole. Place the bulbs on top, spacing them 3 to 4 inches apart, pointed ends up. Gently push them into the soil. If you aren't going for the big display, at least plant a group of seven to eleven bulbs. Cover with the remaining soil, gently firm it with your hands, and water well.

Growing Tips
Keep the soil lightly moist in spring. Fertilizer isn't necessary.

Care and Maintenance
Add 2 to 3 inches of organic mulch when the ground freezes. Be sure to remove it in late winter so the bulbs get through. You will notice Siberian squills start to flower almost as they are out of the ground. The stem slowly elongates during flowering. After bloomtime, let the leaves die back on their own. You can leave this plant on its own for years as it naturalizes and will continue to spread.

Companion Planting and Design
It is a sturdy bulb under trees where grass won't grow—under a dogwood (*Cornus* spp.), magnolia (*Magnolia stellata* and other species), or cutleaf Japanese maple (*Acer palmatum ornatum* 'Dissectum'). The leaves make an attractive cover of green after the flowers are spent. One of my favorite pairings is with glory-of-the-snow (*Chionodoxa luciliae*) with a few early yellow daffodils mixed in to accent the blues.

I Also Recommend
'Spring Beauty' is more floriferous, with larger and darker blue flowers than the species. Although it is sterile and does not set seed, it produces offsets that proliferate. 'Alba' is a white-flowered cultivar.

Snowdrop
Galanthus nivalis

When, Where, and How to Plant
Snowdrops are only available as bulbs. Like other early blooming bulbs, they have a tendency to dry out if they are not planted quickly. Plant them within two weeks after you get them. In the meantime, store them in a paper bag in a cool dry space. Snowdrops grow best in part shade in light, rich, moist, well-drained soil. Plant the bulbs 3 inches deep and 3 inches apart, in groupings of fifteen or more. Water well. (See page 47 for more on planting.)

Growing Tips
Keep the soil lightly moist in spring. Do not let the soil dry out in summer, either. Fertilizer is not necessary.

Care and Maintenance
Add 1 to 2 inches of fine organic mulch when the ground freezes. Some of the mulch will decay over the winter, and the flowers will grow through it. If you use a coarse mulch, remove it in mid- to late January. You can lay pine boughs over the plantings, which can be easily removed at the appropriate time. Snowdrops naturalize well. If the clumps get too big or you want snowdrops in another area of the garden, dig them up and divide the cluster with a knife or shovel. Replant the divisions at the same level they originally grew. Although it is recommended to divide the plants right after flowering, I have done it successfully just as the plant starts to flower.

Companion Planting and Design
Snowdrops pair well with colorful snow crocus (*Crocus tommasinianus* and *Crocus chrysanthus*). Plant several different species and cultivars of snowdrops together.

I Also Recommend
'Flore Pleno' grows to 6 inches tall, bearing unusual, slightly upturned double flowers. It blooms a bit later than the species. Although its flowers are sterile, it naturalizes well from offsets. Giant snowdrop (*Galanthus elwesii*) can grow up to 11 inches high with 1- to 1 1/2-inch flowers. The flowers of 'Scharlockii' are quite interesting—more slender than the species with the outer petal split in two. 'Viridapicis' has a very long central spathe and green markings on the outer petals.

Snowdrops are the true heralds of spring—the first bulbs to bloom. Snowdrops have small white nodding flowers, one to a stem. The inner three petals are shorter than the outer three and are tipped with green. They are extremely hardy and will push up through the frozen ground and snow in late winter or early spring. However, layers of ice will impede their progress. Snowdrops are greatly influenced by exposure or warm spells, so in a protected nook they may even bloom in late February. Like the other early bulbs, often referred to as "minor bulbs," they are best when they are massed—plant dozens or hundreds. The blooms are lightly fragrant. I make an adorable flower arrangement in a 2-inch cobalt blue vase.

Other Common Name
Common Snowdrop

Bloom Period and Seasonal Color
White from late winter to early spring.

Mature Height and Spread
3 to 4 in. × 3 to 4 in.

Tulip
Tulipa spp.

Tulips offer an array of colors, shapes, sizes, and bloom times that no other spring-blooming bulb can come near to matching. With hundreds of species and thousands of cultivated varieties, tulips are classified into fifteen divisions by type and/or bloom time. This includes single early, single late, fringed, parrot, viridiflora (with green stripe), double early, lily-flowered, and more. The low-growing species tulips are the first to bloom: Tulipa biflora, only 4 inches high, opens fully to a yellow-centered white star shape. Greigii tulips, which bloom a little later, have purple striations on their leaves. Darwin (golden yellow 'Golden Apeldoorn') and Triumph hybrids ('Princess Irene', a gorgeous blend of purple and orange) are midseason bloomers. The tallest and showiest are generally among the last to flower, including peony-flowered 'Angelique'.

Bloom Period and Seasonal Color
Every color of the rainbow in single, bicolor, or tricolor from early to late spring.

Mature Height and Spread
4 to 28 in. × 5 to 12 in.

Zone
4

When, Where, and How to Plant
You will find tulip bulbs for sale everywhere; the greatest selection is through mail-order nurseries. Tulips thrive in fertile, neutral to slightly acid, well-drained soil in full or afternoon sun. Tulips have a reputation for being a lot of work (due to lifting and replanting them) or not coming back if left in the ground. They regrow each year in Zones 4b, 5, and 6. If you are in a colder zone, it is worth trying. Plant the bulbs in early autumn, pointed end up. I plant tulips 3 to 4 inches deeper than recommended (three times the bulb's height). Avoid planting them in soldierly rows. Space them 2 to 5 inches apart, depending on the variety. Water well.

Growing Tips
Keep the soil lightly moist until hard frost. Foliar feed every three to four weeks during the growing season.

Care and Maintenance
To prevent root and bulb rot, especially in clay soil, add an inch of builder's sand at the bottom of the planting area and then plant the tulip. Deadhead the flowers as they finish blooming. If you are going to dig up the bulbs, do not foliar feed after flowering. Dig the bulbs up 6 weeks after the leaves turn yellow or when they die back. Put them on a screen to dry for a week. Cut the stem back and store in a warm, dry place until planting time in the fall.

Companion Planting and Design
With the plethora of types and cultivars, plant them with each other. Tulips pair well with daffodils (*Narcissus* spp.). Interplant early bloomers with pansies (*Viola* × *wittrockiana*) and later types with forget-me-nots (*Myosotis sylvatica*).

I Also Recommend
Tulipa praestans 'Unicum' grows 12 inches with bouquets of red flowers above yellow-edged leaves. Lady tulip (*Tulipa clusiana*), shown in photo, grows 12 inches with pink candy cane stripes. 'Spring Green' is 16 inches and blooms ivory white with a central feathery green stripe on the petals. 'Menton' grows 24 inches and blooms rose pink with pale orange edges outside, white veined, bright red inside. 'New Design' grows 18 inches, has pale yellow melding to pale pink petals, and cream-edged leaves.

Variegated Dalmatian Iris

Iris pallida 'Variegata'

When, Where, and How to Plant

Variegated Dalmatian iris is available as a growing plant at nurseries and garden centers, as well as through mail-order merchants. It grows best in rich, moist soil in full sun to part shade. Although you may find the plants in spring, it will perform much better if you plant it in late summer to early fall. In the northern portion of the Prairie Lands states, midsummer is the best time to plant it since the plant needs time to get its roots established before the cold weather sets in. If the pot has several plants growing in it, you can simply unpot and put it all (soil too) in the ground. Or, you can remove the soil and plant each (if there is more than one) rhizome separately, spaced 3 inches apart. Plant the rhizome horizontally with the fan of leaves facing up so that the rhizome is just barely below soil level. Press it gently into the soil. Water well.

Growing Tips

Keep the soil moist. Do not let it dry out. Fertilizer is not necessary.

Care and Maintenance

If the clump gets too large or you want more iris in other places in the garden, you can divide the rhizomes—either in early spring or late summer to early fall. If you make divisions in spring, the plant may not bloom that season. Variegated Dalmatian iris is relatively pest and disease free, but be on the lookout for signs of borers in the rhizomes when you divide the plant. Discard and destroy any infested or suspect rhizomes.

Companion Planting and Design

Variegated Dalmatian iris is beautiful with other bog plants such as Japanese iris (*Iris ensata*), marsh marigold (*Caltha palustris*), and drumstick primrose (*Primula denticulata*).

I Also Recommend

Iris pallida 'Aurea Variegata' is quite similar, except its leaves are pale green with golden yellow striping. The species, *Iris pallida*, has gray-green leaves and is the hardiest of the bunch. The flowers have distinctive silvery, papery bracts.

Variegated Dalmatian iris is a welcome addition to any damp or low-lying area. Its blue-green, swordlike leaves with white variegation (striping) grow 8 to 24 inches tall, enlivening a semi-shaded area with their color contrast. It is considered semievergreen. In mild winters, the leaves will remain, adding color and architectural interest to the bleak landscape. Branching flower stalks rise 8 to 12 inches above the leaves, each bearing two to six fragrant, deep lavender flowers with yellow beards. It is an excellent cut flower—longer lasting than most iris if you cut 1/4 inch off the bottom of the stem and change the water daily. Orrisroot, which is the ground up dried rhizome of the species, is used as a fixative in potpourri.

Other Common Name
Variegated Orris

Bloom Period and Seasonal Color
Dark lavender from late spring to early summer.

Mature Height and Spread
8 to 36 in. × 8 to 16 in.

Zone
4

Groundcovers & Vines
for the Prairie Lands

Groundcovers and vines are often grouped together because the categories overlap and interlink. Many of the plants can serve dual purposes. Generally, people think of groundcovers as relatively flat plants, growing close to the ground and spreading horizontally, and of vines as climbing plants that grow vertically. Yet, many vines can be used as groundcovers if they are trained to grow horizontally. English ivy is a good example; it covers many of the colonial brick buildings in the Northeast. In addition, it is one of the most common groundcovers when allowed to spread. It is an unusual plant because what we usually see is the juvenile or immature vining form. When it matures and flowers, it sends up shoots and is shrublike. If you take cuttings of it in that stage, you can grow ivy in a shrub form.

Growing Where Others Won't

Groundcovers are more utilitarian than most plants as they are grown with the purpose of covering an area of bare earth. They are used to prevent soil erosion, especially on slopes. Groundcovers make good skirts around large trees—a sort of living mulch. Creating a groundcover usually consists of a mass planting of low-growing plants, such as myrtle, creeping phlox, or bearberry, that will fill in an area to the exclusion of any other plants leaving no bare soil. Exceptions are the erstwhile weed and bulbs that can be planted to grow up through the groundcovers in spring.

To me, a groundcover is a low-growing plant, usually no more than twelve to sixteen inches high. I have seen books on the subject that include shrub roses as groundcovers. With a few exceptions, I would consider them a barrier or hedge rather than a groundcover.

Groundcovers may be evergreen or deciduous. For many gardeners, an evergreen groundcover is more desirable, especially when creating large swaths of plants; however, a deciduous groundcover, such as creeping phlox is ideal for a small place, growing in the spaces between stones on walls or walkways.

Clematis

Vines are plants with long stems with a built-in means of supporting themselves as they grow upward. One of the greatest assets of vines is that they have no gentically preset form. This allows them to fit into the tiniest spaces of ground—provided they have room to root—and then grow vertically and/or horizontally among a bevy of other plants. Vines are phototropic—growing to the light. Some are heliotropic—their stem, shoot, or leaf movement is influenced by light and the movement of the sun. Another group, including sweet peas, is thigmotropic—their tendrils grow in response to physical contact, making them twine around the nearest support.

Vine Categories

Vines can be categorized as clinging and nonclinging. There are several basic methods clinging vines use to attach themselves to whatever is nearby on their upward journey. Virginia creeper, for example, has flat adhesive disks at the ends of it branching tendrils. The disks allow it to cling well to most surfaces, so it can easily cover the side of a building or a large area of ground. However, do not let it grow on a wood-shingled building since it can creep between the shingles and even get into the house.

Wintercreeper, trumpet vine, and English ivy have rootlike holdfasts along their stems that cling to rough surfaces. They easily scale trees, stucco, and brick buildings. You can even use these vines to hide an unsightly chain-link fence. If you have an *older* brick house, do not plant this type of vine as it can send its holdfasts into the mortar. This is not a problem with new mortar since it is not as porous. No doubt if you pulled the ivy off any of the old beloved ivy-covered brick buildings that are so prevalent in New England, the building would come down as the rootlets have so embedded themselves into the mortar.

The non-clinging vines also have several different ways of being upwardly mobile based on their growth habits. Twining vines circle upward around a support. This spiraling method is called circumnulation and can be clockwise or counterclockwise. No doubt, you have had the experience of trying to wrap a morning glory around a trellis. You put it on one way, and the next day it is back on the ground. That is because its natural twining is in the opposite direction. If you have curled the vine one way, it may even uncurl and retwine itself in its proper direction. In addition to the entire vine twining, some vines have parts that twine. For example, with grapes and garden peas, the leaf or a part of the leaf is transformed into a tough tendril that corkscrews its way around a support.

The final group of vines is not truly climbers but is more correctly called scramblers. Scramblers like climbing roses and tomatoes have no physical means of keeping themselves upright, so they need support to keep them on the right path. The easiest way is to tie them *loosely* with string or twine (not metal twist-ties). A good method is to cut a six-inch length of string and make a loose figure eight around the stem and the support. Tie it off at the support. That way, there is room for the stem to grow.

Show Support for Clingy Friends

Most of the groundcovers and vines you will grow will come as potted plants. You can follow the basic planting instructions found in the main introduction to this book on page 15. On rare occasions when you're planting a large number of plants, it is more cost-efficient to grow the plants from seed or cuttings. A few large plants can yield dozens of cuttings in a fairly short time.

Remember to always have the support in place—a stake, arbor, pergola, trellis, or twine attached to an overhang—before you put the plant in the ground. In the case of a stake, plant both at the same time. Find out how long the vine will grow, whether it is annual or perennial, and herbaceous or woody. A tall stake is fine for a tomato that dies back at the end of the year, but a climbing hydrangea that can soar sixty feet in the air needs a very strong support. If the plant you are growing gets six feet tall, you want a support that is a least seven or eight feet tall, since at least twelve inches of the support must be underground.

Bearberry
Arctostaphylos uva-ursi

Bearberry, known to the Native Americans as kinnikin-nick, is a handsome prostrate groundcover. It is an evergreen branching shrub (woody plant) that only grows 12 inches tall, with stems up to 6 feet long. It is unique because the stems root at the joints, making it easy to propagate. It has thick, leathery green leaves and bears pink-tinged, waxy white flowers in summer. Pea-sized, smooth red fruits accent the plant from August through late winter, if they are not eaten. As the name implies, its berries are favored by bears. The leaves turn a beautiful shade of bronze in winter, adding color interest when there is little or no snow. Native Americans brewed a tea from the leaves and used it as a diuretic.

Other Common Name
Kinnikinnick

Bloom Period and Seasonal Color
White with pink tinge in summer.

Mature Height and Spread
8 to 12 in. × 5 to 6 ft.

When, Where, and How to Plant
Bearberry plants can be found at some nurseries and are available through mail-order nurseries. They grow best in sandy or rocky, acidic, well-drained soil in full sun to part shade. Space plants at least 2 feet apart. Since our soil is likely to be alkaline (get your soil pH tested by your local Cooperative Extension Service), it needs amending for bearberry to thrive. Dig a hole twice the width and depth of the potted plant, putting the soil on a tarp or in a wheelbarrow. Add equal parts of builder's sand and fine sphagnum moss to the soil and mix well. Put enough soil back in the hole so that it will be at the same level it was growing in the pot. Loosen roots, if necessary, and place the plant in the hole. Fill in around it with the remaining amended soil. Water well with transplant solution.

Growing Tips
Keep the plant lightly moist until it is established. Fertilizer is not necessary.

Care and Maintenance
Once established, it is fairly drought tolerant, so rains should provide ample water unless there is prolonged drought. Bearberry is slightly susceptible to fungal diseases. At the first sign of a problem, spray tops and bottoms of leaves and the entire plant with baking soda spray. (See page 231 for directions on making the solution.) Propagate in spring or late summer by cutting the stem 2 inches long on either side of a rooted node. Carefully dig up the nodes and roots; and replant.

Companion Planting and Design
Bearberry is a good edging plant, alongside a walkway or between stepping-stones. It can stand up to foot traffic and is very handsome with other low-growing evergreen groundcovers such as mother of thyme (*Thymus serphyllum*) and Corsican mint (*Mentha requienii*).

I Also Recommend
'Massachusetts' (6 to 12 inches) has white flowers tinged with pink, is slow growing and vigorous. Birds flock to eat the red berries in autumn. 'Vancouver Jade' bears glossy green leaves that turn deep red in autumn.

Bishop's Hat
Epimedium × versicolor 'Sulphureum'

When, Where, and How to Plant
In spring, you may be able to find bishop's hat plants at some nurseries and garden centers. However, the greatest selection is available through mail-order nurseries. Bishop's hat grows best in rich, moist, well-drained soil in part sun to part shade. Although it will also tolerate sun and dry shade, it will not grow nearly as well as in its ideal conditions. Plant bishop's hat in spring after danger of frost has passed. Refer to page 15 for more planting information. Mix in several handfuls of compost or other organic matter into the soil before planting. Plant it at the same soil level as it was growing in the pot. Space plants 12 inches apart. Water well.

Growing Tips
Keep the soil lightly moist. Be patient, it is slow to grow. You do not need to fertilize the plant as long as it is growing in rich soil.

Care and Maintenance
Do not let the soil dry out. Add a 3- to 5-inch layer of organic mulch on the plant once the ground freezes. Some of this will break down, enriching the soil. Remove the mulch in early spring. As the new shoots are emerging, cut any overwintered stems or leaves.

Companion Planting and Design
Bishop's hat contrasts nicely with the rounded, shiny leaves of the lower growing European ginger (*Asarum europaeum*). For added height, include one or more bleeding heart (*Dicentra spectabilis*), Dutchman's breeches (*Dicentra culcullaria*), or the long-blooming, fringed bleeding heart (*Dicentra eximia* 'Snowdrift').

I Also Recommend
'Rose Queen' has white-spurred, red flowers that reign supreme. Vigorous 'Snow Queen' is breathtaking with showy white blooms. 'Lilafee' is unusual with its purplish flowers and violet-tinted young leaves. Other species of *Epimedium* include *Epimedium × rubrum* (red barrenwort) with white-spurred, bright pink to crimson blooms; its foliage turns bronzy purple in fall. *Epimedium × youngianum* 'Niveum' (snowy epimedium) is very showy with white flowers held above the wavy foliage.

Bishop's hat is one of my favorite spring-blooming perennials—a little gem that you come across in a partially shaded portion of the garden. In time, it forms a thick, impenetrable matrix of roots, where no weeds can penetrate. The leaves are compound, comprised of nine heart-shaped, 1¹/₂- to 2¹/₂-inch-long leaflets borne on wiry stems that form a leaf about 12 inches long. When they first open, the semi-evergreen leaflets are coppery red, and then turn green. The flowers on this species are small—1 inch. To me, the flowers look like a cross between a daffodil and a columbine nestled among the leaves. The common name bishop's hat refers to the spurred petals that resemble a bishop's mitre.

Other Common Names
Barrenwort, Longspur Epimedium

Bloom Period and Seasonal Color
Yellow with white-tipped spurs in mid- to late spring.

Mature Height and Spread
8 to 12 in. × 24 to 36 in.

Zone
5

Bishop's Weed

Aegopodium podograria 'Variegatum'

If you are looking for a fast-growing perennial ground-cover to enliven a partly shady area, bishop's weed is the plant of choice. It is grown for its handsome variegated leaves (three leaflets that form a 4- to 8-inch-long leaf) of sage green with irregular creamy white, slightly toothed edges. It sends up small flat umbels of creamy white flowers in early summer, but they are insignificant in their appearance. Many consider bishop's weed a real weed, as it can be invasive. However, for covering a large area, especially providing erosion control for a hillside or bank, that is a positive attribute. Bishop's weed is a beautiful container plant and is thus controlled. The cut leaves are handsome in small arrangements, making a soft background for bold-colored flowers.

Other Common Name
Goutweed

Bloom Period and Seasonal Color
Creamy white in early summer

Mature Height and Spread
12 to 24 in. × indefinite spread

Zone
4

When, Where, and How to Plant
In spring, container-grown plants of bishop's weed are readily available at nurseries, garden centers, and home stores. You probably have a friend or neighbor that has some growing and would be happy to have you dig up a square. Bishop's weed is easy to grow in ordinary soil. Although it prefers partial shade, it tolerates sun. The use of transplant solution is optional. Plant it at the depth it was growing in the container—or where it was in your neighbor's yard. Water well.

Growing Tips
Water the soil, keeping it lightly moist until the plant is established. Water when the top $1^{1}/_{2}$ inches of soil is dry. Bishop's weed is a vigorous plant that does not need any fertilization.

Care and Maintenance
As beautiful as it is, without some forethought and planning, bishop's weed can easily grow out of control as it spreads both by underground rhizomes and from seed. Cut the flowers when they bloom to prevent seeds from forming. Too keep it in bounds, you can plant it in a large container and sink it into the ground, with the top 2 inches above soil level. Another method is to grow it in decorative containers and place it wherever you want a light accent. If you want bishop's weed within a defined space, edge the area with a metal or plastic barrier that goes at least 4 to 6 inches into the ground and rises 2 inches above soil level. Alternatively, you can let it grow as much as you want and pull it out when it goes beyond bounds.

Companion Planting and Design
Bishop's weed pairs well with a variety of hostas, especially ones in shades of green or blue, such as bluish *Hosta* 'Halcyon'; green-edged chartreuse 'Gold Standard'; cup-leafed, green, edged with creamy white 'Patriot'; or deeply veined, blue-green leafed 'Krossa Regal'. Add a vibrant splash of color with one of the many impatiens (*Impatiens walleriana*).

I Also Recommend
Grow only this cultivated variety.

Bugleweed
Ajuga reptans

When, Where, and How to Plant
Containers of bugleweed are readily available at nurseries, garden centers, and home stores, however the choices are limited. Mail-order nurseries offer a greater range of cultivated varieties. Plant bugleweed in spring after all danger of frost is passed. It grows in average, well-drained soil in part sun to shade. It tolerates sun, but the leaves may burn—turning brown. The soil needs no preparation. Simply plant the bugleweed at the same level as it was growing in the container. Water well with transplant solution. Refer to page 15 for more on planting.

Growing Tips
Bugleweed is a low-maintenance plant that needs regular watering until established. After that, water when the top $1/2$-inch of soil is dry. Fertilizer is not necessary.

Care and Maintenance
If the plant starts to look scraggly, you can mow it down and it will come back looking even more handsome. It is easy to divide as the stems roots. Simply dig up several plants and move them to the new location. Before long, they will spread out to form a lovely mat.

Companion Planting and Design
Bugleweed is such a beautiful mat-forming groundcover that it often does not get the attention it deserves. Use it in a windowbox, a container, or raised bed where you can appreciate the unique loveliness of the flower spires without having to get on you hands and knees. Bugleweed makes a nice transitional plant from lawn into a woodland garden, or an edge to a flagstone walkway. It consorts well with creeping phlox (*Phlox subulata*) and basket of gold (*Aurinia saxatilis*)

I Also Recommend
There are numerous fancy-leaf cultivated varieties. 'Burgundy Glow' has silvery leaves suffused with burgundy; its deep blue flower spikes and attractive rich burgundy foliage. 'Catlin's Giant' has the largest leaves of any bugleweed, up to 6 inches in beautiful purplish-bronze hue, and an 8- to 10-inch bright blue flower spike. 'Bronze Beauty' has attractive glossy bronze foliage; it blooms in spring or early summer with 6-inch spires of very rich, violet blue flowers.

Bugleweed is a wonderfully hardy (to Zone 3) perennial that forms a dense, carpet-like mat, even in shady areas. The stems often self-root, so it spreads easily, making it easy to propagate or move to a new area. The dark green leaves are opposite, growing low to the ground, up to 2$1/2$ inches long. Much breeding has been done in the past decade, and the results are new, mixed colors in the leaves, making the plant even more desirable for a shady area. The 3- to 6-inch flower spikes are composed of blue to lavender, two-lipped, $1/4$-inch florets in spring or early summer. Cut the flower spikes to use in mini arrangements or put them in a napkin ring for a festive look.

Other Common Names
Carpet Bugleweed, Carpet Bugle, Common Bugleweed

Bloom Period and Seasonal Color
Blue to purple in late spring to early summer.

Mature Height and Spread
3 to 6 in. × 2 to 3 ft.

Canadian Wild Ginger
Asarum canadense

Canadian wild ginger is a marvelous perennial ground-cover, surviving even in our coldest regions (hardy to Zone 2). Deciduous, it loses its leaves in autumn. Shade loving, it is a wonderful accent in a woodland garden. It spreads by rhizomes, and since it spreads rather quickly, you can use it for erosion control on a partially shaded bank. The dark, matte green leaves are 2 to 4 inches long and have a rounded heart shape. The leaf stalks are slightly hairy, growing 6 to 12 inches in length. The rhizomes have a pungent gingery smell; however, it is not edible—Native Americans used it for birth control. The flowers are inconspicuous, growing under the leaves. In spring, lift up a leaf and look for a bell-shaped, brownish-purple flower. Spreads by rhizomes.

Other Common Name
Wild Ginger

Bloom Period and Seasonal Color
Inconspicuous brownish-purple in spring.

Mature Height and Spread
6 to 8 in. × 6 to 8 in.

When, Where, and How to Plant
A very hardy (Zone 2) woodland perennial, Canadian wild ginger is more likely found through mail-order sources. Unfortunately, many nurseries and garden centers tend to carry the more showy European variety rather than the native species. Canadian wild ginger grows best in rich, humusy, moist, neutral to acidic, well-drained soil in part shade to full shade. Plant it in spring after all danger of frost has passed or in late summer to early fall (if available) at the same level it was growing in the container. Space 6 inches apart. Water well with transplant solution.

Growing Tips
Keep the soil uniformly moist; do not let it dry out. Canadian wild ginger does not need fertilizer.

Care and Maintenance
If slugs appear, let them be as they pollinate the flowers. However, if they are feasting on the leaves, go out at night with a flashlight and hand pick and destroy them if you can handle that. Or, put several shingles nearby—their cool shade will attract the critters in the daytime. Canadian wild ginger naturalizes easily, spreading by its creeping rhizomes and from seed. In a few years, it can cover a large area. Control its spread by digging it up when it has gone out of bounds.

Companion Planting and Design
Canadian wild ginger belongs in a woodland garden or along a shady path. Its rounded-heart-shaped leaves form a lovely woodland carpet It mixes well with other woodland wildflowers such as Canada mayapple (*Podophyllum peltatum*), Jack-in-the-pulpit (*Arisaema triphyllum*), and Christmas fern (*Polypodium achrostichoides*).

I Also Recommend
Other *Asarum* species include European wild ginger (*Asarum europaeum*), which is less hardy (Zone 4) and has glossy dark green 2- to 3-inch-long leaves. *Asarum europaeum caucasicum* has leaf tips that are tapered and more extended than the species. *Asarum shuttleworthii* 'Callaway' (hardy to Zone 6, but I have grown it in a south-facing, sheltered location in Zone 5) is worth trying for its broadly heart-shaped, 1- to 4-inch, silvery mottled green leaves.

Creeping Juniper
Juniperus horizontalis

When, Where, and How to Plant
Potted plants of creeping juniper and some of its cultivars are available at nurseries, garden centers, and home stores. A greater variety is available through mail-order nurseries. Plant it in spring after danger of frost has passed or in late summer to early fall (look for a bargain). Creeping juniper grows best in full sun and thrives in dry, rocky places. If you have rich or clayey soil, add builder's sand to make it drier. An alternative is to dig a hole about two inches larger and deeper than the pot of juniper and fill it with cactus potting mix that has been lightly moistened with transplant solution. Plant the juniper in this mix at the level it was growing in the original container. Water well.

Growing Tips
Until the plant is established, do not let the soil dry out completely. Feeding is unnecessary.

Care and Maintenance
Prune it, if necessary, to keep it within bounds. When pruning, leave its natural overlapping habit; do not try to shape it. Mulch around the plant (within an inch of the stem) with sand or gravel to increase drainage and prevent rot.

Companion Planting and Design
Before planting creeping juniper, plant a few daffodils (*Narcissus* spp.) that will add an interesting color accent in spring. One of the most striking plant combinations I have seen is 'Bar Harbor' juniper with a dwarf bamboo (*Bambusa* spp.) growing up through it. Creeping juniper is lovely trailing over large rocks.

I Also Recommend
'Bar Harbor' (to 12 inches) has a dense mat of steely blue needles that turn a lovely silvery purple in winter. 'Wiltonii' (to 6 inches) is also known as blue rug juniper as it forms a silvery blue carpet; it is one of the best trailing junipers. 'Plumosa Compacta' (1 to 2 feet × 4 to 8 feet) is also known as compact plumosa juniper and has grey-green foliage that turns light purple in winter; it is fast growing. 'Prince of Wales' has a plum-colored winter color.

Creeping juniper is one of the more unusual groundcovers. It is a low-growing (to 12 inches) bluish gray-green, evergreen shrub that is drought tolerant and will grow in some of the worst soil—rocky and sandy—quickly covering a large area. The branches overlap, so from a distance, it looks like a small, wavy ocean. In fall, it turns bronzy. The inconspicuous berries are dark blue. It is an excellent plant for erosion control on hills or banks. Creeping juniper's glaucous gray-green needles are somewhat pointed, making the plant excellent for defining boundaries—at least keeping children and small animals at bay. Deer unfortunately are not deterred but consider it a delicacy. Juniper berries are used as a flavoring in gin.

Bloom Period and Seasonal Color
Evergreen

Mature Height and Spread
8 to 12 in. × indefinite spread

Goldflame Honeysuckle

Lonicera × *heckrotti* 'Goldflame'

I first fell in love with 'Goldflame' honeysuckle during an outdoor photography workshop. Wandering around an arboretum, we each had to choose one flower and photograph it from all angles, depths, and distances. I spied the eye-catching clusters of 1¹/₂-inch-long tropical-looking flowers and knew it was my choice. The tubular, two-lipped flowers are peachy pink outside and buttery yellow inside, making a cheery display even in the rain. A lightly fragrant plant, I see hummingbirds at the flowers, going for their nectar, and bees buzzing around them as well. The leaves are handsome as well—1- to 2¹/₂- inch blue-green ovals with whitish undersides. It is a loosely twining perennial vine and looks lovely on a lattice where you can weave it from one side to another.

Bloom Period and Seasonal Color
Peach with yellow blooms late spring to summer.

Mature Height and Spread
10 to 12 ft. × 2 to 4 ft.

Zone
4

When, Where, and How to Plant
Container-grown 'Goldflame' honeysuckle plants are readily available at nurseries, garden centers, and home stores. It grows best in rich, well-drained soil in full sun. Plant after all danger of frost has passed, following general planting instructions on page 15. Grow within 6 inches of a support, using an arbor, trellis, or pergola. Place the support before you plant the vine.

Growing Tips
Water well at planting and keep lightly moist until the plant is growing. Foliar feed or apply manure tea to the soil monthly during the growing season.

Care and Maintenance
Loosely tie the stem to the support since it is not a strong twining vine and needs help to keep itself upright. Alternatively, weave it through a lattice or trellis. Deadheading often results in a second, smaller flush of bloom in later summer to early autumn. Spray with baking soda solution (see page 231) if powdery mildew is a problem.

Companion Planting and Design
As a rather delicate-looking vine, it is best left to climb alone; however, you can enliven it by painting its support. It is handsome against white, but cobalt blue is outstanding, as are sage green and purple. For a subtle look, paint the support a very pale yellow—too much yellow may not be the right color match for the flowers. Grow one of the yellow and peach lantanas at the base of the vine for color at ground level.

I Also Recommend
Trumpet (or coral) honeysuckle (*Lonicera sempervirens*) grows to 40 feet and is hardy to Zone 4). It is a great hummingbird plant with clusters of 2-inch-long, tubular flowers—bright red orange outside, yellow inside—from late spring through summer. Winter honeysuckle (*Lonicera fragrantissima*) grows to 6 feet by 10 feet and is hardy to Zone 5. It has a sweet lemony scent that emanates from pairs of ¹/₂-inch, 2-lipped, creamy white flowers in winter and early spring. It is a bushy honeysuckle that is good in the background, as it is not showy.

Hosta

Hosta spp.

When, Where, and How to Plant

Although container-grown hostas of all types are readily available at nurseries, garden centers, and home stores, the greatest selection is through mail-order nurseries. Browse the catalogs and pick the perfect one for your garden. Make sure the light in your planting spot is right for the hosta you choose. Hostas grow best in rich, moist, well-drained soil. Plant after the last frost date at the same level it was growing in the pot. Be sure to allow enough space for its mature size. Water well. Mulch to within 1 inch of the crown with organic matter to keep the roots cool and maintain soil moisture. Water the mulch.

Growing Tips

Once established, hostas are fairly drought tolerant, withstanding weeks with no rain. Foliar feed the plant when you first see the flower spikes appear.

Care and Maintenance

Cut flower stalks for fragrant indoor bouquets. Slugs and snails love hostas. Deter them with an inch-wide ring of diatomaceous earth around the plant. Hostas with cross-venation or rippled varieties are less appealing to these slimy pests. Dig the plant up and divide it in the spring if the hosta gets too large.

Companion Planting and Design

You can make an entire garden from hostas in all their variations. In part shade, they mix well with ferns, bleeding heart (*Dicentra spectabilis* and other *Dicentra* spp.), and foamflower (*Tiarella cordifolia*). Use them to line woodland paths.

I Also Recommend

'Crispula' (to 20 inches by 36 inches) has heart-shaped, deeply channeled white-edged, green leaves that taper and twist at the ends. 'Francee' (to 22 inches by 36 inches) has heart-shaped olive-green leaves irregularly edge white. 'Frances Williams' (to 24 inches by 36 inches) yields glaucous blue-green leaves with irregular wide chartreuse margins. 'Shining Tot' (to 2 inches by 8 inches) has shiny, thick, deep green leaves. *Hosta sieboldiana* (to 36 inches by 40 inches) is the king of the blues with heart- to ovate-shaped, thick, puckered, glaucous leaves—blue on top, paler on the underside.

Hostas have been the epitome of perennial shade plants since Victorian times. They are so long lived that some of the plain green hostas lining the walkways of Victorian homes may indeed be the original plants put in when the houses were new. The amount of hosta breeding during the past decade has been tremendous. Today, you can find hostas that grow in full sun to full shade—and everything in between. Although hostas are mainly grown for their attractive leaves, they send up flower spikes in summer; some are fragrant. Plants range in size from 2 inches to over 5 feet. Leaf colors are phenomenal—from solid green, chartreuse, or blue, to variegations with the aforementioned colors plus white and cream.

Other Common Names
Funkia, Plantain Lily

Bloom Period and Seasonal Color
White to mauve to purple in summer (depending on variety).

Mature Height and Spread
2 to 36 in. × 6 to 60 in.

Zone
3

Jackman Clematis

Clematis × jackmanii

Clematis is often called the queen of the climbers for its regal form and flower. If so, Clematis jackmanii is the perennial king with its lusciously deep purple, velvety, 4- to 6-inch blooms. It is somewhat historic, as it was the first large-flowered hybrid clematis to be developed. Yet, it still reigns supreme as one of the most popular of all clematis. There are many species and cultivars of clematis, but the large-flowered ones are the overall favorites as they are so showy. Even the seedheads are attractive after they have finished blooming—an interesting-looking whorl. Although most people grow clematis formally on an arbor or trellis, I have seen them supported and still showing off growing through a dogwood, shrub rose, or an evergreen.

Bloom Period and Seasonal Color
Deep purple in summer.

Mature Height and Spread
8 to 10 ft. × 2 to 3 ft.

Zones
4

When, Where, and How to Plant
Jackman clematis is widely available at nurseries, garden centers, and home stores. Clematis is a bit fussy, liking its roots shaded and its leaves and flowers in full sun. Clematis grows best in rich, moist, slightly alkaline, well-drained soil. Dig a hole twice the depth of the roots; put the soil on a tarp. Amend it with equal parts of organic matter (compost, well-rotted manure, leaf mold); mix well. Check the pH; 7.0 is ideal. Adjust if necessary by adding lime to acid soil (pH less than 7.0) and bone meal to alkaline soil (pH less than 7.0). Put half the amended soil back in the hole. Water with two cups of transplant solution. Place the support before you plant the vine. Plant the clematis so the crown is 2 to 3 inches deep and cover with soil. Firm the soil gently with your hands. Water with 2 cups of transplant solution. Mulch with 3 to 4 inches of organic matter, keeping the mulch at least 1 inch away from the stems.

Growing Tips
Water regularly. Foliar feed every six weeks with a solution of kelp or fish emulsion.

Care and Maintenance
Clematis stems are fragile; handle them gently. Tie them loosely to a support. In the coldest areas, it will die down to the ground in late fall but will regrow in spring.

Companion Planting and Design
Jackman clematis is stunning paired with a pink climbing rose (*Rosa* 'Handel', 'New Dawn', 'Climbing Tiffany', or 'Cecile Brunner') growing up white arbor or trellis. Plant a white or pink daylily (*Hemerocallis* 'Sunday Gloves', 'Pink Flirt', 'White Temptation', or 'High Lama') near enough to the clematis to shade its roots but not steal nutrients. Before planting, track the sun so the daylilies shade the clematis in the heat of the day—noon to 5 p.m.

I Also Recommend
Other clematis cultivars include 'Henryi' (8 inches across) with stunning pure white flowers. 'Carnaby' (3 to 4 inches) has fuchsia petals fading to white edges. 'Ernest Markham' (4 inches) produces vivid magenta blooms.

Kamtschatika Sedum

Sedum kamtschaticum

When, Where, and How to Plant

Kamtschatika sedum has become more popular, so you are more likely to find it at nurseries and garden centers. Read the tag; some growers are making up common names, so look for the proper botanical name. There are many excellent mail-order sources as well. Often, the cultivar 'Rosy Glow' is easier to find than the species. Kamtschatika sedum grows best in full sun to light shade. Good drainage is of utmost importance, especially in winter. Unless you have sandy soil, dig the planting hole 2 inches deeper than the container. Put 1 inch of gravel at the bottom of the hole, add 1 inch of builder's sand on top of that, and then add soil, placing the plant at the proper soil level.

Growing Tips

Water once a week until the plant is established. Sedum is quite drought tolerant, but water if the leaves begin to look puckered. Fertilization is unnecessary.

Care and Maintenance

It needs little care. Propagation of sedum is very easy. If you want fast results, dig up the plant, make divisions, and replant them. If you are patient, remove a leaf, put it the cut end 1/3 of the way into the ground, and in time it will grow a new plant.

Companion Planting and Design

Kamtschatika sedum is at home in a rock garden. With the numerous varieties of sedums, you could make an entire rock garden ranging from the larger, familiar *Sedum* 'Autumn Joy' (to 24 inches) to the smallest *Sedum humifusum* (1/2 inch tall), all of which have a wide range of leaf colors, sizes, shapes, and formations.

I Also Recommend

'Rosy Glow' (to 12 inches tall) has blue leaves with a rosy tinge and bears pink flowers from summer to autumn. 'Variegatum' (to 4 inches) has creamy-edged, pink-tinted leaves, bearing yellow flowers in summer that age to crimson. 'Weinhenstephaner Gold' (to 4 inches) has a more trailing habit, with yellow blossoms in summer that mature to orange.

Kamtschatika sedum is a sunny perennial delight in the garden. I first saw it in the garden of a friend who was having trouble with flooding and erosion on a somewhat sandy hillside leading to a Japanese garden. A landscaper had added stone steps, but even they washed away as nothing anchored the soil. Another friend suggested planting Kamtschatika sedum around and between the steps to anchor them—and it worked. It is such a darling plant—much smaller (only 4 inches tall) than the common sedums like 'Autumn Joy'. In late summer, clusters of pink buds open to reveal 1/2-inch, yellow star-shaped flowers. In autumn, I am delighted to see young swallowtail butterflies competing with bees for the flowers' nectar. Its succulent leaves add year-round interest.

Other Common Name
Stonecrop

Bloom Period and Seasonal Color
Yellow in late summer.

Mature Height and Spread
3 to 4 in. × 8 to 10 in.

Zone
4

Morning Glory

Ipomoea tricolor 'Heavenly Blue'

My first childhood garden memory is the sky blue 'Heavenly Blue' morning glory twining its way up the trellis with large, heart-shaped leaves. On a sunny summer day with low humidity and a few puffy clouds, it was easy to see how the annual vine got its name. The white in the center of the funnel-shaped 3-inch flowers echoed the clouds in the heavenly sky, with a dash of yellow for the sun. As a small child, watching morning glories grow awed me like sunflowers did—I could see their progress day by day. When they reached the top of the trellis and still wanted to grow taller, my father would lift me up so I could twine the vine to grow across; it eventually filled the entire trellis.

Bloom Period and Seasonal Color
Sky blue with white centers from summer to frost.

Mature Height and Spread
10 to 12 ft. × 6 to 15 in.

When, Where, and How to Plant
Morning glory seeds have tough seed coats. For best germination, nick the seeds with a knife or soak overnight in lukewarm water. Morning glories grow best in full sun, in ordinary to dry soil—even sandy soil. Once the soil is above 65 degrees Fahrenheit in spring, plant the seeds 1 inch deep, spaced 2 to 6 inches apart. Water well.

Growing Tips
Keep the soil lightly moist until two sets of leaves appear. After that, it is fairly drought-tolerant. Drooping leaves signal a need for water.

Care and Maintenance
Give morning glory ample support and room to grow, and watch it head for the sky. Foliar feed monthly.

Companion Planting and Design
Traditionally, morning glories are trained up a trellis or on strings hung from a gutter to the ground. For a change of pace, let 'Heavenly Blue' trail from a hanging basket. Morning glories are perfect for growing on fences, up walls, on mailboxes, and up lampposts. Let them trail to hide an unsightly tree stump or just ramble across the ground. Try a combination of morning glory (it closes by noon), cardinal climber (*Ipomoea quamoclit*) with small red flowers that open in the afternoon, and moonflower (*Ipomoea alba*) with flowers of an almost luminescent white that opens at dusk.

I Also Recommend
Flying Saucers' (6 to 8 feet tall, 2 to 3 inches wide) has blue- to mauve-streaked white flowers. 'Milky Way' (to 15 feet) has white flowers accented with carmine-rose down the center of each petal; it blooms until midday. *Ipomoea* × *imperialis* 'Tie Dye Blue' (6 to 8 feet tall) has $5^1/2$ to 6 inch flowers; each large lavender bloom is uniquely striped and streaked with deep purple. *Ipomoea purpurea* 'Star of Yelta' (8 to 10 feet tall) has $2^1/2$ inch blooms and is an heirloom variety with masses of rich purple bloom with central bright pink area and white dot; unlike most morning glories, it remains open most of the day.

Moss Pink

Phlox subulata

When, Where, and How to Plant

Container-grown moss pinks are available at nurseries, garden centers, home stores, and through mail-order nurseries. They grow best in average, well-drained soil in full sun. Plant it in the spring one week before the last frost date. Dig a hole the same size as the container. Pour a cup of transplant solution in the hole and then plant the moss pink so it is growing at the same level it was in the pot. Water it with an additional 1 to 2 cups of transplant solution. Allow 8 to 12 inches between plants.

Growing Tips

Keep the soil lightly moist until the plant is established. It is fairly drought-tolerant, but water when the top 3 inches of soil is dry. Foliar feed with a solution of fish emulsion or kelp once a month after flowering.

Care and Maintenance

If you want a denser plant, cut the stems halfway back after they have flowered. Plants are long-lived. If the center dies out, dig up the entire plant and divide it, discarding the dead part, and replant the divisions. Water early in the day at ground level to prevent powdery mildew.

Companion Planting and Design

Moss pink grows well in a rock garden or a mixed border. It is impressive planted with airy pasque flower (*Pulsatilla vulgaris*), basket of gold (*Aurinia saxatilis*), and species tulips, such as *Tulipa batalini* or *Tulipa bakeri*. Let it grow between stones or railroad ties in a vertical wall—it has a magical effect and softens the look.

I Also Recommend

'Emerald Blue' ("Emerald Cushion Blue') has a compact habit with bright green leaves and blue flowers. 'Emerald Pink' is the same as 'Emerald Blue' but with vivid pink blooms. 'McDaniel's Cushion' has bright pink flowers. 'Bonita' yields shiny leaves and bright pink blossoms. 'Candy Stripe' has white flowers striped pink down the center of each petal. 'Red Wings' produces deep crimson flowers with dark red centers. 'Apple Blossom' has light pink blooms. 'Coral Eye' has pink flowers with a coral center (eye).

When I was little, my father created a free-form rock garden on our front lawn (a corner property)—unheard of in the 1960s. The plant selections were fewer then, but the plants that left lasting impressions on me were the moss pinks. (He called them mountain pinks.) We had the three colors—purple, white, and pink, each in its special nook—purple in a hole he made in the top stone, filled with soil, and planted. It carpeted the top of the garden and softened the edge. Pink grew in several places between rocks, and white transitioned the garden into the green carpet of lawn. After blooming, the evergreen perennial creepers added interest and did not give away any secrets of the garden. It is deer resistant.

Other Common Names
Ground Pink, Mountain Phlox

Bloom Period and Seasonal Color
Purple, pink, or white in spring.

Mature Height and Spread
3 to 6 in. × 12 to 20 in.

Zone
3

Myrtle
Vinca minor 'Bowles'

'Bowles' is one of the larger-flowered varieties of myrtle. Myrtle is one of the "big three" evergreen perennial groundcovers for shade, including ivy (Hedera helix) and pachysandra (Pachysandra terminalis), but it is the only one included here as it is the hardiest— thriving in Zone 4—while the others are better for warmer-winter climates. Although there are not as many cultivated myrtles as the ivies, 'Bowles' is my favorite with its five-petaled, 1¹/2-inch, lavender-blue flowers. Its shiny, broadly lance-shaped, deep green leaves grow on thin, wiry stems. Since it's an evergreen, 'Bowles' myrtle is as attractive in winter as it summer. The plant is versatile, equally handsome hanging from a deep windowbox as it is a mat-forming groundcover growing at the edge of woodland.

Other Common Names
Periwinkle, Vinca

Bloom Period and Seasonal Color
Lavender-blue in mid-spring; intermittent rebloom in late summer.

Mature Height and Spread
8 to 12 in. × indefinite spread

Zone
4

When, Where, and How to Plant
'Bowles' is one of the most popular varieties of myrtle and is readily found at nurseries, garden centers, and home stores. As your interest in myrtles, head straight for the mail-order nurseries. Bluebird Nursery has the most complete selection (see nurseries in back of book). Although myrtle tolerates sun (requiring more watering), it grows best in part sun or part shade in rich, moist, well-drained soil. Plant in spring after all danger of frost has passed. You can buy flats of rooted cuttings (good for large areas) or a container-grown plant. Plant at the depth it was originally growing, according to instructions on page 15. Water well.

Growing Tips
Keep lightly moist until well established. Foliar feed once a season.

Care and Maintenance
Cut back hard in early spring to restrict growth, resulting in a denser plant.

Companion Planting and Design
Its trailing, spreading habit makes a fine groundcover, rock garden, border, or container plant. Interplant autumn crocus (*Colchicum autumnale*) or daffodils (*Narcissus* spp.) for added interest. For rock garden use, plant it in poor to average, well-drained, gritty soil.

I Also Recommend
Unless noted otherwise, all of these varieties have shiny, deep green leaves. 'Golden Bowles' has bright yellow-edged, blue flowers. 'Bowles White' has pinkish white buds that open to white flowers. 'Alba' has white flowers, and 'Alba Variegata' has leaves edged in pale yellow with white flowers. 'Argenteo Variegata' is also found labeled as 'Variegata'; its leaves are creamy with white margins and has pale blue-violet blooms; 'Atropurpurea' is also known as 'Purpurea' and 'Rubra' and has dark purplish-red flowers. 'Azurea Flore-Pleno' is also seen as 'Caerulea Plena' and has double sky blue blooms. 'Honeydew' has unusual with its chartreuse leaves that contrast with pale blue flowers; it is outstanding for shade, lighting up even the darkest corner. Illumination® is a newly patented variety with unique golden variegated leaves and blue flowers.

Spotted Dead Nettle
Lamium maculatum 'White Nancy'

When, Where, and How to Plant
'White Nancy' is available at most nurseries, garden centers, and home stores as are some other cultivars. Many, however, are available only through mail-order nurseries. When buying, check to see if roots are growing through the drainage hole, indicating a rootbound plant. Plant 'White Nancy' after the last frost. It prefers moist, well-drained soil and part sun to shade. After unpotting the plants, loosen roots if necessary. Plant it at the same level it was growing in the pot. Allow 8 to 12 inches between plants. Water it well with 2 cups of transplant solution.

Growing Tips
Keep the soil lightly moist; do not let it dry out. It does not need to be fertilized.

Care and Maintenance
It is a relatively care-free plant. If it starts growing out of bounds, dig up the unwanted area. You can either replant it elsewhere, divide it and share with friends, or take it to a plant swap. It is slightly susceptible to powdery mildew; use a baking soda spray (see page 231) at the first sign of problems.

Companion Planting and Design
Plant 'White Nancy' with low-growing, early-blooming bulbs like species tulips, crocus, and grape hyacinths in deciduous woodlands. It will not come up until the bulbs have finished blooming and will hide their ripening foliage.

I Also Recommend
'Album' has white flowers. Shell Pink' has white-marbled, green leaves and the palest pink blossom. 'Variegatum' has a silver stripe down the middle of the leaf. 'Beacon Silver' has narrowly green-edged, silver leaves and pink blooms. 'Beedham's White' is a new variety with bright yellow leaves and white flowers. 'Aureum' (to 6 inches) has golden leaves with a central white stripe and pink flowers. 'Chequers' will grow in full sun and is also known as false salvia; it has heavily white-marbled green leaves and rose-pink flowers. Orchid Frost® (6 to 12 inches) is a patented variety with a mounded habit, blue-green edging on silvery green leaves, and vivid orchid pink flowers.

'White Nancy' is a beautiful perennial groundcover for a shady area. It was discovered as a white-flowering sport of 'Beacon Silver'. Its elegant silver leaves have narrow green margins, which show them off well. If the leaves were completely silver, the plant would have the appearance of a silvery carpet; the green edging gives it more definition. In summer, the plant bears spikes of whorled pure white, 2-lipped flowers, each less than 3/4 of an inch long. In general, dead nettles are fast-growing groundcovers, considered invasive by some, because of the rhizomes and stolons that easily root and spread. 'White Nancy' is more demure, and not an aggressive grower. It is a beautiful woodland plant, eye-catching amongst evergreens or growing below a deciduous canopy of trees.

Bloom Period and Seasonal Color
White in early summer.

Mature Height and Spread
7 to 9 in. × 3 to 3 1/2 ft.

Sweet Autumn Clematis
Clematis paniculata

Sweet autumn clematis has gone through a number of botanical name changes. Depending on what resource book you use, you can find it listed as Clematis ternifolia, Clematis dioscoreifolia robusta, Clematis maximowicziana, *or* Clematis paniculata *(the name listed in* The Royal Horticultural Society Dictionary of Plants, *which is my top reference book for plant taxonomy). This clematis by any name smells delightfully sweet from late summer through fall. Its 1- to 1½-inch flowers nearly cover the mighty vine, which is deceivingly dainty looking. In milder winter areas, it is evergreen. Wonderfully whorled seedpods follow the flowers, then dry and last well into the winter. I find it a very versatile vine for growing up, down, or across.*

Bloom Period and Seasonal Color
White from late summer through fall.

Mature Height and Spread
15 to 20 ft. × 6 to 10 ft.

Zone
4

When, Where, and How to Plant
Sweet autumn clematis is available from spring through early fall. In autumn, the delicate flowers and sweet aroma entice you to purchase the plant, although it is better to plant it in spring. Like other clematis, it grows best with its roots shaded and the leaves in full sun. It prefers slightly alkaline, rich, moist, well-drained soil. Dig at least twice the depth and width of the container. Put the soil on a tarp or wheelbarrow and mix in equal amounts of organic matter (compost, well-rotted manure, leaf mold, humus). Adjust the pH so it is 7.0 (add lime if the pH is lower, bone meal if it is higher. Install a support near the planting site. Fill the hole halfway with the amended soil. Water it with 2 cups of transplant solution. Place the plant so that its crown is 2 to 3 inches below soil level. Fill in around the plant with the amended soil. Firm the soil around the plant. Water it with a quart of transplant solution. Add 3 to 4 inches of organic mulch around the plant; be sure to keep it an inch away from the stems. If it touches the stems, there is likelihood of rot, disease, or insects getting into the plant.

Growing Tips
Do not let the soil dry out. Foliar feed in late June or early July with a solution of kelp of fish emulsion (mixed according to package directions).

Care and Maintenance
Loosely tie the stems to the support. You can prune right after it finishes blooming or in spring when the buds swell.

Companion Planting and Design
Sweet autumn clematis is a great cover for a fence, trellis, or arbor, or use it as a groundcover. Plant some fall bulbs such as autumn crocus (*Colchicum autumnale*) or saffron crocus (*Crocus sativus*) near its base.

I Also Recommend
I only recommend the species.

Sweet Potato Vine
Ipomoea batatas

When, Where, and How to Plant

Unlike regular sweet potatoes grown from slips, ornamental varieties are easily grown from potted plants. Some cultivars are found at nurseries and garden centers, while others are only available through mail-order nurseries. Sweet potato vines need full sun and rich, loose, well-drained soil. Amend the area where they will grow—not just the planting hole—with plenty of organic matter. Unpot the plant and unwind the roots (they grow so quickly they easily become rootbound). Dig a hole deep enough for the roots; add 1 cup of transplant solution. Make a cone of soil for the plant, with the roots splaying down so it is growing at the same level it was it the pot. Fill in with soil and gently firm it. Water it with 2 cups of transplant solution. Allow at least 15 to 24 inches between plants.

Growing Tips

Once they are established, which takes less than a week, the plants are fairly drought tolerant. No fertilization is necessary.

Care and Maintenance

If you have other plants growing in the same bed, you will want to direct the vines (and prune them if necessary) to grow where you want them. To harvest tubers, gently dig them when the vines die back. Cure for two weeks in a warm humid space. Store above 55 degrees Fahrenheit.

Companion Planting and Design

Sweet potato vine is an excellent accent plant in the garden or tumbling out of a container. It's fast-growing as a skirt plant around a tree or shrub.

I Also Recommend

'Ace of Spades' has dark, spade-shaped leaves, edible white tubers. 'Blackie' ('Blacky') has deeply lobed, 8- to 10-inch, purplish black leaves and large white edible tubers. 'Lady Fingers' yields deeply cut, dark green leaves with rich purple stems. 'Marguerite' ('Marguarita', 'Sulphur') has 5- to 8-inch, deeply lobed, chartreuse leaves and produces large, tasty deep orange tubers. 'Tricolor' ('Pink Frost') has irregularly triangular, 2- to 5-inch, white, pink, and green variegated leaves.

Sweet potato vine has come into popularity within the past decade. For Prairie Lands gardeners and northern gardeners, it is part of the increasingly trendy "banana-canna craze"—growing a tropical looking garden in a temperate region. Most people grow it for its large, exotic, colorful leaves, not necessarily realizing what a great groundcover this annual plant is. I put out four plants of 'Blackie' in late June, and by early August, they had completely covered a 10-foot by 10-foot area, nearly smothering the existing plants. I have to prune around the roses, dwarf conifers, and coleus in the same bed. When planting there in early September, I discovered the bonus—edible sweet potatoes. Even here, especially with our hot summers, many varieties will produce edible tubers.

Other Common Names

Sweet Potato, Ornamental Sweet Potato

Bloom Period and Seasonal Color

Does not flower in our climate; grown for the foliage.

Mature Height and Spread

15 to 20 ft. × 2 to 4 ft.

Virginia Creeper
Parthenocissus quinquefolia

Virginia creeper is a deciduous, perennial vine that is handsome in summer but really glows in autumn when its leaves turn scarlet. It is not a dense vine that can be used to cover a fence or make a good groundcover; however, its dainty qualities are evident when it is grown on a wall because you appreciate the vine as well as the bare space. I love its look in winter—it is like seeing the skeleton of the plant, and it is the best time to see the way it attaches itself with disk-like suction cups at the ends of the tendrils. It is easily differentiated from its cousin, Boston ivy (Parthenocissus tricuspidata), as it is composed of five leaflets, while Boston ivy has three.

Other Common Name
Woodbine

Bloom Period and Seasonal Color
Inconspicuous in summer; grown for foliage.

Mature Height and Spread
30 to 50 ft. × 1 to 3 ft.

When, Where, and How to Plant
Virginia creeper is readily available at nurseries, garden centers, and home stores. The other recommended varieties will be found through specialty and mail-order nurseries. When choosing a plant, look for one that is the most spreading and the sturdiest. Virginia creeper is not fussy, but it will develop more vigorously in moist, fertile, well-drained soil. It will grow in sun or shade but produces the most brilliant fall foliage color when it is growing in full sun. Plant Virginia creeper within 3 to 6 inches of its support. You may need to guide it initially by loosely tying it with a string or with a nail on one side of the stem bent across it, until the suckers have a chance to take hold. After that, it is self-supporting. Allow 6 to 12 inches between plants. Water well with transplant solution. (See page 15 for more on planting.)

Growing Tips
Keep the plant lightly moist until the suckers are attached and growing well. Fertilization is not necessary, but a 3-inch mulch of compost in the winter will keep the plant nourished.

Care and Maintenance
Although there are a number of pests and diseases that Virginia creeper can develop, it is uncommon. If you see any evidence of a problem, check with your local Cooperative Extension Service. Prune, if necessary, to keep within bounds.

Companion Planting and Design
Virginia creeper is most handsome growing up a light-colored wall where it can be appreciated year-round. Train it up a tree—evergreen or deciduous—for a natural look. It is especially handsome growing on a crabapple, with the fruits and leaves showing off their fall beauty. Watch the wildlife that comes to feed on the blue berries in late summer and early fall.

I Also Recommend
Parthenocissus quinquefolia var. *engelmannii* has smaller leaves than the species. *Parthenocissus quinquefolia* var. *hirsuta* has leaves and young stems with softly white pubescence. *Parthenocissus quinquefolia* var. *saint-paulii* has leaves that remain on the plant longer before dropping than on the species.

Wintercreeper
Euonymus fortunei

When, Where, and How to Plant

Wintercreeper is readily available at nurseries, garden centers, and home stores. Shop mail-order nurseries for some of the cultivars I recommend. Wintercreeper is not fussy about soil, growing equally well in clay or sandy soil, in full sun to part shade. When purchasing, look carefully to be sure you are getting the vine, as some are sold as mature plants that will be bushy while others are obviously juvenile and vinelike. Allow 1 to 2 feet between plants. Water it well with transplant solution. Mulch with 3 to 4 inches of organic matter, keeping it at least an inch from the stem.

Growing Tips

Once it is established, wintercreeper is fairly drought tolerant, but keep it lightly moist until that time. Fertilizer is not necessary.

Care and Maintenance

Mulch is essential only until the plant is established. At that time, the dense leaf cover keeps weeds from germinating. It can sunburn in winter from reflected snow and/or ice glare. Cover it lightly with burlap to protect it, removing the burlap in early spring. To maintain an even look, prune out bushy mature branches as soon as they appear. Prune in spring to direct its growth or to keep it within bounds.

Companion Planting and Design

Wintercreeper is ideal for erosion control or growing on a slope as it roots easily along its stem if the soil is moist and well drained. Intersperse spring-blooming bulbs when planting wintercreeper for added color.

I Also Recommend

'Silver Queen' is a favorite with shiny leaves edged in white. 'Colorata' has green leaves that turn purple in cold weather. 'Gracilis' produces green and cream variegated leaves that turn pink as the temperatures drop; it is slow-growing. 'Minima' (baby wintercreeper) has small ($\frac{1}{2}$-inch) leaves that make it a choice fine-textured groundcover; it is equally lovely trained on a low wall. 'Vegeta' is a mounding, shrubby form with large leaves; it grows to 4 feet tall by 15 to 20 feet wide and is good for hiding ugly walls.

Wintercreeper is an attractive, evergreen vine with shiny green leaves. The leaves cover the spreading stems, almost hiding them completely. Wintercreeper has root-like holdfasts that enable it to climb on any rough surface; however, it should not be grown on a shingled or brick house as the holdfasts can creep between shingles, loosening them or growing the plant through the wall. The holdfasts can penetrate older mortar, making the bricks unstable. Wintercreeper has two forms—juvenile and mature. As a juvenile, the slender clinging stems have small leaves. Mature branches are bushy in form, have larger leaves, and bear inconspicuous flowers and bright red fruit. If you root a cutting from a mature branch, you will get a shrublike plant.

Bloom Period and Seasonal Color
Inconspicuous flowers on mature form

Mature Height and Spread
8 to 20 ft. × 3 to 5 ft.

Zone
5

Edible Groundcovers and Vines
Some Notable Choices

Cucumber

Cucumis sativus

Annual Vine or groundcover

(Zone 4, requiring 48 to 70 frost-free days)

There are three types of cucumber: pickling (short and blocky), slicing (cylindrical—the most common), and burpless (very long and ridged, also sold as English or hothouse cucumbers). They all have the best flavor when picked young and small. Cucumbers range beyond the typical green. Heirloom 'Lemon' is round and lemony yellow, while the European 'De Bouenil' is white.

Hardy Kiwi

Actinidia arguta

Perennial Vine

(Zone 4)

Although available year-round, why bother with store-bought kiwis with hairy skin that needs peeling when you can grow the smaller, tastier hardy kiwis, which don't need peeling? Just pop hardy kiwis in your mouth like grapes. Hardy kiwi is a vigorous grower, needing support of an arbor, pergola, or fence. Grow 'Issai', which is self-fertilizing, otherwise; you will need a male and female for fruit (fruits are borne only on the female plant).

Malabar Spinach

Basella malabar

Annual Vine

Also known as Indian spinach, Ceylon spinach, pasali, and pu-tin-choi, malabar is not a spinach at all. However, its glossy, heart-shaped leaves can be cooked and eaten like spinach. The great benefit to this 6- to 10-foot vine is that it loves the heat. When true spinach has wilted and quit, this beauty is just getting into its glory. If you keep picking leaves it regrows. I especially favor 'Rubra' for its red stems and red-veined leaves. It is lovely on an arbor or trellis.

Melon

Cucumis melo

Annual Groundcover or vine

(to Zone 4, requiring 68 to 95 frost-free days)

As most melons are large-fruited, they make good groundcovers. However, I have also seen small watermelons trained on a chainlink fence with old stockings tied to the fence to support the fruits. The juicy summer treats are perfect for growing where there's plenty of room for them to sprawl. Among the many types of melons (each with variations of size and color) are watermelon, apple melon, cantaloupe, Casaba, Crenshaw, honeydew, and muskmelon. Do not grow them near each other or near cucumbers, squash, or gourds, as they can crossbreed, often with inedible results.

Runner Bean

Phaseolus coccineus

Annual Vine

At last, Americans are learning what the English have for years—runner beans aren't just ornamental, they are edible. The flowers have a lovely sweet flavor. The pods can be eaten like pole beans when they are less than 4 inches long. Or, let the beans mature and wither and harvest the dried beans, which themselves are beautiful (white with black and dark pink markings). 'Scarlet Runner' is particularly eye-catching on an arbor with its scarlet flowers.

Squash

Curcubita pepo

Annual Groundcover:

(Summer Squash—Zone 3, requiring 45 to 65 frost-free days;

Winter Squash—Zone 4 requiring 85 to 110 frost-free days)

There are innumerable shapes and colors of squashes: summer (soft skinned fruit), and winter squash (tough-skinned fruits that keep well for eating through the winter). Summer squashes include yellow or green zucchini, round 'Gourmet Globe Hybrid' with green and yellow striping, yellow crookneck, and white, yellow, or green ruffle-edged patty-pan. Kuta hybrid squash crosses the barrier—picked young like a summer squash or left on the vine like a winter squash. Winter squashes include green or orange acorn squash, green striped sweet dumpling, yellow spaghetti, 'Blue Hubbard' with an unusual warty look, oblong 'Delicata' with ivory and green stripes, and beige butternut. All squash blossoms are edible, and delicious stuffed with cheese or breadcrumbs and sautéed.

Sweet potato

Ipomoea batatas

Annual Groundcover

(Zone 5, requiring 90 to 120 frost-free days)

One of the hottest new plants in the past decade is actually a sweet potato cultivar. 'Blackie' sweet potato vine, with its deep-burgundy fingerlike leaves, will produce edible tubers. Yet, the common edible sweet potato is a handsome groundcover. 'Vardaman' has the prettiest heart-shaped, green to burgundy leaves and is delicious. Once planted, it needs little care. Gently dig the tubers after the first light frost.

Tomato

Lycopersicon esculentum

Annual Vine

Some people let tomatoes sprawl on the ground, but their yield is lower this way, with greater pest and disease problems. Instead, stake or cage them, or use another means of support. Since the supports go into the ground with the small plants, I paint the supports bright colors—cobalt blue is a favorite—adding early color that will last all season. There are literally hundreds of tomato varieties (heirlooms and modern hybrids) including white, yellow, orange, green, purple, green-striped, orange, yellow-striped, and other color variations. Their size ranges from a tiny species no bigger than a pea, to the bite-sized cherry tomato, to the beefsteak, sandwich-sized two-pounders. Tomatoes may be round, elongated, or pepper-shaped, and solid with flesh or almost hollow.

Herbs *for the Prairie Lands*

By definition, an herb is a useful plant. Over the years, herbs have been used for many purposes. Today, herbs are generally divided into three categories: culinary, medicinal, and dye plants.

The medicinal use of herbs dates back to prehistoric times when the medicine woman (or man) of the clan picked and stored herbs for use year-round. She or he knew how to use these herbs because of the information passed down orally from generation to generation. During the Dark Ages, monks kept much of the information and grew the plants in monastery gardens. With the Renaissance, the knowledge, lore, and the plants passed back into the hands of special people—herbalists. These herbalists were sought after, much as we would get a consultation with a doctor. They made mixtures, tinctures, poultices, and tonics and used the plants fresh or dried. Today, health food stores are stocked with herbal products for medicinal, cosmetic, and culinary uses. Many modern medicines are derived from herbs or synthetically created to mimic herbs.

Culinary herbs are the focus of this section. Some of these herbs may have uses that extend beyond the kitchen—these will be noted and discussed. A number of the plants have edible flowers; this too will be highlighted. Unless noted in the individual entry, pest and diseases are not problems with most herbs.

Do you know the difference between an herb and a spice? Herbs and spices are often grouped together and considered interchangeable, as they are both seasonings. Nevertheless, there is a difference. Generally, an herb is the leafy portion of a temperate climate plant (herbaceous, soft-tissued, not woody), while a spice is derived from the seeds or bark of tropical plants (most often trees).

'Hidcote' Lavender

Growing Herbs

Herbs include annuals, perennials (although our climate dictates that we grow some as annuals or overwinter indoors), and biennials. Some of the most common herbs, such as rosemary, sage, thyme, and oregano, are native to the Mediterranean region and need to be grown differently than parsley, basil, anise hyssop, or chives. What they all have in common is that they like well-drained soil.

Mediterranean Herbs

These herbs grow best in full sun and poor to sandy soil that is very well drained. They are well suited for growing in containers, where it is easier to control the soil mix than in the ground. In the Prairie Lands states, the soil is rarely sandy; it tends to be very rich and more clayey. When growing Mediterranean herbs in the ground, you might consider making a grouping of them and digging out the existing soil to a depth of twelve inches—going at least six inches wider the planting area. Mix that soil with about a gallon each of builder's sand and compost to give it a rougher, more friable texture. Replace the soil then plant each herb one at a time. Most herbs are available as young plants, whether from a nursery, garden center, home store, or mail-order nursery. To plant a container-grown herb, start by mixing a gallon batch of transplant solution in a bucket. Let the potted herb sit in the solution for a minute or so. Remove the plant from the pot. If it is rootbound, loosen the roots so they hang free. If this is a plant growing in a cell pack, tear off the bottom half-inch of roots and gently loosen the side roots. Dig a hole the size of the plant, pour in a cup of transplant solution, place the plant in the hole, fill in with the soil from the hole, firm gently, and water with an additional cup of transplant solution. Add a half-inch layer of inorganic mulch (sand, gravel, grit, small stones) to within an inch of the stem, and surround the plant extending as far as its mature spread. If you are planting individually, follow the same directions, making the hole about three inches wider than the existing pot. Water regularly until the plant is established, then once or twice a week as needed (when the top inch of soil is dry).

All Other Herbs

With the exception of sweet woodruff, the other herbs also grow best in full sun. Unlike Mediterranean herbs, they generally prefer somewhat fertile, well-drained soil. If you are planting an herb bed, you can do the same thing—dig out the soil for the bed. For these herbs, however, mix in some compost or leaf mold and add a few handfuls of peat moss (to lower the pH of our alkaline soil). Mix well, put the soil back in the planting area, and proceed as above; do the same for individual plants. However, when it comes to mulching, use organic mulch such as barley hulls, pine straw (needles) barley straw, finely shredded bark, or small wood chips. You can use cocoa hulls, which have the delightful smell of chocolate. I used them until I realized that, since they were imported, they were fumigated before entering this country. In addition, cocoa (chocolate) is second only to cotton in the amount of fertilizers and pesticides used. For me, the use of cocoa hulls defeated the purpose of my organic garden, so I stopped using them. Whatever mulch you choose, you want a fine mulch that water can percolate through—not two-inch wood chips. I prefer dark-colored mulch, but that is an individual choice.

Even if you don't cook, include herbs in your garden since they are beautiful plants. If nothing else, try using a little bit of an herb as a garnish or toss it in a salad. You might discover that you like the flavor and decide to go a step further with them—mix them in with foods. Put a few sprigs of rosemary in the cavity of a roasting chicken. Toss some chopped chives into egg salad or add dill to tuna salad. Experiment. I always grow two containers of herbs right outside the kitchen door. For me, convenience is the key to using anything from the garden. If I can open the kitchen door, snip some basil, sage, rosemary, and chives—even if it is pouring rain, I am much more likely to use the plants than if I have to walk out into the garden. I have additional herbs in my mixed garden for their beauty and to use in the kitchen.

Anise Hyssop

Agastache foeniculum

If you like licorice, anise hyssop is an herb for you. Both the heart-shaped leaves and the tiny light purple florets are edible. The leaves are best made into a tasty tea. Pick the purple florets off the flower spikes; small as they are, they pack a lot of flavor—reminiscent of Good 'n' Plenty candies at Saturday movie matinees. Anise hyssop is a handsome perennial that forms stiff, well-branched stalks. In summer when the flower spikes appear, you'll hear softly buzzing bees and whirring hummingbirds and see a variety of butterflies and even sphinx moths in early evening—all seeking the sweet nectar. The florets are excellent in shortbread and ice cream. Mix them with sugar for use in baking during the off-season.

Bloom Period and Seasonal Color
Lilac from summer into fall.

Mature Height and Spread
24 to 48 in. × 18 to 24 in.

Zone
4

When, Where, and How to Plant
Potted plants are readily available in spring. Anise hyssop prefers ordinary garden soil and full sun. Plant after all danger of frost has passed. Allow 2 feet between plants. Although a mass planting is breathtaking, one or two plants are ample for my needs. Water well. (See page 91 for more planting information.)

Growing Tips
Until the plant is established, keep the soil lightly moist then water deeply twice a week—depending on the weather. Any sign of leaf drooping is a call for water. I foliar feed it once in mid-June when I feed most of the garden, but that is probably unnecessary unless your soil is poor.

Care and Maintenance
Anise hyssop is pest and disease free. If growing it in an exposed area, you might want to stake it to prevent breaking in the wind. Harvest the leaves at any time; the younger leaves have a fresher licorice flavor. Use them fresh, or dry them in a dark, warm, well-aired place for several days. When dry, the leaves will crumble easily in your hand. Store dried leaves in airtight containers for making tea throughout the year. Pluck the individual florets off the flowerspike; they make delicious custard or mix them in with vanilla ice cream for a lovely anise end to the meal. Cut spent flowerspikes back to the next lowest branching stem. New spikes will keep coming until hard frost. Cut the plant to the ground. It is a prolific self-sower, emerging in late spring. Wait to weed until you are sure you have plants growing; they transplant or pull out easily.

Companion Planting and Design
Anise hyssop is companionable with sunflowers of any size—the colors are complementary. It is eye-catching surrounded with 'Lemon Gem' marigolds in a large container.

I Also Recommend
'Tutti Fruti' is a surprise with its raspberry pink flowers taking me back to the old-fashioned taste of tutti-frutti gum. Grow 'Firebird' for the color impact of its coppery orange flowers rather than as an edible.

Basil

Ocimum basilicum

When, Where, and How to Plant

Potted plants of many basil varieties are available in spring at garden centers, nurseries, and through mail-order. Some varieties are only available as seed, but you may find plants at an herb farm, farmers market, plant swap, or plant sale at a botanical garden. Sow seed indoors in peat pots in lightly moistened seed-starting mix, eight weeks before the last frost date. Keep lightly moist. (See page 91 for more planting information.) Grow on a south-facing windowsill or under gro-lights. Plant outdoors at the same time as tomatoes, spacing plants 1 to 2 feet apart depending on variety. Water well.

Growing Tips

Until basil is established, keep the soil lightly moist then keep it well watered. Water monthly with compost tea.

Care and Maintenance

Basil thrives in hot weather. Remove the flower stalks to keep the leaf flavor dynamic. Discard or use the florets in cooking and as beautiful, flavorful garnishes.

Companion Planting and Design

Basil pairs well with tomatoes; they are mutually beneficial for keeping pests away. In a container, basil is beautiful with trailing petunias (*Petunia* hybrids) and vervain (*Verbena bonariensis*).

I Also Recommend

'Genovese', with good-sized leaves is the best for pesto. Newly introduced 'Italian Pesto' is the next contender—preferable if you've had real Italian pesto. Lush-growing 'Mrs. Burns' Lemon' is the best lemon basil, sweet with no acidic aftertaste. I add a half-dozen crinkly leaves of 'Salad Leaf" to any green salad and add olive oil and white balsamic vinegar to finish the dish. 'Cinnamon' excels for spicy flavor and its purple-flushed stems and blossoms in the garden. 'Spicy Globe', with a perfectly rounded shape and 1/4-inch leaves is ideal for containers. 'Magnificent Michael', an All-America Selections winner in 2002, has dark, fragrant, somewhat spicy foliage and handsome, compact purple flowerspikes. 1997's All-American Selections winner, 'Siam Queen', is a purple-stemmed, green-leaf Thai basil—the best for Asian cuisine.

Herb of the Year in 2003, basil has been used in Asian and European cuisine since ancient times and was even declared the royal herb of France in the 1700s. Its popularity is growing—especially in America—as evidenced by new varieties introduced each year. Both leaves and flowers are edible. A traditional use of the leaves is in pesto (ground with pine nuts, Parmesan cheese, and olive oil). There are numerous varieties of basil, each with a distinctive flavor. Some, like 'Thai' or 'Siam', indicate which cuisine favors its use. The flowers reflect the flavor of the leaves but in a lighter, sweeter form. Make creamy-colored flower pesto—beautiful on spinach pasta. Infuse white wine vinegar with flowers or leaves to make basil vinegar. Strain after two weeks.

Other Common Name
Sweet Basil

Bloom Period and Seasonal Color
White, pink, and purple from summer to frost.

Mature Height and Spread
8 to 24 in. × 8 to 30 in.

Bronze Fennel
Foeniculum vulgare 'Purpureum'

Bronze fennel is a must-have plant. The first sign of the leaves reminds me of a 2- to 6-inch-long, light-brunette ponytail. Cut the leaves and stems for cooking to enjoy this visual feast over and over. As this handsome perennial grows, the ponytails relax, becoming fine-leafed, feathery, purplish-bronze leaves. The crowning glory: airy, chartreuse umbels of flowers appear, opening to flat, rounded, 4-inch flowerheads composed of delicately spaced yellow florets, followed by fragrant, rice-sized seeds. Bronze fennel is entirely edible—leaves, stems, flowers, and seeds—with a light anise flavor. Steam or stir-fry the stems as a vegetable. The leaves and florets add pizzazz to salads, pork, vegetables, cheese, and soups. Fennel seeds are a digestive aid and are yummy in cookies, stews, and cakes.

Bloom Period and Seasonal Color
Yellow from midsummer to frost.

Mature Height and Spread
2 to 4 ft. × 15 to 18 in.

Zone
5

When, Where, and How to Plant
Bronze fennel is available as plants, but it is easy—and economical—to grow it from seed. It grows best in average, moist, but well-drained soil in full sun. Sow the seed in place in spring after the last frost date. Cover with 1/4 inch of soil and water lightly.

Growing Tips
Keep the soil lightly moist until the plant is established. Once it is up and growing well, thin plants out to allow 18 to 24 inches between plants (center to center). Use the thinnings (cut off the roots) in a mixed greens salad with the juice of a freshly squeezed orange as the only dressing. Keep the plant well watered with regular deep watering. I foliar feed with a solution of kelp or fish emulsion (mixed according to package directions) in mid- to late June.

Care and Maintenance
Bronze fennel is one of the host plants for the caterpillars (black and yellow striped) of black swallowtail butterflies, so grow enough for them to eat and you to enjoy. The caterpillars will feast voraciously for a short time, but the plant bounces back with new growth. Bronze fennel freely self-sows unless you harvest all the seeds. After the first year, you will find it cropping up around the garden. I often let it grow, just to enjoy the ponytails. The plant is easy to identify and weed out if necessary. Cut flowers for fragrant indoor arrangements.

Companion Planting and Design
Those who subscribe to the concept of companion planting (some plants are beneficial to others, while different plants can retard growth) advise to keep fennel away from tomatoes, dill, caraway, bush beans, kohlrabi, and coriander. Bronze fennel is beautiful in a container or in the garden with parsley. It makes an airy companion to bold 'Purple Majesty' millet (*Pennisetum glaucum* 'Purple Majesty') and 'Gateway' Joe-Pye weed (*Eupatorium purpureum* 'Gateway').

I Also Recommend
'Smokey' has slightly taller, coppery-bronze fronds. Like 'Purpureum', the leaves and seeds make a delicious tea, especially soothing after a big meal.

Chives

Allium schoenoprasum

When, Where, and How to Plant

Although you can readily buy chive plants or seeds, it is easier to get a piece of someone else's plant. No doubt, you have seen chives growing in a friend's or neighbor's garden. Most people are willing to share, and you will probably return home with more than just chives. Follow your friend's instructions for dividing the plant—everyone has his or her own idiosyncrasies. Immediately put your portion in a pot half-filled with lightly moistened potting soil. Take it home and plant it right away, or put in a shady spot, keep it moist, and plant it within several days. Chives grow best in average to fertile, well-drained soil in full to part sun. Dig a hole the size of the root mass, fill it with transplant solution, and let it drain. Place the plant at the same soil level it was before, filling in with soil if necessary. Water with a cup of transplant solution.

Growing Tips

Keep the plant lightly moist until it is established. Chives need regular watering.

Care and Maintenance

Keep picking the flowers, and they will keep producing. Shear the plant back to stimulate new growth if necessary. Pick young flowers for cooking, and deadhead older ones; they can pack the gustatory wallop of an entire bulb of garlic.

Companion Planting and Design

My cat Sebastian had his own little garden of chives in a whiskey barrel where he spent many hours. You may want to use the same combination he had. We combined (*Dianthus* spp.), and cat-mint (*Nepeta* × *fassenii*).

I Also Recommend

'Forescate' is larger than regular chives, with 24-inch-long leaves. Large (to 3 inches across), deep purplish pink blossoms rise up to 6 inches above the foliage. 'Fine Leaf' is a relatively new introduction, prized by chefs and cooks for its slender leaves that don't get tough with age as other chives do. Its lilac-pink blossoms are sweet, yet mildly onion flavored—like a 'Vidalia' onion.

Chives are indispensable. When I lived in an apartment, I had chives on my windowsill. Now, I have half a dozen clumps throughout the garden to keep me—and my neighbors—well supplied throughout the growing season. Both flowers and leaves are edible. Chives are fine textured, with rounded clumps of deep-green, 1/4-inch-diameter, hollow, round leaves, which reach 12 inches long, tapering at the tip. For me, the flowers are the best part of the plant, beginning with a big burst of pink to lilac to pale purple (variable) florets gathered into 1-inch flavorful spheres rising above the leaves. The younger the flower, the sweeter the oniony flavor. As it ages, the flavor intensifies greatly. Don't use whole flowers; break them into individual florets.

Bloom Period and Seasonal Color
Lilac-purple from late spring to early summer.

Mature Height and Spread
12 to 24 in. × 12 to 18 in.

Dill

Anethum graveolens

In the garden, dill can be confused with fennel. Both have blue-green stems and threadlike, ferny leaves, but dill has domed flower umbels while fennel umbels are flat. Fennel has a distinctive anise scent and flavor; dill is tangier. Dill is an annual; fennel is perennial. Dill leaves, flowers, and seeds are edible. Try the fresh leaves in bread, vinegar, with chicken or fish. Fresh and dried flowers are eye-catching in arrangements. Dill flowers are borne in umbels; pick individual florets for use in salads, with devilled eggs, a flavorful cream cheese dip, and more. For more than 3,000 years, dill seeds have been used as a digestive aid; in addition, they are a natural breath freshener. The seeds are best known for use in pickling cucumbers.

Bloom Period and Seasonal Color
Deep yellow from midsummer to frost.

Mature Height and Spread
3 to 5 ft. × 3 to 4 ft.

When, Where, and How to Plant
Dill needs full sun and prefers humus-rich, moist, well-drained, slightly acid soil. After the last frost date, sow seeds outside 1/4-inch deep and thin to 10 inches apart. (See page 91 for more on planting.) Rather than planting in rows, I incorporate dill into my landscape. Keep the soil lightly moist until the plants are up and growing.

Growing Tips
If you pickle, make consecutive sowings every three weeks for a continuous dill supply. Keep the plants well watered. Feed monthly with compost tea.

Care and Maintenance
Cut leaves as needed for the kitchen. For flower arrangements, cut the flower stem just as the flower is opening—before it fully opens. For culinary use, pick the flowerheads when fully open. For dried arrangements, allow flowers to dry on the plant and then cut. Collect dry seed for pickling (put a bag around the flowerhead and shake it so the seeds fall in the bag). Store seeds in a waterproof container in a cool, dry, dark place. In the caterpillar stage (yellow- and black-striped) black swallowtail butterflies feast on dill leaves; let them be. After feeding time, the plant will grow back.

Companion Planting and Design
Dill is delightful with the airy purple flowers of tall vervain (*Verbena bonariensis*), or makes a handsome backdrop for any of the many brightly colored coleus (*Solenostemon scutellarioides*). It is pretty with pink flowers such as purple coneflower (*Echinacea purpurea*) and garden phlox (*Phlox paniculata*).

I Also Recommend
'Dukat', harkening from Denmark, bears an abundance of blue-green, sweetly flavored leaves that last longer when cut than other dills. Slow to bolt, it's a late bloomer that's equally delicious fresh or used for pickling. An All-American Selections winner only 18 inches tall, 'Fernleaf' is well suited for containers or the front of the garden. Although small, it has all the flavor and fragrance of its larger brethren. 'Tetra' is four feet tall, late flowering, and slow to bolt. 'Vierling' grows 4 feet tall with strong stems and blue-green foliage.

Greek Oregano

Origanum vulgare hirtum

When, Where, and How to Plant

Caveat emptor - buyer beware. Read the label carefully; much of the oregano sold is *Origanum vulgare*, which has little or no flavor. You can find plants at specialty nurseries, herb farms, and mail-order nurseries. Greek oregano needs average, well-drained soil and full sun. Plant Greek oregano after all danger of frost has passed, following the directions for Mediterranean herbs (starting on page 90). Allow 18 inches between plants (center to center), or plant closer for a matlike effect. It is also a good container plant.

Growing Tips

Water when the top inch of soil is dry. Feeding is not required.

Care and Maintenance

Cut whole stems for flower arrangements and drying. Cut leaves as needed for culinary use. For maximum harvest, cut the entire plant to 3 inches above the crown before it blooms. Cut the flower stalks and pull off individual florets for cooking. Mulch with pine boughs in early winter to improve survival rate.

Companion Planting and Design

With its spreading habit, it is an excellent plant for patio planting—in the French style—between bricks, pavers, or flagstones. Do not plant it between steppingstones. I did that one year and had to leap over its flower stalks—dangerous in wet weather. In the garden, create a low-growing contrast of textures and leaf colors—and long season of bloom—by growing it with maiden pinks (*Dianthus deltoides*), sea thrift (*Armeria maritima*), and 'Silver Posie' thyme (*Thymus vulgaris* 'Silver Posie'). I plant Greek oregano in a lower side pocket of the large strawberry pot near the kitchen. It trails downward to the ground, hiding the edge of the pot and thus integrating it into the garden. Strawberry pots will crack in our winters, so plant the hardy plants in early fall or pot them up and overwinter indoors under gro-lights. Bring the pots indoors.

I Also Recommend

'Variegatum' (also known as *Origanum vulgare* 'Gold Tip') has yellow-tipped leaves, which add a glow to the evergreen plant in winter. It has a tendency to spread more than the species.

Greek oregano is the oregano of pizzas and Mediterranean cooking—the aromatic and flavorful herb. There is much confusion when it comes to oregano in general. Some call it marjoram, and vice-versa. The botanical names are a web of disagreement as well. Generally, the best way to guarantee the plant is Greek oregano is to taste it, but it may have been chemically sprayed. Instead, let your nose guide you. Break and rub the leaf, and if the aromatic spice scent wafts to your nose, you have the right plant. Many named varieties have little flavor, but if looks are what you are after, that is fine. Greek oregano is a compact plant with slightly hairy, green leaves and white flowers, both of which are edible.

Other Common Name
Oregano

Bloom Period and Seasonal Color
White in summer.

Mature Height and Spread
12 to 28 in. × 8 to 18 in.

Zone
5

Lavender

Lavandula angustifolia 'Hidcote'

'Hidcote' is one of the hardiest lavenders and is low grow-ing (only 15 to 18 inches tall), perhaps accounting for its hardiness. The beautiful dark purple florets, with the delightfully clean, floral scent associated with the herb, grow along velvety, silver spikes. The narrow silvery foliage gives it a dainty look, perfect for the front of a bor-der or a container. The fresh flowers are edible and add unique flavor to tea, ice cream, and other desserts. Caution: a little lavender goes a long way, too much and it tastes soapy. Pick spikes of lavender as they open for fresh or dried arrangements. Let them dry and weave them into wands, or pull off the flowers and put them in a sachet bag to freshen sheets and lingerie.

Other Common Name
'Hidcote' English Lavender

Bloom Period and Seasonal Color
Dark purple in summer.

Mature Height and Spread
15 to 18 in. × 15 to 20 in.

Zone
5

When, Where, and How to Plant
Potted plants are readily available locally or through mail-order nurseries. All lavenders need full sun and average to sandy, well-drained, alka-line soil. In our region, plant the lavender "high" rather than trying to create ideal soil conditions. After the last frost date, form a 3- to 4-inch-high (and 1 inch wider than the pot) mound of soil in the garden. Plant the lavender in the mound, with the plant at the same soil level atop the mound as it was in its pot. Water in with a cup of transplant solution. Mulch with 3/4 of an inch of turkey grit, sand, gravel, or small stones to increase drainage, keep the mound intact, and drain water away from the plant.

Growing Tips
Water regularly until the plant is established. By then, it is quite drought tolerant, as are most silver- or gray-leafed plants. Do not fertilize.

Care and Maintenance
In late spring, prune back any shoots that had been frozen; they will look dead. For continuing bloom, cut back spent flower stalks. Cut flower spikes for drying or using in arrangements when the flowers start to open. For culinary use, cut them when the flowers are fully open. Prune the plant if it gets leggy. Do not prune after mid-August, as any new growth will die back in winter.

Companion Planting and Design
Lavender, with red or pink old-fashioned roses such as 'Gertrude Jekyll' is a delightfully fragrant pairing. Grow lavender with other herbs with the same soil requirements, including sage, rosemary, and thyme. It is lovely in a large container sur-rounded by clove pinks (*Dianthus caryophyllus*).

I Also Recommend
'English Munstead' or 'Munstead' is equally hardy and compact (12 inches high) with spikes of laven-der-blue flowers. 'Twickle Purple' grows 2 to 3 feet high with highly fragrant flowers on the spikes in a fanlike cluster. Handsome planted behind 'Munstead', it blooms after 'Munstead' finishes flowering. 'Betty's Blue Lavender' has an unusual dome shape to the 18-inch plant. Its large, deep blue flowers are highly fragrant.

Parsley
Petroselinum crispum

When, Where, and How to Plant
Curly parsley plants are readily available in spring; Italian parsley is more challenging to find. Follow the planting directions on page 91. Many parsley varieties are available as seed. Soak the seeds overnight in hot water before planting $1/2$-inch deep in peat pots inside a lightly moistened seed-starting medium. Keep the medium lightly moist. Parsley grows best in rich, moist, well-drained soil in full to part sun but will tolerate average soil. Slowly harden the plants off before planting. Tear the sides off the peat pot to just below the soil level inside and plant the whole thing. If the peat pot sticks out of the soil, it will wick moisture from the soil. Water in well with transplant solution.

Growing Tips
Keep plants evenly moist. Feed by watering at ground level with compost tea once a month.

Care and Maintenance
In the second year (parsley is biennial), cut off the flower heads as they appear since they are not edible. This will prolong leaf production. Cut as necessary for culinary use. It is best cut early in the day as the dew dries. Parsley is beautiful in small flower arrangements.

Companion Planting and Design
Grow tall, late summer- and fall-blooming plants such as dahlias (*Dahlia* spp.), Japanese anemone (*Anemone hupehensis*), or snakeroot (*Actea simplex* 'Brunette') through parsley.

I Also Recommend
Italian or flat-leaf parsley (*Petroselinum crispum* var. *neapolitanum*) may not be as showy in the garden as the better-known curly parsley, but its flavor is exceptional. Don't waste it as a garnish; use it in soups, stews, with potatoes, and other vegetables. Add it to a greens salad for some extra zing. 'Gigante Italian' is an heirloom with extra large, shiny green leaves and a mellow, slightly sweet taste. For a great show in the garden, as well as exceptional flavor for curly leafed parsley, 'Crispum' is the standard with its crinkled leaves. 'Sweet Curly', a new introduction from France, has double curled leaves and a unique nutty sweetness.

Parsley is a beautiful biennial, grown for its edible green leaves. For decades, curly parsley (Petroselinum crispum 'Crispum') garnished millions of dishes in restaurants—from diners to 5-star restaurants. It usually went back to the kitchen untouched. Finally, we discovered that parsley is more than just a pretty embellishment—it's quite tasty. Perhaps we had to get past eating 'Iceberg' lettuce salads, changing to mixed greens with arugula and mesclun mixes (often with Italian parsley) and flavors that are more complex before we dared to eat the garnish. Perhaps parsley was more familiar than the newer garnish of edible flowers. In the garden, it is an exceptional edging plant, lining the pathway to a front or kitchen door. Its magnificent emerald foliage is lovely skirting taller plants.

Bloom Period and Seasonal Color
Yellow-green in its second summer.

Mature Height and Spread
8 to 14 in. × 8 to 12 in.

Peppermint

Mentha × piperata

Peppermint brings back fond childhood memories. A patch grew in a friends' garden. My treat was to pick a single leaf. I slowly chewed and savored its distinctive aromatic oils as they infused my mouth and nasal passages—peppermint's smell and flavor are forever melded in my mind. When the grownups drank cocktails, I had iced ginger ale—each ice cube encased a mint leaf—garnished with a spray of mint flowers. I picked the tiny florets one by one, savoring their sweeter, lighter flavor. Peppermint is one of my comfort foods. It is recognized for its mood-elevating quality and is used in aromatherapy. A handsome plant growing an average of 2 feet tall with purple-tinged stems, it bears 2-inch, dark green leaves and spikes of lilac-pink florets.

Bloom Period and Seasonal Color
Lilac-pink in summer.

Mature Height and Spread
12 to 36 in. × 18 to 36 in.

When, Where, and How to Plant
Potted peppermint plants are readily available in spring. It is invasive, so unless you want a minty hillside, contain it (see below). Peppermint thrives in rich moist soil and full sun. In poorer, drier soil, it is less invasive. If you want mint to spread, plant it as you would any other herb, allowing 2 feet between plants. Whichever planting method you choose, water the plant well.

Growing Tips
To control it in the garden, grow it in an 8- to 10-inch pot. Cover the drainage hole with fine screening. Add an inch of builder's sand and plant the mint in potting mix. Dig a hole to accommodate the pot, but 1 inch shallower. Sink the pot so that 1 inch, or the height of the rim, is above ground. An alternative is to plant the mint within a 12-inch deep surrounding barrier. The easiest deterrent is to grow it in a decorative pot placed on a deck or patio—not on soil as roots will grow through. When the top inch of soil is dry, give the plant a deep drink of water. Fertilization is unnecessary.

Care and Maintenance
When mint grown in the ground gets gangly, mow it down. It will return more lush and healthier. Pick the tender upper leaves for cooking (essential in mint juleps). Mint is a flavorful complement to lamb, potatoes, peas, and oranges, and it makes great jelly. Use the flowers in fruit salads and mix them in with any chocolate dessert. Mint tea is a traditional stomach calmative. Chop flowers and/or leaves, mix with a small amount of water, and freeze in ice cube trays. Put the frozen cubes in a freezer bag to use throughout the winter.

Companion Planting and Design
It is believed that peppermint may improve the growth of tomatoes and cabbage. It is striking planted with purple cabbage or red lettuces.

I Also Recommend
'Chocolate' grows 18 inches tall and tastes like the chocolate-mint Girl Scout® Cookie.

Rosemary
Rosmarinus officinalis

When, Where, and How to Plant

Plants are available at garden centers, and nurseries, but for variety, go to mail-order sources. Although most rosemary is not hardy here—most varieties are Zone 8—you can grow it as an annual (follow planting directions for Mediterranean herbs starting on page 90). Harden it off and plant after the last frost date. Rosemary thrives in a container.

Growing Tips

Water regularly. Feed with compost tea every two weeks during the growing season.

Care and Maintenance

Cut stems as needed for culinary use. Bring potted rosemary inside after the first frost into a cool bright room to overwinter. Avoid overwatering— let the soil stay fairly dry. Keep an eye out for any pests (i.e. aphids, spider mites, mealybugs). Spray immediately with insecticidal soap, drenching the plant, including the tops and bottoms of leaves. (Do not eat for a week or more after spraying.) Do any hard pruning in early spring, before setting it back outside. Take it back outdoors on the last frost date in spring.

Companion Planting and Design

Planted near carrots, it reportedly deters carrot flies. Include rosemary with other Mediterranean herbs including lavender, sage, and thyme. If you grow herbs in a strawberry pot, plant rosemary at the top. As I often grow it in a container, I move it around the garden depending on my whims to wherever I want it for the moment. I have grown many varieties in pots. Unlike most other garden herbs, I get to enjoy and use it year-round.

I Also Recommend

'Arp' (2 to 4 feet tall) is one of the hardiest—to Zone 6—but may survive in Zone 5 when grown in a sheltered location against a south-facing wall. It has handsome light gray-green leaves. 'Tuscan Blue' (2 to 5 feet tall) has a columnar form with short thick, deep green leaves that are extremely flavorful—my favorite for cooking. 'Haifa' (a trailing rosemary 2 to 3 feet tall) is a new introduction with pale blue flowers and narrow, deep green leaves. It is an ideal container plant.

Rosemary is a handsome evergreen shrub that has aromatic, needlelike, gray-green to deep green leaves that range from $1/2$ to $1^1/2$ inches long. Its edible leaves (and flowers if you get them) have a piney, resinous flavor that adds zing to Mediterranean dishes, grilled meat, breads, soups, eggs—even sorbet—and for flavoring oils and vinegar. Use rosemary sparingly as the flavor is intense. Its stems are lovely and fragrant in small bouquets. Dry the leaves for out-of-season cooking. Dried leaves lose some of their flavor, however, and may be better suited for potpourri. Grown in a container, rosemary will last for many years, summering outdoors and wintering inside. Rosemary is easily trained and is a favorite for all types of topiary.

Bloom Period and Seasonal Color
Blue in early spring (indoors).

Mature Height and Spread
3 to 6 ft. × 3 to 5 ft.

Zone
6

Sage
Salvia officinalis

I savor sage more for its flowers than its leaves. Perhaps growing up in a seaside town with clam chowder overseasoned with dry sage (a gray powder in a spice jar) prejudiced me. Even when I "discovered" the plant and used the leaves, the flavor was good but a bit strong for my taste. In the flowers, I found a lighter, sweeter version of the unique flavor, and I was hooked. Sage brochettes (a 4- to-6 inch flower stalk, with leaves, dipped in a light tempura batter and quickly fried) are an addiction of mine through the flowering season—shared by my friends. Sage is semi-evergreen with grey-green leaves and gorgeous spikes of purplish-blue blossoms. It is a natural phytoestrogen (no hot flashes when it's blooming).

Other Common Name
Garden Sage

Bloom Period and Seasonal Color
Purplish blue from late spring through early summer.

Mature Height and Spread
30 to 36 in. × 30 to 36 in.

Zone
5

When, Where, and How to Plant
Plants are readily available in spring. Look for specialized cultivars at mail-order nurseries. Plant sage after the last frost date, following the instructions for planting Mediterranean herbs starting on page 90. Water with transplant solution. Grow near the south-facing wall of your house to protect the plant and to provide a warmer microclimate.

Growing Tips
Water when the top inch of soil is dry. Feed with compost tea every two weeks during the flowering season to encourage bloom.

Care and Maintenance
In spring, cut branches as needed to shape the plant. Dry the leaves for later use. Cut flower spikes as needed for culinary use. Cut the spike back to the next set of branching stems to stimulate more flowering. Even if you don't eat the blossoms, prune out the faded flowers stems. In the coldest areas after the first hard frost, protect sage by covering it loosely with barley straw (less likely to sprout weeds than regular straw). Remove the mulch in early spring and cut back any dead or broken stems.

Companion Planting and Design
Grow sage with other Mediterranean herbs such as rosemary, lavender, and thyme. In the garden, the color contrast of its blue flowers with yellow pot marigolds (*Calendula*) is brilliant. Its gray-green foliage is versatile in a mixed border, cooling down hot colors, highlighting whites, and separating contrasting plants. It is also effective in an evening garden. Combine it in the garden or in a container with more colorful sages including 'Icterina', 'Purpurascens', and 'Tricolor'.

I Also Recommend
'Berggarten' is a charmer with broader, rounded, bluish-green leaves but is less flavorful than the species. The colored and bicolored sages are generally grown for their beauty, as their flavors are variable. Most won't flower. 'Icterina', with lovely yellow and green leaves, and 'Tricolor', with outstanding variegation of white, purple to pink, and green, are hardy to Zone 7. 'Aurea' has golden leaves that brighten the garden on a rainy summer day. 'Purpurascens' ('Purpurea') bears reddish purple leaves. Both are Zone 5 hardy.

When, Where, and How to Plant

You can find many varieties of thyme. Before buying, break a leaf to determine its scent. Not all thymes are edible; they are not toxic, they just have an unpleasant taste. Flavor is often a reflection of the scent. Thyme needs full sun and average, well-drained soil. Plant it out after the last frost date, following the directions for Mediterranean herbs starting on page 90.

Growing Tips

Water when the top 1/2-inch of soil is dry. Feed with compost tea every six to eight weeks.

Care and Maintenance

Cut flower spikes as needed. Run your hand along the spike to pull the tiny flowers off. Cut pieces or whole stems for cooking. The stems are a fragrant addition to a small bouquet. Dry or freeze the leaves for culinary use in winter. Make moth-repellant sachets of dried leaves. In spring, cut back any dead or broken branches.

Companion Planting and Design

Be sure to add thyme to your Mediterranean herb garden or the strawberry pot near the kitchen door. Depending on the variety, put it in a lower "pocket" of the strawberry pot so it can cascade downward. Thyme is a good container plant, making a lovely skirt for a small tree. Creeping thymes are ideal for placing between steppingstones. They can stand up to light foot traffic, which releases their scent. Thyme is a good edging plant for a border or raised bed where it can fall loosely, softening the edges.

I Also Recommend

'English' grows 18 inches tall, bearing lovely mauve flowers. It is a common seasoning in chowders, soups, and stuffing, and it enhances the flavor of pork and veal. Diminutive 'French'—only 12 inches high with an upright form—is used in French cuisine and is essential in a *fines herbes* mix. 'Aureus' has leaves splashed with yellow. Lemon-scented thyme (*Thymus × citriodorus*) is a rounded shrub with lemon-scented leaves and pale pinkish-lavender leaves—also lightly lemony and especially good for sorbet. Mother of thyme or wild thyme (*Thymus serphyllum*) is a beautiful mat-forming species with many cultivars.

One of the most versatile and varied herbs, with dozens of species and hundreds of cultivated varieties, thyme is another one of my garden must-have plants. It is perennial, often with woody stems (termed a subshrub). Common thyme, highlighted here, has a bushy, cushion-forming habit, growing no more than 12 inches high. Look closely at its small (1/4 to 1/2 inch) aromatic leaves to see the fine hairs. It bears whorls of tiny white to deep purple florets, depending on the variety. Many gardeners use thyme as an insect repellant; planted near members of the cabbage family, it deters cabbage moths. Indoors, it is a moth repellant for pantries and clothes closets. Thyme is essential in cooking—both the leaves and flowers are edible.

Other Common Names

Common Thyme, Garden Thyme

Bloom Period and Seasonal Color

Lilac to purple in summer.

Mature Height and Spread

6 to 12 in. × 12 to 16 in.

Zone

4

Ornamental Grasses
for the Prairie Lands

When most people think of prairies, they envision lots of tall grasses and some flowering plants, such as black-eyed Susans, purple coneflowers, goldenrod, and sunflowers. In fact, a few robust native grasses and hundreds of wildflowers dominated the original prairies. Indeed, this region was the original habitat of many grasses. The five most resilient and adaptable are big bluestem, little bluestem, Indiangrass, switchgrass, and prairie dropseed. Four of these groups are included in the selections in this chapter, as they are well-suited to a home garden, while the fifth is larger and requires more space than the average gardener has.

A number of the grasses we now consider ornamental are not just native to America but also to other temperate regions. When a hybridizer or breeder finds one that is slightly different or better in some way from the original species, it is given a "name" and is often more prized than the original plant. It is interesting how some native American plants—some we even considered weeds at one time or another—travel to Europe and then return to America with cultivars for which we are willing to pay a pretty penny. Goldenrod is a good example, as are many of the grasses we now classify as ornamental. Many blue fescue hybrids were developed in Germany. Some still retain the original German cultivar names, such as *Festuca* 'Blau Silber' (also known as 'Blue Silver' fescue) and *Miscanthus sinensis* 'Goldfelder' (a.k.a. 'Gold Feather' Japanese silver grass).

The Growth of Ornamental Grasses

Ornamental grasses started catching on as garden plants in the mid-1980s. More than anyone, the East Coast design team of Wolfgang Oehme and James Van Sweden helped to familiarize the public with ornamental grasses. They popularized the use of grasses through examples of their own designs in both public and private gardens, and through their writing and speaking. The time was right for a change in gardening ideas and design. The naturalistic garden became popular, and ornamental grasses naturally were a part of the movement.

Before long, ornamental grasses from other countries were introduced. I remember the first time I saw Hakonechloa macra 'Aurea'. I fell instantly in love with this small gem that flowed like a golden river through the garden. Its cascading leaves, variegated with yellow, and small stature give you a sense of a small rivulet of gold. It took quite a while to find a source for the plant, but I was willing to pay what I considered a fortune for each of the three small plants that arrived at my door a week later. I looked at them and compared them to the photograph I had taken of the marvelous garden. I remembered one of the mottos of gardening—especially on a budget when you buy smaller plants—patience is a virtue. I was virtuous for three seasons before the hakonechloa finally took off and started to give me the flowing lines I was anticipating. I find it interesting that for many years it had no common name, everyone just called it hakonechloa (with a lower-case *h*). Within the past few years, it's been called Hakone grass, which I suspect is a marketing ploy as the botanic name sounds like some rare disease. Today, hakonechloa has come down in price significantly, and I see it in garden centers, nurseries, and even home stores. However, you still must be patient, as its rate of growth has not changed.

Some of the grasses in this chapter are annuals and some perennials, but they are such a special group that I felt they deserved their own space in this book, rather than mixing them among the other plants. There are many reasons why you should grow ornamental grasses. First of all, if you are a proponent of growing native plants, you should have at least one of the original prairie grasses. Second, they are generally tough plants, especially if you are not trying to push the hardiness envelope. They are drought tolerant, heat resistant, and resilient to hash winters—three qualities that make a plant stand out as a must-have for my Iowa garden.

Planting Your Selections

Most ornamental grasses come in pots or bare root from a mail-order source. To plant them, first place the pot in a bucket with several inches of transplant solution (made up according to the manufacturer's instructions). Dig a hole about the size and depth of the pot. Be sure that you are putting the plant where it will get the light and soil it needs. Also, be sure there is ample room between it and existing plants, as most ornamental grasses will get much bigger than the cute plants you purchase. Remove the plant from the pot, pour a cup of transplant solution in the hole, loosen the roots gently, and place the plant in the hole so that it's growing at the same depth it was previously. Gently press the plant down, adding soil around the edges, so there are no air holes. Water with an additional cup of transplant solution.

Ornamental grasses are very low maintenance. Some gardeners do not like the flower plumes on some of the smaller grasses, such as the fescues, but you simply cut them off as they appear. Otherwise, let them be. For me a big plus is that most of them add winter interest—some are even evergreen. Some provide food and shelter for birds during the fall and winter months, so even if they do need to be cut back, wait until spring. Otherwise, you have an empty place in your garden where you could have had a beautiful six-foot clump of wheat-colored leaves and seed plumes and watched the wildlife come and go all winter.

No matter what size your garden, there is at least one ornamental grass for you—small or tall; rounded or upright; green, blue, or variegated—to grow in your garden or in a container. Believe me, you will get years of enjoyment from this group of plants.

Prairie Dropseed

Big Bluestem
Andropogon gerardii

How appropriate that the largest and most widespread grass of the North American Prairie is the first listed. Prairie sod, which made sod houses, was formed from this grass. When I first saw it at a reclaimed prairie, I was overwhelmed—literally—as it towered above me. Walking through that prairie, I was in awe at the abundance of Nature before humans disturbed the land. I was fortunate to see big bluestem with its distinctive turkey feet—3-part seedheads—reaching for the sky. With a recent frost, the lush green leaves were turning into the magnificent coppery red that lasts well into the winter. Although my garden is a front yard, I plan to include big bluestem next year, perhaps as a privacy screen, in homage to our heritage.

Other Common Names
Turkeyfoot, Beardgrass, Bluejoint

Bloom Period and Seasonal Color
Bronze to deep purplish-red in late summer to early autumn.

Mature Height and Spread
4 to 8 ft. × 2 to 3 ft.

Zone
4

When, Where, and How to Plant
Although you might find big bluestem at some garden centers, mail-order nurseries are the best sources. Big bluestem needs full sun; it grows in most soils—even clay. Plant it in mid- to late spring. (See page 105 for planting instructions.) Keep it lightly moist. Although you might expect it to rocket skyward, Nature knows best. A true survivor, it takes its time growing an extensive root system that allows it to ward off drought after several years in the garden.

Growing Tips
Water weekly during the first year (when it doesn't rain) to encourage root growth. Feeding is not necessary.

Care and Maintenance
Depending on your soil and moisture, big bluestem will vary in height. In rich soil with plenty of moisture, it can soar to 10 feet. In poorer soil, with less water, it will grow only 4 to 6 feet tall. In early spring, before new growth appears, cut the entire plant down to within 4 to 6 inches of the ground. Spring is also the ideal time to divide the plant. Dig up a clump, cut it into smaller pieces, and replant it or share with friends and neighbors. Big bluestem is mostly pest free.

Companion Planting and Design
Although big bluestem is tall, it is not thick with leaves. In fact, I would include it in the group of plants I call veil plants, such as Russian sage (*Perovskia atriplicifolia*) and vervain (*Verbena bonariensis*)—with which it makes a striking late summer duet. These plants are tall, but you can see through them. Big bluestem works equally well in the middle of a bed or border or in the back. It enhances the look of other prairie plants such as purple coneflower (*Echinacea purpurea*), prairie coneflower (*Ratibida pinnata*), Maximillian sunflower (*Helianthus maximilliani*), and the myriad asters (*Aster* spp.).

I Also Recommend
'The Blues' has a more erect form combined with handsome blue-gray foliage. 'Roundtree' grows to only 6 feet and blooms earlier in the season, a benefit for more northerly gardeners.

When, Where, and How to Plant

Potted plants are readily available in spring. Plant a week after all danger of frost has passed (see page 105 regarding planting). It prefers average to rich, very well-drained soil. Mulch with pebbles or sand (not organic matter) to increase drainage. If there's no rain, water weekly until it is established. If you are daring, grow plants from seeds collected in summer. The resulting plants will have fun differences in color, size, or form.

Growing Tips

Blue fescue rarely needs watering. Do not fertilize.

Care and Maintenance

Blue fescue is a short-lived perennial—about three years. If you don't like the look of the blue flower spikes, which turn brown as they mature to seed, cut them down. If it looks shabby or loses its compact habit, cut it back. In spring, give it a good pruning, to within 3 inches of the crown; it will come back refreshed. If it goes dormant in summer, cut it back to the crown, and it will regrow when the weather cools. As the plant ages, the mound dies out in the center. Dig the plant up, cut it into sections, and replant. Increase or share your supply of blue fescue by taking small divisions from established plants in spring. It is relatively pest free.

Companion Planting and Design

With its neutral color, blue fescue works as a buffer between strong and brightly colored flowers. Use it between two plants whose colors you would not necessarily mix, such as deep purple petunias and bright red zinnias. Blue fescue cools down hot colors, enlivens pastels, and intensifies whites.

My Personal Favorites

'Blau Silber' ('Blue Silver'), with intense blue-gray foliage, is evergreen even in our harsh winters and stands up to our summers. It has a smaller (6-inch) clumping form, making it a good edging plant. 'Elijah's Blue' is one of the palest blue fescue cultivars with a lovely silvery blue tone. 'Sea Urchin' forms lovely spring-green clumps with extra fine leaves that sway at the slightest breeze like its underwater namesake.

Blue fescue is one of the most popular ornamental grass—for good reasons. It is relatively small, so it can be incorporated in almost any type of garden—a rock garden, bed or border, contemporary garden, and even a formal garden. It makes a good edging plant. Unlike many other grasses, blue fescue has a neat habit, with fine leaves. From a distance, it resembles a cushion. The blue appearance is from a thin, gray, glaucous coating on the leaves, which easily rubs off on your fingers. Often after a rough winter, blue fescue is green, but the glaucous coating returns. Its popularity in the garden is expressed by the number of cultivated varieties available (many only through mail-order nurseries), too many to mention here.

Bloom Period and Seasonal Color

Blue-gray in late spring to early summer.

Mature Height and Spread

8 to 18 in. to 8 to 12 in.

Zone

4

Eulalia Grass

Miscanthus sinensis

Imagine a perennial over 100 years old. Documentation exists for Eulalia grass growing in front of Victorian houses today that was planted in the original landscapes. Its blue-green leaves grow in a vase shape—up and arching gracefully outwards. In summer, flower stems rise above the leaves, gleaming in the sun, then opening to fluffy sprays of silvery gray highlighted in shades of maroon. In autumn, the seedheads and the leaves turn a soft golden tan, which persists through the winter. Birds come to eat the seeds. The foliage provides shelter for birds and other creatures. My cat Sebastian loved the grass as he could lie in sun or shade, play with the leaves, and look at birds, all while watching me swim laps in the pool.

Other Common Name
Japanese Silver Grass

Bloom Period and Seasonal Color
Light silvery-gray with maroon or purplish-brown accents in summer.

Mature Height and Spread
3 to 4 ft. × 3 to 4 ft.

Zone
4

When, Where, and How to Plant
Eulalia grass comes in 4-inch pots to 5-gallon containers. Choose based on cost versus instant impact. Caution: If you opt for a small-sized plant, allow the same spacing as for larger ones—18 to 24 inches (center to center) for a hedge or tight planting, 24 to 36 inches for an airier feel. Wear gloves; the edges of the leaves can be sharp. Grow in average to rich, well-drained soil in full sun. Especially when putting in a larger plant, set the pot where you want it and wait several days before planting to be sure it's in the right space. Once Eulalia grass is established, it takes a lot of muscle to dig and move it.

Growing Tips
Keep the soil lightly moist until it is established. Do not fertilize.

Care and Maintenance
Cut the entire plant down to within 3 to 5 inches of the ground in spring.

Companion Planting and Design
Eulalia grass pairs well with other *Miscanthus*. I created a privacy screen at one end of our swimming pool using five different variegated varieties. It consorts well with shrub and landscape roses, including David Austin™, Flower Carpet™, and 'The Fairy' roses. Add it as an accent in a mixed or perennial bed.

I Also Recommend
'Strictus' (porcupine grass) grows 6 to 8 feet tall with horizontal yellow banding on the leaves. It grows well in wet areas, standing up to heavy rains. 'Gracillimus' (slender maiden grass) is tall and arching (to 8 feet), yet dainty, with narrow leaves with a central white stripe, bearing coppery-red flower tassels in fall. 'Morning Light', growing 4 to 5 feet high and hardy to Zone 5, is a smaller version of 'Gracillimus', with the coloring reversed—the leaf margins are white. Catching a breeze early in the morning, it glows like threads of silver. 'Puenktchen' (Little dot maiden grass—Zone 5) grows only 3 to 4 feet tall, has zebra-like gold banding on the narrow leaves, and doesn't flop with heavy rains.

Feather Reed Grass

Calamagrostis × acutiflora 'Stricta'

When, Where, and How to Plant
Plant feather reed grass in spring, after the danger of frost has passed (see page 105 for planting information). It will grow best in humus-rich, moist, clayey soil, but it will tolerate almost any type of soil. It thrives in full sun but will grow in partial sun.

Growing Tips
Keep the plant well watered until it is established. Fertilization is not necessary.

Care and Maintenance
Feather reed grass is low maintenance and pest free. Allow the foliage and seedheads to remain for winter interest. Cut them back to within 4 inches of the ground in early spring. Feather reed grass is easy to propagate. If it gets too big or if you just want more plants, dig it up in spring and cut in half or quarters. Replant each piece immediately or put it in a pot with garden soil and keep lightly moist and in the shade until you are ready to plant it.

Companion Planting and Design
Its stature and straight form make feather reed grass perfect for the back of a bed or border. It is striking enough to have a space of its own (a group of three plants) in the lawn as a specimen plant, much as you would a special tree. It combines with plants that have a looser more relaxed habit, such as Joe-Pye weed (*Eupatorium fistulosum* 'Gateway'), 'Fireworks' goldenrod (*Solidago* 'Fireworks'), and Shasta daisy (*Leucanthemum superbum*).

I Also Recommend
The flower stalks of 'Karl Foerster' make it a strongly vertical plant. Unlike 'Stricta', its leaves are very slender and wiry, growing up to 3 feet tall. Its flower stalks spike through the center of the leaves, rising 2 to 3 feet above the clump in early summer. The flowers and seedheads are very narrow, resembling pipe cleaners. Watch as they turn from gold to silver in autumn. 'Sierra' is another upright feather reed grass, which becomes a lovely golden brown late in the summer. Like 'Karl Foerster', leave it to enjoy through the winter.

The dense, 2-foot tall clumps of green grass with ¼- to ½-inch-wide leaves are lovely in spring but not very impressive. When it sends up its flowering stems in a vertical column in late spring, it makes a remarkable exclamation point in the garden. The flowering stems provide the height, as they rise militarily straight 3 to 4 feet above the leaves. In contrast, the actual plumes of flowers are golden, open, and airy. In autumn, the leaves turn a breathtaking golden orange. They remain colorful through the winter, adding much-needed bold color to what could be an otherwise dreary landscape. A clumping grass, it is slow to spread, so there is no worry of it taking over the garden.

Bloom Period and Seasonal Color
Purplish-brown in late spring to early summer.

Mature Height and Spread
5 to 7 ft. × 20 to 24 in.

Zone
5

Golden Hakonechloa

Hakonechloa macrantha 'Aureola'

Golden hakonechloa is one of my all-time favorite plants—and one of the few grasses for shade. Perhaps it is slow growing because is it a cliff-growing plant native to the island of Honshu, Japan that spreads by creeping stolons. Its 10-inch-long, lemony yellow leaves are lightly streaked with green. They grow from wiry stems, gracefully spilling over and hiding the stems in one direction, giving the illusion of a golden waterfall. Unlike many grasses, it is not a single mound, but as it expands, it becomes a series of cascades. In autumn, the leaf color slowly transforms to pink, starting at the tip and edges and working its way in until the entire plant has a warm pinkish red tone. This glorious color lasts well into winter.

Other Common Name
Golden Hakone Grass

Bloom Period and Seasonal Color
Pale green from midsummer to fall.

Mature height and spread
1 to 2 ft. × 15 to 18 in.

Zone
4

When, Where, and How to Plant
Plants are available at some nurseries and garden centers, as well as mailorder nurseries in spring. Plant it after all danger of frost has passed. Golden hakonechloa grows best in rich, moist, well-drained soil with ample organic material. Dig the hole several inches larger than the pot. Mix in 2 cups of compost, leaf mold, or well-rotted manure with the soil removed from the hole. Add the enriched soil at the bottom of the hole and pour in a cup of transplant solution (mixed according to manufacturer's directions). Set the plant so it is at the same soil level it was in the pot. Use the remaining enriched soil to fill in around the plant. Firm the soil around the plant. Water with 2 cups of transplant solution.

Growing Tips
Keep the plant lightly moist for the first growing season. After that, water it deeply when there is little rain. In spring, spread a 1-inch layer of compost around the plant, and then mulch it with finely shredded hardwood bark, taking care to keep the mulch an inch away from the stems.

Care and Maintenance
This plant is very low maintenance. Simply cut back any old foliage when it looks ratty. Do *not* cut the entire plant back in spring. Pests are not a problem.

Companion Planting and Design
Golden hakonechloa can light up a partly shady area and add movement as no other plant can. In a Japanese-style garden (or a rock garden), it makes a simple statement planted above a rock where it can flow onto the stone. It is also perfect under a cut-leaf Japanese maple (*Acer palmatum ornatum* 'Dissectum'), echoing its graceful leaves. For contrast, plant it with ferns with upright form such as cinnamon fern (*Osmunda cinnamomea*) or ostrich fern (*Matteuccia strutheopteris*). It makes a handsome edging to a bed of mixed hostas.

I Also Recommend
The species hakonechloa (*Hakonechloa macra*), also known as Hakone grass, is less showy, with spilling, refreshing rich-green leaves. Its leaves change to rusty-orange in autumn.

Little Bluestem
Schizachyrium scoparium

When, Where, and How to Plant
Little bluestem is readily available for purchase. It is a tough plant, thriving in most soils in full to part sun. A native, it flourishes in hot weather, high humidity, and drought. Plant it in spring after the last frost date. You can also grow it from seed for a large area (see page 105 for instructions). After broadcasting the seed, use a water-filled roller to push the seeds down into the soil. Keep the soil lightly moist until the seed has sprouted and is established. Allow 5 to 6 inches between plants when growing it as a groundcover.

Growing Tips
Once it is established, little bluestem can survive on the water Nature provides. Do not fertilize. On a large scale, it is excellent for erosion control or as a groundcover for dry areas.

Care and Maintenance
Seeds attract small birds such as sparrows, and it looks beautiful in snow and ice, so let it remain throughout the winter. If you must cut it back in fall, use the leaves in bunches to add softness and color in dried arrangements or twist it in making holiday wreathes. Cut back to within an inch of the crown in early spring. It usually does not self-sow. Pests are not a problem.

Companion Planting and Design
It is a beautiful addition to a mixed border. Little bluestem is handsome with soft-textured perennials such as astilbe (*Astilbe* spp.), queen of the prairie (*Filipendula rubra*), Russian sage (*Perovskia atriplicifolia*), meadowsweet (*Thalictrum* spp.), and New England aster (*Aster novae-angliae*). Use it as a transitional plant between cultivated and naturalized areas of the garden.

I Also Recommend
'The Blues' grow somewhat taller than the species (to 4 feet high). Its gray-blue foliage is held in erect clumps, making a semi-bold vertical statement. 'Blaze' is more compact, growing only 1 to 2 feet tall, but it is broad (2 to 3 feet wide). It is prized for its brilliant fall and winter color, ranging from purplish-orange through russet to reddish-purple.

Little bluestem's name is misleading. It usually ranges from 2 to 3 feet but can reach 5 feet tall. As for the blue, there is a touch of blue near the base of the slender green leaves. Name aside, it is a terrific addition to the garden—especially for its autumn color. The transformation from green to burnished orange is spectacular. The color is echoed by the hues of many trees and shrubs at that time of year. The flowers of summer become fluffy seedheads that last well into winter—sparkling in snow or with a light coating of ice. The leaves maintain their autumn hue through winter, heating up the garden with their color. They can be used in dried arrangements or twisted onto wire forms for making wreaths. The seeds attract sparrows and other small birds.

Bloom Period and Seasonal Color
Green to purplish from late summer to mid-fall.

Mature Height and Spread
2 to 3 ft. × 12 to 18 in.

Zone
5

Northern Sea Oats

Chasmanthium latifolium

Northern sea oats is outstanding because it thrives in sun or shade. A clump-forming grass, it has broad, close-set leaves. The drooping clusters of green flowers appear in summer and quickly become seedheads, closely resembling oats. They are the main attraction for me. The little time I have to truly enjoy my garden is in the evening, which sets the tone for the northern sea oats. A breeze often arises and catches the leaves, making a swishing sound. The unique light rustling sound of the seedheads in winter and fall is music to my ears. Both the leaves and seedheads turn a lovely tan in fall, persisting through the winter. The flowers are excellent cut for dried arrangements and can last a year with no preservatives.

Other Common Name
Spangle Grass

Bloom Period and Seasonal Color
Green in late summer to early fall.

Mature Height and Spread
3 to 5 ft. × 2 to 2¹/2 ft.

Zone
4

When, Where, and How to Plant

Northern sea oats are readily available in spring. It grows best is rich, moist, well-drained soil in full sun, but it also performs in part shade and poor or dry soil. Plant it in spring after all danger of frost has passed. Space the plants 24 to 30 inches apart if you are growing several plants, 2 feet apart for a mass planting. Water with transplant solution. You can also grow northern sea oats from seed collected (or purchased) the previous fall. Sow the seed ¹/2-inch deep at planting time, spaced 6 inches apart. Keep the seedbed lightly moist. Once the plants are 4 to 6 inches tall, thin them to the proper spacing. I often dig the thinnings—if they are strong plants—and transplant them to another area of the garden. To do that, dig up the plant with a spade, getting at least 4 inches of soil around the plant, going 6 inches deep. Dig a hole in the new location. Pour in 2 cups of transplant solution and place the transplant in the hole. Add extra soil, if necessary, so that it is growing at the same height it was originally. Use your hands to gently firm the soil around the plant. Make sure the soil stays lightly moist for several weeks.

Growing Tips

Keep the plants well watered until they are established. You do not need to feed northern sea oats. Sea oats are self-seeders.

Care and Maintenance

Cut the plant down to within 3 to 4 inches of the ground in early spring. For drying and using in arrangements, cut the seedheads down to the ground in late summer. Pests and diseases are not a problem.

Companion Planting and Design

Northern sea oats makes a lovely border along a path, softening any hard edges. It is charming in a fall garden with 'Autumn Joy' sedum (*Sedum* 'Autumn Joy'), 'Alma Potschke' aster (*Aster novae-angliae* 'Alma Potschke'), and 'Fireworks' goldenrod (*Solidago* 'Fireworks').

I Also Recommend

I only recommend the species.

Prairie Dropseed
Sporobolus herterolepis

When, Where, and How to Plant
Purchase prairie dropseed from mail-order nurseries. It needs full sun and will grow in a range of soil types from sandy to loamy—even rocky soil. For good definition, space plants 18 to 24 inches apart; for a prairie effect or as a groundcover, allow 15 inches between plants. It may be shipped in containers, as bare-root plants (dormant), or as plugs (ideal for large plantings). Follow instructions on page 105 for planting container plants and plugs. Soak bare-root plants in half-strength transplant solution (following label instructions) overnight. Cut off any broken or overly long roots. Dig a hole the size of the root mass. Make a slight mound of soil at the bottom of the hole and place the plant so the crown is just below ground level. Fill in with soil and firm gently. Water with 2 cups of the diluted transplant solution. Keep the soil lightly moist until the plant grows a healthy mound of leaves. Alternatively, grow prairie dropseed from seed sown directly on well-raked soil in fall or early spring. Water gently to avoid disturbing the seedsKeep the soil lightly moist until seedlings are well established. Thin to the proper distance.

Growing Tips
Keep the plant well watered until it is established. It is drought tolerant but does need some water. When the top 3 inches of soil is dry, give it a slow, deep watering. It does not require any fertilizer.

Care and Maintenance
A covering of Reemay® or other floating row cover will protect seeds while preventing the sun from drying out the soil too quickly. Have patience; prairie dropseed is slow to grow but worth the wait. Once established, it is very long-lived and trouble free.

Companion Planting and Design
Prairie dropseed is a distinctive and well-defined plant for inclusion in a perennial or mixed border. Planted en masse, it makes a handsome groundcover, which can be used effectively for erosion control on a slope.

I Also Recommend
I only recommend this species.

If you have never grown an ornamental grass, start with prairie dropseed. It is small, elegant, has superb color, and is easy to grow. It forms a graceful mound of emerald green, fine-textured leaves turning orange-highlighted gold in fall, fading to pale copper in winter. In late summer, airy panicles of small pink flowers rise 2 to 3 feet high. The flowers are lightly fragrant—an aroma that is diversely perceived and described by people as sweet, an unmistakable scent of cilantro, the unique smell of burnt buttered popcorn, pungent, or even odorless. Cut the fresh flowers for a unique accent in any flower arrangement. It's fun to see how guests perceive the scent. Native Americans made nutritious, delicious flour by grinding the seeds.

Other Common Name
Northern Dropseed

Bloom Period and Seasonal Color
Pale pink in late summer to fall.

Mature Height and Spread
18 to 36 in. × 18 to 36 in.

Zone
4

Purple Majesty Millet
Pennisetum glaucum 'Purple Majesty'

This All-America Selections Gold Medal winner in 2003 was a real attention grabber in my garden—and for good reason. Passersby stopped to stare at the plant; growing it in a large pot made it even more impressive, putting it at eye-level or above. If grown from seed, the foliage starts out green, then the leaves and stem spikes turn deep purple once it is growing outside. It sends up several 3- to 4-foot tall, deep purple flower spikes that look very much like purple cattails. As the spike matures, tiny lemony yellow, pollen-filled florets appear along and around the flower spike, making a striking color contrast. Finches flock to it from late summer well into fall. An annual, it did not self-sow in my garden.

Other Common Name
Purple Millet

Bloom Period and Seasonal Color
Deep burgundy with yellow from summer to fall.

Mature Height and Spread
4 to 5 ft. × 1 to 2 ft.

When, Where, and How to Plant
One of the hottest new plants on the market, 'Purple Majesty' is readily available growing in containers. It prefers fertile, moist, well-drained soil and full sun to part sun. The color is deeper and richer in full sun. Plant store-bought purple millet two weeks after the last frost date. Allow 16 to 24 inches between plants. You can also grow the plant from seed. Start the seeds in peat pots indoors 6 to 8 weeks before last frost date. Cover seed lightly with seed-starting mix, and water well. If you place the pots on a seed mat, which provides bottom heat (70 degrees Fahrenheit is ideal), and keep the soil lightly moist, the seed will germinate quickly. Transplant seedlings into the garden a week after all danger of frost has passed. You can also sow seed directly in the garden two weeks before the last frost date. Keep them lightly moist until it is established.

Growing Tips
Water regularly; avoid wetting the seedheads. Fertilization is not necessary.

Care and Maintenance
This is a maintenance-free plant. Watch finches come to it in late summer and early fall. Since it is an annual, you can pull it up at any time it starts to look tired. Pests are not a problem.

Companion Planting and Design
It was a real attention-grabber in my garden—growing in a container with 'Tilt-a-Whirl' coleus (*Solenostemon scutellarioides*). It is an awe-inspiring backdrop plant and mixes surprisingly well with deep pink to red roses.

I Also Recommend
If you favor dark-colored ornamental grasses, purple fountain grass (*Pennisetum setaceum* 'Rubrum'), a cousin of 'Purple Majesty', is a must-have. Grown as an annual, it is diminutive, reaching only 3 to 4 feet tall. Not only is the burgundy foliage eye-catching but the long, gracefully arching flowers open a purplish-red and mature to a reddish purple, finally turning tan in autumn. 'Rubrum Dwarf' is similar—but smaller—growing less than 2 feet tall—a perfect plant for a container or an edging plant.

Silver Variegated Japanese Sedge

Carex morrowii 'Variegata'

When, Where, and How to Plant

Plants are readily available in spring. It grows best in fertile, moist, well-drained soil and performs equally well in full sun to part shade. Wait to plant it until after the last frost date. Allow 2 feet between plants—center to center—for a beautiful edging. Give it more room if you are planting only a few plants among other perennials. Water well. (See chapter introduction for more on planting.)

Growing Tips

Silver variegated Japanese sedge needs regular watering. Do not let the plant dry out. As its leaves are pendulous, drooping is not a sign of dryness. Soil should be lightly and uniformly moist. Foliar feed once in early July with a half-strength solution of liquid kelp or fish emulsion (following package instructions).

Care and Maintenance

Cut back the flowering stem—if you let it stay on the plant—when it finishes blooming. If the foliage looks weather-beaten after the winter, cut it back to the crown; however, if it is still looking good, comb through it with your fingers to remove any brown or dead leaves. It is relatively pest free.

Companion Planting and Design

Silver variegated Japanese sedge is handsome as an edging plant for a sunny border, shady path, or near a pond. Among pink-flowered roses, such as 'Simplicity', 'Carefree Beauty', or 'Gertrude Jekyll', it is one of the most innovative combinations I have ever seen.

I Also Recommend

'Aureo-variegata' is striking for its deep green leaves with a central yellow stripe. 'Ice Dance' is a relatively new introduction that is very appealing in the Prairie Lands states, as it is hardier—to Zone 4—and fully evergreen. Its leaves are wider with more prominent creamy white margins than 'Variegata'. *Carex grayi* (gray sedge) is another new kid on the block, hardy to Zone 5. Unlike other sedges, its seedheads are the show-stoppers, although the green leaves are also attractive. Shaped like spiked balls or medieval maces, the seedheads add unique interest in late spring; they last throughout the gardening season.

Unlike the other ornamental grasses, silver variegated Japanese sedge is outstanding for its 12- to 16-inch-long foliage. The grasslike leaves are the principal players; the flowers are the extras. The leaves are beautiful and graceful—dark green outlined with white. They bring life to a semi-shady area, especially when a wafting breeze sways the leaves. In late spring, the 15- to 18-inch-long flower stems rise up above the leaves, bearing spiky green and brown panicles of flowers. I often cut the spikes for an arrangement or just cut them back so I can appreciate the foliage even more. Although it is not listed as a plant for wildlife, I have seen baby bunnies and mice run for its protective cover when pursued by a predator.

Bloom Period and Seasonal Color
Green and brown in late spring.

Mature Height and Spread
12 to 16 in. × 8 to 12 in.

Zone
5

Switch Grass
Panicum virgatum

One of the five main grasses of the North American Prairie, it is easy to see why it has remained popular in the cultivated garden world. Its history attests to its toughness and reliability as a perennial, since it returns every year no matter how cold the winter or hot and dry the summer. Switchgrass forms attractive, narrow, green clumps that are flat, linear, and slender, growing upright to 24 inches. In midsummer, the real show begins as the flower panicles emerge. When first open, they range in color from dark reddish-purple to silvery white, looking like clouds 12 to 16 inches above the leaves. In autumn, the foliage gradually turns bright yellow, gold, or orange, keeping their color through the winter while the conical seedheads become golden yellow.

Bloom Period and Seasonal Color
Reddish purple through silvery white from midsummer to fall.

Mature Height and Spread
3 to 7 ft. × 2 to 3 ft.

Zone
5

When, Where, and How to Plant
Switchgrass is readily available in spring. Versatile, it grows equally well in full to part sun and most soils—wet or dry, rich or poor. Plant it in spring after all danger of frost has passed, allowing 24 to 30 inches between plants. Water well. (See page 105 for details on planting.)

Growing Tips
Keep the soil lightly moist until the clumps are established. Switchgrass does not need fertilizer.

Care and Maintenance
Keep switch grass in the garden through the winter to show off its beautiful coloration. It also serves as a winter cover for wildlife. Cut it down to within 3 to 4 inches of the ground in spring. The plant is easy to propagate (or control if it spreads). Dig up clumps divide with a knife or shovel. Replant these at the same soil level as they were growing. Water well with transplant solution (mixed according to package directions). It may self-sow, but not reliably. Pests are no problem.

Companion Planting and Design
En masse, it makes a lovely vertical screen, useful for hiding unattractive views or for defining spaces in the garden. It is beautiful growing in a meadow-like setting (even a small 3 foot by 3 foot area in the garden) with beebalm (*Monarda didyma*), purple coneflower (*Echinacea purpurea*), and brown-eyed Susan (*Rudbeckia triloba*)—all plants that provide food for birds. Add a cutleaf staghorn sumac (*Rhus typhina* 'Dissecta') for a taller accent.

I Also Recommend
'Heavy Metal' has stunning, upright, metallic-blue leaves that go through an amazing transformation to yellow in autumn. By winter, the leaves have bleached out to tan. It is hardier, growing to Zone 4. It is gorgeous in the garden planted with vibrant colors like nasturtiums (*Tropaeolum majus*) and Mexican sunflower (*Tithonia rotundifolia*), or keep it cool with other silvery plants like fine-leafed 'Powis Castle' artemisia (*Artemisia* 'Powis Castle') and Miss Wilmot's ghost (*Eryngium giganteum*). 'Strictum' is similar to the species but more narrowly upright in its habit.

Tufted Hair Grass
Deschampsia caespitosa

When, Where, and How to Plant
Plants of tufted hair grass are available at some garden centers and nurseries as well as through mail-order nurseries. It grows best in rich, moist soil in part sun or part shade. It isn't nearly as impressive in full sun. Planting it in a low area, along a bog or lake, should provide ample moisture for the plant. It is also well suited for planting at the edge of a woodland. Space the plants 2 feet apart. Water well. (See page 105 for more on planting.)

Growing Tips
Tufted hair grass needs to be kept moist. Do not allow it to dry out. It does not require fertilization.

Care and Maintenance
If summer and fall winds have made the flower panicles look ragged, cut them down. Otherwise, let them be and enjoy their beauty throughout the winter. Cut the leaves all the way down to the crown in early spring. It seems extreme, but you'll quickly be rewarded with new healthy growth. If the plant get too large or you want more, you can propagate it in spring. Dig the plant up out of the ground—roots and all. Cut it with a shovel or knife into smaller portions and replant or share with friends. It occasionally self-sows and is relatively pest free.

Companion Planting and Design
A unique combination is planting it with low-growing lady's mantle (*Alchemilla mollis*). The light on dewdrops or raindrops on lady's mantle leaves echoes the sunlit blooms of tufted hair grass. It consorts well with colorful shade- and moisture-loving perennials including red cardinal flower (*Lobelia cardinalis*), pink turtlehead (*Chelone obliqua*), and yellow marsh marigold (*Caltha palustrus*). It also adds early color to a late-winter or early spring woodland planting with shrubs like witch hazel (*Hamamelis* spp.) and winterhazel (*Corylopsis spicata*).

I Also Recommend
'Gold Pendant' ('Goldgehange'), with rich golden yellow puffs of blooms. 'Bronze Veil' ('Bronzeschleier') bears golden brown, hanging panicles that nearly cover the leaves. 'Schottland' grows tufts of leaves that are only 2 feet tall.

A cool-season grass, tufted hair grass greens up early. It forms tussocks or mounds with attractive 24-inch long, rough, linear, stiff green leaves. The real reason for growing tufted hair grass is not for the foliage—it merely sets the stage for the tall flowers that rise 18 to 48 inches above the leaves. The flowers are cloudlike; the airy panicles open a pale greenish-yellow, quickly turning purple-tinged silver. In autumn, they turn a lovely golden tan color. In the soft, warm light of early morning or late afternoon, especially when grown with deep green plants such as evergreens that provide a dark backdrop, the flower plumes appear to be sun-kissed. The leaves are semi-evergreen, and the flower plumes will remain for added winter interest.

Other Common Name
Tussock Grass

Bloom Period and Seasonal Color
Silvery with purple tinge from late spring through summer.

Mature Height and Spread
2 to 3 ft. × 2 to 2¹/₂ ft.

Zone
4

Perennials *for the Prairie Lands*

As people get into gardening, they usually start off by adding annuals to whatever is existing on their property—marigolds, impatiens, begonias, and coleus are among the most popular. After a few years, they graduate to perennials, which, as their name implies, come back year after year.

You can get into interesting discussions with people from different areas of the country about whether a plant is an annual or perennial. Having spent time with friends and relatives in southern California, and being a plantaholic (the one addiction for which many of us are grateful there is no Twelve-Step program), I often buy plants impulsively. I do read the tag, but unfortunately, too many plants are just labeled annual or perennial without stating the hardiness zones. I soon learned that many of the plants in the perennial section in a California nursery are perennial—in California—in Zone 10. To be perfectly clear and technically correct, many plants we call annuals should really be labeled as "Perennial usually grown as an annual" or "Perennial in Zones 9 to 11."

Daylily 'Silent Entry'

The perennials included in this section are hardy in all of the Prairie Lands states and zones, unless I have mentioned a *specific* zone, which means that plant is hardy only to that particular zone. I chose plants that span the seasons, require the least maintenance, and perform well in this area. Many of the plants are natives, which means they can thrive despite the great temperature fluctuations—extreme cold in the winter, hot and humid in the summer. They range from tall prairie plants to more dainty cultivated varieties. Whether you are looking to create a woodland garden, grow a wildflower meadow, recreate a prairie, make a formal garden, or design a cottage garden, there are many choices available for you.

Containers Add Versatility

It is important to choose the right plant for the right place. Trying to grow a woodland plant like Jack-in-the-pulpit (*Arisaemia*

Aster

triphyllum) that requires moist soil and part shade next to black-eyed Susan (*Rudbeckia fulgida* 'Goldsturm') that likes well-drained soil full sun is a recipe for failure—if you try to grow them in the ground next to each other. However, you can get away with some interesting combinations by growing plants—even perennials—in containers. There you can control the soil type, moisture level, and place it where it gets the required sun it needs. In the previous example, place the pot with Jack-in-the-pulpit where it is shaded by a taller plant—an ornamental grass, perhaps—or even in the shade cast by a bigger container.

You can have a lot of fun mixing and matching plants in a container. One favorite from last year's garden was 'Purple Majesty' millet (*Pennisetum glaucum* 'Purple Majesty') and 'Tilt a Whirl' coleus (*Solenostemon scutellarioides* 'Tilt a Whirl') with a dozen stems of silk forsythia early in the season to add interest until the other plants grew up. The fact that it was in a three-foot pot made a huge difference. The millet was all the more impressive for being in your face early in the season and above your head in the fall. Varying the heights in the garden adds a great deal of interest because you look up, down, and around to take it all in; this is easily accomplished by using containers of different sizes. Do not just rely on the size of the container. A small blue and white ceramic container with red impatiens would not have been noticed if it had not been raised up on a green plant metal plant stand. The same kind of stand that I use indoors in winter I find even more versatile in summer as it raises the container up towards eye level, but the green of the stand blends into the garden. If I had wanted to make a bold statement, I could have painted the stand cobalt blue to match the blue in the container.

However, most perennials should be removed from the container and planted in the ground several weeks before the first frost date. Otherwise, you should sink the container in the ground or move it into a cool, dark place for winter where it can go into dormancy (about 40 degrees Fahrenheit—not down to freezing).

Sedum 'Autumn Joy' with Petunias

Buying Perennials

Unfortunately, growers are now producing perennials that are in bloom when you purchase them—at a nursery, garden center, or home store. Moreover, people are buying them up because as the adage goes, "What you see is what you get." This has been the practice used in marketing annuals for a number of years, which I don't like, but you can make up for that when you get the plant home by cutting off the flowers and buds to encourage root growth. Annuals rebloom and, in most cases, continue to bloom through the growing season. This is not true for perennials. Most have a limited flowering season and although a few will rebloom if you cut them back, the majority will not. What that means is that when you buy all your perennials in mid-spring—in bloom—they will look pretty in the garden for a short time (most have bloom times from two to six weeks). However, when summer comes or whatever the normal bloom time is for the plant, it has already put on its show, and you will have to wait until the next year to see flowers. Seek out plants that are not in bloom—unless it is their season. Even then, you would have been better off buying and planting the perennial earlier so that it could establish a strong root system. If the place where you regularly buy your perennials offers only plants in bloom, ask them for ones that are in their proper season and not forced to bloom early. If enough people demand this, the growers—even for the large chains—will respond. Many small nurseries propagate and grow their own plant material; plants there should be in their proper stage of growth for the season. Of course, if you shop through mail-order catalogs, you are almost guaranteed to get plants at the right time. I have learned, however, to make a large note on the order form (or tell the operator if I'm doing it by phone or make a comment if I'm ordering online) of the shipping date I want. The shipping date is generally a week or so after the last frost date since mail-order nurseries in warmer zones than ours sometimes ship too early for me to plant.

Planting

Since a perennial will be in place for many years (I know of hundred-year-old peonies), it is worth taking the time to prepare the soil so that it suits the need of the plant. Dig a hole twice the size of the root mass and put the soil on a tarp or in a wheelbarrow. Amend the soil as needed, depending on the plant's needs—pH, drainage, moisture, and nutrients. Almost any plant will benefit from the addition of organic matter —compost, well-rotted manure, humus, or leaf mold. Fill the hole partway with the amended soil. Remove the plant from the container and gently loosen the roots. If it was shipped bare-root, soak it in muddy water for at least four hours or overnight. Form a cone of amended soil in the hole so that the crown of the plant is just below ground level and the roots spread out around the cone. Set the plant in the hole and water with one quart of transplant solution. Fill the hole with the remaining amended soil and firm the soil by pressing with your hands. Water with an additional two quarts of

transplant solution. Mulch the plant (keep the mulch one inch away from the stem(s) with an organic mulch, unless the plant is a succulent or one that prefers day soil. In that case, use sand, gravel, or pebbles—any material that will keep the plant drier. Unless noted in the plant entries to follow, winter mulch (on top of the plant) is not necessary.

Oriental Poppy

121

Beebalm
Monarda didyma

Oswego Indians introduced beebalm to the colonists in the northeast and taught them to make a tea from the leaves and flowers. Beebalm has a slightly spicy minty flavor; the edible flowers are sweeter than the leaves. It has an unusual flower form, with 1½-inch whorls of red florets, with prominent stamens, and red-tinged bracts. Often one flower will grow above another when the lower one is finished blooming. Its square stems identify it as a member of the mint family. Pick individual florets for eating or cooking—it makes delicious ice cream, pound cake, and an interesting sauce with fish or chicken. Both butterflies and hummingbirds flock to the plant for its nectar, adding to its attraction.

Other Common Names
Oswego Tea, Bergamot

Bloom Period and Seasonal Color
Red, pink, or purplish in mid to late summer.

Mature Height and Spread
2 to 4 ft. × 2 to 3 ft.

Zone
4

When, Where, and How to Plant
Beebalm plants—the species and many cultivars—are readily available at nurseries, garden centers, and home stores. You will find a wider choice of cultivated varieties through mail-order catalogs. Beebalm grows best in rich, moist, well-drained soil in full sun to dappled shade. Plant beebalm in spring after all danger of frost has passed following the directions in the chapter introduction. Be sure to allow ample space around the plant so it will have breathing room; this can help prevent powdery mildew. Water well.

Growing Tips
Do not let the plant dry out. When watering, water the soil, not the leaves. If you do have to water overhead with a sprinkler, do so early in the day so any water on the leaves dries out. Foliar feed once a month with a solution of kelp or fish emulsion.

Care and Maintenance
Beebalm is susceptible to powdery mildew, so allow plenty of room around it for air to circulate. At the first sign of powdery mildew remove the infected leaves. Spray the plant every seven to ten days with baking soda solution (see page 231 for directions). Be sure to spray both tops and bottoms of the leaves.

Companion Planting and Design
Beebalm makes a bright combination with sunny yellow tickseed (*Coreopsis* sp.) and 'White Swan' coneflower (*Echinacea* 'White Swan'). Keep it away from other plants prone to mildew, such as garden phlox (*Phlox paniculata*) and black-eyed Susan (*Rudbeckia* spp.). Thin in spring to allow air circulation. Deadhead to extend bloom time.

I Also Recommend
Always taste any of the cultivars before using them in cooking as some have a flavor reminiscent of mothballs. Next to the species, 'Cambridge Scarlet' (36 to 42 inches) with bright red blooms has the best flavor. 'Violet Queen' (30 to 36 inches) is more resistant to powdery mildew and has purplish-violet flowers. 'Croftway Pink' (30 to 36 inches) has a soft rose color. 'Snow White' is a rare white cultivar.

Black-Eyed Susan

Rudbeckia fulgida 'Goldsturm'

When, Where, and How to Plant

'Goldsturm' black-eyed Susan plants are readily available in spring at nurseries, garden centers, and home stores as well as through mail-order nurseries. It grows best in average, lightly moist, well-drained garden soil in full sun to part shade. Plant it after the last frost date in spring or in late summer. Follow the planting instructions on page 121. Water in well with transplant solution.

Growing Tips

Keep the plant lightly moist until it is established. Do not let it dry out. Water at soil level or early in the day. If the soil is poor, top-dress with 1 to 2 inches of compost around the base of the plant in spring. Do not fertilize regularly, as that will result in soft, floppy growth, making it more susceptible to powdery mildew.

Care and Maintenance

Deadhead the first flush of flowers to encourage reblooming. Leave the later flowers on the plants to mature so that the birds can eat the seeds in fall and winter. When plants get too large, dig up and divide in spring or late summer. To defend black-eyed Susan against powdery mildew, do not plant it near beebalm, zinnias, lilacs, or other plants susceptible to this; give it room for air to circulate. See beebalm on the previous page for tips on dealing with powdery mildew.

Companion Planting and Design

Black-eyed Susan is handsome with annual melampodium (*Melampodium paludosum*) and chrysanthemums (*Leucanthemum superbum*). It is lovely in a meadow planting.

I Also Recommend

Rudbeckia hirta (a native, also known as black-eyed Susan or Gloriosa daisy) resembles 'Goldsturm'. Many of its cultivars are charming. 'Bambi' (to 12 inches) has golden yellow petals with bronzy-brown centers. 'Green Eyes' ('Irish Eyes' 24 to 30 inches) has a pale green center surrounded by bright yellow petals. 'Goldilocks' (20 to 24 inches) yields golden orange semi-double to double blooms. 'Rustic Dwarfs' (20 to 24 inches) has brown centers surrounded by mixed colored petals—golden yellow, deep orangish-red, bronzy orange, and some bicolors as well.

Black-eyed Susan is one of the original native prairie plants, a rhizomatous perennial that spread by self-seeding. 'Goldsturm' is one of the most popular hybrid forms because of its large flowerheads. Black-eyed Susans are easy to grow, brightening the garden from midsummer to fall with its 3½- to 5-inch flowers comprised of golden ray florets (petals) surrounding the conical brown disk florets (center). It is wondrous to watch the bees and butterflies attracted to it while it is in bloom. Refrain from cutting down the spent flowerstalks because birds, especially colorful finches, will come to the garden and feed on the seedheads. It is a well-branched plant, producing an abundance of flowers—enough for enjoying outside and cutting to bring inside for arrangements and bouquets.

Other Common Name

Coneflower

Bloom Period and Seasonal Color

Yellow with brown centers from midsummer to fall.

Mature Height and Spread

22 to 26 in. × 15 to 18 in.

Zone

4

Blanket Flower
Gaillardia grandiflora

Few perennials add as much color, for as long a time, to free-wheeling flower beds as the pretty-as-a-blanket native flower named after M. Gaillard de Charentonneau, an eighteenth-century French magistrate and patron of botany. This freely seeding hybrid of two prairie natives is a must near the front of a sunny perennial border, where its loose, low-growing habit can weave among other flowers. The plant is a bushy rosette with rough, hairy gray-green foliage that appears on flower stems. Each branch is topped continually for many months by 3- to 5-inch wide single or double daisy-like flowers, each a tapestry of reds and yellows with contrasting tips and sometimes orange or maroon bands. The flowers are outstanding for bees and butterflies and make long-lasting cut flowers as well.

Bloom Period and Seasonal Color
Blends of warm colors from early summer to frost.

Mature Height and Spread
2 to 3 ft. × 15 to 24 in.

When, Where, and How to Plant
This prairie native tolerates poor soil as long as it is well drained. In late winter or spring, sow seed directly onto loose, bare soil in full or part sun. Wet the area down to start seed germination and expect seedlings to sprout quickly and to flower the first season. Foliar feed when the seedlings appear, then water only as needed to keep young plants growing —usually once every seven to ten days. Gradually begin to withhold water to allow the plant to harden off into a tough survivor. You can buy blanket flower at nurseries, garden centers, and some stores. Follow planting directions on page 121.

Growing Tips
Little or no fertilizer or water is needed for established plants.

Care and Maintenance
Blanket flower has few major pests; however, watch for and control slugs and snails around young plants. Avoid over-watering, which only encourages leaf spots and fungal infections including powdery mildew and rust. Water only during extreme drought. Deadheading (cutting off faded flowers to prevent seed formation), while not necessary for continued bloom, will promote more flowers more quickly. Collect and save seed to sow in other garden spots.

Companion Planting and Design
Plant blanket flower with naturalistic perennials such as gayfeather (*Liatris* spp.), dame's rocket (*Hesperis matronalis*), false indigo (*Baptisia australis*), and native grasses. To help make naturalistic plantings more realistic and interesting throughout the summer and even through the normally bare winter, include a bit of hardscape, such as a wagon wheel, section of split-rail fence, or other rustic ornamentation.

I Also Recommend
Many compact and larger-flowering selections of *Gaillardia* are now available, including deep red 'Burgundy'; 'Torchlight' (yellow flower bordered with red); 'Goblin' (1-foot tall, deep red flowers bordered in bright yellow); and the tiny (7 to 8 inches tall) red-and-yellow 'Baby Cole'.

Bleeding Heart
Dicentra spectabilis

When, Where, and How to Plant

Bleeding heart is available in spring at nurseries, garden centers, and home stores. For unusual varieties, look to mail-order catalogs. It grows best in moist, fertile, humus-rich soil in partial shade. It will grow in full sun if the soil is consistently moist. Plant after all danger of frost has passed. Dig the planting hole several inches larger and deeper than the root mass. Put the soil on a tarp. Mix in several cups of peat moss. Lightly moisten the soil mix with transplant solution. Put several inches of the mix in the hole. Loosen roots and soil of the plant gently. Place it in the hole so that it is at the same soil level it was growing in the pot. Fill in all around the plant with the amended soil. Firm gently with your hands. Water with 1 quart of transplant solution. Add a 3-inch layer of organic mulch around the plant, keeping it at least 1 inch from the stems.

Growing Tips

Keep the soil lightly moist. Do not let it dry out. Fertilization is not necessary if you add 1 or 2 inches of compost around the plant every spring. Water it in well and add a fresh layer of mulch.

Care and Maintenance

Bleeding heart will bloom for four to six weeks in partial shade if not too warm. You can divide overgrown clumps as they go dormant or in the early fall. Bleeding heart has no pest problems.

Companion Planting and Design

Plant it to hide the dying foliage of daffodils and tulips. Since bleeding heart's foliage dies down by midsummer, surround it with plants that will cover the bareness. Bleeding heart is lovely with hostas and ferns; both have luxuriant foliage that grows to fill the space. Cinnamon fern (*Osmunda cinnamomea*) and the huge blue-green leafed *Hosta sieboldiana* 'Elegans' are good companions.

I Also Recommend

'Alba' has pure white flowers. 'Gold Heart' has new foliage that is yellow flame-colored, gradually turning bright golden yellow; by summer, it is lime green.

Bleeding heart is a beloved, wonderfully old-fashioned, shade-loving perennial that never goes out of fashion. Blooming in spring (continuing into summer in the colder parts of the Prairie Lands states), its tall, gently arching stems with strings of 1-inch, deep pink hearts with white points are the mainstay of most spring woodland gardens. Although it is generally thought of just as a garden plant, both the handsome fernlike foliage and the wands of valentines are exquisite in flower arrangements. Did you know that the heart can transform into a lady in a bathtub? Remove a flower, turn it upside down, and gently pull down the two pink portions to expose more white. When they are level, it resembles a woman in an old-fashioned tub.

Bloom Period and Seasonal Color
Pink and white in late spring to early summer.

Mature Height and Spread
24 to 36 in. × 18 to 24 in.

Butterflyweed
Asclepias tuberosa

Butterflyweed is summer-blooming perennial that, as its name implies, attracts butterflies—monarch butterflies in particular. Common milkweed (Asclepias syriaca), a close relative, is one of the plants the monarch caterpillars eat. If you grow both, you will be sure to have butterflies in your garden. It stands out in the garden with its 1½- to 2-inch umbels of vivid orange, red, or yellow flowers. Growing 2 to 3 feet tall, it has hairy, thick, unbranched stems with 4- to 5½-inch, lance-shaped leaves that spiral up the stem. The flowers are borne in the leave axils and at the ends of the stems. A native American plant of dry fields and roadsides, its seedpods are not as prolific or showy as milkweed.

Other Common Names
Butterfly Milkweed, Pleurisy Root

Bloom Period and Seasonal Color
Orange, yellow, pink, vermilion in summer.

Mature Height and Spread
2 to 3 ft. × 8 to 12 in.

Zone
4

When, Where, and How to Plant
Butterflyweed is readily available at nurseries, garden centers, and home stores in spring. They often are included in "butterfly plant" collections since monarch butterflies flock to the nectar. Unless you are an avid gardener with a heated bench and grow-lights indoors, purchase container-grown plants. Butterflyweed needs full sun and well-drained soil. The soil can be average or rich, dry or lightly moist—as long as it drains well. Take care when planting as butterflyweed has a long, brittle taproot. Follow basic planting instructions on page 121. Gently remove it from its pot, disturbing the soil as little as possible, and place in the planting hole (loosen the soil several inches deeper than the pot). You may find sale plants at the end of summer at a good bargain. That is also a fine time for planting, and a bargain as well. Water in with transplant solution. Mulch with pebbles or grit.

Growing Tips
Keep lightly moist until the plant is established. After that, water when the top inch of soil is dry. Fertilization is not necessary.

Care and Maintenance
Because of its long taproot, butterflyweed does not transplant well. It is slow to emerge in spring. Mark its spot so that you do not accidentally disturb it or overplant it with something else. Butterflyweed will self-seed. It has no pest problems.

Companion Planting and Design
Butterfly weed is an excellent plant in a meadow-type or naturalistic garden. It consorts well with ornamental grasses, such as crinkled hairgrass (*Deschampsia flexuosa* 'Tara Gold'), fountain grass (*Pennisetum alopecuroides* 'Hameln' or 'Little Bunny'), black-eyed Susan (*Rudbeckia fulgida* 'Goldsturm'), beebalm (*Monarda didyma*), and wild bergamot (*Monarda fistulosa*). It also looks handsome in a perennial border. Be sure to include some milkweed (*Asclepias syriaca*) nearby so the monarch butterfly caterpillars have a food source. After they pupate, they will dance all over the butterfly weed. For another butterfly attractant, plant butterfly bush (*Buddleia davidii*).

I Also Recommend
'Gay Butterflies' has red, orange, and yellow flowers.

Cardinal Flower

Lobelia cardinalis

When, Where, and How to Plant

Cardinal flower plants are available in spring at garden centers, nurseries, and home stores. It needs wet soil; cardinal flower plant thrives in wet, boggy soils—even up to 4 inches of water. It grows best in deep, rich soil in full to part shade. Allow 12 to 18 inches between plants. Grow in groups of three, five, or more for the most drama. If you are growing cardinal flower in water, pot the plant in a $1/2$-quart or 1-gallon container in heavy, acidic soil. Add peat moss to increase acidity and to retain water. Place 1 inch of fine pebbles on top of the soil to keep it from leaching into the pond. Place the pot so the top is 1 to 4 inches below water level. Alternatively, if you have a clay pond, just plant it at the appropriate depth without a pot.

Growing Tips

Keep the plant moist. Do not let the soil dry out. Foliar feed garden plants every six weeks with a solution of kelp or fish emulsion. Use special aquatic plant food tablets for potted plants in the water; follow package instructions.

Care and Maintenance

On the flower stalk, the lower, spent flowers may have ripe seed while the upper flowers have yet to bloom. Cardinal flower is a short-lived perennial that self-seeds freely. It needs dividing every two to three years. Lift the clumps in early fall, remove the new rosettes of leaves, and replant immediately in amended soil. When the ground freezes, add 4 to 6 inches of organic mulch; remove in spring when the temperature is moderate. Cardinal flower is pest free.

Companion Planting and Design

Cardinal flower is ideal as a waterside planting, in a low-lying wet area, or in a boggy spot where not much else will grow. It consorts well with bigleaf ligularia (*Ligularia dentata*), daylilies (*Hemerocallis* spp.), Japanese iris (*Iris ensata*), marsh marigold (*Caltha palustris*), and Siberian iris (*Iris siberica*).

I Also Recommend

'Alba' has white flowers, and 'Rosea' has pink blooms.

Cardinal flower's brilliant red color is magnificent, especially when backlit by early morning or late afternoon sun. Look closely at an individual flower and you can see how it got its name; it looks like its namesake bird taking flight. Cardinal flower is one of my favorite perennials because it is so versatile. Masses of ruby red flowers adorn slender, purplish, 24- to 30-inch spikes from late summer through early autumn. It can grow in that low damp spot at the edge of the mixed border or it can even grow in a water garden. Thriving in light shade, it is gorgeous highlighting the edge of a woodland, blooming with the brilliance of a stained glass window with the sun radiating through the blooms.

Bloom Period and Seasonal Color

Brilliant red blooms from midsummer to autumn.

Mature Height and Spread

2 to 4 ft. × 12 to 18 in.

Zone

2

Compass Plant
Silphium laciniatum

This is a "ship's mast" flower native to our fields and open woodlands. The clump-forming plant shoots hairy stems up from a large, deep underground root, to nearly twice as tall as I am. Its common name arises from how the fern-like leaves point north and south, with their flat sides facing east and west. It inspired Longfellow to write, "Its leaves are turned to the north as true as the magnet: This is the compass flower." The sandpapery leaves and stems are sticky with a resin that smells like turpentine; pioneer families used the dried tacky resin as a crude chewing gum. Stems are topped with narrow clusters of nodding yellow sunflower-like blossoms up to 5 inches across, and many birds love its seeds.

Other Common Names
Pilot Plant, Rosinweed

Bloom Period and Seasonal Color
Yellow in late summer and early fall.

Mature Height and Spread
10 to 12 ft. × 24 to 30 in.

When, Where, and How to Plant
Compass plant grows best in full sun or open woodlands, in moderately fertile heavy or clay soils that are alkaline or neutral pH. Seeds may be sown in containers as soon as they are ripe in the fall, or mature plants may be divided in the spring. However, bring an extra shovel—the taproot is really deep, even in very heavy soils. When setting out nursery-grown plants, loosen potting soil and roots, then water deeply, not frequently, to encourage wide-ranging and deep root development.

Growing Tips
Foliar feed twice in the spring and water during long dry spells.

Care and Maintenance
Compass plant has few major insect and disease problems, which is good because sprays would harm the many butterflies, other insects, and birds that feed on both pollen and seeds. During wet summers, foliage diseases such as powdery mildew or rust may cause leaves to look bad or even shed, but no control is needed.

Companion Planting and Design
Use this and other tall perennials towards the back of a perennial border or mixed planting, partly because their flowers tower above other plants, and partly to hide their leaves which may not be very attractive during wet seasons. Their distinctive height and welcome color at an otherwise bare time of year provide a dramatic flair to prairies, glades, wetlands, and ditches. Compass plant is also excellent for naturalizing in fields and a wild or woodland garden where it can catch and sway in breezes, especially when loaded with butterflies. In the late fall and early winter, goldfinches and other seed-eating birds feast on the small seed.

I Also Recommend
Another great, tall *Silphium* is cup plant (*S. perfoliatum*), which is a robust, strongly upright perennial with remarkable square stems. The leaves, which grow in pairs on the stem, are joined at their bases to form cups. The plant bears an abundance of yellow, sunflower-like blossoms in mid- to late summer and attracts large numbers of butterflies.

Cranesbill
Geranium spp.

When, Where, and How to Plant
Although you can find cranesbill at nurseries, garden centers, and home stores in spring, to really explore the true variety and range of this plant, go to mail-order catalogs or the Internet. The larger, clump-forming geraniums and most hybrids thrive in fertile soil in full sun to part shade. It is tolerant of most soil types if they are well drained. Mulch with 3 inches of organic matter. The smaller varieties need humus-rich, sharply drained soil in full sun. To improve soil drainage, mulch with 2 inches of sand, grit, pebbles, or gravel. Plant in spring after all danger of frost has passed. Water both types well with transplant solution before adding mulch.

Growing Tips
Keep well watered during the growing season. Foliar feed in spring and early summer with a solution of kelp or fish emulsion.

Care and Maintenance
Removing flower stems as they wither and cutting off old leaves encourages new growth. Some varieties may stop blooming in the heat of summer and rebloom in fall. Divide in spring (share varieties with friends and neighbors). Cranesbill has no pest problems.

Companion Planting and Design
In shady areas, cranesbill looks good with bleeding heart (*Dicentra spectabilis*), Canada mayapple (*Podophyllum peltatum*), and wake robin (*Trillium* spp.). In the garden, mix it with Jacob's ladder (*Polemonium* 'Lambrook Mauve'), foxglove (*Digitalis* spp.), and heucheras (*Heuchera micrantha* 'Palace Purple is superb).

I Also Recommend
Bloody cranesbill (*Geranium sanguineum*—3 to 18 inches by 6 to 16 inches) is clump-forming with spreading rhizomes; it has lovely deeply cut—almost fernlike—leaves. 'Alpenglow' has red blooms in spring and summer. Bigroot cranesbill (*Geranium macrorrhizum*—to 20 by 24 inches) has strongly scented leaves. 'Album' has pink stamens in white flowers in early through midsummer. *Geranium incanum* is a mounded evergreen with aromatic leaves. 'Johnson's Blue' (12 to 18 inches by 20 to 24 inches) is an all-time favorite, forming a dense mat of lobed leaves; it has 2-inch, mid- to lavender-blue flowers blending to pink centers.

Not to be confused with the typical red-flowered container plant called geranium (botanically a Pelargonium), cranesbill includes dozens of species and hundreds of cultivars. It is cherished by gardeners for the range of size from 4-inch tall bloody cranesbill to the stout 24 by 36-inch 'Wargrave Pink'. Other benefits are its colors (single, bicolor, striated, eyed in hues of white, blue, purple, pink, magenta), its long bloom time, beauty of the leaves, and ability to grow in most soil types. Geraniums are versatile—equally at home and appropriate in a cottage garden, woodland walk, formal bed or border, rock garden, as a groundcover, and especially in a collector's garden. Some are even evergreen, which adds year-round interest to the garden.

Other Common Name
Geranium

Bloom Period and Seasonal Color
White, red, rose, pink, purple, or blue in late spring to summer or autumn.

Mature Height and Spread
4 to 24 in. × 1 ft. to indefinite

Zone
4

Creeping Phlox
Phlox stolonifera

Generations of gardeners have grown creeping phlox, a hardy native from the mountains of the southeastern United States, for its lustrous foliage and dazzling drifts of color along well-drained woodland slopes and cascading from rock gardens. Named "Perennial Plant of the Year" in 1990 by the Perennial Plant Association, it is easy to propagate and share and even easier to grow. Its mat-forming stems are covered with somewhat narrow leaves most, if not all, of the year, and it bursts into a cheery profusion of clusters of inch-wide flowers shortly after the spring's first real thaw. Underground stems or stolons spread readily even in dry woodland soils, and aboveground stems root wherever they touch the ground, yet the plant never becomes weedy or invasive.

Bloom Period and Seasonal Color
Blue, purple, pink, or white in early spring.

Mature Height and Spread
4 to 6 in. × 1 ft. or more

When, Where, and How to Plant
Creeping phlox thrives in neglected soils in sun or moderate shade and tolerates summer heat, drought, and even the high humidity in the Prairie states. Underground stems of creeping phlox spread best in loose, well-drained soil, so add a moderate amount of organic matter when preparing the soil. When planting between existing plants, loosen soil outside the immediate planting area to help new stems spread. Encourage new roots to grow deep by soaking the area really well, but allow soil to get completely dry before watering again. Mulch lightly to help keep weeds from sprouting until phlox begins to cover the area. Feed at half-strength until plants are established.

Growing Tips
Water plants deeply once a week for a month or two after planting.

Care and Maintenance
Creeping phlox has no major insect or disease problems. Propagate by removing and immediately replanting well-rooted sections of stems from mature clumps.

Companion Planting and Design
When in full bloom, creeping phlox creates a stunning show all by itself. It is also very effective when not in flower because its lustrous green foliage makes a loose but tidy contrasting groundcover for iris, liatris, and other linear-foliage perennials such as maidenhair (*Adiantum pedatum*) and taller woodland ferns. Since it needs little water during the summer, it also makes an excellent summer and fall cover for dormant bulbs such as daffodils and tulips, which would rot when planted under fussier summer flowers. It spreads well under small trees.

I Also Recommend
Popular cultivars include 'Sherwood Purple', lavender blue 'Blue Ridge', pink 'Home Fires', and 'Bruce's White' and 'Ariane', both of which have pure white flowers with yellow eyes.

Dame's Rocket

Hesperis matronalis

When, Where, and How to Plant

Dame's rocket, which grows best in light shade, is very easy to start from seed sown directly onto freshly prepared soil in the spring. The small seeds need light to germinate, so do not cover them with soil and do not mulch freshly-seeded areas. For double-flowering forms, add compost or leaf mould to the planting soil. Thin seedlings to 1 foot or more apart. Water newly-set out plants, but do not keep them soggy wet or you will risk "damping off" disease. If the growing season is long enough, it can flower the first year from seed; otherwise, it will form an attractive rosette of leaves the first year and bloom the next.

Growing Tips

Feed lightly and regularly after they are established, and water deeply only when very dry.

Care and Maintenance

Over watering and heavy feeding can cause plants to get leggy and floppy and to be in need of staking; it can also contribute to leaf disease, especially mildew. Keep plants "lean and mean" like the weeds they can be. Occasionally, flea beetles will make "shotgun holes" in leaves, and snails and slugs can be problems in moist areas that are heavily mulched. Larvae of some butterflies may also chew holes in leaves, but they are easily controlled with insecticidal soap that won't harm adult butterflies.

Companion Planting and Design

The clumps of spoon-shaped leaves contrast nicely with other flowers, which in turn help hide the leaves if insects attack. Flowering stems will stand above many other flowers, so plant Dame's rocket in the middle ground of flower borders or as a medium-height filler in wild or naturalistic gardens, especially in light shade.

I Also Recommend

The white-flowering form of dame's rocket, *Hesperis albiflora*, will come true to seed if it is isolated or planted far enough away from other color variants to reduce cross-pollination. 'Alba Plena' has double white flowers, 'Liacina Flore Plena' bears double lilac flowers, and 'Purpurea Plena' has double dark lilac or purple flowers with neatly arranged petals.

The intense late afternoon and evening fragrance of this mustard relative conjures memories of grandmother's cottage garden, and its habit of self-seeding around the garden ensures that it will come back for many years—so much that in some areas it is considered an invasive weed! Native to stony sites and wastelands from Europe to Siberia, its rosettes of leaves are very attractive to tiger swallowtails and cabbage white butterflies. Loose clusters of 4-petaled, cross-shaped lilac, purple, or sometimes white flowers are real stand-outs in the spring and summer, yet in spite of it being grown for its excellent cut flowers (especially the double-flowering varieties), it is also an excellent, if tangy, pot herb. Cook its young leaves or add its flowers to salads and fruit dishes.

Other Common Names

Sweet Rocket, Damask Violet

Bloom Period and Seasonal Color

Purple, pink, or white from spring to midsummer.

Mature Height and Spread

3 ft. × 18 in.

Daylily
Hemerocallis spp.

A thousand new varieties of the popular daylily are introduced each year. They are easy to grow and beautiful in single and double flowers of varying shapes—triangular, circular, star, spider, and ruffled— in rainbow hues (single, bi- and tricolored). The American Hemerocallis Society touts them as tough—growing in water, drought, salty soil, even planted in winter. California uses it for firescaping—surrounding property to protect it from wildfires since it does not burn easily. Every part of the plant is edible. Add 6-inch-long new shoots in spring to salads or stir-fries, prepare buds sautéed or steamed (can be used dried in Chinese cuisine), use flower petals in salads, hors d'oeuvres, and sorbets. Rhizomes of Hemerocallis fulva *in autumn can be used as a water chestnut substitute.*

Bloom Period and Seasonal Color
Rainbow hues, and also peach, pink, ivory, and mauve; single, bi- and tricolors from late spring to late summer.

Mature Height and Spread
10 to 48 in. × 1 to 4 ft.

When, Where, and How to Plant
Daylilies are readily available at nurseries, garden centers, and home stores from spring through summer. You will find the greatest variety through specialty mail-order nurseries. Plant anytime. Although they thrive in full sun and fertile, moist, well-drained soil, they will grow and flower in most any soil, but not in shade. Once you start growing them, you won't be able to stop.

Growing Tips
From spring until buds form, water freely. Foliar feed every two to three weeks.

Care and Maintenance
Deadhead and remove flower stalks to encourage rebloom. Pick day-bloomers in midafternoon for cooking that evening. Remove pistils and stamens. Daylilies are excellent cut flowers, as each scape will open a new flower each day. To maintain vigor, divide plants in spring every three to five years. Trade divisions with friends. Daylilies have no pest problems.

Companion Planting and Design
Daylilies are lovely with many varieties planted en masse and are an excellent addition to a cottage garden.

I Also Recommend
Hemerocallis fulva (to 3 feet by 4 feet) is the ordinary 2$\frac{1}{2}$- to 4- inch, orange daylily (known as ditch lily). It is simple, elegant, delicious, and the traditional daylily used in Chinese cuisine. 'Flore-Pleno' is a double flowered form. *H. lilio-asphodelus* (formerly *H. flava*, to 3 feet x 3 feet) is usually the first to flower in spring; it is night-blooming, fragrant, and sweet tasting with 3$\frac{1}{2}$-inch, star-shaped yellow blooms. 'Stella de Oro' (to 12 x 18 inches) is a very popular cultivar as it blooms early and, if kept picked, keeps blooming throughout the growing season. It's lovely two 12-inch bright yellow flowers are perfect for stuffing with a flavorful dip as an hors d'oeuvre. *H. citrina* (to 48 x 30 inches) is night-blooming and is citrus-scented with a sweet citrus flavor and star-shaped, pale yellow 3$\frac{1}{2}$- to 5-inch blooms. Siloam hybrids are diploids, very well branched, and often have tricolored petals (green throated) with ruffled edges.

False Indigo
Baptisia australis

When, Where, and How to Plant

Plant false indigo in a sunny, very well drained sandy or sloping soil, where it can remain for many years without needing to be disturbed or moved. Seed may be sown directly onto the ground or in pots as soon as they are ripe in the late summer; set potted plants out the following spring. Deep-rooted false indigo grows naturally in dry soils and, being a bean-family legume, is able to "fix" or make its own nitrogen fertilizer literally from thin air. Follow planting directions on page 121.

Growing Tips

False indigo requires little or no supplemental water or fertilizer.

Care and Maintenance

Mark or cage the area where plants are buried to prevent stepping on or digging into young shoots before they emerge in mid-spring. Divide young clumps in the spring and water just enough to get them started. Stake taller flowering clumps, especially when they are grown in light shade. Removing spent flowers may encourage more flower stalk production and shapes the plant. Leave seeds for wild birds and then cut back the top growth after the first frost of fall. In unusually wet seasons, false indigo may require staking, and some minor leaf spot diseases may appear for which treatment is ineffective and unnecessary. Weevils may penetrate seedpods and eat the seeds.

Companion Planting and Design

Grow false indigo for its foliage alone. Its leaves and flower stalks make it ideal as a specimen plant, in informal borders, on open hillside meadows, on dry banks, or grouped in wild-flower plantings. Plant false indigo with other meadow perennials to extend the flower season, such as earlier-blooming *Coreopsis* and later-blooming goldenrod (*Solidago* spp.). It also makes a terrific spiky companion to roses.

I Also Recommend

Baptisia perfoliata has gray-green leaves and bright yellow flowers in the summer. *Baptisia pendula* is an erect bush with many branches densely topped in late spring with white flowers followed by hanging black seedpods.

False indigo, so-named by Native Americans and pioneers who used it as a poor substitute for dye-making indigo, is a striking meadow and woodland-edge perennial. Each multi-branched plant stands out in flower above the still-small midseason native grasses in wild meadow hillsides and in the poorest soils along hedgerows and beside roadsides. It has lupine-like foliage (with each bluish-green leaf fully divided into three clover-like leaflets) and tall, branched stems covered in the heat of summer with many pea-like indigo-blue flowers followed by drooping black, inflated seed pods, the stems of which make attractive additions to seasonal flower or dried arrangements. This very tough, long-lived, heat- and cold-resistant plant develops unusually long, deep, fleshy taproots which enables it to survive prolonged drought in even very gravelly soils.

Other Common Names
Blue False Indigo, Wild Indigo

Bloom Period and Seasonal Color
Blue from early to midsummer.

Mature Height and Spread
3 to 5 ft. × 2 to 3 ft.

False Sunflower
Heliopsis helianthoides

False sunflower is one of the brightest rays of sunshine in the summer garden. It is hard to miss—growing 3 to 6 feet tall. False sunflower is a bushy, well-branched plant with 2- to 3-inch, all-yellow daisylike flowers. In the daisy family, it is the earliest bloomer—from late spring through midsummer. Its leaves are unusual, with a triangular shape. It is a native prairie plant, so you know it is tough enough to put up with harsh winters, floods, drought, heat, and humidity—and still look great. Enjoy it indoors as well; heliopsis is an excellent and long-lasting cut flower. It is a versatile plant that looks as good in a perennial border as it does in a naturalistic meadow or restored prairie setting.

Other Common Names
Ox-eye, Sunflower Heliopsis

Bloom Period and Seasonal Color
Golden yellow from summer to fall.

Mature Height and Spread
30 to 72 in. × 20 to 30 in.

When, Where, and How to Plant
You can find false sunflower at nurseries, garden centers, home stores, and mail-order nurseries in spring. Heliopsis (its name derived from the Latin *helios-* meaning "sun") grows best in full sun, although it can tolerate part sun. It prefers fertile, moist, well-drained soil. As a prairie native, it can tolerate drier soil; however, it will not be as floriferous. Plant according to the chapter introduction after all danger of frost has passed. The taller species may require staking; put the supports in at the same time as the plants. Leave ample room around the plant for good air circulation. Water in well with transplant solution. Mulch with 2 to 3 inches of organic matter.

Growing Tips
Water when the top 2 inches of soil are dry or if the plant shows any signs of wilting. Fertilization is not necessary, but you can add a 2-inch layer of compost around the plant in spring before renewing the mulch.

Care and Maintenance
False sunflower is susceptible to powdery mildew and rust. At the first sign of infection, use baking soda solution (see pages 233) and continue to spray weekly. Heliopsis that is grown in rich soil needs to be divided every two to three years; in poorer soil, divide it only as necessary to rejuvenate the plant or to keep it within bounds.

Companion Planting and Design
False sunflower is beautiful in a cottage garden, adds brightness to a long bed or border, and fits in perfectly in a naturalistic meadow. It consorts well with other prairie plants including gayfeather (*Liatris spicata*), tickseed (*Coreopsis* spp.), and goldenrod (*Solidago* spp.).

I Also Recommend
Subspecies *scabra* (to 3 feet x 3 feet) is less floriferous than the species and has coarse, hairy leaves. 'Golden Plume' ('Goldefeider' to 4^1/$_2$ feet) has double flowers with golden ray flowers around green disk florets. 'Summer Sun' ('Sommersonne' to 36 inches) has single or double flowers with deep yellow ray flowers, occasionally with an orangish-yellow flush, and brownish yellow disk florets.

Fringed Loosestrife
Lysimachia ciliata 'Fire Cracker'

When, Where, and How to Plant
Grow this perennial in full sun or partial shade in humus-rich, preferably moist but well-drained soil that does not dry out in summer. Sow seed in containers outdoors in spring then transplant into the prepared garden site, or buy plants at nurseries, garden centers, or home stores. Little or no fertilizer is needed for new plant establishment. See page 121 for planting directions.

Growing Tips
Keep the soil lightly moist, not wet. Once it is established, water only during extreme drought. Foliar feed monthly in the spring. Fertilize with leaf mulch in the fall.

Care and Maintenance
Divide every few years to keep mature clumps thriving, and transplant the extras or share them with friends and neighbors. Overfeeding, followed by a lot of rain or over watering, may cause flowering stems to be weak and floppy, and it is difficult to stake entire clumps.

Companion Planting and Design
It is the perfect complement to midsummer clumps of ornamental grasses. Set divisions along with northern sea oats (*Chasmanthium latifolium*) just above water's edge around a pond or creek bank to lend a deliberate look to grasses and other volunteer plants that are so irritating to trim. Use it in a bed or ditch that stays a bit too wet for other perennials. Let it naturalize at the sunny edge of a woodland or wildflower garden.

I Also Recommend
'Atropurpurea' is a cultivar with burgundy-red leaves. Dense-flowered loosestrife (*Lysimachia congestiflora*) 'Outback Sunset' is a mat-forming plant with red-tinged, yellow-variegated leaves and yellow flowers with red centers in spring and summer. Whorled loosestrife (*L. punctata*) has erect flowering stems with whorls of yellow flowers in late summer and fall, but it may be invasive. Popular *Lysimachia*, particularly gooseneck loosestrife (*L. clethroides*) and creeping Jenny or moneywort (*L. nummularia*), can become quite a weedy nuisance, especially in moist, well-drained garden bed soils. Use them only if you are willing and able to keep them in bounds.

Don't hold the common name "loosestrife" against this gorgeous clump-forming perennial—it is not the seriously invasive "purple loosestrife" (Lythrum salicaria, a pink-flowering wetland weed) you've read about. This slow but steadily-spreading plant is perfect for planting at the edges of areas bothered with "regular" weeds, like along ponds, wet ditch banks, and other low areas. Its midsummer flowers will help make the scene look to neighbors like you are doing the "naturalistic thing" on purpose. The plant may spread a little, but the blooms are spectacular, which is why we put up with plants like these! 'Fire Cracker' is a my favorite cultivar, for its heat-of-the-summer purple-bronze foliage adorned with bright yellow, nodding blooms. It has been described as "lemon yellow on chocolate leaves." Gorgeous!

Bloom Period and Seasonal Color
Yellow from early to midsummer.

Mature Height and Spread
2 to 4 ft. × 2 ft. or more

Garden Heliotrope
Valeriana officinalis

For legal reasons, I avoid giving advice about the medicinal use of plants. So let us overlook how garden heliotrope has been used since the time of Hippocrates in the fifth century B.C. as a mild sedative and how its nutrient-rich roots are still used in England prepared in a broth. Latin valere means "to be strong," referring to both the health virtues of the plant and its distinct odor. Garden heliotrope has divided leaves with many pairs of lance-shaped leaflets; its several hollow stems are topped with a dense head of intensely fragrant white flowers. Seeds have fluffy crowns that help them spread by wind. The fresh root looks like a mop—a mass of long, white, and relatively unbranched rootlets. Fresh valerian root has a much more pleasant odor than the dried; it has even been used in perfumery.

Other Common Names
Valerian Root, All-heal

Bloom Period and Seasonal Color
White from late spring to midsummer.

Mature Height and Spread
4 to 6 ft. × 2 to 3 ft.

When, Where, and How to Plant
Garden heliotrope, native to sunny and partly shaded western European marshes and streams, prefers wetter conditions than many other herbs. The seed are slow to germinate. Sow them in spring under glass or plastic and plant out in summer in a well-prepared, moist bed. Plants are available at garden centers, nurseries, and home stores. (Follow directions on page 121 for planting.)

Growing Tips
Keep evenly moist, mulched, and fed lightly in the spring and summer.

Care and Maintenance
Garden heliotrope needs to be kept a bit damp, especially if grown in full sun. It has few pests but may suffer from leaf diseases during an unusually rainy season. It may require staking if the soil is very rich or fertile. Mature plants may be divided in spring or autumn, but don't disturb them when in summer bloom. Keep plants moist, not wet, until established.

Companion Planting and Design
Use garden heliotrope as a specimen or accent beside an arbor or towards the back of an herb garden. A tall plant in a narrow bed looks awkward unless planted near a pole, statue, wall, or similar feature; limit the height of tall plants to half the diameter of the garden, or trim to a lower size. Garden heliotrope can be naturalized along lightly shaded creek banks or ditches in moist but well-drained soil. Grow it in a container, or interplant it with other moisture-loving perennials such as blue star (*Amsonia tabernaemontana*) and canna (*Canna* spp.).

I Also Recommend
Don't confuse this tall herb with the common red valerian (*Centranthus rubra*) often seen in cottage gardens. *Valeriana* 'Aurea' is a clump-forming, spreading perennial with soft yellow leaves in the spring that turn to lime- or mid-green by summer. In early summer, branching stems bear rounded clusters of small white flowers.

Garden Phlox

Phlox paniculata

When, Where, and How to Plant

Many varieties of garden phlox are available at nurseries, garden centers, and home stores in spring. Use mail-order nurseries for the greatest selection. Garden phlox grows best in rich, lightly moist soil in full to part sun. In my experience, there is less chance of powdery mildew if phlox is grown in full sun. Follow planting instructions in the chapter introduction. For good measure, stake tall varieties when you plant them. Allow 12 to 18 inches between plants for good air circulation, another mildew preventative. Water them in with transplant solution.

Growing Tips

Keep the soil lightly moist; do not let it dry out. Water at ground level, using soaker hoses to avoid wetting the leaves. If you must water overhead, do so in early morning on a sunny day. Water well with compost tea in spring.

Care and Maintenance

To encourage larger flowers, remove the weaker shoots in spring when the growth is small. Deadhead the clusters of flowers regularly to encourage rebloom. Because they are prone to powdery mildew, keep them away from similarly prone plants. Use baking soda spray as a preventative every seven to ten days, but do not spray when the temperature is over 80 degrees Fahrenheit. When it is finished blooming, cut the plant down to the ground.

Companion Planting and Design

Garden phlox is an essential cottage garden plant and is also lovely in beds and borders. Grow it with any of the number of shorter varieties of dianthus (*Dianthus* spp.). It pairs well with Japanese iris (*Iris ensata*) and variegated orris (*Iris pallida* 'Variegata').

I Also Recommend

Mildew resistant varieties include: lavender-blue 'Chattahoochee', lavender 'Katherine, crimson-eyed pink 'Bright Eyes', and white 'David'. Other charmers, although not necessarily mildew resistant, are: 'Fujiyama' ('Mt. Fujiyama', 4 feet)—white that does not need staking; 'Orange Perfection' (2 feet)—salmon-orange blooms; 'Nora Leigh' (3 feet)—white variegated leaves, pale lilac blooms with deep lilac-pink eyes; and 'Sir John Falstaff' with-wine-red eyes on deep salmon pink blooms.

I remember the sweet scent of garden phlox from childhood visits to my grandmother. The varieties were limited then compared to today. Much breeding has been done since then, especially for mildew resistance. The flowers were just at nose-height for me. I'd walk through them in the early evening inhaling their perfume, comparing one to another, fascinated with what my grandmother called the "eye" (the darker center of some). Fragrant in the daytime, they were more so at night. I'll never forget the evening she made me sit still, promising me magic. The fireflies were out, but they were not the show. I heard a soft whirring sound that I thought were dozens of hummingbirds, our common day visitors. They were sphinx moths pupated from tomato hornworms (garden enemies nevermore).

Other Common Name

Summer Phlox

Bloom Period and Seasonal Color

White, pink, magenta, to dark lilac—some with a contrasting colored center from summer to midautumn (or frost).

Mature Height and Spread

3 to 4 ft. × 24 to 40 in.

Zone

4

Globe Thistle

Echinops ritro

Talk about unusual—globe thistle looks nothing at all like the aster family from which it hails. It looks more like a big blue sweetgum ball on a stick! Its effect in a garden is simply awesome, as it provides startling spiny foliage texture, tight roundish clusters of flower bracts to contrast with other garden favorites, and of course its intense blue color, which is always welcome in any summer garden. Native to dry mountainsides from the Mediterranean to Africa and India, it is well suited for summer droughts, though after a couple of months of high humidity its large, spiny, jagged leaves may start looking a bit ragged. The flowers are easily worked into any garden setting or in a vase with other cut or dried flowers.

Bloom Period and Seasonal Color
Blue-gray from mid- to late summer.

Mature Height and Spread
2 to 4 ft. × 2 to 2$^1/_2$ ft.

When, Where, and How to Plant
Globe thistle grows best in sunny, dry rock crevices, rock gardens, and dry raised beds. The foliage resents high humidity, so choose a sunny spot where air circulation will be good, or plant them behind smaller plants to hide fading foliage. Propagate by seed, division, or root cuttings; sometimes even small (2 to 3 inch) pieces of roots left in the ground during division can sprout into new plants. Plants are more reliable, and are available at garden centers, nurseries, and home stores. (See page 121 for planting information.)

Growing Tips
Globe thistle needs light fertilization and occasional deep soakings during extreme drought.

Care and Maintenance
Avoid excessive watering and winter wet, and protect plants during harsh winters with mulch. Aphids may be a problem some summers; rinse the plants with soapy water in the morning so foliage will dry quickly, or spray an insecticidal soap that won't harm visiting butterflies (or just let the little spiders have them). Cutting faded flowers causes more flowers to form and reduces seed dispersal.

Companion Planting and Design
It is interesting how *Echinops* and *Echinacea* are often listed side by side in garden books, because they also grow so well together in the garden. The spiny round balls of globe thistle complement purple coneflower's spiny orange centers and hot pink ray flowers. Globe thistle also contrasts well with daylilies (*Hemerocallis* spp.), and its sometimes-ratty foliage can be hidden by that of iris or yarrow (*Achillea* spp.). For flower arrangements, cut flowers when they are just beginning to open, at the peak of blue, strip off the prickly leaves, and hang the stems upside down in a dark but dry, airy place until completely dry. It will hold its blue color well.

I Also Recommend
Common cultivars of globe thistle include deep blue 'Taplow Blue', 'Blue Globe', and small reblooming 'Veitch's Blue'.

Goldenrod

Solidago spp.

When, Where, and How to Plant

You can find a few goldenrods (mainly 'Fireworks' with its dazzling long flowerheads) at nurseries, garden centers, and home stores. Mail-order nurseries have a complete array of these underutilized native plants. Goldenrod grows best in sandy, poor to moderately fertile, well-drained soil in full sun. Plant according to instructions in the chapter introduction in spring after all danger of frost has passed. Water in with transplant solution. Mulch with sand or gravel.

Growing Tips

Goldenrod is quite drought tolerant. Water when the top 2 to 3 inches of soil are dry. Fertilization is not necessary.

Care and Maintenance

This is an easy-care plant. Divide if necessary or if you simply want more plants in early spring or mid-fall. It may get a fungal problem. Treatment is not necessary but you could use baking soda spray if desired (see page 121).

Companion Planting and Design

One of the most striking plant combinations I have ever seen was 'Fireworks' goldenrod (to 30 x 18 inches; long, spiky racemes radiating outward) with 'Purple Dome' aster (*Aster novae-angliae* 'Purple Dome'). The brilliant hues of each were a perfect match. Grow goldenrod in a wildflower or meadow garden. Add it into a cottage garden, mixed with asters, or use tall varieties in the middle or back of a mixed border.

I Also Recommend

'Goldenmosa' (to 30 x 18 inches) is compact, bushy, and vigorous and has an upright flower habit with unusual wrinkled leaves; it has a tendency to be invasive. 'Crown of Rays' (to 24 x 18 inches) has 10-inch-long flattened, radiating panicles of flowers and blooms mid- to late summer. *Solidago virgaurea* subsp. *minuta* (2 to 8 inches x 6 to 8 inches) has a moundlike form with leathery, lance-shaped leaves and 1¼-inch-long, spiky racemes of deep yellow florets; it is perfect for a rock garden but needs more moisture than most goldenrods. *S. sphacelata* 'Golden Fleece' (to 18 x 24 inches) is one of the latest goldenrods to bloom, and is well-branched with lance-shaped mid-green leaves.

Let us clear up two misconceptions. Goldenrod is not a weed, unless it is growing where you do not want it. (There are more than 80 indigenous species and many hybrids.) Most important, it does not cause hay fever; however, in the wild it often grows with ragweed (an allergen) that has tiny, inconspicuous flowers. Goldenrod is a beautiful yellow-flowered plant with elongated flowerheads comprised of numerous florets in summer to fall. Many varieties are sweet smelling. Native Americans made a delicious tea from the flowers and made flour from the pollen. In the wild, it grows in poor soil—in wastelands, ditches, near beaches—and can be invasive. Goldenrod thrives in a cultivated garden, and hybrids are well behaved. It makes an excellent cut flower.

Bloom Period and Seasonal Color
Yellow from midsummer through fall.

Mature Height and Spread
2 to 72 in. × 10 to 36 in.

Zone
5

139

Jack-in-the-Pulpit
Arisaemia triphyllum

One of the most exotic-looking shade-loving plants we can grow, Jack-in-the-pulpit is a tuberous perennial native to our moist woodlands that gives us a perfect excuse to not rake leaves. Just after the last frost, a single stalk pushes up through forest leaf litter, topped by one or two large, deeply divided arrow-shaped leaves, sometimes mottled with purple. Then the mysterious-looking flower appears with a large, blowsy pale green hood (called a spathe) that hides a single slender, pale, finger-like projection (the spadix) that produces a dense cluster of berries. The plant dies down by midsummer, but the stem of berries, which slowly turn red, remains to give us something to ponder into fall. Autumn leaves bury then slowly decompose to feed this wonder plant.

Bloom Period and Seasonal Color
Green from spring to early summer; red berry spikes in the fall.

Mature Height and Spread
18 to 24 in. × 6 to 8 in.

When, Where, and How to Plant
It is always best to buy Jack-in-the-pulpit from reliable sources that specifically state that theirs are "nursery propagated" (grown from seed at the nursery), as opposed to "nursery grown," which usually means collected from the wild. This shade-loving perennial grows best in moist bottomland soils, which may stay wet part of the season but dry in the summer and fall. Seed collected in the fall from plants on your property may be sown in pots kept in a cool protected area and transplanted the following summer, or plants may be dug and their small bulblike offsets removed and replanted. It is very important to keep small plants moist through the first summer, but little or no fertilizer is needed, just a natural leaf mulch.

Growing Tips
Little care is needed if it is planted in a woodland setting that stays fairly moist.

Care and Maintenance
Other than needing protection from slugs during moist seasons, this hardy native pretty well takes care of itself. It tends to spread slowly by offsets, and seeds that sprout in leaf mulch, so it is important not to rake autumn leaves from the area. Some attention to weed control will be needed to help slender stalks of young plants find their way up into the light of day.

Companion Planting and Design
Naturalize Jack-in-the-pulpit in shaded, leaf-littered gardens. It grows well with and complements small *Hosta*, woodland phlox (*Phlox divaricata*), dead nettle (*Lamium* sp.), and Virginia bluebells (*Mertensia* sp.). The large leaves of *Arisaemia* species come and go above those plants, but the stalks of red berries remain. If planted close to hostas, it can look as if the *Arisaemia* berries are growing from hosta plants.

I Also Recommend
Other members of this interesting genus include dragon root (*Arisaemia dracontium*) and several Asian species that have variegated leaves and very large, showy spathes, some of which are purple, burgundy, or striped with green, white, yellow, pink, mauve, or maroon.

Joe-Pye Weed

Eupatorium maculatum

When, Where, and How to Plant

Joe-Pye weed is available at most nurseries and garden centers. It grows best in average to rich, moist soil in full or part sun. Plant in spring after all danger of frost has passed. Follow planting instructions on page 121. Water in with transplant solution. Mulch with 3 to 4 inches of organic matter, taking care to keep the mulch at least 1 inch away from the stems.

Growing Tips

Keep the soil moist. Do not allow it to dry out. Fertilization is not necessary.

Care and Maintenance

Joe-Pye weed may be big, but it is an easy-care plant. It often takes two years for Joe-Pye weed to reach its full size. Once established, it will spread outward to form a dense, good-sized, bushy clump. If the clump gets too large, you can divide it in spring or fall. You will need a knife or heavy-duty shears to cut through the tough crown. Cut the plant down to the ground after it has finished blooming in fall. Joe-Pye weed is free of pests.

Companion Planting and Design

Since Joe-Pye weed likes moist soil, it thrives near a pond or stream or in a boggy area. It is equally at home in a cottage garden setting as part of a woodland area or a naturalized bog. Other moisture-loving plants that works well with Joe-Pye weed include these spring bloomers that add interest while Joe is growing: Jack-in-the-pulpit (*Arisaema triphyllum*), marsh marigold (*Caltha palustris*), and trout lily (*Erythronium americanum*). Summer bloomers include rose mallow (*Hibiscus moscheutos*), blue flag (*Iris versicolor*), and cardinal flower (*Lobelia cardinalis*). Summer to fall bloomers include turtlehead (*Chelone obliqua*), New England aster (*Aster novae-angliae*), sneezeweed (*Helenium autumnale*), gayfeather (*Liatris spicata*), and bugbane (*Cimicifuga racemosa*).

I Also Recommend

'Gateway' (likely a cross between *Eupatorium purpureum* and *E. maculatum*, growing only 3 to 4 feet tall) has foamy rosy purple, lightly scented flowerheads. *Eupatorium coelestinum*, known as hardy ageratum, looks like an overgrown annual ageratum, but it's a different genus and species.

Named in honor of the Native American medicine man who utilized it for healing, Joe-Pye weed is impressive for its massive size—growing 5 to 7 feet tall topped with large clusters of purplish-pink flowers. I first saw it growing at the back of a mixed border about six feet deep. What I did not realize until I saw the steps at the end of the long border was that it cleverly disguised a steep bank. Atop the bank, Joe-Pye weed was enormously tall. It has a light fragrance, and you will often see bees and butterflies at the flowers, taking in the pollen and nectar. Unfortunately, it usually blooms too late for hummingbirds. It is a fabulous, long-lasting cut flower for a striking arrangement.

Other Common Name

Sweet Joe-Pye Weed

Bloom Period and Seasonal Color

Pinkish-purple from midsummer to early autumn.

Mature Height and Spread

5 to 7 ft. × 3 to 4 ft.

Zone

4

Meadow Rue

Thalictrum aquilegifolium

Assuming you don't step on new shoots before they come up in mid-spring, meadow rue's clump of foot-long, blue-green ferny foliage looks like a large columbine. It quickly shoots up flowering stems of puffs of small flowers, each consisting of four sepals and a prominent cluster of stamens. The clouds of white, rosy lilac or purplish stamens (which appear on male plants only) remain for weeks after the white or yellow sepals shed. Spent flowers are followed by attractive, long-lasting seed heads. Found naturally along streams and in low bottomland meadows and other moist, shady areas, its tall flower stems are fluffy flags waving in the spring.

Bloom Period and Seasonal Color
White, rosy lilac, or purplish from mid- to late spring.

Mature Height and Spread
3 ft. or more × 18 to 24 in.

When, Where, and How to Plant
Because meadow rue grows best in moist, humus-rich soils, amend garden soil if needed with acidic peat moss before planting. It prefers light shade or at least protection from hot midday sun. Mature plants are easily divided as soon as they begin growing in the spring; divisions may be slow to re-establish. Buy plants at garden centers, home stores, and nurseries. See page 121 for planting.

Growing Tips
Foliar feed in the spring. Keep moist, not wet, during dry weather.

Care and Maintenance
Few pests seriously bother meadow rue, though slugs may chew on new growth as it appears in mid-spring. Because the plants need damp conditions to really thrive, powdery mildew and other leaf diseases may appear; use fungicides as needed. Tall flowering stems of some species and cultivars may need staking or protection from strong winds. Mature clumps perform best if divided every four or five years.

Companion Planting and Design
Meadow rue is superb for an airy effect, as a pleasing contrast to sturdier perennials. Its delicate tracery of leaves and flowers is particularly effective against a dark background such as is found along edges of woodland gardens. Its foliage is also good in flower arrangements.

I Also Recommend
True meadow rue has several cultivars, including 'Album' with white stamen; 'White Cloud' with yellow-tipped white stamen; and 'Thundercloud' (sometimes called 'Purple Cloud') with dark purple stamen. Other members of the *Thalictrum* genus include small ones well suited for alpine and shady moist rock gardens, such as fernleaf meadow rue (*T. adiantifolium*) and yellow meadow rue (*T. flavum* 'Illuminator') that has bright yellow-green leaves and lemon-yellow flowers. Chinese meadow rue (*T. delavayi*) is tall with thin, dark purple stems (that need support), and its heat-tolerant flowers have violet sepals and yellow stamens which last two months or longer. 'Hewitt's Double' lacks stamens but has lots of mauve sepals, forming pom-pom like flowers.

New England Aster

Aster nova-angliae 'Purple Dome'

When, Where, and How to Plant

'Purple Dome' aster is readily available at nurseries, garden centers, and home stores. Although it is sometimes seen in spring (probably bought through a mail-order catalog), like chrysanthemums, it is more often available in summer as smallish plants or full-grown container plantings. It grows best in deep, fertile, moist soil in full to part sun. Plant it as soon as it you get it, following the instructions on page 121. Water in with transplant solution. 'Purple Dome' is a good container plant. If you purchase it already growing in a 6-inch or larger container, upsize it to a container at least 2 inches wider, for a single plant, as it may be rootbound. If you grow it in a container, look for a potting mix that has moisture-holding crystals. You can also mix in finely shredded peat moss to the potting mix. Lightly wet the mix before putting it in the pot to ensure even moisture. Mulch with fine bark to maintain moisture.

Growing Tips

Keep the plant well watered. Do not let it dry out. Foliar feed every three weeks with a solution of kelp or fish emulsion, following the package instructions.

Care and Maintenance

Attention to deadheading rewards you with a multitude of continuous blooms. If you get the plant in spring, pinch the stems back to the next lower set of leaves every three weeks until mid-July to create a bushy plant. New England aster is free of pests.

Companion Planting and Design

'Purple Dome' is majestic in a cottage garden, eye-catching at the edge of a woodland or included in a butterfly garden. As mentioned before, 'Purple Dome' is outstanding with 'Fireworks' goldenrod (*Solidago* 'Fireworks'). Plant it with other asters in varying hues. It also mixes well with chrysanthemums (*Dendranthema* spp.).

I Also Recommend

'Alma Potschke' (3 feet) has cerise blooms. 'Barr's Pink' (4 feet) needs staking for its semidouble rose-pink blossoms. 'Harrington's Pink' (3 to 5 feet) requires staking for its salmon-pink late blooming flowers.

'Purple Dome' is the most impressive of the New England aster hybrids as evidenced by its ever-growing popularity. It's appreciated for its magnificent sprays of 2-inch flowers comprised of royal purple, double petals surrounding a small yellow center. It is eye-catching and long-lasting, beginning in midsummer and often lasting (with deadheading) until frost. It is a compact plant that from a distance looks just like a large hemisphere of purple. The flowers are so profuse you barely see the hairy stems or lance-shaped leaves. For most of the growing season, it just blends into the background of the garden—until it begins to bloom. Many people treat it as an annual, purchasing the plant in midsummer just before it flowers.

Other Common Name
Michaelmas Daisy

Bloom Period and Seasonal Color
Deep purple from late summer to fall.

Mature Height and Spread
15 to 18 in. × 24 to 30 in.

Oriental Poppy
Papaver orientale

A planting of oriental poppies is absolutely eye-popping, especially with the low rays of the early morning or late afternoon sun illuminating the crepe-paperlike, brilliant orange petals. Look closely at the 4- to 6-inch, cup-shaped flowers. The base of the petals is usually black, surrounding a prominent central ring of black stamens. You will often hear buzzing before you get close to the flowers, which attract a bevy of buzzing bees. The blossoms are borne singly on hairy stems rising above hairy, gray-green leaves. After the flower blooms, an attractive 1-inch seedpod forms, which you can let ripen or cut for adding to flower arrangements. The plant goes dormant in summer, disappearing altogether. It is very drought-tolerant with a deep taproot that makes it difficult to transplant.

Bloom Period and Seasonal Color
Orange in late spring to early summer.

Mature Height and Spread
18 to 24 in. × 2 to 3 ft.

Zone
4

When, Where, and How to Plant
You can buy young potted plants in the spring at nurseries, garden centers, and home stores. Oriental poppies need deep, fertile, well-drained soil and full sun. Because of its brittle taproot, take care when planting. Allow 15 to 18 inches between plants. Dig a hole the size of the potted poppy, but 4 inches deeper. Add 4 inches of builder's sand to the hole to ensure that the root will not become waterlogged when the plant is dormant. Dipping the potted poppy in transplant solution for a minute can help keep the soil mass intact. Carefully remove the plant from the pot, and insert the entire soil mass into the hole. Add extra soil if necessary and firm gently with your hands. Water in with transplant solution.

Growing Tips
Oriental poppies are very drought-resistant; normal rainfall should suffice. In case of drought, when the top three to four inches of soil are dry, water the plants. Fertilization is not necessary.

Care and Maintenance
The poppy will probably not bloom the first year, but it will leaf out. By midsummer, the leaves die back and the plant goes dormant. Then add several inches of organic mulch to keep the soil temperature cool. Buy spring, the mulch will have broken down and will feed the plant. It may take two or three years for the plant to bloom, but it is well worth the wait. If you want to use oriental poppies in flower arrangements, cut the flower and immediate sear the cut end with a match. After several minutes, you can put it in water. Oriental poppies are pest free.

Companion Planting and Design
Oriental poppies are beautiful with blue- and purple-flowered plants such as false indigo (*Baptisia australis*), speedwell (*Veronica* spp.), and bellflowers (*Campanula* spp.).

I Also Recommend
'Allegro' (18 inches) has bold black basal markings on bright orange petals. 'Beauty of Livermere' ('Beauty of Livermore') has crimson-scarlet flowers with prominent black stamens. 'China Boy' sports bicolored white petals with broad, irregular orange edging.

When, Where, and How to Plant

Container-grown peonies are available in spring at nurseries, garden centers, home stores, and mail-order nurseries. Peonies grow best in deep, fertile, moist, well-drained soil in full to part sun. Peonies do not like to be disturbed, so choose your location well. If transplanted, it may be several years before they bloom. Double-flowered varieties need support (use peony hoops) as wind and rain added to their own weight can knock them down. Dig the hole about 1¹/₂ times the size of the potted plant and put the soil on a tarp or in a wheelbarrow. Add plenty of organic matter (compost, well-rotted manure, leaf mold, humus) to the soil. Put enough amended soil into the hole and place the plant so the eyes (buds) are no more than 2 inches below the soil surface. Fill in with the remaining soil and tamp it down with your hands. Water well with transplant solution. Allow at least 3 feet between plants.

Growing Tips

Keep the soil lightly moist. Do not let it dry out. In spring, 2 inches of compost around the plant will feed the soil during the growing season.

Care and Maintenance

Cut the leaves down as they die off in the fall. Add a 4-in layer of mulch after the first freeze to keep the plant from heaving during winter thaws. Remove mulch in spring. Peonies are relatively pest free.

Companion Planting and Design

Peonies are beautiful with foxgloves (*Digitalis* spp.) against a white picket fence in a cottage garden. A backdrop of lilacs heralds their bloom. The emerging foliage of peonies will hide browning leaves of early bulbs like crocus (*Crocus* spp.) and grape hyacinths (*Muscari* spp.).

I Also Recommend

'Sarah Bernhardt' has double, rose-pink flowers. 'Festiva Maxima' sports double, red-flecked white blossoms. 'Karl Rosenfeld' has double, dark crimson blooms. Fernleaf peony (*Paeonia tenuifolia*, 12 to 18 inches) is gorgeous for its ferny foliage and 2¹/₂- to 3-inch-wide ruby red blossoms; 'Rubra Plena' has magnificent double blooms and is hardy to Zone 3.

Peonies are the very essence of late spring. Their sweet perfume is the precursor to the roses that will bloom within several weeks. Peonies are among the longest-lived perennials. I used to reside at the end of a long drive, 100 feet of which was lined on both sides with twenty or more different peonies that were planted in 1906. They are still blooming in profusion with little attention, although the names of most of the varieties were lost over time. The large, 3- to 6-inch wide, rounded single or double flowers rise above the handsome shiny lobed leaves. Both leaves and flowers are superb in arrangements. All too often, a heavy rain or unseasonably early heat shortens the season. Pick the flowers to keep the plant blooming.

Other Common Names
Common Garden Peony, Chinese Peony

Bloom Period and Seasonal Color
White, pink, and red in single and bicolors from late spring to early summer.

Mature Height and Spread
18 to 36 in. × 2 to 3 ft.

Zone
2

Purple Coneflower

Echinacea purpurea

Purple coneflower is one of the quintessential native plants of the Prairie Lands states. The numerous varieties attest to its popularity among gardeners throughout America. It is a versatile, handsome plant that is at home in any type of garden—prairie restoration, wildflower meadow, cottage garden, or even a cutting garden. In summer, butterflies, bees, and the occasional humming-bird visit the flowers. The plant is well branched and shrubby, usually growing 2 to 4 feet tall. The coarsely leafed stems bear dozens of flowerheads comprised of pur-plish-pink ray flowers and a central brown cone of disk flowers. One of the reasons I love purple coneflower is that it is the lazy gardener's flower. In fall, just leave the flower stems and birds will come eat the seeds.

Bloom Period and Seasonal Color
Rose-pink in summer.

Mature Height and Spread
2 to 5 ft. × 15 to 18 in.

When, Where, and How to Plant
Purple coneflower is readily available at nurseries, garden centers, and home stores in spring. Some of the more diverse cultivated varieties are only available through mail-order nurseries. Purple coneflower grows best in rich, loamy, well-drained soil. Plant it in the spring after the last frost date. Allow at least 18 inches between plants for good air circulation. Water in with transplant solution. See chapter introduction for more on planting. Mulch with 3 inches of organic material, taking care to keep it at least 1 inch away from the stems.

Growing Tips
Keep the soil lightly moist until the plant is estab-lished. Purple coneflower is susceptible to powdery mildew, so water at ground level or early in the morning. Once established, it is quite drought tol-erant since it grows a long taproot.

Care and Maintenance
At the first sign of powdery mildew, spray the leaves with baking soda solution (see page 233 for complete directions). Continue spraying every seven to ten days. Otherwise, purple coneflower is care-free. Division is not recommended (or needed), as plants that have been divided are bushier but far less floriferous.

Companion Planting and Design
Due to its susceptibility to powdery mildew, do not grow it with other susceptible plants, including beebalm (*Monarda didyma*), garden phlox (*Phlox paniculata*), black-eyed Susan (*Rudbeckia* spp.), zin-nias, (*Zinnia elegans*), or lilacs (*Syringa vulgaris*). It is lovely in a cottage setting with chrysanthemums (*Dendranthema* spp.), 'Moonbeam' coreopsis (*Coreopsis verticillata* 'Moonbeam'), and valerian (*Centranthus ruber*). It works well with ornamental grasses, especially growing in front of any of the *Miscanthus* species.

I Also Recommend
'Alba' (to 3 feet) has white flowers. 'Cygnet White' ('Baby White Swan'—20 inches) is compact with horizontal white petals; it's good for containers. 'Leuchtstern' ('Bright Star'—2 to 3 feet) has bright rosy-red, fine flowers. 'Magnus' (1998 Perennial Plant Association Plant of the Year) is an excellent plant with intense dark purplish-pink.

Queen of the Prairie
Filipendula rubra

When, Where, and How to Plant

Queen of the prairie can be found at many nurseries, garden centers, and home stores in the spring. A broader choice is available through mail-order nurseries. Queen of the prairie grows best in moderately rich, consistently moist soil in full sun to light shade. It thrives in the soil along lakes, ponds, streams, or by your own water garden. Plant Queen of the prairie after the last frost date in spring (see page 121 regarding planting). Allow at least 3 feet between plants. Water in with transplant solution. Mulch with 3 inches of organic material, taking care to keep it at least 1 inch away from the stems.

Growing Tips

Keep the soil evenly moist. Do not let it dry out. Fertilizing is not necessary.

Care and Maintenance

Clumps can spread rapidly by creeping stolons. Lift and divide clumps in fall if they have overstepped their bounds or if they are getting too large. If the clump is old, you will need a sharp knife or heavy-duty shears to separate it. Replant the divisions 3 feet apart. To encourage the plant to rebloom, cut back any spent flowerheads. Once the blooms are finished for the season, you can either cut them down or let them be and enjoy their beauty as they sway with the breeze. This plant is pest free.

Companion Planting and Design

Thriving in wet or boggy soil, Queen of the prairie mixes well with astilbe (*Astilbe* cvs.), bergenia (*Bergenia* spp.), Japanese iris (*Iris ensata*), Siberian iris (*Iris siberica*), forget-me-not (*Myosotis scorpioides*), primroses (*Primula* spp.), meadow rue (*Thalictrum* spp.), cardinal flower (*Lobelia cardinalis*), and great blue lobelia (*Lobelia syphilitica*).

I Also Recommend

'Venusta' ('Magnifica'—6 to 8 feet) is vigorous with feathery plumes of deep rose pink florets in midsummer that fade to soft pink as they age. *Filipendula vulgaris* 'Plena' (meadowsweet) has fully double white flowers on 24" plants. *Filipendula palmata* (Siberian meadowsweet—3 to 4 feet) is a compact plant with 4- to 5-inch open clusters of pink florets.

With its majestic size and shape, Queen of the prairie is a well-deserved name. Its foliage is bold with 8-inch-wide, 3-lobed, toothed leaves. In early and midsummer, its branching red stems bear 6-inch, feathery clusters of closely packed, deep peachy pink florets. As I consider that it is one of the native plants of the tall prairies, I continue to be in awe of our forefathers (including some of my forbearers) who traveled the Prairie Lands states to settle or move further west. One can only imagine how awesome it must have been traveling on foot or in wagons and going through these plants that are larger than life. Queen of the prairie is a water-loving plant that is perfect for a boggy area.

Bloom Period and Seasonal Color
Deep peachy pink from early to midsummer.

Mature Height and Spread
6 to 8 ft. × 3 to 4 ft.

Zone
3

Russian Sage
Perovskia atriplicifolia

Russian sage is one of those wonderful plants I call a veil plant. Although it is tall—growing 3 to 4 feet high—it is slender and not sparse. You see through it as if you were wearing a blue-gray veil. Plantings behind it take on a more interesting appearance as you view them through the willowy silvery stems and long slender panicles of small tubular violet-blue flowers. Russian sage is a shrubby plant with a delicate air about it. For that reason, it works equally well in the front, middle, or back of a garden bed. Its hardiness rating has been under-rated, listed as Zone 6 in many books. Although it will die back to the ground, it will come back reliably in Zone 4.

Bloom Period and Seasonal Color
Violet-blue in late summer to early autumn.

Mature Height and Spread
3 to 4 ft. × 30 to 36 in.

Zone
4

When, Where, and How to Plant
Russian sage is readily available at nurseries, garden centers, and home stores. The cultivated varieties can be found through mail-order nurseries and on the Internet. Russian sage grows best in poor to average, well-drained soil. It requires full sun. Plant Russian sage after all danger of frost has passed, according to instructions on page 121. Allow at least 3 feet between plants if you want to maintain a light veil effect. If you choose a shrubbier, thicker look, plant them 2 feet apart and there will be plenty of overlap between plants. Mulch with 2 inches of grit, gravel, sand, or pebbles. Keep the mulch at least 1 inch away from the stems.

Growing Tips
Water lightly until the plant is established. Silver or gray foliage is a good indicator that a plant is drought tolerant. Water when the top two inches of soil are dry. Fertilizing is not necessary.

Care and Maintenance
Russian sage is low maintenance and rarely needs dividing. There are no pest or disease problems. The only chore is to cut the stems down to 1 inch after you have had a hard frost. The plant may die completely to the soil level. Have no fear; it will resprout in the spring. Russian sage goes through three seasonal stages: soft grayish green shoots in springtime, followed by tiny violet-blue flowers in summer, and finishing the growing season with silky gray seedheads in fall.

Companion Planting and Design
Russian sage, with its silvery foliage, can be used to cool down hot-colored plants, separate blatant colors, or warm a cooler palette. It is beautiful with 'Europa' rose, which has dark burgundy-green stems and velvety red flowers.

I Also Recommend
'Filagran' (to 30 inches) has more finely cut leaves. 'Longin' is narrower, more erect, with less toothed leaves than the species. 'Blue Spire' (to 4 feet x 3 feet) has an upright form with violet-blue flowers on 12-inch panicles. 'Hybrida' (to 36 × 30 inches) has dark lavender-blue flowers on 16-inch panicles.

When, Where, and How to Plant

Sedum 'Autumn Joy' is likely the most popular sedum. It is readily available at nurseries, garden centers, home stores, and even grocery and hardware stores that sell plants in spring. 'Autumn Joy' prefers average to rich, well-drained soil but will grow in most any well-drained soil in full sun. Wait until several weeks after the last frost date to plant. Follow planting instruction in chapter introduction, and allow 2 feet between plants. Water in with transplant solution. Mulch with 3 inches of gravel, sand, grit, or pebbles. Keep the mulch at least 1 inch away from the stems.

Growing Tips

Water lightly until the plant is established. Sedum 'Autumn Joy' is drought tolerant. Water when the top 3 inches of soil are dry. Fertilizing is not necessary.

Care and Maintenance

'Autumn Joy' is a relatively carefree plant. It is virtually pest and disease free. Butterflies swarm to it in late summer and early fall. In spring, cut any broken stems. It may need dividing after several years—you will know this if the center opens and splays out. Divide and replant divisions, discarding the dead centers.

Companion Planting and Design

'Autumn Joy' is quite versatile—lovely clustered in a cottage garden, handsome in a mixed bed or border, and even elegant enough to make a fine edging for a formal garden. It mixes well with other fall-blooming plants such as New England aster (*Aster novae-angliae*), New York aster (*Aster novi-belgii*), goldenrod (*Solidago* spp.), and berried shrubs like rockspray (*Cotoneaster horizontalis*), Japanese barberry (*Berberis thunbergii* 'Atropurpurea'), and bearberry (*Arctostaphylos uva-ursi*).

I Also Recommend

'Matrone' is similar to 'Autumn Joy', but its flowers are deeper red with white edge. 'Ruby Glow' (to 10 inches x 18 inches) has red stems with green-purple leaves and clusters of small, star-shaped, ruby-red flowers from midsummer to fall; it is hardy in Zone 5.

Sedum 'Autumn Joy' is truly a joy to behold—in all four seasons. It is a bushy, succulent-leafed perennial with slightly glaucous (waxy whitish) green stems and 3- to 5-inch-long, glaucous green, oval leaves with slightly serrated edges. The flower clusters begin to form in summer, looking like light green heads of broccoli. As the season begins to turn, so do the 8-inch wide clusters of tiny, 1/2-inch, star-shaped florets that gradually turn deep pink. As autumn progresses, they become pinkish bronze and then a coppery red. By winter, they fade to a coppery brown but last through all but the toughest winters. The leaves slowly disappear. Then in spring, suddenly there appear small rosettes of leaves that start the process all over again.

Bloom Period and Seasonal Color
Pink in late summer through autumn.

Mature Height and Spread
18 to 24 in. × 18 to 24 in.

Speedwell
Veronica spicata

Speedwell is one of those special perennials that add visual zest to gardens from spring to fall, with solid foliage topped with many narrow, pointed spikes studded densely with flowers of blue, white, purple, red, or pink. The blooming stems are great as cut flowers—and the more you cut, the more will grow back. When in flower, which seems to be all spring, summer, and fall, it is a powerful attractant for butterflies, and it grows well in poor soils similar to the scrabbly rocky hillsides and dry meadows of its native Europe. It is somewhat drought-tolerant as well, meaning it will not be a chore to keep alive in the heat of summer when nearly everything else—including the gardener—has faded.

Other Common Name
Veronica

Bloom Period and Seasonal Color
Blue, pink, red, or white from spring to fall.

Mature Height and Spread
6 to 24 in. × 12 to 15 in.

When, Where, and How to Plant
Veronica grows best in sunny or mostly sunny beds in well-drained soils; work organic matter and either grit or very sharp sand into planting holes. Divide mature plants in spring or fall, or sow seed in summer or fall in containers. When setting out nursery-grown plants, loosen their potting soil and spread the roots into the planting hole. See page 121 for planting information.

Growing Tips
Water deeply but only occasionally; fertilize lightly and infrequently.

Care and Maintenance
After flowering, deadhead to promote fresh new growth with more flowers. Fertilize sparingly and water only during prolonged droughts. Root rot is its biggest problem and is usually caused by heavy rainfall, over watering, or plants being sited in poorly drained or clay soils. Species and cultivars with densely hairy or fuzzy leaves should be protected from excessive winter moisture. There are few insect pests, and these can be pruned out during routine deadheading.

Companion Planting and Design
Veronica is at its best when used near the front of a mixed flower bed, where its attractive foliage provides a groundcover effect, and its tight spears of flower spikes contrast with nearly all other flowers, especially small daylilies (*Hemerocallis* spp.), daisies (*Aster* spp.), hosta, peony, black-eyed Susan (*Rudbeckia* spp.), and blue fescue grass (*Festuca glauca*). Veronica grows well in rock gardens, large containers, and alpine meadow gardens.

I Also Recommend
'Sunny Border Blue', the Perennial Plant Association's 1993 Plant of the Year, bears sturdy dark violet-blue flower spikes up to 7 inches long, from early summer to late fall. Old standards include the patriotic trio 'Red Fox', 'White Icicle', and 'Crater Lake Blue'. A brand-new introduction from Europe, 'Royal Candles' is a 3-inch tall, tight clumping rock-garden-sized plant. Starting in spring, it is topped with dozens of thin but sturdy 15-inch tall pale blue flower spikes which begin opening with blue-purple flowers at the base and move steadily upward like a lit fuse.

When, Where, and How to Plant

Preferring full sun and relatively poor soils, sundrops can be grown from seed sown directly onto the soil from spring to late summer or in pots to be kept over the winter. (Place in a cool or protected area and set into the ground in the spring.) Follow planting instructions on page 121. Feed very lightly at transplanting time.

Growing Tips

Foliar feed monthly every spring, but water only during extreme drought.

Care and Maintenance

Sundrops spread by underground rhizomes into neighboring soils; use metal or plastic edging to keep colonies under control or simply remove unwanted plants in the fall before they get too established. Few pests bother sundrops, and the leaf spots which occasionally appear in wet seasons are relatively minor problems. No control is recommended. Root rot can occur in wet soils. Divide existing plantings in the spring by digging smaller plants and their short "runners" from outer edges of mature colonies.

Companion Planting and Design

Sundrops spreads into a thick, rosette-forming groundcover for the middle of flower borders, where its flowers can rise above smaller plants in the foreground but the foliage is hidden and doesn't detract. When planted against a dark backdrop, its flowers really shine. Good combinations include winter and spring bulbs, which need to be kept dry in the summer, and yarrow (*Achillea* spp.), which has complementary ferny foliage and flat, round flowers. Sundrops and other *Oenothera* species are excellent for naturalistic or wildflower gardens.

I Also Recommend

Sundrops cultivars include clear yellow 'Highlight', 'Fireworks' with red buds opening to yellow flowers, bright-red foliage 'Summer Solstice', and 'Yellow River' with red stems and large, canary-yellow flowers. Relatives include tall, fragrant evening primrose (*Oenothera biennis*), small, clump-forming species (*O. perennis, O. pumila, O. pallida,* and *O. macrocarpa,* which may spread), and a groundcover (*O. speciosa,* with large pink or white flowers).

Some garden experts say we shouldn't grow certain plants because they are invasive—meaning they so easily spread that they tend to colonize nearby areas. This is not a problem with sundrops, which is simple to pull or dig and share with less fortunate garden neighbors! The prairie native blooms so dependably, it's worth the risk of having too much of a good thing. Moreover, unlike its evening primrose cousin Oenothera biennis (a night-blooming biennial with fragrant flowers), we can enjoy sundrops and its butterflies during the day while we—and the sun—are out in the garden. Not a true primrose, this spreading perennial has knee-high, or higher, spikes of clear yellow flowers, sometimes tinged with red, from late spring to late summer.

Bloom Period and Seasonal Color
Yellow flowers through summer.

Mature Height and Spread
2^1/$_2$ to 3 ft. × 2 ft. or more

Threadleaf Coreopsis

Coreopsis verticillata 'Moonbeam'

Coreopsis is usually thought of as a basketball-size clump of leaves with many tall, wire-stemmed, daisy-like cut flowers of golden yellow that reseeds freely. But threadleaf coreopsis is a lower-growing, thin-leaf perennial plant, native to the prairies, that spreads steadily by rhizomes into a mass of needle-looking dark green leaves with taller stems of smaller, many-petaled flowers. The Perennial Plant Association named 'Moonbeam' Plant of the Year in 1992, making this cheerful, clear yellow threadleaf cultivar the recipient of rare, one-flower-a-year honor from the nation's only organized group of perennial plant growers and researchers. Flowers of this easy-to-propagate sunflower relative attract bees and butterflies, and small birds such as titmouse, goldfinch, and sparrows favor its tiny nutlet-like seeds.

Bloom Period and Seasonal Color
Yellow from late spring to early fall.

Mature Height and Spread
10 to 18 in. × 12 in. and spreading

When, Where, and How to Plant
Prepare soil in full sun by adding organic matter and perhaps some coarse or sharp sand, then lightly scatter seed of coreopsis in the spring, summer, or fall, and water the area to begin germination. Plants are available at garden centers, nurseries, and home stores. Follow directions on page 121 for planting. Water only to prevent wilting, and fertilize lightly to get plants started.

Growing Tips
Water deeply but infrequently, and fertilize lightly in spring and early summer.

Care and Maintenance
Coreopsis needs very little care, other than regular deadheading to remove seedpods, which produces more flowers. Divide mature clumps every three or four years to maintain vigor. There are no major insect or disease problems, except fungal diseases caused by over-watering or rainy spells. No control is needed, as new buds will appear quickly during drier, hotter weather.

Companion Planting and Design
Coreopsis grows well as a specimen beside steps, and in wildflower plantings. Combine with other plants in flower borders, especially veronicas (*Veronica* spp.) and daylilies (*Hemerocallis* spp.). They are tidy enough to include in rock gardens and drought- and heat-tolerant enough to cascade from containers on hot decks in the summer sun. Because coreopsis grows new foliage in the spring and blooms in the summer, it is perfect planted over winter and spring bulbs, such as daffodils (*Narcissus* spp.), which are summer-dormant.

I Also Recommend
The lemon-yellow flowers of 'Moonbeam' make it a favorite of mine. Other threadleaf coreopsis include a deeper golden-yellow, drought-resistant 'Zagreb', and 'Golden Shower' (sometimes called 'Grandiflora') with dark yellow flowers. *Coreopsis rosea* looks like threadleaf coreopsis but has mauve-pink flowers from summer to early fall and naturalizes well on dry slopes.

When, Where, and How to Plant

Valerian grows in poor, dry soils nearly anywhere else except damp shade. It does poorly in prolonged heat and humidity, so choose a spot with good air circulation and protection from the reflected heat of brick or concrete walls, and paved decks and walks. In the spring, set out nursery-grown plants, divide mature plants, or sow seed. Water until it's established, then gradually water more deeply but less frequently to allow the new plants to grow deeper roots.

Growing Tips

Water as needed, but avoid allowing plants to dry to the wilting point.

Care and Maintenance

Cut off old flowering stems to shape the plants, to encourage more blooms to form, and to prevent a good bit of the seeding. Replace plants every three to four years to prevent them from getting ragged as they turn woody and begin to decline. Valerian is relatively pest free. Do not use insecticides when plants are in flower, or you will risk killing pollinating butterflies and moths.

Companion Planting and Design

In most gardens, valerian can become a successful weed because it is pretty and good for wildlife without being too invasive or hard to pull. It is a great choice for a far-away bed that you just can't get water to. In fact, it is often listed as a xeriscape or dry-garden plant. It is suitable for flower borders, especially when surrounded with white flowers or foliage plants; however, valerian grows best in crevices in crude walls and on stony roadside or garden embankments, even in chalky or limestone soils. It is a good companion for ornamental grasses, *Sedum* 'Autumn Joy', and daylilies (*Hemerocallis* spp.).

I Also Recommend

Cultivars include 'Albus', a compact and bushy plant with dense white flower clusters along the stems; 'Coccineus', with large, carmine-red to deep crimson flowers; and rose-pink, nearly magenta 'Roseus'. 'Snowcloud' is of course white. Note: Valerian does not have the medicinal value found in the herb valerian (*Valeriana officinalis*), also known as garden heliotrope, which I've included on page 136.

One of our most trouble-free perennials, red valerian gives a long, showy flower display in difficult garden spots, including poor or alkaline soil. The sometimes-common plant grows along roadsides and in rocky banks. The stems are tall and bluish-green, with a waxy surface. The bushy clump has many erect, branched stems of 4-inch long bluish green waxy-looking leaves, topped in spring and summer with dense ball-like clusters of half-inch long, fragrant funnel-shaped flowers of white, rose pink, or dusty crimson. They are fragrant and attractive to butterflies and bees. In France, it is called honeysuckle because of its importance as a nectar source. The plant self-sows prolifically by way of seeds with dandelion-like parachutes, even into rock piles and crevices in walls and walks.

Other Common Name

Jupiter's Beard

Bloom Period and Seasonal Color

Deep pink from late spring to late summer.

Mature Height and Spread

2 to 3 ft. × 1 1/2 to 2 ft.

Virginia Bluebells

Mertensia virginica

A relative of forget-me-not (Myosotis), Virginia bluebells is a native of the woodlands of the eastern United States. It has broadly oval, bluish green leaves in loose clumps that send up leafy, 2-foot tall stems bearing loose clusters of nodding, 1-inch flowers. Buds are usually pink to lavender but open to blue bells, sometimes with a pinkish cast. The flowering stems are almost succulent like impatiens and nearly hollow, so they are fragile. The plant "comes and goes" rather quickly, appearing and flowering in the spring, but it dies down to the ground soon after going to seed, usually by midsummer. Each clump will spread slowly, and seedlings will appear in nearby areas where leaf litter has turned to composted mulch. If left undisturbed, it will thrive and form large colonies.

Bloom Period and Seasonal Color
Blue in mid-spring.

Mature Height and Spread
1 to 2 ft. × 8 to 24 in.

When, Where, and How to Plant
Virginia bluebells thrive in moist but well-drained, humus-rich soil in with light or dappled midday shade. Add organic matter to your native soil to get plants started and then let natural leaf litter replenish your soil every fall and winter. Start seeds in the fall or spring in pots in a shady spot outdoors but covered with plastic or glass to prevent the soil from drying out. Seedlings come up readily but may take two or three years to reach blooming maturity. Virginia bluebells are available at garden centers, nurseries, and home stores. Follow directions on page 121 for planting.

Care and Maintenance
Water to keep the soil moist, but not wet. Feed plants only lightly.

Growing Tips
Watch for slugs, which can be a serious problem to new growth. Powdery mildew can sometimes ruin the foliage for a few weeks. Transplant volunteer seedlings in the early spring or divide mature clumps in the fall or carefully in the spring without damaging the early new growth. Instead of spraying, cut the foliage down, hold back on watering frequency, and see if new growth comes up without the disease symptoms. Protect plantings from strong winds that can literally shred the delicate leaves and flowers.

Companion Planting and Design
True blue is a hard color to come by in gardens, so Virginia bluebells fills an important color niche. It is best planted en masse and left undisturbed in shady woodland, wildflower or native plant gardens. Clumps may be sprinkled in borders or rock gardens. Because of its ephemeral up-and-then-down short season of growth and flower, Virginia bluebells makes a good companion for myrtle (*Vinca minor*), Jack-in-the-pulpit (*Arisaemia* spp.), bleeding heart (*Dicentra spectabilis*), columbine (*Aquilegia canadensis*), creeping phlox (*Phlox stolonifera*), and ferns and hosta which expand as the growing season progresses. Use summer annuals such as caladium and impatiens to fill the void when plants die back.

I Also Recommend
Try the variety 'Alba', which has white flowers.

Willow Blue Star
Amsonia tabernaemontana

When, Where, and How to Plant

Willow blue star loves sunlight but tolerates a good bit of shade and grows well in heavy soils. The easiest way to get started is to divide a big chunk of root and stems in the late winter or early spring. If the plants are in full bloom or it's summertime when you need a piece of the plant, simply cut back the stems before digging off a nice size chunk of the roots. Softwood cuttings taken in early summer, after flowers have faded, root well in moist potting soil kept humid and out of direct sunshine for two or three weeks. Sow collected seed in containers in the late summer or fall when they ripen.

Growing Tips

Water only during extended periods of drought, and fertilize sparingly.

Care and Maintenance

Willow blue star grows under great duress, needing no care at all, other than perhaps cutting down the faded foliage after a hard freeze or snowstorm. It has no major insect or disease problems, although rust may cause some discoloration on some of the foliage.

Companion Planting and Design

Plant blue star in low wet areas, near the bottoms of ditch banks, alongside a pond or water garden, or any other place that stays pretty wet in the winter and spring, even if it dries out in midsummer. Companions that complement blue star and tolerate wet or heavy soils include ornamental grasses such as *Miscanthus* or upland sea oats (*Chasmanthium* sp.), cardinal flower (*Lobelia cardinalis*), canna, and elderberry (*Sambucus* spp.). Its fall colors also sets off hardy chrysanthemums when they come into bloom.

I Also Recommend

Willow-leaf amsonia (*A. hubrectii, A. ciliata*) has very soft, fine, needle-shaped leaves crowded on each stem. *Amsonia illustris* has shiny, leathery leaves. A compact form, *A. tabernaemontana* 'Montana', is more compact than the species, its leaves are slightly wider, and the flowers, which bloom up to two weeks earlier than the species, are a deeper blue.

This refined milkweed relative resembles in growth habit and flower shape a miniature, blue, spring-flowering garden phlox (Phlox paniculata). Willow blue star grows naturally in some of the most miserable places, such as clay-based ditches, and spots that are wet all winter and spring but cracked and dry in summer. Its many unbranched stems have narrow, willow-like leaves, and each stem is topped in mid-spring and summer with loose but showy clusters of small, star-shaped, pale or sky-blue flowers. Its seed pods are narrow and not showy, but the bright yellow fall color is a bonus. Flower clusters are on long stems, which make them easy to cut and use in flower arrangements; be careful when stripping off the narrow leaves—some people are allergic to the sap.

Bloom Period and Seasonal Color

Blue in late spring through midsummer.

Mature Height and Spread

2 to 3 ft. × 2 to 3 ft.

Yarrow
Achillea millefolium

One of the first plants new gardeners found to be nearly too hard to kill, this pungent-smelling perennial was brought to this continent by settlers who used it as an herbal wound wrap. It was named in honor of the Greek hero Achilles, who is said to have used it on the battlefield to staunch the bleeding of his men's wounds. The plant spreads slowly but surely and is tough enough in all weather extremes to grow from along railway tracks in Alaska to beaches of the Gulf Coast. Most form matted clumps of feathery or fern-like foliage and send up slightly leafy stalks of very showy, flattened round heads of white, pink, yellow, gold, or red flowers that are outstanding in both fresh or dried arrangements.

Bloom Period and Seasonal Color
White, pink, yellow, gold to red from late spring to fall.

Mature Height and Spread
1 to 2 ft. × 2 ft. or more

When, Where, and How to Plant
Sun-loving yarrow will tolerate light shade but requires well-drained (never soggy) soil. Follow planting instructions on page 121. Some yarrow is so prolific with seed that it spreads around like weeds. Yarrow is available at garden centers, nurseries, and home stores.

Growing Tips
Until new plants are established, water only to prevent plants from wilting, and feed new plants at half-strength. After that, apply light fertilization in the spring every year or two, and never water at all!

Care and Maintenance
Little or no care is needed for yarrow, other than occasional dividing to reinvigorate old clumps. Few insects or diseases affect the plant or its flowers. Its pungent foliage can irritate the skin of some gardeners.

Companion Planting and Design
Yarrow planted in masses forms good ferny groundcover in sunny beds and under small, airy trees. Its round, flat flowers contrast beautifully with spiky perennials, such as blazing star (*Liatris* spp.) and iris, as well as tone down clumpier perennials such as daylily (*Hemerocallis*). As its foliage begins to billow up in the spring, it holds up and then hides the floppy leaves of daffodils (*Narcissus*) and other spring-blooming bulbs. Its flowers are good for cutting and retain their colors well when dried.

I Also Recommend
There are many species of *Achillea*, each with slightly different growth habits. Some I like include 'Moonshine' with its finely-divided gray-green leaves and light yellow flowers with darker centers, and 'Cerise Queen' which forms a mat of dark green leaves with bright magenta-pink flowers that fade to medium pink with age. 'Gold Plate' and 'Coronation Gold' are popular yellows, but the bright red flowers with yellow eyes of 'Fanal' are real knockouts. Instead of the flattened, disk-like flowers of most yarrow, *Achillea ptarmica* 'The Pearl' has unusual tight, button-like, double white flowerheads.

When, Where, and How to Plant

Any sunny, well-drained, dry soil with moderate to low fertility will serve yucca quite well. There is no need to water or fertilize at planting time. Yucca plants are available at nurseries, garden centers, and home stores. See page 121 for planting instructions.

Growing Tips

These xeriscape plants can thrive without water. Fertilize lightly in the spring.

Care and Maintenance

Tolerant of prolonged dry spells, Yucca is fine with normal rainfall. Young plants grow slowly at first; they fill in and usually become quite solid. Divide clumps in the spring by removing suckers or "pups" from the base of plants. Root in moist potting soil, or bury root sections of stems in sandy soil in the fall. Remove faded flower stems, after leaving a few long enough for birds to perch on. Occasionally, foliage will be mottled from a heavy infestation of spider mites or scale insects; control with a dormant oil application in late winter.

Companion Planting and Design

Yucca grows well in tight, dry, sloped spots or small areas next to pavement with reflected heat where not much else can survive. Grown for its bold, linear leaves, its coarse clump-forming habit, and its strikingly tall flower stem, yucca can be used effectively either as a specimen by itself, in showy groups, or as a fabulous contrast with more traditional garden plants such as coneflowers, daylilies, grasses, and the like. Its winter form can help define a bed, even in the winter.

I Also Recommend

Though the commonly grown plain green yucca can be very effective, there are several stunning cultivars, which add "oomph" to the landscape. The particularly showy 'Bright Edge' has yellow edges. 'Variegata' has blue-green leaves with creamy-white margins that turn pinkish in winter, and 'Golden Sword' has a yellow stripe down the middle of each green leaf. Other kinds of yuccas are not hardy in the Midwest or Prairie states but can be grown outdoors during summer and fall as potted plants to be brought in for the winter.

Yucca has a bad reputation, partly because everyone gets warned not to poke out their eye on one. Actually, soft-tipped native kinds are not dangerous, and since their bold forms and striking flowers are such useful accents for architectural or tropical effects, they are nearly over-used. Spreading rosettes of slender, sword-like leaves up to 2 or more feet long with sharply pointed but soft tips grow in whorls from a short trunk. Each mounding clump has several crowns of these rosettes; leaf edges are fringed with small filaments, like threads from a brand-new shirt. In the summer, nearly every crown sprouts a 4- to 6-foot tall spire with dozens of 2- to 3-inch-wide fragrant, white with pink tinge, perfectly edible bell-shaped flowers.

Other Common Name
Adam's Needle

Bloom Period and Seasonal Color
White in midsummer.

Mature Height by Spread
2 to 4 ft. × 3 to 5 ft.

Roses *for the Prairie Lands*

Roses are among the most ancient of flowers, with fossil evidence dating them back more than forty million years. No wonder they are so beloved and have so much symbolism attached to them. It is curious that although people around the world grow roses today, roses are native only to regions north of the Equator. No species roses are indigenous to the Southern Hemisphere.

The Chinese were the first in recorded history to cultivate roses. This was during the Sen Nung Dynasty about 2737 to 2697 BC, and rose cultivation reached a high degree of sophistication during the Han dynasties from 206 BC to 9 AD. In the western world, the ancient Romans took rose cultivation seriously. They were attracted to roses not just for their fragrance and beauty but for their medicinal and culinary properties as well. They strewed the floors of their bacchanals with roses, perfumed their baths with them, used the essential oil as a skin emollient, incorporated roses into their culinary repertoire, and perfumed themselves with roses.

Roses declined with the fall of the Roman Empire. The Church looked upon them as examples of Roman excesses. For nearly a thousand years, only a few monasteries cultivated roses. In the 1200s, the Church reversed its position and embraced the symbolism of the rose—white for the Virgin Mary's Immaculate Conception and red (the briar rose) for the blood of Christ. Beads were made from a heated mixture of cut rose petals, water, and salt. This was then rolled out to the desired shape. These beads were strung together, making a rosary (meaning a gathering of roses).

The ancient Greek poet Sappho gave roses the appellation "Queen of Flowers" more than 2500 years ago. The strong bond between humans and roses has lasted for millennia. When asked what they want to plant in their garden, most people pick the rose. With all the modern scientific techniques, like gene splicing and cloning, at our fingertips, who can tell what the future of roses will be? Disease resistance has been an important factor in breeding for years. Perhaps in the future—maybe even in our lifetimes—we will be able to purchase an everblooming (year-round), large-flowered, frost-resistant, cold-hardy, fragrant, pest- and disease-resistant, thornless rose that changes colors through the seasons. Yet, for me, that would take a lot of fun out of growing roses. For me, the joy is in the challenge—growing a vigorous rose without chemicals (especially in the Prairie Lands states), discovering a new fragrance or a new color, and most importantly, getting my hands into the soil and becoming one with the rose and the earth.

Cultivating Roses

If you follow these four guidelines, you should be successful at growing roses.

1. Choose a location with at least four to six hours of direct sun a day, good air circulation, and away from trees and large shrubs which cast their shadows on the roses and compete for soil nutrients.

2. Select the best possible rose with at least three healthy canes. Ideally, the plant should be grown on its own rootstock and rated hardy for your zone.

3. Provide good, rich soil with good drainage.

4. Give the plant a lot of TLC (tender loving care). This includes, mulching, feeding, watering, weeding (often not necessary if the plant is mulched well), pruning, preparing the plant for winter dormancy, and controlling pests and diseases.

Selecting A Rose

Before setting out to purchase a rose, do a little research. First, walk around your neighborhood and notice what people have growing. If you see something that catches your eye, ask about the plant. Most gardeners are more than happy to share information. What's the basic information you should ask for? Get the name, type of rose, hardiness (how well does it survive the winter, does it need any special protection), how long the person has had the plant (gives you idea of its long-term performance), and its history of pest and

'William Baffin' Climbing a Fence

disease problems (ideally you want a rose that is free of these). If there is an arboretum or botanical garden nearby, go visit it. Usually the staff is willing to answer your questions. Finally, contact your local Cooperative Extension Service. They often have pamphlets or brochures on specific plants—especially roses suited for your area.

You can purchases roses locally (at a nursery, garden center, home store, and even some hardware stores and supermarkets) or order them on the Web or through a mail-order catalog. The main advantage of getting the rose locally is that you can pick and choose the best rose, but the selection is by far greater through mail-order nurseries (as is the case with all other plants).

Specific information on roses including planting, pruning, and preparing for winter can be found in the back of this book starting on p. 225. In that section, I've also included some information on the language of roses and suggested roses for beginners.

Alchymist Rose

Rosa 'Alchymist'

'Alchymist' is classified in several rose categories—large-flowered climber, modern shrub, and shrub. It was bred by Kordes in Germany (known for his breeding of cold-hardy roses) and introduced in 1956. It is a stunning rose, growing 8 to 12 feet high. It can be trained on an arbor, fence, or pillar. It blooms early in the season with outstanding 3½- to 4-inch double blooms (sometimes quartered—like old-fashioned roses) in shades of apricot from the deepest part of the center, fading at the outer petals. Strongly perfumed, if its size and color don't draw you to it, the fragrance will. Not only can it handle our cold winters, it thrives in the heat of the summer.

Bloom Period and Seasonal Color
Apricot blend in early summer.

Mature Height and Spread
6 to 12 ft. × 6 to 8 ft.

Zone
4

When, Where, and How to Plant

'Alchymist' is available as a container-grown or bare-root plant. If you buy bare root, look for an "own-root" plant, which means the entire plant—crown, canes, and roots—are all 'Alchymist' (as opposed to being grafted onto hardier rootstock). Plant bare-root 'Alchymist' when the soil can be worked in the spring. Container-grown plants available later in spring should be hardened-off and can take the chill, even before the last frost date. Water well at planting with transplant solution.

Growing Tips

Keep the plant well watered until it is established. Mulch well to keep the soil moist. Foliar feed once a month.

Care and Maintenance

'Alchymist' may be prone to blackspot, a fungal disease that manifests as small black spots on the leaves. At the first sign, remove and destroy any afflicted leaves. Check the stems for spotting. If they are affected, cut them off and destroy them. Clean up around the plant, picking up any dead leaves on the ground. Blackspot is spread by spores when you water the plant from above and by rain. It starts on the lowest branches. When a water droplet hits mature spores, they are hurled to leaves above. Removing all the mulch around an affected plant and replacing it with fresh mulch also helps since spores may have lodged in the mulch. At the first sign of blackspot, or if it has been a problem in the past, spray with baking soda solution as soon as the plant leafs out. Re-spray the entire plant, including tops and bottoms of leaves and canes, every seven to ten days. Do not spray if the temperature is over 80 degrees Fahrenheit. Since this rose does not rebloom, take advantage and cut plenty of flowers to enjoy indoors.

Companion Planting and Design

'Alchymist' is beautiful sharing the same trellis with 'Goldflame' honeysuckle (*Lonicera* × *heckrotti*).

I Also Recommend

'Buff Beauty' (6 feet) is a hybrid musk shrub rose with slightly paler blooms in midseason.

Bonica Rose

Rosa 'Bonica'

When, Where, and How to Plant

'Bonica' is readily available as an own-root, container-grown plant at nurseries, garden centers, and home stores. You can also purchase bare-root plants through mail-order nurseries. Follow detailed planting directions starting on page 226. This tough plant can be put in the ground before the last frost date as long as the ground is workable, the soil is not too wet, *and* the plant is dormant. If it has already leafed out, keep it in a cool, bright place until danger of frost has passed, and then plant it. Otherwise, the tender leaves and buds could freeze. Whether it's container-grown or bare root, be sure to water at planting with transplant solution.

Growing Tips

Keep the soil lightly moist until the plant is established. A thick layer of mulch helps retain moisture and prevents weeds. Unless it is very hot and dry, weekly watering will suffice.

Care and Maintenance

This rose is very care-free since it is not bothered by pests or diseases. Cut the faded blooms to encourage rebloom (I wait for the last in the cluster to finish blooming). Always cut at a 45-degree angle just above an outward-facing leaflet that has 5-to-7 leaves. This makes the new growth develop outward from the shrub, rather than crowding the center. After the 15th of August, do not cut back the faded flowers. Let them develop into the bright orange fruit (rose hips) that will attract birds and other creatures. You can cut the hips and use them in fresh or dried flower arrangements.

Companion Planting and Design

'Bonica' is beautiful paired with the airy blue spikes of Russian sage (*Perovskia atriplicifolia*). Planted in front of tall ornamental grasses, it adds color and softens their strongly vertical lines.

I Also Recommend

'Cecile Brunner', which is the true 'Sweetheart Rose', is also an excellent shrub rose, although it may need winter protection in the colder regions. Unlike 'Bonica', its flowers are lightly fragrant. Flowers are a paler pink than 'Bonica'. It is disease resistant.

'Bonica' is a shrub rose developed by the famous house of Meilland in France in 1982. In 1987, it became the first shrub rose ever to be named an All-America Rose Selection. It rightly deserves that and the other prestigious honors that have been bestowed on it. It is a care-free rose, being very disease resistant. The 1- to 2-inch-wide, double flowers (with more than forty petals) are in rosette form, borne in clusters. The blooms are medium pink, fading to a lighter pink at the slightly frilled edges. The canes are strongly arched, and flowers are produced along their length throughout much of the summer. It is a good repeat bloomer. The glossy leaves are handsome—an unusually coppery light green. Perfect for small gardens, but note that it has no fragrance.

Bloom Period and Seasonal Color
Medium pink in summer.

Mature Height and Spread
3 to 5 ft. × 2 to 4 ft.

Zone
4

Carefree Beauty Rose

Rosa 'Carefree Beauty'

'Carefree Beauty' is one of the most popular Buck roses, with long, pointed buds that open to slightly cupped medium pink flowers averaging five inches across with a pleasant fragrance. Edible spherical orange hips follow the flowers. The vigorous plant is bushy, well clothed with large, leathery dark green foliage. No book that includes roses for the Prairie Lands states could be complete without highlighting the super-hardy landscape roses developed by Iowa State University rose hybridizer Dr. Griffith Buck. Working with all sorts of parent roses, including hardy antiques and modern hybrids, he carefully crossbred for beauty and sturdiness. From over 80 of his best constant-blooming shrubs, dozens of "own root" (not grafted) cultivars have proven themselves to be solid performers, year in and year out, and are becoming more popular for gardeners with every season that passes.

Bloom Period and Seasonal Color
Shades of pink from late spring to fall.

Mature Height and Spread
2 to 6 ft. × 3 to 4 ft.

When, Where, and How to Plant
Plant Buck roses in at least half a day of sun, in a wide hole dug into well-drained soil slightly amended with organic matter (just enough to get roots started). Fertilize lightly at planting time, and encourage important deep root growth by watering deeply only every two or three weeks. Mulch to help control weeds and to prevent soil from crusting and compacting in the sun and rain.

Growing Tips
Foliar feed in spring and mid-summer, and water deeply as needed to keep plants from drying out in the sun and wind. Overwatering can lead to problems. It is best to water in the morning, or late enough in the afternoon for foliage to dry by dusk. 'Carefree Beauty' has very little black spot or powdery mildew (the two most common rose diseases).

Care and Maintenance
Prune ever-blooming Buck roses only if they get too large, by shearing the previous year's growth by about one third. Water deeply right before the winter's first hard freeze, and mulch to reduce the freeze/thaw cycle that can damage roots when there is little snow cover.

Companion Planting and Design
Shrub roses can be used wherever a small ever-blooming shrub is required, including in perennial borders, small hedges, or even mass-planted as a bedding plant.

I Also Recommend
Great selections of Buck roses include 'Apple Jack', 'Pearlie Mae', 'Prairie Flower', 'Prairie Harvest', and 'Winter Sunset'. These and most of the others can be seen at Reiman Gardens, located just south of the ISU football stadium in Ames, Iowa. Many are widely available through hardy rose nurseries—locally or through mailorder sources.

David Austin™ Rose

Rosa 'Heritage'

When, Where, and How to Plant

A site with light mid-afternoon shade helps thick-flowering roses retain their fresh look longer. Plant David Austin™ roses in at least half-day sun, in a wide hole amended well with organic matter. Follow planting instructions starting on page 226. Fertilize lightly at planting time, and encourage fast, deep root growth by watering deeply only every two or three weeks (do not over water!). Mulch to help control weeds and prevent soil from crusting and compacting in the sun and rain.

Growing Tips

Fertilize lightly in spring and mid-summer, and water deeply as needed to keep plants from drying out in the sun and wind. Water deeply right before the winter's first hard freeze.

Care and Maintenance

Mulch to reduce the freeze/thaw cycle that can damage roots when there is little snow cover. Prune ever-blooming shrub roses if they get too large by shearing the previous year's growth by about one third. Insect and disease problems are usually not serious enough to warrant routine spraying. Problems increase if the shrubs are watered too often. Water in the morning, or late enough in the afternoon for foliage to dry by dusk. For fungal problems, try baking soda spray (see page 233).

Companion Planting and Design

Some English roses tend to grow more like hybrid teas than old garden roses, which is why Austin suggests grouping two or three plants on 18-inch centers for the full old rose bush look. Use them as specimens, in the back of perennial borders, or as a thorny hedge. I am delighted by my favorite, 'Heritage', if only because the petals have a delightful lemon fragrance. It's a vigorous rose with infolding, double, cupped, $4^{1}/_{2}$-inch blooms that are set off by its dark green leaves.

I Also Recommend

The hardiest David Austin™ roses include 'Gertrude Jekyll', 'Mary Rose', 'Winchester Cathedral', 'Graham Thomas', and 'Windrush.' These and others are widely available through hardy rose nurseries and mailorder sites.

More than a decade ago, when English rosarian David Austin began introducing new hybrid shrub roses, he started a trend that has led to incredible choices for gardeners. He combined the romantic shape, fragrance, hardiness and disease resistance of "old garden" roses with the everblooming and cut-flower qualities of modern roses. There are now quite a few such roses from other breeders, but Austin claims the cachet of being the first to successfully give us the best of both the old and the new. While most of his roses perform best from Zone 5 and farther south, quite a few, especially the 'Heritage' strains, do well in our hot summers and tolerate, with good siting and some protection, our cold winters. And, they smell—and taste—so good!

Bloom Period and Seasonal Color

Light pink from late spring through summer.

Mature Height and Spread

3 to 4 ft. × 3 to 4 ft.

Zone

5

Flower Carpet® Red Rose

Rosa 'Flower Carpet® Red'

I was given five specimens of Flower Carpet® Red for trial in my garden a year before they came on the market in 1990 Carpet®. The catalog copy made it sound like it was a revolutionary new type of rose, and as a landscape or groundcover rose, indeed it was. When it was first marketed, you couldn't miss its bright pink pots. I planted it in full sun, part shade, clay soil, sandy soil, and good garden soil. It performed beautifully in every place I tried it. From a plant 6- to 8-inches across, it grew almost like an octopus—sprawling in one area at least 8 feet. A profusion of bright 3-inch, double red flowers adorned shiny green leaves all summer long. Best of all, I discovered it tasted delicious.

Bloom Period and Seasonal Color
Deep pink from summer through fall.

Mature Height and Spread
18 to 24 in. × 4 to 6 ft.

Zone
5

When, Where, and How to Plant
Flower Carpet® Red was first introduced in signature hot pink pots with growing directions and a packet of slow-release fertilizer attached. Follow the directions on your plant's instruction tag. Basically, all you need to do is dig a hole the size of the pot, remove the rose from the pot, put it in the ground, water it, and let it grow. I mulched it (I hate to weed). However, this was unnecessary, as it grows thick enough to keep any weeds from sprouting. My roses were established and growing in no time.

Growing Tips
When you purchase the plant, the slow-release fertilizer is already mixed in the soil; the fertilizer packet is for the following season. Watering every seven to ten days is usually ample.

Care and Maintenance
Flower Carpet® Red is a self-cleaning rose. When the flowers finish blooming, the petals drop by themselves. Prune it, if necessary, to keep it within bounds. If you're in Zone 5, mulch in winter. Remove the mulch in spring. In early spring, prune it back to half its size.

Companion Planting and Design
Flower Carpet® Red is ideal for patio pots, borders, and walkways where a blast of color brightens the landscape. It is beautiful as a groundcover under a tree and can protect the tree by keeping pets and children away.

I Also Recommend
Flower Carpet® White (to 30 in. × 36 in.) is another award winner, including the 'Golden Rose of The Hague', which is highly coveted in the world of roses. Flower Carpet® Pink (to 30 in.) is an almost iridescent rose pink, and is lightly fragrant. Flower Carpet® Coral has clusters of single coral- pink flowers and is lightly fragrant. Flower Carpet® Apple Blossom (to 30 in.) yields an abundance of soft pastel pink, small, cup-shaped flowers that show off against shiny green leaves; it is lightly fragrant. Flower Carpet®Yellow (to 30 in.) has bright yellow, small, cup-shaped flowers blooming in abundance on a tidy, groundcover plant.

Harison's Yellow Rose

Rosa × harisonii 'Harison's Yellow'

When, Where, and How to Plant

This rose is most often found through a mail-order nursery or on the Internet. It has several distinguishing characteristics that make it appealing. It will grow in sandy soil, rocky soil, clayey soil, and even good garden soil. An added bonus is that it will grow in full sun or partial shade—a rare characteristic for a rose. It's no surprise settlers in the mid-1800s brought it west with them; some are still growing today where they planted it. Plant it as soon as you get it, as long as the ground can be worked. Follow planting instructions starting on page 226. It is such an early bloomer that it may not bloom until the next year since it may have already bloomed at the grower's facility. Water it well. Mulch with 3 to 4 inches of wood chips.

Growing Tip

This is a tough plant and quite drought tolerant. However, in the heat of summer, when there is no rain, water once every ten to fourteen days. As an alternative to monthly foliar feeding, lay an inch of compost around the base of the plant in spring. It will decompose and slowly feed the soil, which feeds the plant.

Care and Maintenance

Its bloom season is early and short. Take advantage by cutting some of the deep yellow, 2- to 2¹/₂-inch blooms to perfume the indoors. Be careful, as it is quite a thorny plant.

Companion Planting and Design

'Harison's Yellow' has an arching shape, good for the back of a border. After flowering, the thorny, dark mahogany brown canes add interest when espaliered against a light-colored wall. Emphasize its tenacity with dandelions around its base (*Taraxicum ruderalia* 'Catalogna Special' has tasty greens). Follow the yellow theme with the shrubby Japanese rose (*Kerria japonica*).

I Also Recommend

'Golden Showers' (Zone 5) is a slightly later blooming, lovely, bright yellow, large-flowered climbing rose.

'Harison's Yellow Rose' was thought to be from Texas, as it is known there as 'The Yellow Rose of Texas'. Research by Stephen Scaniello, former rose curator at the Brooklyn Botanic Garden, discovered that it was first found—and named—growing on George F. Harison's farm in Manhattan in the 1830s. It was such a tough rose (hardy from Zones 2 through 9), that settlers took it with them as they moved west. It can be found still growing on abandoned homesteads. The infatuation with this rose is not for its looks—it is rather gangly. However, it is the first rose to bloom, often in spring at the same time as lilacs or peonies. It's very fragrant and is a brilliant yellow that is a portent of the upcoming summer.

Other Common Name

The Yellow Rose of Texas

Bloom Period and Seasonal Color

Bright yellow in late spring.

Mature Height and Spread

5 to 7 ft. × 5 to 7 ft.

Zone

4

Queen Elizabeth Rose

Rosa 'Queen Elizabeth'

For many years hybrid tea roses reigned supreme with their long stems, high centers, and beautiful flowers. Try growing them in our region, and you often find yourself growing the equivalent of high-priced annuals. In the 1920s, breeders in northern Europe developed a new class—floribunda—with clusters of smaller, harder blooms. Hybridizing continued, crossing floribunda with hybrid teas in the expectation of getting the best qualities from both kinds. 'Queen Elizabeth', introduced in 1953, was the first grandiflora. Although not as hardy as was hoped, they are hardier than hybrid teas with large, high-centered (often fragrant) blooms in clusters. Regal, pink Queen Elizabeth' is still one of the best-selling roses today. Ironically, the British never accepted grandiflora as a class, although they grow the queen.

Bloom Period and Seasonal Color
Pink in early summer

Mature height and spread
4 to 6 ft. × 5 to 7 ft.

Zone
5

When, Where, and How to Plant
'Queen Elizabeth' is so popular, you will find this marvelous grandiflora rose everywhere, including mail-order nurseries. Buy and plant a bare-root in early spring when the ground can be worked or purchase a container-grown, self-root plant in late spring. Avoid plants with waxed stems—the spring sun may not be hot enough to melt the wax, so the plant may not come out of dormancy properly. Avoid container-grown plants already in bloom and those in cardboard "self-plant" boxes. (Follow planting instructions on p. 226).

Growing Tips
Keep the plant evenly moist until it is established. Then water weekly or as needed according to rain. Foliar feed monthly early in the day with a solution of kelp or fish emulsion (following package directions).

Care and Maintenance
For a bare-root plant, remove the extra soil above ground level when the plant begins to show the first signs of leaves and buds. Add a 3-inch layer of organic mulch around the plant, keeping the mulch at least an inch away from the stem. However, if there is a threat of a freeze after the soil has been removed and the plant is still relatively tender, cover it with row cover or a light blanket for the night. Remember to remove the covering the next day—midmorning is ideal—as you don't want to overheat the plant during the day.

Companion Planting and Design
'Queen Elizabeth' is lovely used in a grouping to set off a piece of garden art, sculpture, an armillary, or even a birdbath. It looks spectacular planted with lavender (*Lavandula* 'Lady' or other cultivars).

I Also Recommend
The unique 'White Lightnin' (to $4^1/2$ ft.) has a delightful citrus fragrance, and double, 4-inch, white flowers tipped with a hint of pink on gently scalloped petals; it's borne in clusters, and is disease resistant and hardy. 'Shining Hour' (to $4^1/2$ ft.) is highly floriferous with classic hybrid tea form; it keeps blooming and has vivid yellow double flowers that are "lit" from within. It is disease resistant and hardy.

Redleaf Rose

Rosa glauca

When, Where, and How to Plant

You might find redleaf rose as a container-grown plant at a local nursery or garden center. Otherwise, mail-order nurseries carry bare-root plants. Choosing the right place for this plant is critical-it is not like your typical garden hybrid tea or floribunda rose. Treat it like a specimen plant, giving it a special place to be viewed and admired from all sides. Its size—with branches arching to 8 feet—would look out of place in a typical rose garden with 4- or 5-foot plants. Give it room to expand. Unless you are trying to make a hedge, one redleaf rose (or two in a mixed bed or border) is ample. Plant it as soon as you get it (see planting instructions on page 226). Plant bare-root specimens as soon as the soil can be worked.

Growing Tips

Keep redleaf rose well watered until it is established. Unless it is very hot and dry, water once a week. Although I foliar feed most plants, redleaf rose's leaves are one of its highlights, so I do not want to risk discoloring them. Instead, I water every three weeks with compost tea.

Care and Maintenance

This is one of the most care-free roses I have ever grown. The only reason I prune is to keep the shape balanced, which it usually does by itself. You can prune it partway back to encourage a more bushy form; however, its canes were not meant to stand upright. So, unless you can enjoy a lush, lax rose with interesting, colored leaves and stems, stick with the regular garden roses.

Companion Planting and Design

Rosa glauca is lovely with dainty early spring bulbs such as snow crocus (*Crocus tommasinianus, Crocus chrysanthus*), Dutch crocus (*Crocus vernus*), snowdrops (*Galanthus nivalis*), and glory-of-the-snow (*Chionodoxa luciliae*). In fall, autumn crocus (*Colchicum autumnale*) adds a colorful accent at ground level. All of these recommended bulbs highlight the color of the canes and leaves.

I Also Recommend

Plant only the species.

Rosa glauca, *formerly Rosa rubrifolia, is extremely hardy (Zone 2). Both names refer to its coloration of arching, reddish-green, long (up to 14 feet) stems and grayish-purple leaflets (five to nine per leaf). This is one of the few roses not grown for its flowers, although when the clusters of flat, 1 1/2-inch, bright pink flowers bloom in late spring or early summer they are a delight. However, they are fragile and fleeting, with the petals easily blown off during a rainstorm or high winds. Just let the plant do its own thing, and by late summer to early fall, you will be rewarded with a plethora of spherical reddish-orange hips (the fruit). An added bonus is the creatures it attracts.*

Bloom Period and Seasonal Color

Pink blooms in early summer.

Mature Height and Spread

4 to 8 ft. × 4 to 6 ft.

Zone

2

Rugosa Rose
Rosa rugosa

The rugosa rose is lovely and versatile. When I was growing up on Long Island, where it grew wild on many of the beaches, I assumed it was native. However, rugosa came here from Japan. First and foremost, rugosa is the best-tasting of roses, excellent for ice cream, sauces, jellies, or just munching as you work in the garden. The flowers of the species are single; some of the hybrids are double. All are delightfully fragrant. Left on the plant, they will become terrific, large orange-red rose hips in fall. If you do not pick them for jelly making, the hips attract wildlife. The botanical name refers to the winsome wrinkled leaves. The thorny canes act as a good barrier hedge.

Other Common Names
Japanese Rose, Beach Rose

Bloom Period and Seasonal Color
Pink, deep reddish-purple, white, or yellow in early summer and fall.

Mature Height and Spread
3 to 8 ft. × 2 to 6 ft.

Zone
2

When, Where, and How to Plant
Rugosa roses—all species and hybrids—are readily available at nurseries, garden centers, home stores, and through mail-order nurseries. Tough (hardy from Zones 2 through 9) and easy to grow, it is tolerant of most soil types, although it will thrive in rich, lightly moist, well-drained soil and full sun. Usually sold as a container-grown "own-root" plant, you can plant it as soon as the soil can be worked in spring. Water at planting with transplant solution. See page 226 for more planting instructions.

Growing Tips
After transplanting, water deeply every seven to ten days. Once, in the heat of summer, one of my rugosas slowly turned brown, appearing dead. I watered and foliar fed it, and cut down one-third of the branches. Within two weeks, there was new growth; soon it was full of blossoms. Because I eat the flowers, I normally do not foliar feed. Instead, in early spring, I put a 2-inch layer of compost around the plant, water it, and cover it with 3 inches of mulch.

Care and Maintenance
Pruning is only necessary to maintain shape or height. Prune in early spring just as the buds appear. Prune at a downward 45-degree angle just above an outfacing bud to keep the plant open and airy.

Companion Planting and Design
Rugosa roses, especially the pink and red varieties, are lovely with blue flowers such as summer-blooming willow blue star (*Amsonia tabernaemontana*), Russian sage (*Perovskia atriplicifolia*), or late summer-flowering bluebeard (*Caryopteris* × *clandonensis* 'Blue Mist'). With its extremely thorny canes, rugosa rose makes a great barrier and hedge which few animals (or children) can get through.

I Also Recommend
Rosa rugosa var. *alba* has pale pink buds that open to 3^1/$_2$-inch fragrant white flowers. *Rosa rugosa* var. *rosea* has rose-pink blooms, and *Rosa rugosa* var. *rubra* yields purplish-red blossoms. 'F. J. Grootendorst' (or 'Grootendorst') sports ruffled, deep red, double flowers. 'Hansa' has reddish-purple flowers with an intensely spicy scent. 'Sarah Van Fleet' has semi-double pink blossoms.

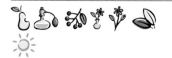

William Baffin Rose

Rosa 'William Baffin'

When, Where, and How to Plant

'William Baffin' may be found in some nurseries or garden centers that specialize in the older, hardy, and well-proven varieties of roses. Otherwise, you can buy it through mail-order nurseries and shop for it on the Internet. As hardy as it is, it should be "own-stock" and not a grafted rose. Plant it as soon as you get it, whether container-grown or bare root. If it is bare root, there should not be any rounded bud union on the stem. Plant it so the bottom 2 or 3 inches of the stem is below ground level. Water with transplant solution.

Growing Tips

Keep the soil lightly moist until the rose is established and is sending out new growth, buds, and leaves. If there's no rain, a slow, deep, weekly watering should be adequate. The size of the plant can be daunting for foliar feeding unless you get a diluter spray attachment for your hose that you can set for the proper dilution ratio. Spray the entire plant as you would when using a watering nozzle.

Care and Maintenance

For the northernmost gardeners in the Prairie Lands states, this may be the only repeat-blooming climber available for you. If it were not so hardy, you would not get the bloom since climbers bloom on old wood (the previously year's growth). It is disease and pest resistant. There is no history of it having blackspot, and even mildew is very rare. If Japanese beetles have appeared in your garden, they will head for other, fragrant roses and ignore 'William Baffin'.

Companion Planting and Design

The best-known of the tough Canadian Explorer roses, 'William Baffin' can quickly cover an arbor, trellis, or pillar and thrive year after year with a minimum of fuss. Provide support to best show it off. Grow a purple Jackman clematis (*Clematis x jackmanii*) with it for color contrast.

I Also Recommend

'Prairie Princess' is another disease-resistant, hardy rose, with semi-double, lightly fragrant coral blooms.

'William Baffin' is a vigorous rose that can be treated either as a climber or as a sprawling shrub. It is one of the most cold-hardy shrub roses, with a hardiness range (Zones 2 to 9) equaled by only a few roses, including 'Harison's Yellow'. The deep strawberry-pink blooms are borne in large clusters of up to thirty flowers and cascade down the plant—a very impressive sight. Each semi-double flower is 3- to 4-inches wide with twenty petals. It is a midseason bloomer with excellent repeat bloom, so the more you cut the flowers to bring indoors for arrangements or bouquets, the more flowers the plant will produce. The glossy green leaves are a gorgeous contrast to the flowers. Unfortunately, it has no fragrance.

Bloom Period and Seasonal Color
Deep strawberry pink in summer.

Mature Height and Spread
6 to 9 ft. × 4 to 6 ft.

Shrubs *for the Prairie Lands*

Many people often confuse a tree with a shrub. One of the easiest ways to tell the difference is that many—but not all—shrubs have multiple main stems, while a tree has a single trunk. Another differentiation is size. A shrub is generally less than twenty feet tall, while a tree is over twenty feet. Again, this can be challenging, as many dwarf varieties of trees are quite low—some even are designated as groundcovers. And of course, there is the English yew, which branches down to the ground and that you keep pruned at a height of five feet. No matter, it is still a tree, just artificially constrained to shrub size.

Dwarf Burning Bush

For me, shrubs are the icing on the cake that is the garden. They can accentuate and highlight the other plantings, especially perennials and trees. Shrubs tie the garden together. Usually larger than perennials but smaller than trees; shrubs are the unifying force.

As with trees, there are evergreen and deciduous shrubs. To me, variety is the spice of life and adds life to the garden, so include both types. When choosing a deciduous shrub, it is a bonus if it has an interesting or unique architectural form that will draw the eye in winter when there is less to see in a garden or landscape. One of my favorite plants, Harry Lauder's walking stick, has such marvelous twisted branches that it looks better

Red Twig Dogwood

in winter than in summer when the interesting branches are hidden by leaves.

Choosing Your Shrubs

It's all a matter of the right plant for the right place. One of the main uses of shrubs is as foundation plants, which are grown around the house, especially the front, to hide the foundation and make the house look more inviting. Find out what the mature height of the plant is (spread as well, although not as important), especially for shrubs in front of windows. You don't want something that is going to grow eighteen feet in front of a picture or bay window, unless for some reason you are trying to obscure the view. A plant like that would require constant pruning to keep it in bounds. First and foremost, that's a lot of work for you. I prefer a landscape I can plant and enjoy, other than the routine maintenance of feeding, watering, or pruning dead or broken limbs. Secondly, such a plant would need pruning constantly. English yews, which naturally grow into 40-foot-high plants, require cutting off new growth. In addition, with other yews, if you cut back the old growth, they often don't fill back in.

Another important consideration for foundation plantings is soil pH. Why should that be more important for a foundation planting than any other garden area? Because the foundations of most houses are concrete. Over the years, some of the lime from the concrete leaches out into the soil, making it alkaline. A serious consideration in much of the Prairie Lands regions is that the soil is already alkaline. It is important to have to soil near the foundation tested for pH. You can get a soil sample and take it to your local Cooperative Extension Service or local nursery where, usually for a small fee, they can test the pH. Alternatively, you can buy an inexpensive pH test kit. You can even use old-fashioned litmus paper (remember that from high school chemistry? It turns red or pink in the presence of acid and blue when the soil is basic or alkaline.) You can find litmus paper that is more specific—within several points of 7.0, which is neutral. Check out a pool supply store, as they often stock it.

If your soil is already alkaline, the leaching of lime can take it over the limit, putting the pH higher than 9, and making the choice of plants limited, if not nearly impossible. You can add organic matter mixed with fine peat moss to lower the pH, making it less alkaline. Between a pH of 7 and 8.5, there is a good choice of foundation plants. However, it certainly doesn't make sense to try and grow a plant such as a rhododendron or azalea, which thrives in a pH closer to 5. You would have to constantly monitor and amend the soil.

Like any other plant, the choices are almost limitless—except for the hardiness limitations. Walk around your neighborhood, drive around your city, and you will spot plants that appeal to you. Don't hesitate to ring the bell and ask the homeowner what a plant is, or if you are shy, leave a note in the mailbox. Visit a local public garden, arboretum, or botanic garden to see some great choice of shrubs that are right for your area. Remember that one of the best sources of information is your local Cooperative Extension Service. They often have printed lists or booklets of the best shrubs for your region. Take their advice; they have plenty of knowledge backing them up.

Most of the shrubs in this chapter are available at garden centers, nurseries, and home stores.

Planting

Planting a shrub is very similar to planting a tree in the trees chapter, except the overall size of the planting hole is smaller and shrubs are usually smaller. Turn to page 189 for explicit directions on planting bare-root, container-grown, and balled-and-burlapped plants. (Balled and burlapped types are rare in shrubs, but are still found with some larger ones).

Shrubs for Difficult Sites

Weigela

Dry Areas:

Fothergilla (*Fothergilla major*)—Zone 5; lovely bottlebrush-like white flower in late spring.

Shrubby cinquefoil (*Potentilla fruticosa*)—Zone 3; long blooming from late spring.

Fragrant sumac (*Rhus aromatica*) and staghorn sumac (*Rhus typhina*)—both Zone 4; tough plants for many places. Great fall color and long-lasting large clusters of small reddish-brown fruit.

Shade:

Fothergilla—see above.

Oakleaf hydrangea (*Hydrangea quercifolia*)— Zone 5; long-lasting white flowers; outstanding fall colors of red to purple; leaves resemble oak leaves.

Hydrangea

Mountain pieris or fetterbush (*Pieris floribunda*)—Zone 5; broadleaved evergreen with clusters of flowers in spring that resemble lily-of-the-valley; needs acid soil. Mapleleaf viburnum (*Viburnum acerifolium*)—Zone 3; good woodland plant for year-round interest; white flowers, black fruit, rosy fall foliage.

All-Around Good Shrubs

Shadbush (*Amelanchier canadensis*)—Zone 3; white blooms in spring; edible fruit; reddish fall foliage; grows well in moist soil. Siberian pea tree (*Caragana arborescens*)—Zone 2; showy yellow blooms; good for hedges or windbreaks. Sweet pepperbush (*Clethra alnifolia*)—Zone 3; fragrant white blooms in mid to late summer; yellow fall foliage; requires evenly moist-well-drained soil as it cannot tolerate drought. Spicebush (*Lindera benzoin*)—Zone 4; small yellow blooms in early spring; dioecious; fragrant leaves; red fruit on female plants; yellow fall foliage. Nanking cherry (*Prunus tomentosa*)—Zone 3; fragrant white flowers in spring; edible red cherries; handsome shiny bark.

American Cranberrybush
Viburnum trilobum

American cranberrybush produces rounded, maple-like, 3-lobed, dark green leaves, 5 inches or longer, which are bronze when young and turn yellow to red in the autumn. In late spring, through early summer, lacecap-like heads are produced, each up to 4 inches across and made of tiny tubular, white flowers surrounded by showy, flat, white sterile florets up to 3/4-inch across. The flowers are followed by tartly edible, round red fruit which are nearly half an inch across and that ripen, depending on cultivar, from late August to October. By choosing three different cultivars of this native American shrub, you can extend your fruit harvest season by weeks. Be careful not to confuse this dry-bog plant with its swamp-growing cousin the lowbush cranberry (Vaccinium macrocarpum).

Bloom Period and Seasonal Color
White in mid to late spring

Mature Height and Spread
15 ft. × 12 ft.

When, Where, and How to Plant
This moisture-loving plant prefers well-drained, moist soil in sun or part shade. Work the soil up with generous amounts of organic matter and be prepared to water young plants through their first summer.

Growing Tips
Foliar feed or fertilize in the spring. Water deeply when the plant begins to get really dry.

Care
Mulch to conserve moisture. Prune to thin wayward stems, or to rejuvenate overgrown plants. There are no major pests on this native tree, but water stress—too much or too little—during extreme drought can cause fruit drop and leaf tip burning.

Companion Planting and Design
Use this small flowering tree in hedges, barriers, or borders, as a background (better to enjoy the gray-brown, waxy winter bark), or as an accent. Plant it where you can reach the fruit! The tree is a good addition to the wildlife garden. Birds ignore the berries until after frost, when they sweeten up considerably. Underplant with groundcovers or shade perennials that can tolerate the watering needed by this fruiting shrub.

I Also Recommend
Cultivars include the dense, broad 'Alfredo', only 5 to 6 feet tall with brilliant red autumn foliage color. 'Andrews' produces fruit very early in its season. 'Hahs' fruit ripens in mid season, and 'Wentworth' has rich red autumn leaf color and produces yellow-red fruit that ripens to bright red. 'Compactum' is perhaps the most common form of the species; this selection is a handsome compact plant that reaches 6 feet tall with upright spreading branches. The plant flowers and fruits well, but the fall color can be a poor yellow instead of the brilliant red of other varieties. 'Bailey Compact' is one of several dwarf forms that are offered in the trade, getting to 6 feet tall with red fall foliage and a good fruit set.

Annabelle Hydrangea
Hydrangea arborescens 'Annabelle'

When, Where, and How to Plant
Whether planted in sun or shade, start with a well-prepared bed. Mix the native soil with generous amounts of organic matter in a planting hole that is much wider than deep. Water newly-set out plants deeply as needed, just often enough to keep young plants from staying wilted, and feed lightly at planting time to get them started.

Growing Tips
Initially water deeply as needed, especially in sunny locations. Feed lightly to keep foliage green. Light fertilization and only occasional deep soakings are all that the shrub will need later. Gardeners who say they have to water all the time usually did not do a good job of soil preparation, or they over-prepared by adding too much organic matter.

Care and Maintenance
Thick leaf mulch will keep roots cool and moist. Stake flowers if they flop. Insect pests are unheard of. Although leafspot may be a problem during exceptionally wet springs and summer, no control is recommended.

Companion Planting and Design
Grow 'Annabelle' as a low hedge. It's great in a mixed flower border to bridge the season between spring flowering shrubs and summer; astilbe, columbine, and other fine-textured late spring and early summer perennials are livened up with the bold flowers and coarse foliage of this small but flower-packed shrub. Daffodils can also be underplanted for spring interest, as long as the bed they share does not get watered so much in the summer that it rots the dormant bulbs.

I Also Recommend
Smooth hydrangea 'Grandiflora' has smaller flowerheads than 'Annabelle' but has larger sterile flowers, making it somewhat showier. Pee Gee hydrangea (*Hydrangea paniculata* 'Grandiflora') is a tall shrub with showy white flower clusters in the summer that turn pink and dry on the plant—making a fine show through winter.

Annabelle hydrangea, named after the town of Anna, Illinois where it was discovered, is one of the most stunning showstoppers in the early summer garden. The small shrubs have large, deep green leaves that serve as platters for foot-wide piles of mashed potato-white flowers so overloaded they often bend over under their own weight, and may need staking. 'Annabelle' accepts almost any soil type, even moderately alkaline, and makes a spectacular show after very cold winters because it blooms on new growth even if cut to the ground. In fact, pruning close to the ground in winter increases the flower size. Flower heads dry beautifully on the plant and they can be used in cut or dried flower arrangements. Try spray-painting them for a fun holiday effect.

Other Common Name
Smooth Hydrangea

Bloom Period and Seasonal Color
Large white flowers from June through August

Mature Height and Spread
3 to 5 ft. × 4 to 5 ft.

Bridalwreath Spirea

Spiraea × vanhouttei

Spiraea smells "dusty" to me—not a bad dusty—it reminds me of old houses and gardens, which is good. Van Houtte spirea, the latest blooming bridalwreath (Spiraea prunifolia is also called bridalwreath), has long been recognized as one of the toughest shrubs. An 1888 garden catalog proclaimed it "the most showy of all the spiraeas, and one of the very best shrubs in cultivation." It was also inexpensive. A 1930's mail-order company offered a dozen 18- to 24-inch Van Houtte spireas for 45 cents. The long fingernail-like foliage is a distinctive blue-green, and the white flowers are borne in late spring, in wide, flat-topped clusters that line stems so thickly the entire shrub appears arched toward the earth.

Other Common Name
Van Houtte Spirea

Bloom Period and Seasonal Color
White in late spring

Mature Height and Spread
6 to 8 ft. × 5 to 8 ft.

When, Where, and How to Plant
Like all spireas, bridalwreath is ironclad, and will grow in nearly any soil, sun or shade, as long as it does not stand in water or go months without moisture. Dig a wide hole, loosen pot bound roots of nursery-grown shrubs, then water enough during the first summer to get the plant established. No fertilizer is needed their first season. Summer cuttings root quite easily and can be planted the same fall or the next spring.

Growing Tips
Water during prolonged drought. Fertilize lightly every 2 to 3 years.

Care and Maintenance
Established plants rarely need any care, (spireas often survive for decades in cemeteries), however, watering deeply during prolonged hot spells can prevent leaf burn. Because heavy snow may break branches, and older plants can get leggy, prune up to $1/3$ of old stems every year or two, close to the ground after flowering. This will stimulate new arching branches. Iron chlorosis and rabbits can be problems, as can foliage diseases in very wet seasons.

Companion Planting and Design
Bridelwreath spirea tolerates de-icing salt, grows rapidly and may be used as a hedge or screen. It is bold enough to stand alone as a specimen along the foundation of an older home. Use it to provide a backdrop to spring and summer bulbs, perennials, and smaller shrubs like Annabelle hydrangea (*Hydrangea arborescens* 'Annabelle').

I Also Recommend
Cultivars include 'Pink Ice' with variegated pink foliage on 4-foot plants. 'Renaissance' is an improved selection with more resistance to almost-rare foliage diseases. Other spireas are nearly as tough, including many white-flowering species, but I really love the unique summer-blooming, pinkish-red-flowered *Spiraea japonica* 'Anthony Waterer'. Other *S. japonica* cultivars include white 'Alba', light pink 'Alpina', 'Bumalda' with bronze foliage and deep pink flowers. 'Goldmound' has contrasting yellow leaves and pink flowers. 'Limemound' bears lime green leaves that turn orange-red in autumn.

Burkwood Viburnum

Viburnum x burkwoodii

When, Where, and How to Plant

This tough shrub grows best in moderately fertile, slightly acidic soil in full sun, although part shade is preferred in areas with long, hot summers. Dig a wide hole and add peat moss to acidify the backfill soil. Water deeply. Fruit production is heaviest if two different cultivars are planted near one another for cross-pollination.

Growing Tips

Keep lightly moist until established. Overwatering can invite root rot. Fresh organic mulch each spring will feed the plant.

Care and Maintenance

Mulch plants to keep roots cool and moist. There are no major pest problems under normal growing conditions, although powdery mildew, leaf spots, and a little twig die back may appear some years. Burkwood viburnum is also susceptible to aphids, scale, and Japanese beetles.

Companion Planting and Design

This upright, fully branched shrub can be used as an accent plant, hedge, screen, or in a mixed shrub border or woodland garden. Wherever you plant it, you can be assured it will attract all sorts of good wildlife. Birds often nest in it in the summer, close to its ripening berries. It is tall enough to be used for good effect against an arbor where its long twigs make it look almost like a climber. Tie, prune, or train it as an espalier against a sunny wall or on a trellis.

I Also Recommend

Cultivars of Burkwood viburnum include the more compact, dense 'Chenault' which is also slightly later blooming. It has bronze foliage earlier in the fall. 'Mohawk' gets a little larger than the species, has very showy red buds long before the white flowers appear, and bright orange-red fall color. In addition it is resistant to some of the leaf spot diseases that sometimes plague viburnums. 'Anne Russell' is a compact cultivar with very fragrant flowers. Many other species of under-used viburnums are available and desirable for their flowers, foliage, and berries.

When a Burkwood viburnum is added to a landscape, everyone will notice. Its rounded form, tough foliage, fragrant flowers, bird-attracting berries, and intense fall colors turn heads in every season. Burkwood is a medium-size shrub with glossy, dark green leaves that have white, fuzzy undersides. The foliage turns orange-red in autumn before shedding to reveal birds' nests left over from the summer. The 4-inch wide, domed clusters of pink florets slowly open into eye-catching white, tubular flowers, each with five petals and showy yellow stamens. Burkwood fragrance is often described as gardenia-like—a welcome spring event. Flattened red summer berries gradually ripen into blue-black fruit valued by birds. Plant guru and author Michael Dirr sums it up, saying this shrub "asks little, gives much."

Bloom Period and Seasonal Color
White in mid-spring

Mature Height and Spread
6 to 10 ft. × 4 to 6 ft.

Burning Bush
Euonymus alata

Few shrubs polarize preening garden designers more quickly than this common Euonymus, which has become one of the most over-planted shrubs beside interstate overpasses. We may dislike its over-use, and the occasional insects or diseases, or how it escapes by seed into our natural woodlands, but gardeners still love it for its extravagent fall show and toughness. The large, bushy, twiggy member of the bittersweet family grows into a shrub ten feet tall or more, and is wide with dull-green summer foliage that turns a searingly brilliant crimson in the fall. Young twigs have corky "wing-like" growths. Small cream-colored flowers in the spring are not showy at all, and birds eat the small fruits before people really even notice they are there.

Other Common Name
Winged Euonymus

Bloom Period and Seasonal Color
Inconspicuous cream colored flowers in summer; vibrant red foliage in fall

Mature Height and Spread
10 to 15 ft. by 8 to 10 ft.

When, Where, and How to Plant
For best fall color, plant burning bush in full sun. Spread out roots of container-grown plants to help get them started out of their "pot" shape, and water only to get young plants through their first summer.

Growing Tips
Feed very lightly every year or two. Soak deeply during extreme drought. Little watering is needed once it is established as it reduces the fall show. Use little fertilizer, as this causes rank growth that either needs pruning or is damaged by hot dry wind and long cold freezes.

Care and Maintenance
The most serious pest to burning bush is powdery mildew, and small, crusty scale insects, which attach to the undersides of leaves and stems and can sometimes completely defoliate the plant. Control scale with heavy pruning to remove infested branches and stimulate sturdy new growth. Apply dormant or summer-weight horticultural oil. Use baking powder solution for powdery mildew (see page 233). *Euonymus* species are all super easy and root quickly from short stem cuttings in the summer or fall.

Companion Planting and Design
Used almost exclusively as a stark specimen or sturdy hedge in a hot, dry spot, or grouped or massed for a spectacular show. This no-care large shrub can be underplanted with any groundcover or summer-dormant bulb that needs little or no summer water.

I Also Recommend
Since the common burning bush is nearly a small tree, try 'Compacta', which turns pinkish red in the fall and still reaches 8- or 10-feet. 'Red Cascade', an 8- to 10-foot cultivar of the European euonymus (*Euonymus europaeus*), has very showy bright red fall fruits.

Butterflybush
Buddleia davidii

When, Where, and How to Plant
With the increasing number of cultivars, you can find butterfly bushes at nurseries, garden centers, and home stores. However, the greatest choice of varieties is through mail-order catalogs. Butterflybush grows best in rich, but not heavy, well-drained soil in full sun. Although tolerant of most soils, it does not like wet feet. It is best in a protected location.

Growing Tips
Butterflybush is fairly drought tolerant once it is established. Water when the top inch of soil is dry, or you see evidence of drooping leaves. Fertilize with a low nitrogen, high phosphate fertilizer, such as 5-10-5, two or three times during the growing season.

Care and Maintenance
This is a plant that unless it is pruned yearly, will be short-lived. Prune back the previous year's wood in late winter to early spring; cut it down almost to the ground and it will regrow—more vigorous and floriferous. Cut back faded flowers to encourage new bloom. There are no major pests or diseases. If you have children or friends who are severely allergic to bees, keep them at a safe distance, as the plant attracts many insects with its nectar.

Companion Planting and Design
A butterflybush makes an excellent specimen plant. Site it where you can enjoy its full benefits. It is also a good plant for a mixed border along with asters (*Aster* spp.) and goldenrod (*Solidago* spp.) for fall interest. Its long branches make it an excellent candidate for espalier—against a wall or trellis, or growing on an arbor or pergola.

I Also Recommend
There is a host of cultivars: 'Black Knight' has very dark purple flowers so the orange eye really stands out. 'Nanho Blue' is a more compact plant with deep blue flowers on gracefully arching stems. 'White Profusion' is a somewhat smaller plant with pure white flowers with yellow eyes. 'Harlequin' has rich purple-red flowers against variegated leaves. 'Pink Spread' bears clear pink flowers, a new Dutch introduction. 'Lochinch' is long blooming with soft lavender-blue flowers.

With the booming interest in wildlife and especially butterfly gardens over the past decade, there has been a boom in sales and introductions of new cultivars of this fragrant, old-time favorite shrub. It is a vigorous plant with slightly arching stems that end in long foxtail clusters of orange-eyed florets. The coarse-textured, lance-shaped leaves are dark green above, soft, and white below. The most common butterflybush is dark purple, but there are many other colored varieties, including hues of white, pink, magenta—all with the distinctive orange eye at the center of each floret. The flowers are fragrant, enhancing the garden from summer to frost. Above all, they attract butterflies by the dozens—and hummingbirds too. The butterfly bush shows nature "in action."

Other Common Names
Orange-eye Butterflybush, Summer Lilac

Bloom Period and Seasonal Color
Purple, white, reddish purple, and pink from summer to fall.

Mature Height × Spread
6 to 10 ft. × 4 to 8 ft.

Zone
5

Dwarf Red Japanese Barberry

Berberis thunbergii atropurpurea

This is not the plain old red Japanese barberry. Sure, there are several interesting cultivars, including 'Aurea' with bright yellow young foliage, tiny yellow barberry-typical flowers, and sometimes-showy red fruit in the fall and winter. What catches my imagination, and designer's eye, is the intense development of this shrub's delightful dwarf cultivars, starting with 'Rosy Glow', that go way beyond the commonly-planted, two-foot 'Nana' or 'Crimson Pygmy' planted in front of every fast-food joint. With this interesting shrub, you can try a new twist on an otherwise familiar, but over-used favorite. I want them all, but like hand-made chocolates stuffed with every filling I could ever imagine, there are just too many new dwarf barberries for this gardener's plate and space.

Bloom Period and Seasonal Color
Yellow in spring, variegated purplish red foliage in fall

Mature Height and Spread
2 to 3 ft. × 2 to 4 ft.

Zone
4

When, Where, and How to Plant
Any well-drained soil in full or part sun will do nicely for barberries. Water deeply to get plants established, but do not keep soggy wet or risk root rot.

Growing Tips
Water when dry. Feed very lightly once in the spring.

Care and Maintenance
Older growth makes the best fall colors, so the less pruning, the better. However, barberry can be selectively thinned. Don't worry about the thorns, which point up and won't snag you like a rose. Put on a good pair of gloves and just snip out a few wayward branches, leaving most untouched, and you will end up with a more relaxed, energetic look than when clipped into a tight box or gumdrop.

Companion Planting and Design
Widely used as specimen shrubs, masses of color, or accents in flower gardens, dwarf barberries have become a mainstay of the garden design world. Their needle-like spines are just stiff enough to help keep peeping neighbors and their pets where they belong.

I Also Recommend
My new favorite, 'Rosy Glow', is burgundy in the spring, but soon turns red-purple flecked with white, like a hastily mixed strawberry milkshake. 'Golden Ring' has very nearly purple leaves narrowly margined with golden yellow, and bears red fruit. 'Dart's Red Lady' is very dark red-purple and turns very bright red in autumn. 'Golden Ring' has reddish purple leaves with a narrow golden margin. 'Roseglow' has rose-pink foliage mottled with pink, purple, and cream. 'Aurea' has yellow foliage and red berries, and grows to only 2 feet tall. 'Helmond Pillar' is upright to 5 feet, only 2 feet wide.

Elderberry

Sambucus canadensis

When, Where, and How to Plant

Elderberry grows and produces best in a moist soil and full sun. When planting nursery-grown cultivars, spread new roots out, and water the fast-growing plant through its first full season.

Growing Tips

Water only during very long dry spells. Fertilization is not necessary.

Care and Maintenance

Keep plants vigorous and within bounds by pruning out older stems at ground level. New canes will quickly replace them. Flowers appear on new growth, so pruning in the winter is acceptable. Berry ripening is affected by long summer drought, so for good berries be prepared to water.

Companion Planting and Design

Elderberry is most easily used as a specimen along a woodland edge or backed up against a wall where its form and flowers can be enjoyed. Or, use it as an accent in a meadow or large wildflower garden.

I Also Recommend

'Adams' is used in wildlife plantings and for culinary use, with berries ripening in early September; 'Scotia' has very high sugar content, and 'Nova' has large, sweet, less astringent berries. 'Laciniata' has lacy, cut leaves, 'Aurea' is a rounded plant with yellow foliage and red fruits, and 'Goldfinch' has leaves both deeply cut and yellow. 'Maxima' is a vigorous cultivar with larger flowers and leaves than the species, and purple flower stalks. There are variegated forms as well. Add ripe elderberries to an apple pie recipe, in a 40/60 elder to apple mix. For a real summer treat, cut an elderberry flower head while in full bloom, remove the florets, and add them into thin pancake batter. Fry in hot oil until light brown, drain and pat dry, sprinkle with powdered sugar and cinnamon.

This prairie native is a large herbaceous shrub with several stems that grow to 10 feet or more in a season. Large leaves have up to eleven narrow leaflets, and each stem is topped in the summer with a large, flat, cluster of small, creamy white, fragrant, edible florets. As berries mature, they turn from reddish to blue to black, and the entire berry cluster will droop downward when it is ripe for harvest. Both its flowers and berries are edible when cooked (elderflower-corn fritters are scrumptious) or made into wine (flowers make a great champagne), but all other parts are toxic. The flowers are a butterfly magnet and birds can strip it of its berries in several days. Grow enough plants to share or net them from the birds.

Other Common Names
American Elder, Sweet Elder

Bloom Period and Seasonal Color
Creamy white in late spring to early summer

Mature Height and Spread
6 to 10 ft. × 5 to 8 ft.

Forsythia

Forsythia × intermedia

Perhaps the most common early spring showstopper around old home places is "golden bells"—an apt descriptive common name for this old-fashioned flowering shrub. Commonly escaped from older gardens to the point where it is considered weedy by some, it can survive where an old homestead has long disappeared. The fountain-shaped deciduous shrub has long, stiff, arching branches arising from a fairly narrow basal clump, with pointed, slender oval leaves up to four inches long produced in pairs. Flowers are inch-long trumpets of lemon to golden yellow, produced in clusters at leaf joints the entire stem length. When in bloom, the entire shrub is an eruption of yellow fireworks. This nearly indestructible shrub also has lovely burgundy fall foliage.

Other Common Name
Golden Bells

Bloom Period and Seasonal Color
Yellow in late winter to early spring

Mature Height and Spread
6 to 10 ft. × 5 to 9 ft.

Zone
5

When, Where, and How to Plant
Forsythia grows in sun or shade, in any kind of soil and in most any place, including abandoned gardens and into the woods. Plant in a wide, loose hole, water two or three times to get new plants established, and move on to other chores. Divide a crowded clump in the fall or winter, or take root cuttings in the late spring or summer.

Growing Tips
Water infrequently if at all once plant is established. Fertilize only sparingly

Care and Maintenance
Few gardeners expect the shrub to get as large as it will. Luckily, forsythia can be pruned by thinning old canes close to the ground or cutting the entire shrub to a few inches tall to force strong, arching, new growth to shoot up over the summer and fall. To rejuvenate an overgrown or unsightly forsythia while achieving the fullest fountain effect, prune a third of the old stems to the ground every year for three years; your patience will be rewarded. Try to avoid tight pruning. Allow it to shoot out into in its natural arching form.

Companion Planting and Design
Forsythia is an excellent specimen plant. It fits in well with conifers and spring-flowering shrubs, including *Spiraea*, *Weigela*, and lilac (*Syringa vulgaris*). It makes a good backdrop to a flower border. It is awesome when massed and makes a great hedge. Cut its long stems while in bud and place in a tall container of water for forcing in mid-winter. Alternatively, wait until it blooms for dramatic indoor flower arrangements.

I Also Recommend
'Lynwood' or 'Lynwood Gold'—the most common variety at garden centers). 'Fiesta' grows less than five feet tall with deep-yellow flowers followed by green and yellow variegated leaves that last all summer. 'Spring Glory' bears pale-yellow flowers. 'Gold Tide' spreads rapidly by suckers, grows only two feet tall. 'Primulina' has pale yellow flowers and foliage that turns mahogany in the fall. 'Karl Sax' has deep yellow flowers and red or purple fall foliage.

Laceleaf Staghorn Sumac

Rhus typhina

When, Where, and How to Plant

Sumacs require super well-drained soils, and have best fall colors when grown in full sun and poor, well-drained soil. Follow planting instructions on page 189. Plants also do well in large containers or raised beds, as long as the soil is not too rich.

Growing Tips

No fertilizer is needed. Only minimal watering should be done to get plants established.

Care and Maintenance

No major insect or disease problems affect this plant. The sumac's problem is gardeners who water and fertilize too much, causing it to lose its fantastic fall colors.

Companion Planting and Design

Because of its round-topped colony-forming habit, sumac is best used as an accent, or planted along a hot, dry fencerow. Grow it on a steep bank where it can spread with abandon with native wildflowers for company. Underplant it with yucca for a year-round naturalistic effect. It's also very good for large containers.

I Also Recommend

'Dissecta' is a naturally occurring staghorn variety similar to 'Laciniata' with finely-divided, almost ferny leaflets and distinct orange fall color, but less vigorous than the species. Fragrant sumac (*Rhus aromatica*) is a spreading, upright groundcover type with three leaflets very similar to poison ivy, to which sumac is related. Illinois Nursery Selection 'Gro-Low' sumac (*R. aromatica* 'Gro-Low') is a two-foot, dense, pachysandra-like groundcover with red, showy fruit in the late summer and good orange-red fall colors. It makes an excellent groundcover, bank cover, or cascade over a wall. Poison sumac has stubby foliage and clusters of white, not burgundy, berries. It is nearly always found in low, wet, boggy soils, not on dry hillsides like "good" sumacs.

Cherished in European landscapes but grown here mostly in botanic gardens, this outstanding native forms small colonies of fast-growing, sparsely branched small trees with furry red new stems. 'Laciniata' is fernier and less aggressive than the species, yet still has almost unbelievably gorgeous orange fall colors. Its greenish-yellow summer flowers, produced in pointy clusters above the foliage, are an outstanding nectar source for bees, butterflies, and hummingbirds. Plants are either male or female; only female flowers form the fuzzy burgundy-red berries held in tight, triangular clusters above branches, which are very showy well into winter. When seeds first begin to from in summer, their sticky fuzz tastes lemony, and can be steeped in water with sugar to make tea. The dried berries are an African spice.

Bloom Period and Seasonal Color
Deep burgundy in summer

Mature Height × Spread
10 to 15 ft. × 12 to 15 ft.

Lilac
Syringa vulgaris

Cold-climate gardeners who move to the West Coast or South often long for lilacs. The first day you get a sweet waft from that bush on a spring day, your spirits soar. Talk about aromatherapy! The old lilac shrub from my grandmother's garden is still alive, though its big leaves are a bit raggedy and there are dead stems in need of pruning. But the dense, conical clusters of single or double flowers—purple, lavender, pink, or white—still fill the air with a perfume so intense I continually cut blooms to bring inside and enjoy. The flowers are edible; some have a perfumed flavor that's great on vanilla ice cream.

Other Common Name
French Lilac

Bloom Period and Seasonal Color
Hues of white, purple, pink, or lavender in spring

Mature Height and Spread
15 to 20 ft. × 12 to 18 ft.

Zone
5

When, Where, and How to Plant
Whether grown in sun or shade, well-drained neutral or alkaline soils for lilac are a must to prevent root rot. See page 189 in Trees for planting information.

Growing Tips
Water lilacs during prolonged drought, and fertilize lightly once every spring.

Care and Maintenance
Always keep a 3-inch layer of organic mulch over the root zone to buffer against sudden temperature swings in the winter, and heat in the summer. Deadhead or cut off faded flower stalks the first season to help young plants put their energy into root growth, not seed formation. Hard pruning will rejuvenate old shrubs by getting rid of old, partly-dead trunks and branches, and stimulating strong, healthy new shoots which quickly get back up to flowering size. There are many minor pests, but powdery mildew can be a real headache to some gardeners. Try baking soda spray (see page 233) to slow the spread to non-infected leaves.

Companion Planting and Design
Lilacs are commonly used as specimen plants or as hedges along property lines. They consort well with forsythia, spiraea, roses, and other flowering shrubs, and provide a deep green backdrop to perennial borders.

I Also Recommend
I must have 'Scentsation' in my garden for its unique deep purple florets edged in white, its great aroma, and its sweet flavor. Other lilacs I enjoy include Japanese tree lilac (*Syringa reticulata*) with reddish brown bark and large panicles of creamy white flowers in the early summer; cut-leaf lilac (*S. laciniata*), a compact but wide-spreading shrub (6 feet x 10 feet) with fern-like, compound leaves and late spring flowers; and *Syringa meyeri*, another compact shrub (6 feet x 4 feet).

Red Twig Dogwood

Cornus alba

When, Where, and How to Plant

Because of its thicket-forming nature, give red twig dogwood room to grow. It has best stem color in full sun, but tolerates even thin, wet soils. Loosen the soil in a wide circle at planting time to encourage wide roots, and mulch after planting to keep roots cool in our hot summers. See page 189 in Trees for more planting details. Root hardwood cuttings in autumn.

Growing Tips

This Siberian native is very low maintenance. Feed very lightly the first summer. After that, it needs only a little water and fertilizer.

Care and Maintenance

This plant has few needs, and pests are not serious. Thin wayward branches in the winter when you can see them better. For a really good show in the winter, cut everything back to within a few inches of the ground in the spring after flowering. Lots of sturdy new growth will come up by the next winter for a more colorful effect.

Companion Planting and Design

This plant is best used as a strong winter focal point in a prominent location. Groups scattered across a nearby hillside or along a sunny drive can be stunning. Mulch well or plant bulbs or an evergreen groundcover such as wintercreeper (*Euonymus fortunei*) underneath to complement stark winter stems.

I Also Recommend

Cultivars of red twig dogwood include 'Aurea' with crisp yellow leaves. 'Elegantissima' (also known as 'Argenteo Marginata') has gray-green leaves irregularly margined with white. 'Kesselringii' has blackish purple winter shoots and red and purple autumn leaves. 'Sibirica' has red autumn leaves and bright red winter shoots. 'Cream Cracker' has green leaves with creamy margins on the older growth; its stems are a purplish-red in the winter. 'Bailhalo', sometimes called ivory halo dogwood, is a compact variegated ball. The small redosier dogwood (*Cornus stolonifera*) is a vigorous, suckering deciduous shrub with dark red winter shoots, which tolerates wet soils. Its 4-inch long, lance-shaped leaves turn red or orange in autumn.

Blood-red twigs poking up out of the snow can be a little off-putting to folks raised in a society obsessed with gumdrop- and meatball-shaped shrubs scattered in front of the house. If ever a plant were to get us excited, red twig dogwood is it. The shrub is a must-have—a vigorous little thicket of upright stems and long, pointy-oval dark green leaves. Even its small but fragrant creamy-white flowers in flat heads are nice, especially behind spring perennials. However, the variegated-leaved cultivars are not as vigorous as those with all green leaves. White berry-like fruits appear sometimes tinged in blue, and red or orange colors in fall. However, the winter twigs are what make this a must-have plant.

Other Common Name

Tatarian Dogwood

Bloom Period and Seasonal Color

White in late spring

Mature Height and Spread

5 to 10 ft. × 5 to 10 ft.

Rose of Sharon

Hibiscus syriacus

This old-garden shrub, which gets both its common and Latin names from the Syrian Plains of Sharon, graces many older neighborhoods out of sheer persistence. Interesting varieties abound which, once set into the garden, quickly become long-lived focal points from summer to fall. Its prolific edible flowers and winter branches tipped with light-brown seed capsules can be used in flower arrangements. Rose of Sharon is vase-shaped to ten feet or more with medium-sized dark green lobed leaves that often turn golden in autumn. The typical hibiscus flowers are produced even in shade. Blooms are single or double, bell-like and up to four inches across, in white, pink, red, lavender, and pale blue. Sometimes there is a contrasting "eye" or flower streaks. The flowers are great bee attractors.

Other Common Name
Althea

Bloom Period and Seasonal Color
White, pink, red, lavender, or mauve through summer.

Mature Height and Spread
8 to 10 ft. × 4 to 8 ft.

Zone
5

When, Where, and How to Plant
Rose of Sharon blooms in sun or light shade. Container-grown specimens can be set out any time you can dig a wide hole. Follow instructions on page 189 for planting. Water and lightly feed new plants to get them established, then gradually withhold water to toughen them up.

Growing Tips
Little or no supplemental watering is needed, and it needs only light feedings.

Care and Maintenance
In general, unless you are training rose of Sharon into a single stem specimen, or espaliering against a wall, prune only to thin unwanted clutter or wayward branches, or to remove seed capsules. Old, overgrown plants can be rejuvenated by cutting them back severely in late winter or spring; flowers will appear on new growth. Sticky black sooty mold is sometimes a problem on plants infested with aphids.

Companion Planting and Design
Rose of Sharon does well as a medium-size accent shrub, singly or in groups, especially where summer color may be lacking in light shade. It also works well as a hedge. Because it prefers dry soils, it can easily be underplanted with daffodils, iris, daylily, and other perennials that tolerate light shade.

I Also Recommend
One of my favorites is the pale blue 'Blue Bird', which may appear a bit lavender in hot summers. 'Woodbridge' bears large rich pink flowers up to 4 inches across. 'Red Heart' produces ruffled white flowers with dark red centers. The National Arboretum introduced sterile (seedless) kinds that don't waste energy forming seeds, and thus have much heavier flowering. The best include low-branched 'Minerva' with ruffled lavender pink flowers having reddish throats; 'Aphrodite' is rose pink with a deep red eye; 'Diana' is pure white; 'Hélène' has white flowers with a deep red eye.

Weigela
Weigela 'Bristol Ruby'

When, Where, and How to Plant
Any well-drained soil will do, but for best foliage and flower color, weigela prefers a good loamy soil, moderate fertility, and full sun. Follow planting instructions on page 189.

Growing Tips
Water only when desperately needed. Fertilize weigela lightly every spring.

Care and Maintenance
Preserve its natural shape by pruning after flowering—if at all. Other than cutting it back by half when I moved, my 'Wine and Roses' has been left alone and is gorgeous with a small burst of bloom in late summer lasting well into fall. If you prune, selectively thin older canes during the late spring and early summer, and leave others to fill in. Weigela has no major pests.

Companion Planting and Design
Weigela provides an excellent color bridge after lilacs and before summer perennials. Use it as a specimen. It softens a fence or breaks up a long flowerbed. Used in groups on a hillside or broad area, the flowers and form can be a stunning focal point. Utilize it as a small screen; it tolerates reflected heat well enough to use around parking areas.

I Also Recommend
'Red Prince' is one of the hardiest weigelas, even into North Dakota. 'Polka' is a Canadian introduction considered the best pink weigela. It blooms from June to September. Others include 'Bristol Snowflake' (white), 'Java Red', 'Variegata' (variegated leaves, rosy red flowers), 'Candida' (white tinged with green), and 'Minuet' (a dwarf variety to around three feet high with purplish foliage and flowers of red, purple, and yellow). My current favorite and traveling buddy is 'Wine and Roses' with burgundy leaves and hot rose-pink flowers.

Some old-fashioned shrubs just won't fade away, including weigela, whose late spring flowers knock my socks off. This outstanding hummingbird shrub has arching branches that give it a fountain-like effect up to six feet tall and wide. Long oval leaves are dark green or variegated. In late spring (and during a small reprise in fall) loose clusters of deep red, rose, lavender, pink, or white 1¹/₂-inch, narrow trumpet flowers appear, weighing branches downward as if to show off the flowers. The florida in its Latin name simply means, "producing abundant flowers." The plant I got in 1997 as a 3-inch cutting has been abused, yet is thriving in my front yard despite being moved in the heat of a 102 degrees Fahrenheit August day. Talk about a tough plant!

Bloom Period and Seasonal Color
Deep-red, rose, lavender, pink, or white in late spring

Mature Height and Spread
4 to 6 ft. × 4 to 6 ft.

Zone
5

Trees *for the Prairie Lands*

Trees are the dominant plants in the landscape—for their mere size alone. The choice of trees can set the tone for the entire landscape. Depending on how the trees are sited, the effect on the home and surrounding property can vary tremendously. The uses of trees are many and varied. Trees can: define the border of the property, line a driveway, shade the house in summer, protect the house from cold winter winds, provide privacy from the road or neighbors, hide an unsightly outbuilding or neighboring property, and muffle road noise. Even a single tree can perform some of those functions.

A special single tree—set apart—is called a specimen tree. Most often, a specimen tree is planted in the lawn away from other plants. This allows it to be shown off. This may be a tree that has a unique form or shape—pendulous, fastigiated, sinuous, dwarf, or angular that provides year-round interest. You may set it apart for its appealing color (foliage, flowers, fruit). Evergreens are good specimen plants as they have appeal all year. Some gardeners are plant collectors and will single out a rare tree as a specimen. Depending on the size of your property, you can have more than one specimen tree. However, on a small lot if you have more than one or two specimen trees, they lose their uniqueness and impact, as they will tend to blend into the surrounding landscape.

Dazzling Cutleaf Japanese Maple in Autumn

Evergreen and Deciduous

An evergreen tree is one that keeps its leaves throughout the entire year, while a deciduous tree sheds its leaves, usually in autumn. We often think of evergreens as conifers—cone-bearing, needled trees such as pines, firs, hemlocks, or spruces. However, there is another group of evergreens—broadleaved evergreens. These include trees such as hollies and some magnolias.

When you are planning your garden, remember that it's more interesting to have a combination of different types of trees. Of course, the evergreens provide winter interest with their color, but seek out variegated varieties for additional appeal. Many deciduous trees are great accents in winter for their form or unusual bark.

Choosing a Tree

When you buy a tree, it may come one of three ways—bare root, container grown, or balled and burlapped. Bare-root trees are most likely to come from mail-order nurseries, while container-grown and balled-and-burlapped trees can be purchased locally. Imagine the shipping costs of trees with all the soil!

When you are purchasing a tree, you may have a limited budget. Unless you have the patience or you are buying a fast-growing tree, it is best to invest in the largest tree you can afford—especially when buying bare-root trees since they are usually smaller, and younger, than container-grown or balled-and-burlapped trees.

If you are buying the tree locally, take the time to check out several nurseries, garden centers, and home stores. You are likely to find quite a difference in price and quality. If the tree is deciduous, it is best to buy it in spring before it leafs out so that there will be less danger of transplant shock. The best planting time is spring; second best is early fall. Check the tree over to make sure that there is no damage to major limbs, that the bark is intact, and that there are no holes that might indicate insect damage or infestation.

Planting

When you receive a bare-root tree, unpack it immediately and soak the roots and about twelve inches of the trunk in muddy water with one tablespoon of undiluted transplant solution overnight. If you cannot plant the tree the next day, heel it in—dig a trench and lay the tree in the trench at an angle so the roots are completely buried. If you keep it well watered, the tree can stay like that for a month.

The method of planting a tree has changed recently due to extensive research done by the Cornell Cooperative Extension and other groups. The old adage was to dig a $50 hole for a $5 dollar plant—that shows how old the adage is. You certainly don't find trees for $5 any more. What it meant was that the soil from the planting hole (twice the width and depth of the root mass) was heavily amended with

Dwarf Alberta Spruce

organic matter as well as with various nutrients. What the researchers found was that the tree did not grow into the surrounding, unamended, soil. The roots just stayed within the rich soil and could even become root-bound. The result was trees with a less than normal lifespan, which were also easily uprooted by heavy winds and storms.

To plant a tree properly, dig a hole about one-and-one-half times the width and depth of the tree and loosen the soil removed from the hole. Add back about one-third of the loosened soil to the hole. If you are planting a bare-root tree, make a cone of soil of a proper height and width so that the roots can spread down around the cone and so that the base of the trunk is at ground level. Place the tree on the cone and make any adjustments necessary. Fill in with remaining soil. Gently tamp the soil down with your hands. Make a three-inch high ring of soil—creating a water basin—around the planting hole. Water in with several gallons of transplant solution. Mulch with a three-inch layer of wood chips, taking care to keep the mulch several inches from the tree trunk. Mulching over the water basin makes it sturdier.

If you are planting a container–grown tree, follow the above directions for digging and loosening the soil. Shovel about one-third of the soil into the hole. Pour in two quarts of transplant solution. While it's still in its container, soak the tree in a bucket of transplant solution for several minutes. Remove the tree from the container. If it is packed in tightly, which indicates it may be rootbound, cut the container from around the root mass with scissors and unwind any roots, if necessary. If it's very pot-bound with roots spreading all over the sides of the container, make four vertical slits, about one-half-inch deep with a knife, equidistant around the root mass to loosen the roots, allowing them to grow into the surrounding soil. Place the tree in the hole, adjusting the amount of soil under it so it is at the same soil level it was in the pot. Hint: you can use a ruler or board and lay it across the hole to check that the levels of the surrounding soil are the same as the remaining soil on the tree that came from its container. Fill the hole following the directions above, including making a water basin and mulching.

Planting a balled-and-burlapped tree is similar to planting a container-grown one; however, do not soak the tree in transplant solution. Once you have dug the hole, return some of the soil to the hole, add transplant solution, and move the tree next to the hole. Some of these trees are quite large and heavy, so you may need help. It has become very difficult to tell real burlap from the semi-plastic type, so it is best to remove the burlap. The real burlap will decay in the soil, but the plastic type inhibits root growth. Once you have replaced the proper amount of soil in the hole so the tree will be at the proper height when planted, loosen the tie or heavy metal twist-tie around the top of the burlap. Place the tree in the hole, and by angling and lifting it—with assistance—remove all the burlap. Sometimes you will find an added surprise under the burlap—a metal or plastic mesh basket. Remove that as well. Once the tree is positioned at the proper height, water with several gallons of transplant solution. Fill in with the remaining soil, firm the soil with your hands, make a water basin, and water with another gallon or two—depending on the size of the tree. Mulch as described above.

Staking

It is good for us that many of the old ways are changing, making tree planting simpler for us. Staking is no longer considered necessary unless the tree is in a windy site or its rootball is too small to keep it upright until it has established a good root system. Researchers have discovered that small amounts of movement of a tree actually help strengthen the trunk and root system. (The same goes for any transplant—even a small annual.)

To stake a tree, you will need heavy wire, some old hose, wire cutters, and three metal tree stakes that are looped (or eyed) at the top. Drive the stakes into the ground about three feet away from the center of the tree (or just outside of the water basin described earlier)—angled slightly outward with the stakes equidistant from each other. Measure the wire: For each stake, the wire must be double the distance from the stake to the trunk at just above the lowest sturdy branch, plus twelve inches. Attach one end of the wire to the stake, looping it around the eye. Cut a 12-inch length of hose and slide that onto the wire. Loop the wire around the trunk, not too tight, with hose protecting the tree from the wire. Attach the other end of the wire around, wrapping it several times. Cut off any excess wire.

Check the stake monthly to be sure it isn't too tight around the trunk. Do not leave the tree staked for more than six to eight months.

American Arborvitae
Thuja occidentalis

Arborvitae is a mighty tree, valuable for lumber. An evergreen conifer, it is unique with flattened branchlets of overlapping, yellowish-green, small fragrant scales—each pair of branchlets at right angles to the pair above and below. Oblong cones, about 1/2-inch-long, are erect on the branchlets. The furrowed, ridged bark is handsome and somewhat fibrous, ranging in color from reddish brown to gray. It has a compact, conical form. Separate male and female cones are borne in spring. The small 1/2-inch, fertilized female cones mature in late summer and are lovely shades of light yellow to cinnamon red. They are fragile and stand erect on the branchlets.

Other Common Name
Northern White Cedar

Bloom Period and Seasonal Color
Reddish-brown (cones) in spring.

Mature Height and Spread
40 to 50 ft. × 15 to 35 to ft.

Zone
2

When, Where, and How to Plant
Arborvitae is readily available at nurseries, garden centers, and home stores. It will grow well in limey, moist, or boggy soil. It grows best in part sun protected from the wind. Plant your arborvitae according to the chapter introduction. Add a 3-inch layer of wood chips as mulch. Be sure to keep the mulch at least an inch away from the trunk. Water in well with transplant solution. Do not fertilize.

Growing Tips
Water lightly until the plant is established. Water it deeply during drought. Arborvitae is happier in slightly moist soil. Do not fertilize for the first two years. After that, you can use the stake-type fertilizer, following package directions for the size of the tree. This type of fertilizer is a solid form, made to look like a stake. There are different types for the various kinds of trees and shrubs. Make sure you use one for evergreen trees. Pound the stake(s) into the ground, and the fertilizer gradually releases into the soil. Fertilize in spring. Arborvitae can be transplanted in spring, summer, or fall.

Care and Maintenance
This is a very low-maintenance plant. It has no pest or disease problems. It is slow growing—about 8 to 10 inches a year. It will tolerate pruning and shearing, but let it keep its natural shape. I like to cut off the lower branches to expose the handsome trunk. On a 15-foot tree, allow about 3 feet of trunk to show. Arborvitae has no serious pest problems.

Companion Planting and Design
Arborvitae makes a beautiful specimen tree all by itself on the lawn. In a grouping, it serves as an excellent windbreak. Arborvitae is even handsome, when kept pruned back, at the back of a mixed border. Plant it where its foliage, which turns bronze in winter, can be enjoyed during the cold months.

I Also Recommend
'Techny' has a perfectly pyramidal shape with dark green needles. *Thuja plicata* (western or giant arborvitae) is not eaten by deer, as is the American arborvitae.

When, Where, and How to Plant

Box elder is readily available in spring at nurseries, garden centers, and home stores. The fancy, variegated-leafed cultivars are usually found through mail-order nurseries. Choose non-grafted plants, which are less likely to revert to the rootstock form. Box elder will grow most soil types in full sun to part shade. Plant as directed in the chapter introduction. Plant box elders 32 feet apart to create a handsome avenue or alee of trees. For an attractive hedge, allow 4 feet between plants—center to center. Add a 3-inch layer of wood chips as mulch. Be sure to keep the mulch at least an inch away from the trunk. Water in well with transplant solution. Do not fertilize.

Growing Tips

Water lightly until the plant is established. Once it is established, it is quite drought tolerant. Water deeply in times of severe drought. Fertilize every other year with fertilizer stakes. (For deciduous trees—following package instructions).

Care and Maintenance

The variegated types benefit from pruning. If you see an all-green shoot on a variegated tree, remove it immediately or the tendency will be to revert to green. Hard pruning in spring is beneficial to variegated box elders. Box elders have no serious pest problems.

Companion Planting and Design

Because box elder is a fast-growing tree, it is ideal as a fill-in tree, especially around a new house with no landscaping, until slower-growing, more desirable trees reach a good height. Kept-well pruned, it makes an excellent hedge. Although it is a short-lived tree, it will withstand the rigors of the Prairie Lands weather.

I Also Recommend

'Elegans' (*Elegantissimum*) has brightly yellow-edged green leaves. It grows smaller than the species and is slightly less hardy. 'Flamingo' is a real eye-catcher with variegated white-bordered, pink and green leaves. *Variegatum argenteovariegatum* is another lovely variety with green and white variegated leaves. It is susceptible to reverting to all green. Var. *violaceum* has handsome purple to violet young shoots. Dark pink, long flower tassels in spring are appealing as is its autumn color.

To look at a box elder, you would not think it was a maple unless you saw it in summer with the winged seedheads that are just like those on other maples. As children we used to split the wing in half, gently open the seed sack, and stick it on our noses for a Pinocchio look. Box elders are native trees, which can thrive in drought. Usually short-lived, they are good for a bare landscape because they are inexpensive and grow quickly into a good-sized shade tree while other trees fill in. Unlike other maples, it has compound leaves composed of three to seven irregularly margined leaflets.

Bloom Period and Seasonal Color
Yellow-green in spring.

Mature Height and Spread
20 to 25 ft. × 20 to 25 ft.

Zone
2

Catalpa
Catalpa speciosa

Big and bold, native catalpa is grown for its big leaves, large clusters of big bell-shaped flowers, and long, bean-like seed pods. Of the several species found in Prairie states, Northern catalpa is the most cold hardy and has the largest leaves and longest beans. Wide, heart-shaped leaves with wavy margins can get a foot long. Individual flowers, which are each two-lipped and over two inches long, are white with throats flecked with purple and yellow, and are produced in large clusters atop the foliage in midsummer, making the tree a real stand-out. Bean-like pods, which hang in clusters, are cylindrical and up to twenty or more inches long and persist into the winter after the huge leaves have fallen and been raked.

Bloom Period and Seasonal Color
White in midsummer.

Mature Height and Spread
30 to 50 ft. × 30 to 50 ft.

Zone
5

When, Where, and How to Plant
Native catalpas prefer woodland edges in rich, well-drained soil. Never plant in soil with standing water. Make sure they have room to spread their full width at maturity. If possible, plant where they are sheltered from strong wind that tatters big leaves. See page 189 for planting specifics. Water to get started and keep moist through the first summer, with moderate amounts of fertilizer to support the production of large leaves.

Growing Tips
Provide regular moisture, but don't allow the soil to stay wet. Fertilize yearly.

Care and Maintenance
If branches are cut back about halfway every year (a tree-pruning technique called pollarding), a catalpa will produce even larger leaves. The big leaves of catalpa are affected in wet years with leaf spots and powdery mildew, but these rarely cause serious problems. Huge, finger-size caterpillars known as catalpa worms (the larvae of the large night-flying sphinx moth) may chew leaves in warm weather. Ignore them as they do not seriously harm the trees; they make excellent fish bait and are magical visitors to the evening garden.

Companion Planting and Design
Catalpa is best used as a specimen tree. Set it where its wide-spread, rounded form and showy summer flower clusters can be better viewed and where leaf problems will less obvious from afar. A consideration is its heavy amount of fall leaf litter. Run the leaves over with a lawnmower for plenty of winter mulch. Catalpa also has been used as a coarse-textured contrast to large shrubs and other trees in across-the-way borders and edges of woods.

I Also Recommend
Southern catalpa (*Catalpa bignonioides*) is hardy in much of the Prairie Lands and has interesting leaf-colored cultivars. 'Aurea' bears bronze new foliage that turns bright yellow. 'Purpurea' has dark blackish purple new leaves that mature to deep green. 'Nana' is a dwarf (6 to 8 foot) rounded shrub that doesn't flower.

Crabapple
Malus spp. and cultivars

When, Where, and How to Plant

Many crabapples are available in spring at nurseries, garden centers, and home stores. The choice varieties are only found through mail-order sources. Plant dormant crabapples as soon as the ground can be worked in spring. Crabapples grow and produce fruit best in full sun in well-drained, average to rich soil. Plant as described in the chapter introduction.

Growing Tips

Keep lightly watered until the plant is established—for the first year and a half. Water deeply if the top inch of soil is dry. Do not fertilize the first year, but fertilize yearly thereafter with fertilizer stakes, following package instructions for flowering deciduous trees. Before you eat the fruit, check the fertilizer label to be sure it is safe for edible plants.

Care and Maintenance

Prune any crossed or rubbing branches to open the center of the tree to sunlight and air circulation, and to promote fruit production. Promptly prune branches damaged by wind or winter storms. Crabapple is susceptible to apple scab and apple canker, both of which can damage leaves and fruit. Remove and destroy any infested portions of the tree.

Companion Planting and Design

Crabapples are beautiful planted with spring bulbs, such as daffodils (*Narcissus* spp.), tulips (*Tulipa* spp.), or Siberian squill (*Scilla siberica*) beneath them. Use a groundcover such a myrtle (*Vinca minor*) as the base and plant the bulbs in the groundcover. Don't grow grass under the tree, as there is too much competition for water and nutrients, as well as potential damage to the trunk from the lawnmower.

I Also Recommend

'Red Jade' has a weeping form, bright green foliage that turns yellow in fall, and flowers that are pink-tinged white. It bears bright red fruits and is a slightly smaller tree than other varieties. 'Bob White' has white flowers and golden yellow fruit. 'Donald Wyman' has white blooms, red fruit, and handsome peeling bark. 'Prairiefire' yields coral-red blossoms, purplish red fruit, and red-tinged leaves turn orange in fall.

We had a crabapple in our garden when I was a child. I wish I knew the variety, as its fruits were large, deep wine-red, and delicious. I was discouraged from eating them, even though we did eat jarred spiced crabapples. I remember what a beautiful tree it was—year-round. In spring, it had clusters of pretty pink flowers followed by bright green leaves. You didn't even notice the fruit—with so many other things going on in the garden, until it colored up in early fall. Some years—depending on how hungry the birds and I were—the fruit persisted into winter. Even the shape of the bare tree, with its horizontal branches, gave architectural interest in winter, especially with snow.

Other Common Name
Flowering Crab

Bloom Period and Seasonal Color
White, pink-tinged white blooms with wine-red, purple-red fruits in mid-spring.

Mature Height and Spread
10 to 26 ft. × 15 to 20 ft.

Zone
4

Dwarf Alberta Spruce
Picea glauca albertiana 'Conica'

Very few plants give the instant eye-appeal of dwarf conifers. As accents, companions to perennials, or as a tough container plants, they're great. And talk about tough—they can be found growing unattended in cemeteries. Dwarf Alberta spruce, a natural miniature form of white spruce (discovered in the wild in Alberta, Canada in 1904), is a bluntly conical bush, very dense yet soft to the touch—almost huggable. Its needles are light green and densely set as they radiate around the stem. It is noted for its naturally formal, semi-dwarf, evergreen, and stately pyramidal appearance. However, being extremely slow growing (only 2 to 4 inches per year), it may take many years to grow from a small plant. Buy one close to your ideal size.

Bloom Period and Seasonal Color
Green foliage year-round

Mature Height and Spread
6 to 15 ft. × 3 to 8 ft.

Zone
2

When, Where, and How to Plant
Dwarf Alberta spruce grows best in full sun in well-drained, slightly acidic soil. Choose a site a few feet away from any other plant, wall, or irrigation to allow sunshine and good air circulation. Shelter it from strong winds. Don't plant near roadways or walkways where winter salt is used. See page 189 for planting instructions.

Growing Tips
Water deeply but infrequently the first summer, just enough to keep deeper roots moist. Dwarf Alberta spruce does not tolerate long dry spells or being irrigated frequently. Little or no water or fertilizer is necessary after the first year, unless there is drought.

Care and Maintenance
Dwarf Alberta spruce is susceptible to spider mites. Lightly shear stem tips to improve its look, encourage new growth and promote thickness. Hard pruning often kills conifers. If you prune a stem back to where no needles remain, it will usually die all the way back to its point of origin.

Companion Planting and Design
Dwarf Alberta spruce is often used in pairs at foundation entranceways or singly as a dramatic lawn focal point. It can provide year-round interest for perennial beds, acting like a sentry around which seasonal bulbs such as daffodils, tulips, and iris come and go. It works well as a long-lived, low-maintenance container plant as long as it is watered during dry spells and the container is large enough so it doesn't freeze solid in winter.

I Also Recommend
'Jean's Dilly' (to 5 ft.) is a shorter variety, with needles that are concentrated at the ends of each season's short stem growth; it has a wonderful distinctive twist to the needles. 'Rainbow's End' (to 8 feet tall) is unique for its second flush of foliage growth in midseason that is chartreuse to creamy yellow.

Eastern Cottonwood
Populus deltoides

When, Where, and How to Plant
Cottonwood will grow in nearly any soil – even sandy or heavy clay—but prefers a moist, well-drained site where it neither dries out in the summer nor stands in water (which can lead to root rot). However, it will not tolerate shade. Nurseries, garden centers, and home stores all have cottonwood and its cultivars. Page 189 provides more on planting. Researchers estimate that a mature tree can produce over 40 million seeds every year, most of which will sprout quickly if planted immediately when they are shed. Seed should not be covered nor pressed into the soil.

Growing Tips
Seedlings are very susceptible to drying out. Keep the seedbed moist for germination and at least one month thereafter. Once it is established, water it regularly. Give the tree a deep soaking during prolonged dry spells. Fertilization is not necessary.

Care and Maintenance
Cottonwood grows fast and has soft wood, making it susceptible to pest and diseases for which there is little practical control. Vigorous roots may invade old tile-style sewer lines and septic fields but cannot penetrate watertight pipes, Expect trees to have some leaf spots, borers, and die-back.

Companion Planting and Design
Cottonwood is frequently planted to give quick shade near homes. Male clones, which have none of the objectionable cotton associated with seed, are preferred. Cottonwoods are good windbreaks.

I Also Recommend
Balm of Gilead (*Populus balsamifera* or *P. candicans*), is a smaller but hardy cottonwood whose two cultivars, 'Siouxland' and 'Mojave Hybrid (with nearly white bark), are male-only clones. Plains cottonwood (*Populus occidentalis)* has slightly smaller, more coarsely-toothed leaves which are more broad than long. It is considered the fastest-growing tree in the Great Plains and provides habitat for over 80 percent of nesting birds on the Prairie Lands. Other good poplars include white poplar (*P. alba*), the tall, strictly narrow Lombardy poplar (*P. nigra* 'Italica'), and quaking aspen (*P. tremuloides*).

Cottonwood is the fastest growing native tree in North America and provides habitat for many bird species. The easy shade tree can quickly reach 30 feet or more, eventually much larger, and typically has a large trunk with thick, deeply furrowed bark. Branches near its base grow into a wide, spreading crown covered with large, glossy, papery leaves which can be a temporary litter problem in small gardens—but they compost quickly. Trees are dioecious (separate male and female). Before leaves appear in the spring, the male trees bear tiny flowers borne on red, hanging catkins from which pollen is shed. The fertilized females produce the prolific fluffy white seeds (the so-called cotton). Unless you want a lot of flying fluff, choose male-only cultivars.

Other Common Name
Necklace Poplar

Bloom Period and Seasonal Color
Inconsequential red flowers in spring.

Mature Height and Spread
60 to 100 ft. × 30 to 70 ft.

Zone
2

Honeylocust

Gleditsia triacanthos

This elegant native, popular as a fast-growing shade or street tree, is prized for its form, fall colors, and winter seedpods. The trunk and zigzag shoots are armed with dangerously sharp, branched thorns up to 6 inches long. The bark is almost black, with long narrow fissures and ridges, and contrasts nicely with snow. Its handsome, glossy dark green leaves are fernlike and composed of many oblong leaflets. They add special elegance in autumn when they turn a lovely shade of yellow. Unlike large-leafed trees, honeylocust does not create leaf litter problems. Flowers are inconspicuous yellow-green clusters, nectar-rich and favored by bees, and produce very interesting groups of unusual, dark brown hanging, flat and wavy seedpods up to 18 inches long.

Bloom Period and Seasonal Color
Inconspicuous flowers in spring.

Mature Height and Spread
80 to 100 ft. × 40 to 70 ft.

When, Where, and How to Plant
Honeylocust are available at garden centers, nurseries, and home stores. Follow directions on page 189 for planting. Full sun is best, as is a well-drained, moderately fertile soil. When preparing the soil for planting, dig a wide hole to encourage side roots and don't add organic matter so the plants can quickly get used to your landscape's native soil. Cuttings are very difficult to root, and seeds require special treatment to sprout. Buy container-grown cultivars at nurseries, garden centers, or home stores.

Growing Tips
Once established, the plants can withstand drought but do not tolerate standing water. Watering mature trees is generally unnecessary. If grown on the lawn as a specimen, any fertilizer for the lawn feeds the tree.

Care and Maintenance
In fall, prune low-growing or wayward limbs and branches at their points of origin to maintain a healthy, open shape. Expect insect problems, including webworm caterpillars, aphids, and other minor pests; however, there is no need to control them in specimen plants set away from patios or walkways. Pull webworm tents down with a long pole. Pruning them out or burning them does more damage to the tree than the worms could.

Companion Planting and Design
Honeylocust is often used as a specimen plant, occasionally grouped for a more massed effect. Urban landscapers use the thornless, seedless forms, which are highly tolerant of urban pollution (including salt from roadways), as neatly groomed street trees to replace elms. Grass grows easily underneath honeylocusts.

I Also Recommend
Though I think the thorns and bean pods are quite attractive, there are several good thornless cultivars. 'Moraine' has golden yellow fall colors and is resistant to webworms. 'Sunburst', with its golden yellow new foliage turning pale green at maturity and changing to yellow in fall, does not fruit at all. 'Rubylace' has dark bronze-red young leaves turning dark bronze-green by midsummer. 'Imperial' is a wide-spreading tree with rounded, bright green leaves and very few seedpods.

Japanese Maple
Acer palmatum

When, Where, and How to Plant
These plants tolerate full sun, but in hot windy summers they will hold their color better and suffer less leaf-tip burn when planted in light afternoon shade. Avoid root damage by providing a deep, well-drained soil with organic matter such as compost or rotted manure added to your native soil, or grow it in slightly raised mounds for extra drainage in the wet seasons. Loosen pot-bound roots at planting time and mulch the soil immediately after planting to shade the soil and keep young roots cool in the summer. Add just a little fertilizer to get new plants started. Don't overdo it, or you will risk rampant leaf growth, which will be unsupported by a struggling new root system.

Growing Tips
Keep soil lightly moist with occasional deep soakings. Fertilize once a year.

Care and Maintenance
Prune only to remove or direct branches and limbs, leaving no stubs that can rot into the trunk. This can be done any time of the year. It has no major pests. Water it during dry spells to prevent leaf-tip burn.

Companion Planting and Design
Large Japanese maples are used as street trees or specimens beside houses, where their leaves are attractive even as they shed in the fall and are colorful additions to leaf piles and compost bins. Small Japanese maples are perfect eye-catchers in flower beds, as accents by entries or turns in garden paths, or as container-grown specimens. They are doubly-stunted when grown in pots, looking all the world like natural but oversized bonsai plants.

I Also Recommend
There are too many dozens of cultivars and selections of Japanese maples to list! Some favorites include 'Bloodgood', which has dark red-purple leaves in the summer turning bright red in the fall. *Acer palmatum atropurpureum* 'Dissectum' has very finely divided burgundy leaves and a weeping form. 'Aureum' is soft yellow-green spring foliage with crimson-purple fall colors. 'Viridis' is all green, while 'Sango Kaku' has an electric combination of green leaves on red petioles and red bark.

Every day of the year, even in winter, Japanese maples are stunningly graceful and colorful and come in such huge array of forms and hues of red or green there should be at least one in every landscape. The small to medium-sized trees, native to Asian forests, have been selected for the most exotic forms, including even shrub-like dwarfs. Their sinuous, dark trunks and branches are exciting in the winter; however, their deeply divided leaves get the attention. Their colors range from light yellow or green to red-tinged, to blood red or deep burgundy, even variegated. The flowers are not showy, just purplish-red clusters in the spring, but they are followed by classic red winged maple seedpods (called samaras) that can be fairly showy.

Bloom Period and Seasonal Color
Inconspicuous red in spring

Mature Height and Spread
3 to 25 ft. × 3 to 30 ft.

Zone
5

Japanese Yew

Taxus cuspidata

Japanese yew is an extremely versatile plant that will grow in most conditions. The species is magnificent given ample space to grow and makes a spectacular specimen tree with lovely brown shredding bark and horizontal or ascending branches. Gardeners who are into topiary like it, as it takes well to shearing and shaping. A gardener I knew took full advantage of its versatility, creating everything from a hedge with dolphins leaping and diving to a miniature (20-foot) Statue of Liberty. It is dioecious — with separate male and female plants. All parts of the plant are toxic. The needles are green on the top, yellow-green beneath, and are arranged in a v-shaped pattern. Fleshy red arils cover the seeds. Many gardeners prefer the smaller, low-growing cultivars.

Bloom Period and Seasonal Color
Evergreen

Mature Height and Spread
30 to 50 ft. × 10 to 15 ft.

Zone
4

When, Where, and How to Plant
The Japanese yew and a number of its dwarf varieties are readily found at nurseries, garden centers, and home stores; however, you need to turn to the mail-order nurseries for some of the more esoteric and interesting cultivars. Japanese yew grows in fertile, well-drained soil, either acidic or alkaline, in full sun to shade. Plant as described in the chapter introduction.

Growing Tips
Keep lightly watered until the plant is established—for the first year and a half. Do not fertilize the first year. After that, water deeply if the top inch or so of soil become dry, and use a fertilizer in spring that is specifically for evergreens, following the package instructions. This tree is generally pest free.

Care and Maintenance
As all parts of the plant are toxic, keep small children away from it. Trim hedges in early summer. Japanese Yew can withstand heavy or rejuvenative pruning. Add a fresh layer of organic mulch each spring, which will break down and become soil, thus feeding the tree. It is susceptible to mealybug and mites. Control with insecticidal soap, following label directions.

Companion Planting and Design
Japanese yew is well suited as a specimen tree. Pruned, it makes a good hedge. Smaller varieties make excellent groundcovers and are also attractive in a mixed border. As a groundcover, wintercreeper (*Euonymus fortunei* 'Aureomarginata') is a lovely companion, with contrasting leaf color and shape, to any of the low-growing varieties.

I Also Recommend
'Aurescens' (1 ft.) spreads to 3 ft. with yellow new shoots. 'Capitata' (10 to 25 ft.) has a beautiful, dense pyramidal form and is excellent as a specimen tree. 'Nana' (3 to 4 ft.) has a wonderful spreading dwarf form that can be used effectively as an evergreen groundcover as it spreads widely. 'Denisiformus' ('Densa'; 3 to 4 ft.) is another lovely dwarf that spreads from 6 to 8 feet across. 'Emerald Spreader' ('Monloo'; 30 in.) has a lovely dark green color year-round and spreads 8 to 10 ft. wide.

Littleleaf Linden
Tilia cordata

When, Where, and How to Plant
In general, it is easier to find a littleleaf linden through mail-order nurseries than most local home stores or garden centers. It grows best in loose, well-drained soil; otherwise, the roots will girdle. Plant as described in the chapter introduction. Do not fertilize the first year.

Growing Tips
Keep lightly watered until the plant is established—for the first two years. After that, it requires deep watering only when the top 2 to 3 inches of soil become dry. Fertilize using tree spikes yearly; follow directions for the number of spikes for the size of the tree. If you plan to use the flowers for tea, make sure to use a fertilizer that is specifically for edible plants.

Care and Maintenance
Add a fresh layer of organic mulch each spring, which will break down and become soil, thus feeding the tree. If given ample space for its roots and kept well watered and fertilized, it is relatively pest free; however, it is susceptible to fungal problems such as anthracnose and powdery mildew. Usually these problems are unsightly, but they don't affect much of the tree. A professional arborist or tree company can examine an infested tree. Make sure their recommended treatment is the least toxic. Watering at the base of the tree (not spraying the leaves) can help avoid fungal problems

Companion Planting and Design
If you have a large lawn, a littleleaf linden is a splendid specimen tree. It is tough and makes a good street tree. A littleleaf linden is a great shade tree to keep the house cool in summer. Plant it far enough away from the house that it doesn't grow too close as it matures. An alee of lindens is beautiful and wonderfully scented in early summer.

I Also Recommend
'Shamrock' has the same pyramidal shape with a more open crown. 'Greenspire' is handsome with its dark green leaves. If your areas has Japanese beetles, do not grow this variety, as it is highly susceptible to these pests.

Littleleaf linden, as its name implies, has the same typical heart-shaped leaves as other lindens but is more diminutive. The deep-green, lustrous leaves are 3 inches wide, with blue-green undersides. In fall, it turns a lovely shade of yellow. For centuries, Europeans have used tea made from the fragrant linden flowers as a calmative. It has a sweet floral flavor and can be made from fresh or dried flowers. The flowers are quite unique—small clusters, highly fragrant, creamy white, with a large bract attached. When the linden is blooming, it's abuzz with bees. The tree is quite handsome and has the pyramidal shape typical of all lindens. It is tough enough to be a street tree and beautiful enough to be a specimen plant.

Other Common Name
Basswood

Bloom Period and Seasonal Color
Yellow in early summer.

Mature Height and Spread
30 to 75 ft. × 15 to 40 ft.

Zone
3

Norway Spruce
Picea abies

Norway spruce is the most widely cultivated evergreen in America. Seen from a distance, when it has space to reach its mature height of 40 to 80 feet, it is breathtaking. Norway spruce has a lovely conical form. It has a single straight trunk with the branches in whorls around the trunk. Each of the ½- to ¾-inch needles is separately attached to the twig, with its base completely surrounding the twig. Male and female flowers, resembling catkins, appear in spring standing upright on the branch. Once fertilized, the female flowers slowly turn downward. By the time they mature in autumn, the cylindrical, pendulous light brown cones have reached a size of four to seven inches. In winter, the scales pull back and release the seeds.

Bloom Period and Seasonal Color
Yellow insignificant blooms in spring.

Mature Height and Spread
40 to 80 ft. × 18 to 36 ft.

When, Where, and How to Plant
Norway spruce and some of its dwarf varieties are available at nurseries, garden centers, and home stores, as well as through mail-order nurseries on the Internet. It grows best in full sun in fertile, well-drained soil but will grow in most any soil, except for very acidic soil or soil that is constantly wet. Plant as described in the chapter introduction. Do not fertilize the first year.

Growing Tips
Keep lightly watered until the plant is established—for the first year and a half. After that, water deeply if the top two inches of soil is dry. It is shallow-rooted, so a weeping hose or drip irrigation is ideal for watering. Fertilization is not necessary.

Care and Maintenance
In winter and early spring, prune out any storm-damaged branches. Adding a new layer of organic mulch each spring will feed the tree as is breaks down. Norway spruce is generally pest free.

Companion Planting and Design
Given ample space, a Norway spruce is an excellent specimen plant. Groupings of Norway spruces create an excellent year-round windbreak—highly valued when the winds come whistling down the plains. Norway spruces planted in a row make a highly visible property line—year-round. The dwarf varieties are lovely included in a mixed border. They also make fine specimen plants. Some gardeners place an actual bird's nest in the depression at the top of the tree, while others utilize that space for a lightweight garden ornament such as a Victorian gazing ball. The dwarf varieties are highlighted by planting small spring-blooming bulbs such as snow crocus (*Crocus tommasinianus*), glory-of-the-snow (*Chionodoxa lucillea*), snowdrops (*Galanthus nivalis*), or late summer to fall blooming autumn crocus (*Colchicum autumnale*).

I Also Recommend
'Pumila' (to 4 feet) has dense, compact needles and branches with a globular form. Bird's nest spruce ('Nidiformus') is slow growing (to 4 feet) and a very popular dwarf variety. It has dense needles and branches with a slight depression at the top, making it look like the perfect spot for a bird's nest.

Redbud
Cercis canadensis

When, Where, and How to Plant

You can find redbud trees at most any nursery, garden center, or home store. For some of the more esoteric cultivated varieties, look to the mail-order nurseries and do a search on the Internet. In the wild, redbuds are understory trees, growing in filtered shade from taller trees; however, if you really want to see a redbud that can show its stuff, plant it in full sun. It will grow in any well-drained soil, acidic or alkaline; however, wet soil will mean a death knell for redbuds. Plant as described in the chapter introduction.

Growing Tips

Keep the tree very lightly watered until the plant is established—for the first two years. After that, it requires deep watering only when the top two inches of soil become dry. It will not tolerate constantly wet soil. Do not fertilize the first year. After that, fertilize yearly using tree spikes—following package instructions for the size of the tree. If you want to eat the flowers, read the fertilizer label carefully. Use a fertilizer that is specifically for edible plants.

Care and Maintenance

Each spring, add a fresh 3-inch layer of organic mulch. There are some pests and diseases to watch out for, such as scale, aphids, leafhoppers, downy mildew, canker, and blight. If the tree is healthy, has good air circulation, is well feed but not overfed, and is not stressed from drought, any of the pests may be present but not in numbers to damage the tree. A weak or overwatered tree, on the other hand, is likely prey. Watering at the base of the tree will help avoid fungal problems.

Companion Planting and Design

A redbud is a lovely specimen tree that is also at home at the edge of a woodland surrounded by wildflowers.

I Also Recommend

'Forest Pansy' bears beautiful purple leaves but is slightly less hardy than the species. Two white-flowered varieties are 'Royal White' and 'Alba'. 'Flame' is outstanding with semidouble purplish-pink (yummy) blooms. 'Pinkbud' and 'Wither's Pink Charm' are pink-flowered.

Growing up on the East Coast, I always had a particular fondness for Eastern redbud, which grew there as a shrub, usually in the 5- to 8-foot range and rarely more than 12 to 15 feet high. It was kind of scraggly and scruffy looking. Part of what endeared me to it was the pink flowers, borne in clusters right on the branches. Redbud is in the pea family. Its flowers are edible (as long as you don't spray the tree with any chemicals), with a surprising crunch and a pea-like flavor. Moving to Iowa, where redbuds are full-blown big, beautiful, full trees, I was dazzled—and overjoyed. The lovely heart-shaped flowers emerge after the flowers fade and give a lovely show of color in the autumn.

Other Common Name
Eastern Redbud

Bloom Period and Seasonal Color
Pink in spring.

Mature Height and Spread
25 to 35 ft. × 25 to 35 ft.

Zone
4

Sargent Cherry

Prunus sargentii

Sargent cherry is an elegantly beautiful tree that is certainly the finest of the ornamental cherries. It is the first really showy tree to flower in the spring. This spreading tree is initially vase-shaped but becomes more rounded with age, eventually getting as wide as it is tall. The copper- or cinnamon-tinted, shiny bark is studded with prominent light-colored bumps (lenticels). Glossy leaves up to 5 inches long are red when young, expanding to dark green by late spring then turning an exquisite orange-red in early autumn. Bowl-shaped, pale pink flowers up to 1 1/2 inches across are produced in clusters in spring and can even tolerate late snow. In early summer, small pea-sized, bitter fruits turn from red to purple-black and are easily found and devoured by birds.

Bloom Period and Seasonal Color
Pink in early spring.

Mature Height and Spread
30 to 50 ft. × 30 to 40 ft.

Zone
4

When, Where, and How to Plant

Sargent cherry can live longer than other flowering cherries. It is available at garden centers, nurseries, and home stores. Plant in lightly moist, well-drained, moderately fertile soil where water never stands, or on a slight slope to create surface drainage away from the trunk.

Growing Tips

Water deeply during dry summers. Fertilize lightly every spring.

Care and Maintenance

Cut a skinny new, young flowering cherry back to about three feet tall, even if it removes all the branches, to force the development of strong multiple trunks that will make it sturdier later. Feed lightly at planting and water to get it established. Prune in the winter or as needed to remove cluttered, crossing, and wayward branches. Most diseases are aggravated by poor growing conditions, including overfeeding. Remember that feeding the lawn also feeds trees. Trunk wounds from mowers or string trimmers also lead to decay. Japanese beetles love the foliage but rarely seriously damage the tree.

Companion Planting and Design

A magnificent specimen tree because of its early flowers and stunning fall colors, Sargent cherry also serves well as a street tree and parking lot tree for its toughness, and because its small fruits are not very messy. The canopy is too dense for grass to grow very well underneath; plant groundcovers or simply spread a neat mulch to dramatically set off its trunk and surface roots.

I Also Recommend

'Columnare' grows tall and narrow—about 30 feet by 10 feet wide. 'Rancho' is another narrowly upright form, 20 to 25 feet tall by 5 to 10 feet wide, with dark pink flowers. Yoshino cherry (*Prunus yedoensis*) has pale pink flowers fading to nearly white, and *Prunus* 'Okame' has carmine-red flowers. Amur cherry (*P. maackii*) has choice peeling, yellow-brown bark. Black cherry (*P. serotina*) bears edible red fruit.

When, Where, and How to Plant

Serviceberry prefers wet woodsy sites, so grow it in acidic, fertile, and moist but well-drained soil in sun or partial shade. Create a naturalistic woodland soil by digging a wide area of native soil at least a foot deep. Thoroughly mix in a 2-or 3-inch layer of a mixture of compost and peat moss, then cover with a thick mulch of natural leaf mixture. Serviceberry is easily found for purchasing.

Growing Tips

Feed new plants very lightly and keep them moist through the first summer. Mulch with natural leaf litter, and water during drought.

Care and Maintenance

It is generally pruned up as a specimen tree, with suckers removed every year or two. Some years when late flowers overlap with those of wild roses or brambles, bees may spread bacterial fire blight to shadblow, but this is rarely a serious problem in the Prairie Land states.

Companion Planting and Design

Grow it as a small group at the edge of a woodland or as a specimen in a shrub border, preferably with a dark background to show off its brief but bright show of flowers, fall colors, and winter form. The noninvasive roots and light shade make this a good tree under which to garden with ferns, trillium, and other woodland perennials. It makes an interesting background addition to a wildlife garden.

I Also Recommend

This serviceberry is nearly indistinguishable from *Amelanchier arboreus*. Cultivars include 'Cumulus', a very vigorous, upright growing plant with orange-red fall color; 'Prince Charles', an upright, oval tree, 30 feet tall and 20 feet wide; and 'Snowcloud', which bears large white flowers. Other species include "Saskatoon" (*A. alnifolia*), which has the 4- to 6-foot, heavy-fruit bearing cultivar 'Regent', and apple serviceberry (*A. grandiflora*) with blue-green foliage that turns orange red in the fall and very white flowers opening from pink buds; it is a good fruit crop.

Native to our woodland creek banks, the suckering tree gets its common name from the settler tradition of holding memorial services for those who died in the winter, when the tree flowered. Shadblow, another common name for serviceberry, refers to its flowering when shad begin swimming up creeks. It is now grown for its hanging clusters of white or pink-flushed flowers and for the sweet, blueberry-looking, pie-quality, summer fruit to which birds race gardeners in June—hence its other common name Juneberry. Its berries formed the basis of pemmican, a Native American trail food; the tree's stems were made into arrows. Its dark green leaves are bronzy purple when new and turn a fine orange or red in autumn. Grayish bark is attractive, and the winter silhouette is airy and graceful.

Other Common Names
Juneberry, Shadblow, Allegheny Serviceberry

Bloom Period and Seasonal Color
White in spring.

Mature Height and Spread
25 to 30 ft. × 20 to 25 ft.

Zone
4

Sugar Maple
Acer saccharum

The main source for maple syrup and countless millions of refrigerator doors festooned with children's leaf rubbings, this "Canada flag" leaf tree has spectacular fall colors which contribute mightily to tourism. Summer leaves are dull green, 3-7 inches wide with three to five rounded lobes, but they really fire up in autumn with brilliant yellows, oranges, reds, and scarlet. Twin seeds arranged in the typical maple helicopter samara are not very showy. The tree is intolerant of road salt or urban pollution, so it should be used mostly in large urban woodland settings, away from roads and traffic. When looking for a good maple for your part of the state, visit a local garden center in the fall when foliage of container-grown trees is changing hue.

Bloom Period and Seasonal Color
Insignificant red in spring.

Mature Height and Spread
60 to 70 ft. × 30 to 40 ft.

When, Where, and How to Plant
Sugar maple is easily found for purchasing. Sugar maple must have a well-drained soil, but it needs ample moisture available for the shallow roots. Prepare a wide planting site with a moderate amount of leaf compost mixed in, preferably on a slope. Planting information is on page 189. (The bottom of a hill has more summer moisture than the top.) Cover fresh plantings with leaf mulch to protect roots the first summer.

Care and Maintenance
No fertilizer is needed the first year; this allows roots to get established before forcing top growth. After that, fertilize lightly in spring. Water only as needed to prevent complete drying out—especially during a drought.

Growing Tips
Mulch the root area every spring. The far-ranging, competitive roots of sugar maple will find fertilizer under any nearby lawn. Feed the lawn, and you feed the tree. Water deeply during hot, dry summers to keep leaves healthy and intact until fall color kicks in. Prune lower and cluttered limbs and branches to shape the tree, but don't leave stubs. Protect the trunk from the lawn mower and string trimmer.

Companion Planting and Design
Sugar maple is not the best choice for a street tree because of its intolerance of road salt, its attractive but bulky leaf litter, and the nuisance of brittle branches dropping on parked cars and sidewalks. It is better planted as a specimen or in groups where it can be enjoyed without interfering with lawn care. Little or no grass can be grown under sugar maple. Edge the lawn in a wide area under the outer reach of maple limbs, cover with mulch, and naturalize bulbs such as snowdrops (*Galanthus* spp), grape hyacinth (*Muscari* spp.), and autumn crocus (*Colchicum autumnale*).

I Also Recommend
My favorites for the hot, dry prairie summers include 'Caddo' (native to Oklahoma). It is more tolerant of alkaline soils than many of its Eastern relatives. 'Green Mountain' tolerates heat and drought, with yellow or orange-red fall color. 'Seneca Chief' has a narrow form suited for street plantings and has an orange to yellow fall color.

When, Where, and How to Plant

Tuliptrees are readily available at nurseries, garden centers, and home stores. Look to mail-order nurseries and the Internet for the cultivars. To help it achieve its true potential, plant a tuliptree in moderately rich, slightly acidic, moist, well-drained soil in full sun. Plant as described in the chapter introduction. Do not fertilize the first year.

Growing Tips

Keep the tree lightly watered for the first two years until it is established. After that, give it a deep watering every three weeks during the growing season. During dry spells, water more frequently. Fertilize yearly using tree spikes, following package instructions. Use spikes that are labeled for flowering trees.

Care and Maintenance

Each spring, add a fresh 5-inch layer of organic mulch. Over time, the mulch breaks down, forming humus, which enriches the soil, thus feeding the tree. Mulch out all the way to the drip line (where the ends of branches reach). Be patient, a tuliptree is often slow to get started growing and may seem to malinger for several years. The flowers do not appear until the tree is at least ten years old. Tuliptrees are generally free of pests.

Companion Planting and Design

As it has a large network of fleshy, shallow roots that are easily damaged, do not try to grow anything under or near the edge of your tuliptree; just keep it well mulched. A tuliptree is a magnificent specimen tree and also looks handsome planted in front of a mixture of evergreens.

I Also Recommend

'Aureomarginatum' (to 65 feet by 22 feet) has leaves edged with bright yellow to greenish yellow. Its edging color fades somewhat in summer; it is less hardy than the species, and late frosts can kill off new spring growth. 'Fastigiatum' ('Arnold', 'Pyramidalis'—to 100 feet by 22 feet) has a columnar or fastigiate form with the same beautiful color and flowers as the species; it is somewhat rare but worth finding as its size is more suitable for a typical yard.

A full-grown tuliptree is truly awesome. With the ability to reach 100 feet in height, it is the tallest native American tree. For Native Americans, its size and its relatively high branches made it a wood source for the best and most watertight canoes. Tuliptrees are named for the flowers which, if you can see them, are usually borne fairly high up in the tree on the ends of branches. The flowers look like—and are the size of—a viridiflora tulip that is greenish cream and striped with orange. I was fortunate once to stay at a bed and breakfast with a second story window (complete with window seat) that looked out into a tuliptree in bloom.

Other Common Names

Whitewood, Yellow Poplar, Tulip Poplar

Bloom Period and Seasonal Color

Greenish-cream with orange in early summer.

Mature Height and Spread

40 to 100 ft. × 26 to 33 ft.

Zone

5

Water Gardens *for the Prairie Lands*

Water gardens are the fastest-growing type of gardening in America today. Almost anyone can have a water garden—a small container on an sunny apartment balcony, a reflecting pool in a front yard urban garden, a burbling recirculating stream, a small formal water garden, a waterfall, a large, naturalistic pond—or a combination of any of these.

Using water in the garden is pleasing to the eye, soothing to the ear (with moving water), and most importantly, calming to the soul. It provides a sanctuary where you can get away from all the cares and worries of the day. It is the antithesis of most any other garden. Most of your time is spent watching and enjoying the water feature, rather than weeding, mowing, watering, pruning, and doing other chores that go hand in hand with other gardens.

Even in our harsh winter climates, plants (and fish if the pond is kept from icing over) will survive with minimal effort only to burst forth the following year—often even bigger and better if the water feature is more than two feet deep. (An electric heater keeps water above freezing.)

Still or Moving

There are so many choices. You can have a still reflecting pool or a birdbath where the only elements are the reservoir and the water. Graduate to moving water—a fountain, stream, waterfall, or a pool with a recirculating pump.

Choosing the right pump (designated by GPH—gallons per hour it can pump) is based on three factors: the pond volume (length × width × depth × 7.5), its use (for filtering, creating a waterfall, or making a fountain), and how far the water has to travel—horizontally or vertically. Most pumps are electric, requiring waterproof outdoor outlets.

No more than the entire volume of the pond should recirculate in an hour. Solar pumps are just coming on the market, but most—like solar lights—do not store energy. Therefore, the pump works only when the sun is shining.

Yellow Flag Irises in Pond

There is also a variety of materials for the water feature, including an earth pond (must be heavy clay soil); earth lined with PVC or flexible EPDM rubber; a preformed polyethylene pond; gunnite or cement; and of course the easiest, a large container. A lovely Prairie Lands garden has a horse trough dug in the center that makes a wonderful water garden. A metal container above ground, however, might conduct too much heat into the water. Above ground, any container without a drainage hole will work, or plug up the drainage hole and waterproof the inside of a large terracotta pot. Faux materials are fun containers, mimicking stone, terracotta, or even a well-worn whiskey barrel. Half whiskey barrels do leak, so special liners are available to convert them into water gardens. Half whiskey barrels are much lighter and can be left outside during the winter without worrying about them breaking.

Once the water feature is complete and pumps, filters, or any other electrical elements are installed, add water to within several inches of the top. Let the water stand for about a week to let any chlorine dissipate before adding fish or plants.

A Delicate Balance

The ideal pond needs no expensive filtration but is a delicate balance of plants, fish, algae, and eating fauna such as Japanese black snails. Use floaters and submerged plants in addition to any ornamental ones you choose. Floaters provide shade, a hiding place for fish from predators, keep the water cool, and their long roots act as biofilters to clean the water. Submerged plants provide food for fish, add oxygen to the water (they are often called oxygenators), and offer a place for the fish to spawn or just hang out.

Like all gardening, once you start looking through the catalogs and visiting nurseries, it is tempting to buy more plants and creatures than your water garden can maintain. Catalogs often refer to plants being suitable for a container or a small, medium, or large pond. This is the translation: a container garden is one to three feet wide, a small pond three to six feet wide, a medium pond six to ten feet wide, and a large pond greater than ten feet wide. A natural pond, with an earth bottom, can be any width but is at least three feet deep.

For a pond with ten square feet of surface area (multiply for the size of your pond) use:

- five black Japanese snails
- four bunches (six stems per bunch) of oxygenators (less expensive at pet stores than at garden centers)
- one small to medium-sized water lily
- two bog or marginal plants
- two small-leafed floating plants

- five two-inch fish (or ten one-inch fish) You may want to start small, as the most common fish—goldfish and koi—will grow quickly

Algae will come by itself, often on some of the plants you purchase.

A pond myth is that without moving water, mosquitoes will be a problem. If you have fish, they will feast on mosquito larvae. I prefer to hand feed the fish, putting my hand in the water then placing a few flakes of fish food on the surface. If the fish are three inches or larger, I use pellets. Eventually, the fish associate the hand with food and will literally eat out of my hand. The most renowned water gardener in Holland, Ada Hoffmann, has one pond with named fish that come when she calls each one by its name. Neither my Dutch nor her English was good enough to explain how she trained them. Yet even when I called one by its name, the fish came—and, of course, was rewarded with food.

When planting for the water garden, use rich, clayey soil or heavy loam. Follow the planting directions for depth of the roots or rhizomes and add a layer of pea gravel or builders sand to keep the soil in the pot. Using pots with drainage holes is ideal, especially if the water level drops, since the plant is assured of staying moist from below.

Different types of plants grow best in certain sized pots. In general, I prefer round pots since they are easier to arrange in the garden, but square or rectangular ones work equally well. The pot should be relatively deep.

A Guide to Pot Sizes for Aquatic Plants

Type of plant	Ideal pot size
Lotus	twenty-four inches wide
Marginal	one gallon
Submerged creeper	Large cat litter pan with holes drilled in the bottom or a special mesh basket available by mailorder
Submerged non-creeper	one gallon
Water lily	one gallon
Water lily-like	one gallon

Many water plants are heavy feeders and require regular fertilization to remain healthy and bloom freely. Tablets or pellets are the easiest to use, as you simply push them into the soil of the potted plant. Always be sure to follow manufacturer's directions for quantity (varies from plant to plant) and frequency of feeding. Although the time-release spikes may sound appealing and timesaving, they do not release the nutrients consistently, often giving off too much fertilizer at the beginning of the season and none by the end.

Any water plant that is a floater or a submerged plant (such as water lettuce, parrot feather, and water hyacinth) gets all the nutrition it needs from the water. These oxygenating plants help clean the pond, eating algae and bacteria.

Insect pests and diseases are generally not a problem with water plants. Their greatest pest is the raccoon. Racoons are attracted to water gardens, as they like to wash their food before eating. There are many delectable treats for them in a water garden. I had a small horse trough that I had sunk into the ground, which made a perfect water garden—complete with plain and fancy goldfish, water lettuce, a water lily, a number of submersed oxygenating plants, and a lizard tail. I was training the fish to eat from my hand. I went out one morning to feed them, and, to my horror, the entire pond had been destroyed by raccoons overnight. They ate much of the plant material, tossed the pots out into the garden, tore up what they didn't eat, and, needless to say, the fish were probably their favorite part of the meal. The water was brown from all the dirt and a total mess. The best control for raccoons is to surround the water garden with a two-wire electric fence. Some people cover the garden with bird netting or chicken wire, but that can prevent the plants from gaining their full height. In addition, unless the wire or netting is strongly anchored, a heavy raccoon can easily walk on it and drop into the water. The worst case scenario is if the raccoon gets caught in the wire or netting; then you must call animal control.

The plants included here will get you started in water gardening. Soon you will find you want to explore more possibilities—and there are many. The greatest choices are available through specialty mail-order companies. (See mail-order sources in the back of this book.) While your enthusiasm builds, I will be out and checking on my two water gardens—a small horse trough dug in the front yard garden and a faux whiskey barrel on the front porch. Between them, I have a resplendence of life with fish (several types of goldfish and koi), oxygenators including parrot's feather, 'Aurora' water lily, water mint, lizard's tail, curly rush, dwarf cattails, variegated iris, and water lettuce.

Tranquil Spot by Water Garden

American Lotus
Nelumbo lutea

Native in most of the Prairie Lands, the American lotus (formerly N. pentapetala) is one of the largest and magnificent plants for any water garden—from a 5- by 5-foot tub to a large pond. Its impressive (1 to 2 feet across), eye-catching, bluish-green leaves capture water droplets, adding to the plant's almost mystical appearance. By midsummer, the huge (up to 10 inches across), lightly fragrant, lilylike flowers rise above the leaves, adding to its beauty. After several days, the flower transforms into a flat-topped seedpod with an interesting cratered look. It matures and dries to a lovely brown color. Although the edible seeds, immature seedpods, and rhizomes (lotus root) are most often associated with Asian cuisine, they were also an important food for Native Americans.

Other Common Names
Water Chinquapin, Yanquapin

Bloom Period and Seasonal Color
Pale yellow in summer.

Mature Height × Spread
3 to 6 ft. × indefinite (unless contained)

Zone
4

When, Where, and How to Plant
Order rhizomes from mail-order catalogs or buy them in nurseries in spring. Once the weather reaches 70 degrees Fahrenheit, fill a round container (1 to 2 feet across and at least 12 inches deep) that has a drainage hole with rich, heavy garden loam. Add distilled water (lotuses are pH sensitive) until there is 2 inches of water above the soil. Put the rhizome in the pot and let it float. Once it starts sprouting leaves, place a flat stone on the rhizome so it touches the soil; do not bury it. Move the container into the water garden.

Growing Tips
When first putting the lotus in the water garden, prop it on bricks so the base of the plant is 2 inches below water level. As the plant grows, remove the bricks. It can thrive with 3 feet of water above the rhizome once it is established. Lotus is a heavy feeders, requiring food every few weeks, but wait to fertilize until there are at least three leaves on the plant. Use a tablet-form fertilizer for water plants. Follow label instructions. Lotus needs a few weeks of 80-degree weather to bloom.

Care and Maintenance
The deeper the lotus (and its container), the better it will overwinter—at least 3 feet is ideal as the tuber migrates down to avoid freezing. If needed, divide lotus in spring. Turn over the pot, wash away the soil, and cut the rhizome 1 to 4 inches past the second joint from the end. Make more divisions; be sure each has two joints. Repot as described above. There are no pest or disease concerns.

Companion Planting and Design
Lotus is often planted alone. Add some fish—koi or goldfish—to dart about the water, adding to the serenity of the scene. In a large water garden, combine it with day- and night-blooming water lilies.

I Also Recommend
The flower of the sacred lotus (*Nelumbo nucifera*) resembles an aquatic peony—single or double—in shades of pink and white on a 5-foot stalk.

Blue Flag

Iris versicolor

When, Where, and How to Plant

Plant anytime from mid-spring to early fall. Blue flag prefers acidic soil; add peat moss to the soil when planting. The peat moss also retains moisture, which is a key to success. Blue flag may be planted directly in an earthen pond or in 1-gallon pots on the top shelf of a preformed pond.

Growing Tips

If the plant is not growing under 2 to 3 inches of water, make sure the soil remains consistently moist. Watch for yellowing of the leaves, which may indicate rot or iris borers. No feeding is needed.

Care and Maintenance

Blue flag may be allowed to grow into large clumps; however, any decline in flower production is a sign that the plant needs dividing. After it blooms, dig up the clump using a shovel or a fork. Use two pitchforks (dug in at the same place but pulling in opposite directions) to divide the plant into smaller clumps once it is out of the ground. Replant the smaller clumps immediately—some in original locations and others in new locations or share them with friends. Replant at the same level they were growing originally. Dig up any suspicious looking plant and examine the rhizome for disease or insect damage. Watch for holes, which indicate borers (or you may see the small grublike creatures), black or brown rotted areas, or green moldy spots. Cut out any problem areas and discard (do not compost).

Companion Planting and Design

The upstanding, swordlike leaves add a vertical element near the edge of a garden. I find that a collection of the various water-loving iris including laevigate iris (*I. laevigata* 'Aureomarginata'), yellow flag (*I. pseudacorus*), variegated yellow flag (*I. pseudacorus* 'Variegata'), and Japanese iris (*I. ensata*), provides accents in a variety of hues, including variegated. The foliage provides a range of flowers from the shallow portions of the pond to the moist banks.

I Also Recommend

'Kermesina', with reddish-purple flowers, is outstanding for small ponds. 'Rosea' sets itself apart with its pink blooms.

Blue flag is one of the prettiest plants that helps to make the transition from traditional garden space into a water garden. Its graceful, narrow, gray-green foliage makes this plant attractive even without its glorious show of flowers. Each stem branches, producing three to five flowers that appear almost iridescent in the light of the setting sun. Look closely and notice the falls (petals that hang down) with their gold and white butterfly-like veined design that begins at the base of the petals and continues into the broader portion where it changes to all purple. Blue flag is a marginal plant, grown in the shallows 6 inches under water, yet I have grown it successfully in a bog garden planted in very wet, peaty soil.

Other Common Name
Wild Iris

Bloom Period and Seasonal Color
Purple, violet, or lavender blue in early to midsummer.

Mature Height and Spread
3 ft. × 2 ft.

Zone
5

Cattail

Typha spp.

I grew up on Long Island, where cattails with their distinctive poker-like flower spikes were indigenous. The rustling leaves were background sounds of my childhood. Those cattails, however, are too large for most home water gardens. Dwarf cattail (Typha minima) fits the bill, with its more diminutive habit, growing only 18 inches tall. The flower spikes are different—slightly more rounded—yet still have male and female flowers on the same spike. Like its larger cousins, the flower stalks of the dwarf cattail are prized for flower arranging. Along with the plant's smaller stature, its leaves are quite narrow, almost grass-like, making that familiar rustling sound in a breeze. It is ideal for a container water garden or a small pond, adding a dramatic vertical element to the garden.

Bloom Period and Seasonal Color
Chocolate brown in summer.

Mature Height and Spread
2/3 to 9 ft. × 1 to 8 ft.

When, Where, and How to Plant
Like other marginal water plants, cattails are best planted in the spring with the rhizomes 2 inches or more below the soil and with 4 to 6 inches of water above the soil level. If it's grown in a round container (at least 12 inches wide and deep), you do not have to worry about them spreading, even if you put the container in a soil-bottom pond. The thick rhizomes thrive in shallow water and, unrestrained, spread readily, bearing narrow, upright leaves and brown flower spikes.

Growing Tips
If you plant any cattail directly in a pond, it will become invasive unless the water is too deep for it. Beware, as the rhizomes are tough and can even grow through a thin pond liner. To keep it within bounds and avoid costly liner repairs, grow it in pots and place the pots in the pond. Cattail does not need fertilizer.

Care and Maintenance
Cattail needs minimal attention. If you want to dry the flower heads for use in flower arrangements, pick them early in the season before they flower, let them dry, and then spray with a fixative or lacquer. Cattail was a favorite of Native Americans. Once the plant was in bloom—you see small yellow female flowers on the upper half of the flower spike—they would shake or rub off the flowers and pollen. This was used as a flour substitute as well as a soothing tea.

Companion Planting and Design
At the edge of a water garden, the tropical looking leaves and exotic white flowers of calla lilies (*Zantedeschia aethiopica*) are a good foil for the stark upright habit of the dwarf cattail. Although not hardy, calla lilies can be dug up in fall and overwintered indoors. 'Crowborough' is a good choice, growing only 24 inches tall, while 'Little Gem' is even smaller (12 inches high).

I Also Recommend
Narrow-leafed cattail (*Typha angustifolia*)—4 to 5 feet tall—is suitable for a larger space garden, yet it retains a dainty look.

Duck Potato
Sagittaria latifolia

When, Where, and How to Plant

Duck potatoes are best planted in late spring in full sun. Plant directly into pond soil or in a round 1-gallon pot filled with rich, heavy garden soil. Place the crown (where roots and stem meet) 1 inch below soil level. If you want to harvest tubers, plant directly in a pond or a long container such as a large cat litter pan with several holes drilled in the bottom. Plan its placement so the crown is 3 to 6 inches below the water surface.

Growing Tips

Don't worry if some of the leaves grow on or even under the water; that is normal. An added benefit of duck potato is that it is an oxygenator—adding life-supporting oxygen to the water. This helps keep the delicate balance of life in a water garden. Fertilizing is not necessary.

Care and Maintenance

If the plant gets too big, divide it in the summer. Dig it up or remove it from its pot and wash away all the soil. The new plants attached to the mother plants will become obvious. Cut off any new plants that have a good set of roots and leaves. Pot them or plant them in the pond with the crown no more than 1 inch below the soil level. Duck potatoes have no pest or disease problems.

Companion Planting and Design

Repetition of leaf shape is pleasing to the eye. Grow duck potato along with the variegated arrowhead, *S. graminea* 'Crushed Ice'. The variegation in its leaves adds contrast during the daytime and is visible after the sun goes down, adding nighttime interest. Lizard's tail (*Saururus cernuus*), also known as American swamp lily, makes a good companion with its gooseneck of fragrant white flowers that last all summer.

I Also Recommend

Double-flowering arrowhead (*Sagittaria sagittifolia* 'Flore-Pleno') is not hardy but is worth growing as an annual. Or dig it up and overwinter it indoors in a cool, but not freezing, space and replant in late spring. Its showy double flowers and strong, up-facing arrow-shaped leaves are outstanding.

Like any of the arrowheads that are commonly seen growing along the edges of ponds and water gardens, duck potato has arrow-shaped leaves. Its leaves are 4 to 12 inches long and rise above the water. Also unique are the triangular, 4-foot flower stems which bear racemes of 1- to 1¹/2-inch, whorled white flowers. Duck potato distinguishes itself by the walnut-sized tubers it produces. These were prized by the Native Americans (as well as by ducks) and were often roasted and eaten like potatoes. If you want to try eating the tubers, do not pull up the plant. In late summer to autumn (if the plant is in earth), root around with your toes, and the tubers will break off easily and rise to the top of the water.

Other Common Name
Wapato

Bloom Period and Seasonal Color
White in summer.

Mature Height and Spread
1¹/2 to 3 ft. × 3 ft.

Zone
5

Parrot Feather
Myriophyllum aquaticum

This plant is all too often overlooked, yet it is so beautiful and plays a vital role in the ecology of a water garden. It is delicate and lacy looking, light green like a wild parrot's feather. I have "grown" it in a small tabletop water garden by just laying several 4-inch long pieces in a 12-inch clear glass bowl. It is so elegant and simple because the parrot feather will float on top of the water and grow below as well. It is often used in fish tanks, as the fish will nibble on it. More important in a water garden, it is an underwater oxygenator, adding that vital element to the water (even more critical if you have fish).

Other Common Name
Diamond Milfoil

Bloom Period and Seasonal Color
Yellow (insignificant) in summer.

Mature Height and Spread
2 to 3 in. × 6 ft. or more

Zone
6

When, Where, and How to Plant
It is so easy to grow. Just drop a piece of parrot feather in water. I have grown it by itself in a glass bowl indoors, near a south-facing window throughout the winter. As it is only hardy in Zones 6 to 10, wait until the temperature has warmed outdoors. Put it in the water about the same time you would plant tomatoes. In a large pond, much of it will sink, providing some nibbles for any fish and giving off oxygen. It can be a decorative marginal plant. To achieve that effect, grow it along the edge of a pond by sticking one end about 1 inch into the soil, or plant it in a 6-inch pot filled with heavy soil with 3 to 12 inches of water above the soil.

Growing Tips
Parrot feather can be an enthusiastic grower and can easily take up too much space above water in a container garden (such as a lined whiskey barrel). Do not worry about cutting it back too much. Just leave an inch of the plant above water and at least 3 inches underwater. Parrot feather gets its nutrition from the water and provides food for fish.

Care and Maintenance
Parrot feather is low maintenance, needing just the occasional pruning. As it is not hardy in the Prairie Lands states, you might want to cut a piece or two and bring them into the house to grow in a bowl during the winter. Make sure it is near a western or southern window for ample light. Although I like the drama of seeing it above and below water by growing it in a clear glass bowl, any bowl or container will do.

Companion Planting and Design
Parrot feather's ferny look pairs well with a more solid plant like water lettuce, which can also be grown in a bowl or in a pond. A word of warning: water lettuce is like rabbits—multiplying profusely. Therefore, you may have to thin the crop.

I Also Recommend
Plant only this species.

Water Hyacinth
Eichhornia crassipes

When, Where, and How to Plant

When the water temperature is 65 degrees Fahrenheit, place water hyacinth in a deep, glass bowl of room-temperature water. Swish it around gently. If you see any tiny two-leafed plants float to the top circulating in the water, that is duckweed, which is invasive, not at all beneficial, and should be removed. Once you are sure the roots are clean, place the water hyacinth into the water garden. If you have one or more pools and a contained stream or small waterfall (that does not go into any waterway), place some in all areas. You can often find a place, even in the running water, where one or two will stay in place. Otherwise put an inconspicuous rock to hold it in place. As the water runs through the roots, the roots filter out impurities, including those from fish waste. I have seen a number of complex water gardens with several pools, stream, and waterfalls run with only the pump that recirculates the water. The balance of fish and plants keeps the water in these magnificent gardens crystal clear.

Growing Tips

As it grows, the "mother" plant puts out offshoots. If the number of plants gets out of control (covering more than two-thirds of the water), separate the plants and discard the mother plants, unless they are about to bloom. Keep the healthiest and best-looking plants. Water hyacinths needs no fertilizer.

Care and Maintenance

Occasionally a plant may develop brown spots or turn yellowish. Pull it out and discard it. Never discard or plant water hyacinth in any stream, river, or lake. Put it on the compost pile or in the trash. Even though we are beyond their hardiness zone, it is possible for them to travel downstream during the growing season and arrive in their ideal climate.

Companion Planting and Design

As floating plants, water hyacinth defies design. It will travel around the water garden with the current and breeze, looking attractive paired with anything in the garden.

I Also Recommend

Plant only this species.

Water hyacinth has gotten a bad name for itself because it is so prolific and invasive that it has clogged waterways in the South. However, it will not winter over in our region. Water hyacinth is a floating plant with a thick stem. The purplish-green roots extend about a foot down into the water. It is unusual looking with three or more balloon-like stalks at the center, which give rise to rounded leaves. Its flowers are magnificent, looking like giant lilac-blue hyacinths with yellow at the centers. It is important in a water garden as it acts as a natural biofilter, helping to keep the pond clean, especially if there are fish. Water hyacinths are now used commercially in water treatment plants.

Bloom Period and Seasonal Color
Violet-blue with a yellow splotch in summer.

Mature Height and Spread
6 in. × up to 18 in.

Water Lettuce

Pistia stratiotes

Like the water hyacinth, water lettuce is invasive; it is even banned in some states. In cold regions, its benefits outweigh any negatives. Like strawberries and water hyacinth, it sends out runners from the mother plant, so one plant can cover a large area. The plant is a beautiful green, floating rosette—looking like the most perfect leaf lettuce. Each runner it sets out is equally perfect. It has a light glaucous coating that makes water droplets from rain or splashing stand up on the leaf, resembling small round diamonds shining back at you. Its long feathery roots are a sight to see, changing color from white to purple, indigo, and finally black. Like those of the water hyacinth, they act as filters, removing impurities from the water.

Other Common Name
Shell Flower

Bloom Period and Seasonal Color
Inconspicuous white flowers in summer.

Mature Height and Spread
4 in. × up to 20 ft.

Zones
9 to 11

When, Where, and How to Plant

Purchase water lettuce in spring once the water is consistently 65 degrees Fahrenheit. Once you get the plant, fill a sink or the tub with room temperature water (about 70 degrees Fahrenheit). Holding the plant gently by its leaves, lightly swish the long roots through the water. Look for any duckweed that may have traveled along on the roots. Duckweed is a tiny (less than $^{1}/_{2}$ inch), two-leafed plant that is very invasive. Because it is so tiny, it is very difficult to remove from a pond once it is there. Remove and throw out any duckweed. Swirl the roots for a few minutes, changing directions, to seek out any hangers-on. Then you are ready to place the water lettuce in your water garden, where it will float and multiply. Put some in each section of the garden. Not only does it filter water, its cover provides a nice hiding place for fish from birds, cats, and raccoons and is a food source.

Growing Tips

As it grows, the "mother" plant puts out offshoots. If the number of plants gets out of control (covering more than two-thirds of the water), separate the plants and discard the mother plants. Keep the healthiest and best-looking plants. No fertilizer is needed.

Care and Maintenance

Occasionally water lettuce turns yellow—indicating chlorosis. It can also be due to the water—too acidic or too alkaline. Often, the addition of fish—if you don't already have them—and oxygenating plants will fix the problem.

Companion Planting and Design

Since water lettuce is a floater, it is difficult to choose plants to grow with it, as it travels on its own around the water garden. It looks beautiful next to the feathery foliage of parrot feather or floating among the lacy leaves of fairy moss, especially late in summer when the fairy moss turns dark red.

I Also Recommend

'Angio Splash' is variegated with splotches of creamy yellow. 'Aqua Velvet' has deep blue-green leaves. 'Rosette' has denser clusters of leaves.

Water Lily
Nymphaea spp., cultivars, and hybrids

When, Where, and How to Plant
Water lilies grow in still water. In late spring, plant the rhizome in a round one-gallon, plastic pot in firm loam covered with a thin layer of soil. Add an inch of pea gravel or coarse sand. Place the pot so that the rhizome is submerged 6 to 10 inches. Small rhizomes require 3 inches of water while large varieties need 20 inches. As the plant grows, gradually lower the pot so that, at maturity, the rhizome is twice its original depth.

Growing Tips
To get the proper water level above the plant, place the pot on bricks or remove them as necessary. For especially vigorous plants, use a special aquatic cage-like container (3 feet wide × 18 inches deep). Feed with pellets according to the manufacturer's label.

Care and Maintenance
Cut off any yellow leaves and deadhead often for longer bloom. Hardy water lilies can remain in the water year-round at maximum depth. Treat tropical varieties as annuals and discard them at season's end or move them to an indoor pool. Alternatively, wait until after several hard frosts to dig up the rhizomes, air dry them for several days, and over-winter them (above 50 degrees Fahrenheit) in damp sand. In spring, restart tropicals and divide hardy water lilies in preparation for summer. Water lilies are susceptible to crown rot, which is evident as the top of the plant starts to die. Remove the affected plants and destroy it immediately.

Companion Planting and Design
Combine tropicals and hardy varieties, day- and night-bloomers. Pair it with water snowflake (*Nymphoides indica variegata*) with its heart-shaped, water lily-like leaves and small, single, white flowers. Or, contrast its horizontal habit with a vertical plant such as one of the flag irises (*Iris* spp.).

I Also Recommend
Try the hardy varieties: 'Charles de Meurville'—fragrant, pink-tipped red flowers; 'Virginalis'—an abundance of white flowers from late spring to fall; 'Georgia Peach'—delicate yellow and pink blended flowers, slightly mottled leaves. Tropicals include: 'Charles Thomas'—sweetly fragrant, periwinkle-blue flowers, purple-blotched leaves; 'Emily Grant Hutchings'—night-blooming, large deep rose-pink flowers, easy to grow.

Water lilies often draw people to water gardening for the first time. It reigns supreme with its elegant flowers and floating leaves. The large multi-petaled flowers (from 5 to 10 inches across in rainbow hues) add a look of romance. When fully open, it reveals the boldly colored stamens in the center. Water lilies are of two major types: hardy (Zone 3) and tropical. Night-blooming tropicals open after sunset, perfuming the night air. The flowers are not the only remarkable parts of the water lily; the leaves are quite sensational as well. Leaves range from deep burgundy to maroon, olive green to dark purple, even purple mottled; heart-shaped and round; smooth, curved, or with raised edges. With so many choices, the decision is not whether to buy a water lily, but how many.

Bloom Period and Seasonal Color
White, pink (from palest to fuchsia), magenta, carmine, red, lilac, yellow, light blue, red-orange, and apricot; from late spring to fall, depending on variety.

Mature Height and Spread
4 to 12 in. × $1^1/2$ to 12 ft.

Zones
3 to 7
10 to 11 (tropicals only)

Lawn Care Tips

Although there is always a great debate on chemical versus organic lawn care experts on both sides agree on one thing: Lawn care should be made to be as simple as possible. It may require some extra work initially to get your lawn in good shape, with healthy soil. After that, you can follow a regular regimen.

Spring

After the snow melts and the warm weather starts to settle in, it is time to get out the rake and give the lawn a good cleanup. Use only a lawn/leaf rake (the kind with the tines spayed out). Get rid of leaves and other debris that may have accumulated on the lawn over the winter. Add this to your compost pile. The raking also raises the mat of the lawn, allowing it to breathe.

Do you lime or sulfur your lawn every year? Before you add anything, determine if it is needed by having your soil tested. Many nurseries do soil tests and there are simple at-home testing kits. For a modest fee, most Cooperative Extension services will do a soil pH test (sometimes these are free for members).

It is important to take a sample that is representative of the lawn area. The sample should come from beneath the sod, in the top two to six inches of soil. The Extension Service recommends that you bring about a $1/2$ cup of soil in a plastic sandwich bag, labeled so you know what area it came from. If you have extensive lawn areas it is a good idea to take samples from several locations, such as front and back lawns and other areas.

John Doyle, a research and development turfgrass specialist, recommends core aeration in spring to help reduce thatch while promoting better root development and improving compacted soil. Experts agree that compaction is a major problem on lawns. People don't think about the soil under the lawn the same way they do about regular garden soil. Gardeners who would never consider stepping in their flowerbeds for fear of compacting the soil, lithely walk across lawns all the time. This is not to say that lawns should be off-limits, but you should recognize the effects of foot traffic. A de-thatching machine can be detrimental to the lawn. Aeration machines punch out 2- to 3-inch plugs of soil every four to six inches.

Some experts recommend adding organic matter to help reduce compaction and improve soil structure. You can spread a $1/4$-inch layer of compost, well-rotted manure, or humus across the lawn and lightly rake it in. If you do this after aeration, it will sink into the ground quicker.

Any existing lawn, especially if is an old lawn, will benefit from overseeding in the spring. Many lawn experts suggest blending grasses; unfortunately there is no perfect grass. Even in a lawn that is all rye grass, for example, you should blend two or three kinds of rye. You can also blend different types of grass together. For example, mix fine fescue with ryegrass for shady areas. Using a variety of grasses cuts down on the incidence of disease and insect problems. Bluegrasses are still the backbone of the lawn industry. They have the advantage of being able to repair themselves and fill in areas. When overseeding you should add about 15 to 18 seeds per square inch.

Fall

In most cases, fall is the best time to fertilize. Otherwise, (contrary to what most lawn care companies, and lawn fertilizer brands would have you believe) you create more work for yourself by fertilizing with a high nitrogen fertilizer in the spring. Cool season grasses have a bimodal growth curve. That is, they have a strong vertical growth period in the spring, go dormant in the summer heat (without watering) and have a moderate growth period in the fall. When you fertilize in the spring, the plant keeps putting out top growth at the expense of root growth. You have to mow earlier and more frequently—a waste of your time and natural resources. Then, in the summer, when drought conditions are likely, the roots don't reach far down into the soil. As a result, you have to water more frequently if you want a green lawn.

When you fertilize in the fall, the plant puts energy into the roots and stores carbohydrates. Doyle explains that a lawn is like a car. As you run the car, the alternator charges the battery so that when you turn off the car, there is energy to start it up. When you feed a lawn with a slow-release fertilizer in the fall, it stores the energy as carbohydrates, ready to get the lawn off to a green start in the spring. I always fertilized my lawn on Thanksgiving Day (even if there's snow). It is a good way to work off that big dinner, and feed another life form and be thankful for the beauty it provides through the growing season.

In a case of a lawn that is not in good shape, however, fertilization in both spring and fall is recommended, preferably with a slow-release, organic fertilizer.

Mowing

All the experts recommend cutting lawns high, especially in hot weather. The length of the blade of grass helps to keep the lawn cooler. It actually shades the roots and helps to conserve moisture. Three inches is the recommended cutting height.

When you cut your lawn, leave the clippings. They will break down and help feed he soil—thus in turn, feed the lawn. When mowing, do not cut off more than a third of the height of the grass. If you have let the lawn go and the clippings are too long and look like windrows, rake them up and add them to your compost pile.

Weeds

As for lawn weeds, if you are concerned about the environment, it is best to accept them. As your lawn becomes thicker and healthier, there is less chance of weeds having a place to take hold. For now, if it is green, enjoy it. Those young dandelion greens are great in salads or stir-fries!

Edible Flowers

Adding beauty and flavor to garden and kitchen.

The 10 Commandments of Edible Flowers

1. Eat only those flowers you can positively identify as safe and edible. Learn the Latin or botanical names, which are universally accepted (common names may vary from region to region).

2. Do not assume that restaurants and caterers always know which flowers are edible. Just because it is on your plate does not mean it is edible (see Rule #1).

3. Eat only those flowers that have been grown organically.

4. Do not eat flowers from florists, nurseries, garden centers or public gardens (see Rule #3).

5. Do not eat flowers if you have hay fever, asthma or allergies.

6. Do not eat flowers picked from the side of heavily trafficked roads.

7. Eat only the petals of flowers; always remove and discard the pistils and stamens before eating. (Except for the tiny flowers like thyme where it would be like performing microsurgery to remove the pistils and stamens.)

8. Not all sweet-smelling flowers are edible; some are poisonous.

9. Eat only the flowers of the recommended plants; other parts may be toxic or inedible, even though the flower may be delicious.

10. Gradually introduce flowers into your diet—one at a time and in small quantities, the way you would new food to a baby.

The Flowers

Common Name	Botanical Name	Flavor
Anise hyssop	*Agastache foeniculum*	Licorice
Apple	*Malus* spp.	Floral
Arugula	*Eruca vesicaria sativa*	Peppery
Banana	*Musa* spp.	Sweet
Basil	*Ocimum basilicum*	Herbal
Bee balm	*Monarda didyma*	Spicy/sweet
Borage	*Borago officinalis*	Cucumber
Broccoli	*Brassica oleracea,* Botrytis group	Spicy
Calendula	*Calendula officinalis*	Slightly bitter
Canary creeper	*Tropaeolum peregrinum*	Peppery
Chamomile	*Anthemis nobilis*	Apple
Chicory	*Cichorium intybus*	Slightly bitter

The Flowers (continued)

Common Name	Botanical Name	Flavor
Chives	*Allium schoenoprasum*	Oniony
Chrysanthemum	*Dendranthema grandiflorum*	Mild to slightly bitter
Coriander (Cilantro)	*Coriandrum sativum*	Herbal
Dandelion	*Taraxacum officinale*	Sweet, slightly bitter
Daylily	*Hemerocallis* spp.	Sweet to vegetal
Dianthus	*Dianthus caryophyllus*	Sweet, clove
Dill	*Anethum graveolens*	Herbal
Elderberry	*Sambucus canadensis*	Sweet
English daisy	*Bellis perennis*	Slightly bitter
Fennel	*Foeniculum vulgare*	Herbal
Garlic chives	*Allium tuberosum*	Garlicky
Hibiscus	*Hibiscus rosa-sinensis*	Mild citrus
Hollyhock	*Alcea rosea*	Mild nutty
Honeysuckle	*Lonicera japonica*	Sweet floral
Hyssop	*Hyssopus officinalis*	Strong herbal
Japanese plum	*Prunus* 'Mume'	Sweet almond
Jasmine	*Jasminum sambac* and *J. officinale*	Sweet floral
Johnny-jump-up	*Viola tricolor*	Slightly minty
Kale	*Brassica oleracea*, Acephala group	Spicy
Lavender	*Lavandula* spp.	Strong floral
Lemon	*Citrus limon*	Sweet citrus
Lemon verbena	*Aloysia triphylla*	Sweet citrus
Lilac	*Syringa* spp.	Floral
Linden	*Tilia* spp.	Sweet
Marjoram	*Origanum vulgare*	Herbal
Mint	*Mentha* spp.	Minty
Mustard	*Brassica juncea*	Spicy
Nasturtium	*Tropaeolum majus*	Peppery
Nodding onion	*Allium cernuum*	Oniony
Ocotillo	*Fouquieria splendens*	Sweet cranberry
Okra	*Abelmoschus aesculentus*	Mild, sweet

The Flowers (continued)

Common Name	Botanical Name	Flavor
Orange	*Citrus sinensis*	Sweet citrus
Oregano	*Origanum* spp.	Herbal
Pansy	*Viola* x *wittrockiana*	Slight minty
Pea	*Pisum sativum*	Pea-like
Pineapple guava	*Feijoa sellowiana*	Sweet tropical
Pineapple sage	*Salvia elegans*	Spicy sweet
Radish	*Raphanus sativus*	Peppery
Red clover	*Trifolium pratense*	Sweet
Redbud	*Cercis canadensis*	Pea-like
Rose	*Rosa* spp.	Floral
Rose of Sharon	*Hibiscus syriacus*	Mild
Roselle	*Hibiscus sabdariffa*	Mild citrus
Rosemary	*Rosmarinus officinalis*	Herbal
Runner bean	*Phaseolus coccineus*	Bean-like
Safflower	*Carthamus tinctorius*	Bitter
Sage	*Salvia officinalis*	Herbal
Scented geranium	*Pelargonium* spp.	Floral
Signet marigold	*Tagetes signata* (*T. tenuifolia*)	Citrusy tarragon
Shungiku	*Chrysanthemum coronarium*	Slightly bitter
Society garlic	*Tulbaghia violacea*	Sweet garlicky
Squash	*Curcubita pepo* spp.	Vegetal
Summer savory	*Satureja hortensis*	Herbal
Sunflower	*Helianthus annuus*	Bittersweet
Sweet woodruff	*Galium odoratum*	Fresh, sweet
Thyme	*Thymus* spp.	Herbal
Tuberous begonia	*Begonia* x *tuberhybrida*	Citrus
Tulip	*Tulipa* spp.	Bean- or pea-like
Violet	*Viola odorata*	Sweet floral
Winter savory	*Satureja montana*	Herbal
Yucca	*Yucca* spp.	Sweet (must be cooked)

Find additional information in *Edible Flowers from Garden to Palate* by Cathy Wilkinson Barash, which contains 280 recipes for 67 different flowers. Also *Edible Flowers: Drinks & Desserts*.

More About Roses

Rose Classification

There are a number of classes of roses. The most common (and ones likely to be grown in our region) include: hybrid tea, floribunda, grandiflora, shrub or landscape, and species.

Hybrid tea roses are the largest group of modern roses and the most widely grown—even in our region. They exemplify the ideal characteristics; long pointed buds opening to elegant, high-centered, fragrant flowers of diverse colors on long, straight stems. However, they are generally the least hardy, needing the most winter protection—some will not survive even with protection. It is a matter of personal choice. I prefer to have as low-maintenance a garden as possible, and as far as roses are concerned, I do not want to have to fuss with winterizing and then worry when we have a warm spell in winter that the roses are overheating with all their insulation.

D.T. Poulson from Denmark first created floribunda roses. His goal was to create a rose that would be hardy, survive the cold winters of northern Europe, be floriferous and constantly blooming, and need little or no special attention. He succeeded, and since his first introduction in 1924, other breeders have improved them. The originals had no fragrance, but many of today's hybrids do. Many also have the high centers and range of colors so prized in hybrid tea roses. Generally, they are not long-stemmed; instead they bloom in clusters, which is very attractive.

Grandiflora is the newest class of roses, created in the United States in 1954 for the rose 'Queen Elizabeth'. (Ironically, the British do not recognize this class; instead they call them floribunda hybrid-tea types.) Grandifloras are crosses between hybrid tea roses and floribundas, with the resulting roses having (ideally) the best characteristics of both. They bloom consistently through the growing season, are floriferous, with an abundance of 3- to 5-inch double flowers— borne singly or in clusters, with stems longer than floribundas but shorter than hybrid teas. Unfortunately, the quality that I look for they did not inherit—cold hardiness. They don't survive winters without protection.

Shrub rose is a bit of a misnomer, as it does not necessarily define size, shape, or habit (as in the preceding classes). A number of roses have been put together in this class. The characteristic common to them all is their toughness. They include true shrub-form roses, landscape roses, and English roses.

Species roses are those that occur naturally in the wild. Most self-pollinate and form beautiful hips (fruit)—often red or orange—that produce seeds that will grow true to the parent plant. Rose hips are high in vitamin C, and make delicious tea and jelly (if roses are grown organically). There are man-made hybrids of the species as well.

Container-grown Roses

Container-grown roses are found locally—often throughout the growing season. The choice of container-grown roses is very limited compared to bare-root plants. However, they are available later in the season—even in bloom—so you can truly judge the vigor of the plant.

Bare-root Roses

The roses you receive from mailorder companies are dormant, bare-root roses, which have been kept in cold storage and sent to you at the proper time for planting (you hope). Some local nurseries also have some bare-root roses in early spring. Check the canes (stems) to be sure they are healthy with green or reddish color and are firm to the touch. Do not buy ones that have dry or broken canes. Neither should you buy ones with a lot of new growth, as they are not in soil, so there is nothing to nourish the plant. Be aware that some of the roses you see in stores in long cardboard boxes are bare root, just wrapped with wood shavings, newspaper, or other moist packing material. You can judge by the heft whether the cardboard-boxed roses are bare root or containerized.

Planting

Roses are heavy feeders and need good, rich, well-drained soil. If you are planting an entire bed of roses, it is best to prepare the soil in the fall and then it will be ready to plant in the spring. Add plenty of compost and about 1 cup of superphosphate per cubic foot of soil and mix in well. Roses prefer slightly acid soil with a pH between 6.0 and 6.5.

Consider spacing before you plant. Allow 12 inches between miniature roses, 24 inches between hybrid tea roses, 30 inches between grandifloras, 36 inches between floribundas, 48 inches between standards (roses grown in tree form, plant them as an annual here), and 7 feet between climbing roses. Adequate spacing allows for good air circulation that prevents fungal diseases, and keeps plants from touching to prevent the possible spread of any disease or pest. Spacing is most important to give you access to the plant.

Container-grown Roses are Easy to Plant

1. Dig a hole a few inches larger than the container.
2. Amend the soil (see above).
3. Add about 6 inches of amended soil to the hole.
4. Remove the rose from the container (even the cardboard ones that say to plant the entire box). Keep the surrounding soil intact as much as possible.
5. Pour in a quart of transplant solution and let it absorb into the surrounding soil.

6. Position the rose at the same level it was in the container. However, if it is a grafted rose (you see a knob-like portion on the stem, which is the bud union where the rootstock and main plant were joined), plant the bud union 2 to 3 inches below ground level.

7. Add soil, filling the hole halfway. Gently firm the soil to eliminate any air pockets. Water with a quart of transplant solution.

8. Add the rest of the soil and water with another 2 quarts of transplant solution.

9. Add 2 to 3 inches of organic mulch (keeping 1 inch away from the stem) around the entire plant.

Bare-root Roses are Worth the Effort

When you receive a bare-root plant, unwrap it and soak it in muddy water for at least eight hours before planting. If you cannot plant it within 24 hours, wrap it in wet burlap or newspaper and store at about 40 degrees Fahrenheit in a dark place for up to a week. If it still cannot be planted, resoak and heel it in a trench at a 45-degree angle. Cover completely with several inches of moist soil and it can remain entrenched for up to six weeks. To plant:

1. Dig a hole at least 12 to 18 inches deep and 12 inches wide—large enough to accommodate the roots of the plant with several inches to spare.

2. Fill the hole with transplant solution and let it soak in. If any liquid is left after an hour or two, dig deeper and add builder's sand and organic matter to increase drainage

3. Amend the soil (see above).

4. Examine the bare-root plant. Prune to three or four healthy canes, removing any that are thinner than a pencil. Cut back any damaged roots or ones that are disproportionately long.

5. Make a mound of amended soil in the center of the hole, forming a cone that will support the roots. Make the cone high enough so that the bud union is 2 to 3 inches below soil level.

6. Position the plant, spreading the roots down around the cone.

7. Add the amended soil, filling two thirds of the hole. Add 2 to 3 quarts of transplant solution and let it soak in.

8. Fill in the rest of the hole and firm the soil gently with your hands.

9. Add moist soil, covering two-thirds of the plant to protect the dormant plant from wind and weather, while providing extra moisture so the plant can develop properly.

10. Check the plant at least once a week. When new growth is 1 to 2 inches long, gently remove the extra soil, smoothing to soil level. Mulch well.

Feeding Your Roses

Roses are heavy feeders. However, do not feed a newly planted rose for at least at month. Species, shrub roses ramblers and climbers need only be fed once in spring, before they leaf out.

Hybrid teas, floribundas, and grandifloras need at least three feedings a year. Give them their first feeding as early in spring as the shrub starts to leaf out. Feed for the second time as soon as the shrub starts to flower, and the final feeding in early August. Feeding too much later that than in our region encourages new growth that won't harden off before frost and will die back.

My approach is to treat your plants as you would your children or pets. Give them nutrition that is as close to natural as possible. If you buy an all-purpose rose fertilizer, read the label carefully; you just want to feed the rose, not kill pests and weeds at the same time. Always follow package instructions. If you don't want a specific rose fertilizer, you can use a granular, general-purpose fertilizer with an N-P-K (Nitrogen-Phosphorus-Potassium) ratio of 5-10-5. Generally, a handful or cupful spread around the base of each plant is sufficient.

I follow a more organic approach and in spring I apply around the base of each plant (keeping it several inches from the canes) 2 to 3 cups of compost or other well-rotted organic matter (leaf mold or rotted manure), $1/2$ cup bone meal, $1/2$ cup bloodmeal, $1/2$ cup greensand). Just to keep track of what I've put down I alternate between dark- and light-colored amendments. I then water plant with a gallon of water in which 1 to 2 Tablespoons of Epsom salts have been dissolved. Finally, I add a 4 to 6 inch layer of organic mulch. I foliar feed once a month with a solution of fish emulsion or kelp, taking care to spray leaves top and bottom, and early in the day. For the last feeding of the season, use a formulation without nitrogen, such as 0-10-10. Nitrogen promotes foliar growth. In late summer and autumn, you want to enhance the root system, not make more leaves.

Pruning Bravely

Pruning is the most intimidating facet of gardening to most gardeners. Believe me, it is rare that you will kill a rose by pruning it. Were it not for pruning, most roses would become a jungle of tangled stems with fewer and smaller flowers. Think of the wild roses you see at the edges of woodlands. Is that what you want your rose to look like? Without pruning, they would.

Cutting Roses

There are several reasons for pruning: to remove diseased or dead wood, to encourage new growth, and to train the plant to grow so that the crown area is as open as possible, allowing for optimal air circulation.

It is important to use the right tool for the size of the cane or stem. It is equally important to invest in a good pair of hand pruners (also called pruning shears or secateurs) that are comfortable for your hand. Hand pruners work well on canes up to $1/2$ inch in diameter. For canes up to an inch in diameter, use long-handled loppers. If you are pruning a very old rose with a larger diameter, use a fine-toothed saw. Wearing leather or rubber-reinforced gloves will help protect your hands from the thorns.

Pruning cuts are made at a 45-degree angle. You can always find a dead cane to practice on if you are nervous. As you prune, look for bud eyes—small nubs on the stems. They can be a bit hard to see in the early part of the season, but once the plant is growing, they are easily found in the crotch between the leaf attachment and the stem. Make the 45 degree cut $1/4$ to $1/2$ inch above an outward-facing bud eye. This encourages the plant to grow outward.

Major pruning is done in spring. Most hybrid teas, grandifloras, and floribundas can be cut back to as low as six inches. Just make sure to cut out all the dead wood. If you are unsure if the wood is alive, rub it gently with your thumbnail. If you see green, it is alive. Little or no pruning should be done after the end of August to mid-September—not even deadheading.

When you cut a rose to bring in for a bouquet or deadhead one that is past bloom that is also a form of pruning. When the plant is in full leaf, make the cut just above the lowest 5- or 7-leaflet leaf. That gives you a nice long stem for flower arranging, and it will grow a new healthy stem where you cut.

Watering

Roses not only need a lot of nutrition, they need a lot of water—the equivalent of an inch of rain a week at the least. The best way to measure—accurately—is with an inexpensive rain gauge.

Several factors influence the amount of water needed. When it is hot and humid, roses get by with less water than when it is hot and dry. Factor in our Prairie Lands "breezes", which increase evaporation, and up goes the water bill.

The best way to tell if a rose needs water is the old fashioned way. Stick your middle finger down into the soil. The soil should feel lightly moist to the touch. If it feels dry more than one inch down, water immediately. Of course, since you mulched well in spring, that mulch which is keeping the weeds down and the soil temperature constant, is also conserving water, and keeping the soil from drying out.

When watering, if at all possible, water at ground level to avoid wetting the leaves, thus avoiding some of the fungal problems of roses. One of the easiest ways to water is to get a leaky hose also known as a soaker hose (the kind where beads of water form on the surface) and weave it around the outer root zone of the plants. I lay it out in spring, and cover it with mulch, so it's invisible. I know what the output of the hose is per hour, so I can set a timer or turn on the hose for time needed, and the roses are watered. If you use an automatic timer system, get one that incorporates a water sensor so you are not wasting valuable water when it is raining. Our winters are too cold to leave the hose out all winter (that's why I prefer it to emitter or other plastic piping systems which are more complicated), so I take it up in winter when I'm winterizing the garden.

Getting Ready for Winter

To a lazy gardener, the main reason to grow Buck roses and the Canadian hardy roses (such as the Brownell sub-zero's) is that you don't have to do anything to get them ready for winter. They are bred to withstand the tough winters.

Hybrid teas and grandifloras need the most attention. Check how hardy your floribundas are relative to your zone and microclimate. At the end of the growing season, after the first light frost, mound up 4 to 6 inches of light soil around established roses. After the first hard frost, when that layer freezes, add another few inches of soil, allowing each layer to freeze before adding another. Top off at about 12 inches. You'll see a broad cone of soil with rose canes sticking up from that. In Zone 4 and below (and for any success with hybrid teas), cover the frozen mound with leaves. Cover any new plant completely or the extreme cold will kill the tender canes.

It's Spring!

As you well know, spring is fickle, so don't be in a rush to remove winter protection. Even light frosts can kill tender growth. Take a look under the mulch to see if any new growth has begun. If the danger of frost has passed, gently remove the mulch, taking care not to injure tender (and small) new growth. Keep some salt hay or barley hay on hand in case of a late freeze. A light covering can make the difference between a plant that thrives and one that succumbs to a late winterkill.

Propogation:
The Art of Making Plants

From a single plant, many can come. That's the basis of propagation. It is a very good way to cut the expense of your garden, especially if you want a lot of a single variety of plant.

If you are planting a large area, you might start by purchasing medium-sized to large plants very early in the season. Make stem cuttings (indoors), grow the cuttings indoors, and when it is the proper planting time, plant the rooted cuttings outside at the proper spacing—or even a bit closer than recommended. A few large plants can yield dozens of cuttings in a fairly short time.

Herbaceous Stem Cuttings

This is the technique to use for annuals and perennials, the easiest, and most common method of propagation. Water the "mother plant" well for several days ahead of time. Take cuttings from the young, vigorous growth on the plant. For annuals and summer- or fall-blooming perennials, the best time is in spring. In summer or early fall, take cuttings of annuals to overwinter indoors, as well as spring-blooming perennials.

When taking a cutting, use a sharp knife or razor to cut off about four to six inches (depending on the plant) of new (flexible) stem growth, including four or more sets of leaves. Make the cut just below a node (where the leaf attaches) at a 45-degree angle. Carefully cut off all but the top one or two sets of leaves, exposing several sets of nodes, and taking care not to cut the stem. If you are doing this outside, put the cuttings in a glass of water or wrap them in a moist paper towel until you get inside.

If you have been propagating any coleus, put the cuttings in the water from the coleus. Otherwise, dip the stem (including the nodes) in powdered rooting hormone, using the proper type for the plant. Fill a 6- to 12-inch pot with lightly moistened seed-starting mix. Use a pencil or dibble to make a hole in the mix. Insert the cutting so that only the leaves are above soil level. Space cuttings 1- to 2-inches apart. Make a u-shape from a piece of metal (wire hangars work well) that is at least four inches taller than the cuttings when it is bent. Push it two inches into the potting mix. Cover the pot with clear plastic—the wire supports the plastic, keeping it from drooping on the cuttings. Secure the plastic around the pot with a rubber band. Set in warm, well-lit place for about 6 weeks (not full sun or you will cook the cuttings; fluorescent lights 8 to 9 inches above the tops of the cuttings are ideal). During this time, they will be making roots. Remove the plastic weekly; check that the mix is still lightly damp. To remoisten, mist gently.

You can tell that the plant is rooted when you try to wiggle it and it stays still. Now it is time to transplant. Before transplanting outdoors, you need to harden off the cuttings. (Assuming that the timing and temperature is right for planting). With the plastic discarded, gradually bring the pot outdoors for an hour in the shade. Gradually increase the time and sun (depending on the plant's particular needs) over a two-week period until it is adjusted to the outdoors.

After they are hardened off, to transplant these rotted cuttings, use a pencil or a dibble to make the hole in the soil (in the garden if it is warm enough) to the right depth (the same level the soil was before). Insert the cutting, and gently firm soil around it. Water the plant with transplant solution. Keep the soil lightly moist until the plant is established.

If it is too early in the season, or if you want larger plants to put out in the garden (or even just grow them in containers), pot up the rooted cuttings into individual pots—usually a 3 to 6 inch pot depending on the size of the transplant. Use regular potting soil, lightly moistened with transplant solution, and make a hole for the transplant as above. Gently add more soil and press in. Keep the plant growing until you are ready to put it in its final place. Take the plant through the hardening off stage before putting it in its permanent new home.

A Word of Caution

More and more growers are patenting, registering, and trademarking their plants (this is especially evident in the world of roses, daylilies, and other perennials, although trademarked annuals are also now on the market). If you are considering purchasing a plant with propagation in mind, be sure to read the label carefully, and look for the description and name in any plant catalogs. If you are unsure, look up the plant on the Internet. If you see ™ or ® symbols, or a patent number, or "patent pending," it is illegal to propagate that plant. Some growers are getting serious about infringements, and taking people to court over patent or trademark infringement. When in doubt, just buy many little plants instead and wait for them to grow—don't risk breaking the law.

Pest and Disease Control

One can get so caught up in all the possible problems there can be with a garden that you almost feel defeated before you start. You can read that this plant gets this disease, another attracts a certain pest, and you might feel you need to call in the militia.

In all my years of gardening, I have taken St. Francis' prayer to heart (note: for those of you who think he is the patron saint of gardening, it is actually St. Fiacre). "God grant me the serenity to accept the things I cannot change, the courage to change the things I can, and the wisdom, to know the difference"—especially when it comes to garden pests and diseases.

I have always had a varied garden, with plants that are evergreens, deciduous, edibles, and ornamentals—a great diversity of plants. For this reason, I believe I have had far fewer pest problems than other folks. This is because there is a balance between the good bugs and the bad bugs. There are places for praying mantis to pupate. There are certain plants (trees and shrubs and many perennials) that have permanent places, while other plants are not in the same place from year to year (like vegetables and annuals that usually invite problems). This keeps soil diseases at bay.

Baking Soda Solution

One persistent problem in the Prairie Lands is powdery mildew, downy mildew, and other fungal diseases. You see it commonly on zinnias and lilac—a white powdery covering to the leaves. It rarely kills the plants, in fact, I have silver-leaved zinnias in full bloom, but it does take its toll. This homemade mixture works, especially when the spraying is started early in the season, before the disease takes hold. This baking soda solution has worked wonders on powdery mildew on zinnias, and blackspot on roses. Mix a solution of 1 gallon of water, 1 Tablespoon of baking soda, several drops of Ivory® liquid soap, and several drops of vegetable oil. Shake well before using. This keeps for weeks at room temperature. Spray the tops and bottoms of the leaves in the early morning every 7 to 10 days. Never spray if the temperature is above 80 degrees Fahrenheit. Good hygiene is important as well. Pick up affected leaves off the ground, and pick them off the plant. When cutting zinnia flowers, dip the pruners in alcohol between each cut to prevent spreading the problem. Note that this solution is NOT the same as insecticidal soap, which kills insects and must be purchased, not made.

Integrated Pest Management (IPM)

In choosing plant material for the garden, I look for plants that are resistant to some of the more common diseases, or more often, rely on the old stand-bys like the heirlooms. With edibles, I know that I may have some tomato hornworms, but I also know what my limit is. If there are only a few, I can tolerate that (especially as they turn into wonderful hummingbird-like sphinx moths). When there are too many and the leaves are being eaten quickly, I go out and handpick them, using tweezers or latex gloves and dropping them in a zipper-type plastic bag, or I drop them on the ground and stomp on them (good for getting out aggressions). There is another caterpillar that will eat the leaves of the members of the carrot family, including dill, parsley, fennel, and carrot. I have learned to plant lots of parsley (both curly and flat make good edgings) and plenty of the other plants. The caterpillars munch away for a few days, but these I leave alone as they turn into swallowtail butterflies.

I try to live peacefully with the other creatures in the garden. However, I do have a good book that identifies the critters, so I know what is good and what is bad. Remember that if you spray an insecticide (even an organic one like insecticidal soap), it kills both good and bad bugs. If you find things out of control, choose the least toxic remedy. What I have described are the tenets of IPM (Integrated Pest Management). Learn to accept the less than perfect apple, lettuce, or dahlia. And rejoice when the butterflies flock to the 'Autumn Joy' sedum in late summer and early fall.

Glossary

AARS: (All-America Rose Selections) Since 1938, winners of 2 year trials in more than 20 test gardens across America. A great honor to be bestowed on a rose.

AAS: (All-America Selections) A network of industry-based trial gardens throughout the country that test new introductions of flowers and vegetables and flowers. Winners are top-notch plants that are sure to be around for a long time.

Acid soil: soil with a pH less than 7.0. This is often found in regions with high rainfall. Most garden plants thrive in a slightly acidic soil with a pH between 6.0 and 7.0.

Alkaline soil: soil with a pH greater than 7.0. Sometimes called sweet soil. Limestone (or concrete leaching from a house foundation can contribute to alkalinity.

All-purpose fertilizer: powdered, liquid, or granular fertilizer with a balanced proportion of the three key nutrients—nitrogen (N), phosphorus (P), and potassium (K). It is suitable for maintenance nutrition for most plants. 10-10-10 is an all-purpose, balanced fertilizer.

Amend: the addition of organic matter (compost, peat moss, manure, etc.) or mineral to improve the soil.

Annual: a plant that lives its entire life in one season. It is genetically determined to germinate, grow, flower, set seed, and die the same year. In our region, there are numerous plants that are perennial in warmer climates that we grow as annuals.

***Bacillus thuringiensis* (Bt):** a biological insecticide (which can kill good and bad insects) that when sprayed at the right stage of an insect's growth, can control caterpillars, cabbageworms, and mosquito larvae. Another species (*B. papillae*), more commonly known as milky spore disease, is used to treat Japanese beetles and other grubs.

Backfill: the soil that is put back into a planting hole after the plant has been positioned. This soil may be native (as is) or amended.

Balled and burlapped: a tree or shrub grown in the field whose rootball was wrapped with protective burlap and twine when the plant was dug up to be sold or transplanted.

Bare root: a dormant plant that has been packaged without any soil around its roots. (Often young shrubs, trees and sometimes perennials purchased through the mail arrive with their exposed roots covered with moist peat or sphagnum moss, sawdust, or similar material, and wrapped in plastic.)

Beneficial insects: insects or their larvae that prey on pest organisms and their eggs. They may be flying insects, such as ladybugs, parasitic wasps, praying mantis, and soldier bugs, or soil dwellers such as predatory nematodes, earthworms, spiders, and ants.

Bicolor: a flower or leaf which has more than one color; in leaves this is often called variegation.

Biennial: a plant that takes two years to complete its life cycle; sprouting and leafing out the first year, flowering, setting seed and dying the second. Many reseed (foxglove, hollyhock) so seem perennial.

Blackspot: a fungal disease of roses that manifests itself as small black spots on the leaves. Leaves eventually turn yellow and fall off.

Bog: a waterlogged area of land, which is usually acidic.

Bones: the hardscape of a garden; the background that provides the structure; all non-plant material in the garden.

Bract: a modified leaf structure on a plant stem near its flower that resembles a petal. Often it is more colorful and visible than the actual flower, as in dogwood.

Bt: see *Bacillus thuringiensis*.

Bud: a small swelling or nub on a plant that will develop into a flower, leaf, or stem.

Bud union: the place where the top variety of a plant (usually a rose) was grafted to the rootstock; on roses this is seen as a rounded area near the bottom of the stem. With roses In the Prairie Lands states, the bud union should be at least two inches below soil level when planted in the ground.

Bush: A small shrub with many branches and no main stem.

Cane: a long pliable stem, such as a grape, but most commonly one of the main stems of a rose.

Canopy: the overhead branching area of a tree, usually referring to its extent including foliage.

Catkin: a dense spike of small flowers without petals, such as on a birch tree or Harry Lauder's walking stick.

Climber: a plant with the ability to wend its way upward, whether by tendrils, rootlets, adhesive pads, or twining stems; needs to be planted near a support.

Cold hardiness: the ability of a plant to survive the winter cold in a particular area.

Compost: organic material that has decomposed that is used as a fertilizer and soil amendment. Every gardener should be making his or her own compost, no matter how small the garden

Compost tea: liquid fertilizer made by steeping compost in water—several days is ideal; good for general watering or foliar feeding.

Composite: a flower that is actually composed of many tiny flowers. Typically, they are flat clusters of tiny, tight florets, sometimes surrounded by wider-petaled florets. Composite flowers are highly attractive to bees and beneficial insects.

Compost: organic matter that has undergone progressive decomposition by microbial and macrobial activity until it is reduced to a spongy, fluffy texture. Added to soil of any type, it improves the soil's ability to hold air and water and to drain well.

Conifer: a tree or shrub with needlelike leaves that forms a cone that holds the seeds. Most (hemlocks, pines, cedars) are evergreen, but a few (larch, dawn redwood, bald cypress) are deciduous.

Container-grown: a plant that has been grown from seed or cutting in a container, usually at a nursery. As opposed to a plant that is dug up from the ground and put into a container with soil.

Corm: the swollen energy-storing structure, analogous to a bulb, under the soil at the base of the stem of plants such as crocus and gladiolus.

Corymb: a cluster of flowers or florets that starts blooming on the outer edges and works its way in.

Crotch: the place where a major stem or branch of a shrub or tree joins the trunk.

Crown: the base of a plant at, or just beneath, the surface of the soil where the roots meet the stems.

Cultivar: a hybrid plant variety (CULTIvated VARiety) that is only reproduced vegetatively (from cuttings) or inbred seed. It is been selected for particular desirable qualities. In a plant name, the cultivar name is always denoted within single quotes, such as a specific lilac—*Syringa vulgaris* 'Scentsation'.

Cutting: 1. a method of propagation where a portion of the stem is cut from the plant and induced to produce roots, eventually growing into a plant on its own. 2. The part of a plant cut off from the parent plant that is treated so it produces roots and becomes a plant itself.

Cyme: a cluster of flowers or florets that is branched; flowers start opening from the center outward.

Dappled shade: the pattern of light cast by trees with branches open enough to let light pass through their leaves, branches, or needles.

Deadhead: to remove faded flowerheads from plants to improve their appearance, prevent seed production, and stimulate further flowering. May be done manually or by pruning. Deadheading, however, will remove seeds that some birds and other animals use as a food source.

Deciduous plants: trees and shrubs that drop their leaves in the fall and send out new leaves in the spring. Plants may also drop their leaves in order to survive a prolonged drought.

Desiccation: drying out of foliage tissues, usually due to drought or wind.

Dibble: a small pointed wooden hand tool used to make small holes in soil for seeding or transplanting small seedlings. Also known as dibber.

Dieback: a stem that has died, beginning at its tip and continuing inward, most often cause by from cold temperatures, but may also be a result of insufficient water, insect attack, nutrient deficiency, or injury.

Dioecious: male or female flowers are on separate plants. A plant of each sex is necessary for fruiting.

Disk flower: the center of a composite flower, composed of tightly packed florets. This is the center of a daisy, black-eyed Susan, purple coneflower and others.

Division: the practice of splitting apart perennial plants to create several smaller-rooted segments. The practice is useful for controlling the plant's size and for acquiring more plants; it is also essential to the health and continued flowering of certain perennials.

Dormant: the state in which a plant, although alive, is not actively growing. For many plants, especially deciduous ones, this is the winter—a survival method for cold or drought. Spring-blooming bulbs are dormant from summer through winter.

Double-flowered: a flower that has more than the usual number of petals, usually arranged in extra rows.

Drip line: the area underneath the farthest-reaching branches of a tree that receives water from rain dripping down the leaves and branches.

Dwarf: a naturally occurring smaller version of a plant, such as a dwarf conifer. The dwarf is small in relation to the original plant, but is not necessarily diminutive in stature.

Established: the point at which a newly planted tree, shrub, or flower begins to produce new growth, either leaves, flowers, or stems. This is an indication that the transplantation was successful and the roots have begun to grow and spread.

Evergreen: perennial plants (woody or herbaceous) that do not lose their foliage annually with the onset of winter. Needled or broadleaf foliage will persist and continues to function on a plant through one or more winters, aging and dropping unobtrusively in cycles of three or four years or more.

Fertilizer: a substance that is used to feed a plant—may be liquid, granular, or solid form.

Firm: to gently press the soil down around a plant after planting in order to eliminate air pockets.

Floret: a small individual flower, usually part of a cluster that comprise the larger flower

Foliar: of or about foliage.

Foliar feeding: spraying the leaves with liquid fertilizer (often kelp or fish emulsion, but may be a other liquid fertilizer diluted according to package directions); leaf tissues absorb liquid directly for fast results, and the soil is not affected.

Genus: (plural genera) a group of species which have certain traits in common. When written, the genus is capitalized, and both genus and species are italicized (*Rosa rugosa*).

Germinate: to sprout. Germination is a fertile seed's first stage of development.

Graft: the area on a woody plant where a plant with hardy roots was joined with the stem of another plant. Roses are commonly grafted. Some plants, such as members of the apple family may be grafted onto a different plant, such as an apricot onto a peach. This technique is often used to produce dwarf plants.

Hardscape: the permanent, structural, nonplant part of a landscape, such as walls, the house, sheds, pools, patios, arbors, and walkways.

Herbaceous: plants having fleshy or soft stems that die back with frost; the opposite of woody.

Hybrid: a plant that is the result of intentional or natural cross-pollination between two or more plants of the same species, variety, or genus.

Leaflet: the leaflike parts that make up a compound leaf.

Low water demand: describes plants that tolerate dry soil for varying periods of time. Typically, they have succulent, hairy, or silvery-gray foliage and tuberous roots or taproots.

Mulch: a layer of material over bare soil to protect it from erosion, slow evaporation of water, to modulate soil temperature, to prevent the soil from heaving due to thawing and freezing in the winter, and to discourage weeds. It may be inorganic (gravel, fabric) or organic (wood chips, bark, pine needles, chopped leaves). Mulch is usually put around plants.

Naturalize: (*a*) to plant seeds, bulbs, or plants in a random, informal pattern as they would appear in their natural habitat; (*b*) to adapt to and spread throughout adopted habitats (a tendency of some nonnative plants).

Nectar: the sweet fluid produced by glands on flowers that attract pollinators such as hummingbirds and honeybees for whom it is a source of energy.

Neutral soil: soil with a pH of 7.0. It is neither acid nor alkaline.

Organic material, organic matter: any material or debris that is derived from plants. It is carbon-based material capable of undergoing decomposition and decay.

Peat moss: organic matter from peat sedges (United States) or sphagnum mosses (Canada), often used to improve soil texture. The acidity of sphagnum peat moss makes it ideal for boosting or maintaining soil acidity while also improving its drainage. It also helps hold moisture.

Perennial: a flowering plant that lives over two or more seasons. Many die back with frost, but their roots survive the winter and generate new shoots in the spring.

pH: a measurement of the relative acidity (low pH) or alkalinity (high pH) of soil or water based on a scale of 1 to 14, 7 being neutral. Individual plants require soil to be within a certain range so that nutrients can dissolve in moisture and be available to them.

Pinch: to remove tender stems and/or leaves by pressing them between thumb and forefinger. This pruning technique encourages branching, compactness, and flowering in plants, or it removes aphids clustered at growing tips.

Pollen: the yellow, powdery grains in the center of a flower. A plant's male sex cells, they are transferred to the female plant parts by means of wind or animal pollinators to fertilize them and create seeds.

Raceme: an arrangement of single stalked flowers along an elongated, unbranched axis.

Ray flower: a flat petal-like floret in a daisylike flower. The ray flowers surround the central disk flower.

Rhizome: a swollen energy-storing stem structure, similar to a bulb, that lies horizontally in the soil, with roots emerging from its lower surface and growth shoots from a growing point at or near its tip, as in bearded iris.

Rootbound (or potbound): the condition of a plant that has been confined in a container too long, its roots having been forced to wrap around themselves and even swell out of the container. Successful transplanting or repotting requires untangling and trimming away of some of the matted roots.

Root flare: the transition at the base of a tree trunk where the bark tissue begins to differentiate and roots begin to form just before entering the soil. This area should not be covered with soil when planting a tree.

Self-seeding: the tendency of some plants to drop their seeds—or have the wind scatter—freely around the yard. These plant, often annuals and biennials, will come back year after year.

Self-sowing: another term for self-seeding.

Semievergreen: a plant that remains evergreen in a mild climate but looses some or all of its leaves in a colder one.

Shearing: the pruning technique whereby plant stems and branches are cut uniformly with long-bladed pruning shears (hedge shears) or powered hedge trimmers. It is used when creating and maintaining hedges and topiary.

Slow-acting fertilizer: fertilizer that is water insoluble and therefore releases its nutrients gradually as a function of soil temperature, moisture, and related microbial activity. Typically granular, it may be organic or synthetic.

Succulent growth: the sometimes undesirable production of fleshy, water-storing leaves or stems that results from overfertilization.

Tamp: when sowing a seed or putting a plant in the ground, the act of gently pressing on the soil with the palms of your hands to make contact of seed and soil, and to help eliminate air pockets.

Sucker: a new growing shoot. Underground plant roots produce suckers to form new stems and spread by means of these suckering roots to form large plantings, or colonies. Some plants produce root suckers or branch suckers as a result of pruning or wounding.

Tuber: a type of underground storage structure in a plant stem, analogous to a bulb. It generates roots below and stems above ground (example: dahlia).

Variegated: having various colors or color patterns. The term usually refers to plant foliage that is streaked, edged, blotched, or mottled with a contrasting color, often green with yellow, cream, or white.

Wings: (*a*) the corky tissue that forms edges along the twigs of some woody plants such as winged euonymus; (*b*) the flat, dried extension of tissue on some seeds, such as maple, that catch the wind and help them disseminate.

Mail-Order Plant Sources

Andre Viette Farm & Nursery
608 Longmeadow
Fishersville, VA 22939
540-943-2315
www.viette.com

*Arnold's Greenhouse
1430 Highway 57 SE
Leroy, KS 66857
620-964-2463

B & D Lilies
P.O. Box 2007
Port Townsend, WA 98368
360-765-4341
www.bdlilies.com

Bluestem Prairie Nursery
Route 2, Box 106 A
Hillsboro, IL 62049
217-532-6344
http://www.midwestplants.com/
    Categories/Natives/Natives
    Stack/nativesstack_3.html

Bluestone Perennials
7211 Middle Ridge Road
Madison, OH 44057-3096
800-852-5243
www.bluestoneperennials.com

Brady's Nursery
11200 West Kellogg
Wichita, KS 67209
316-722-7516

Brent & Becky's Bulbs
7463 Heath Trail
Gloucester, VA 23601
804-693-3966
www.brentandbeckysbulbs.com

Burpee Seed Company
300 Park Avenue
Warminster, PA 18974
800-333-5808
www.burpee.com

Busse Nursery
13579 10th Street NW
Cokato, MN 55321
612-286-2654
www.midwestplants.com/
    Categories/ Natives/
    body_natives.html

Chaplin Nursery
27814 27th Drive
Arkansas City, KS 670015

Forest Farm
990 Tetherow Road
Williams, OR 97544-9599
541-846-7269
www.forestfarm.com

Gurneys Seed & Nursery
110 Capital Street
Yankton, SD 57079
605-665-1930
www.gurneys.com

**Henry Field Seed &
    Nursery Co.**
415 N Burnett Street
Shenandoah, IA
www.henryfields.com

Heronswood Nursery
7530 E 288th Street
Kingston, WA 98346
360-297-4172
www.heronswood.com

Hillside Nursery
2200 S. Hillside
Witchita, KS 67211
316-686-6414
http://www.360wichita.com/tou
    rs/landscaping/hillside.html

Lilypons Water Gardens®
6800 Lilypons Road
Post Office Box 10
Buckeystown, MD 21717-0010
800-999-5459
info@lilypons.com

Matterhorn Nursery
227 Summit Park Road
Spring Valley, NY 10977
845-354-5986
www.matterhornnursery.com

Milaeger's Garden
4838 Douglas Avenue
Racine, WI 53402-2498
800-669-1229 x123

Niche Gardens
1111 Dawson Road
Chapel Hill, NC 27516
919-967-0078
www.nichegdn.com

Nichols Garden Nursery
119 Old Salem Road NE
Albany, OR 97321
541-928-9280
www.nicholsgardennursery.com

Northwind Perennial Farm
7047 Hospital Road
Burlington, WI 53105
262-248-8229
    www.northwindperennial
    farm.com

*Oakcrest Gardens
22871 Kane Avenue
Glenwood, IA 51534
712-527-4974
www.oakcrestgardens.com

Park Seed
1 Parkton Avenue
Greenwood, SC 29647
800-213-0076
www.parkseed.com

Plant Delights Nursery
9241 Sauls Road
Raleigh, NC 27603
919-772-4794
www.plantdelights.com

Prairie Moon Nursery
Route 3 Box 163
Dept. SDIZ
Winona, MN 55987
507-452-1362
nepenthes.lycaeum.org/Commer
    ce/pmn.html

Prairie Nursery
P.O. Box 306
Westfield WI 53964
800-476-9453
www.prairienursey.com

*Ridge Road Nursery
3195 Saint Catherine Road
Bellevue, IA 52031
563-583-1381

Roslyn Nursery
211 Burrs Lane
Dix Hills NY 11746
631-643-9347
roslynnursery.com

Seed Savers Exchange
3076 North Winn Road
Decorah, IA 52101
563-382-5990
www.seedsavers.org

Song Sparrow Perennial Farm
13101 East Rye Road
Avalon WI 53505
800-553-3715
www.songsparrow.com

*The New Peony Farm
St. Paul, MN
Phone: 651-457-8994
General Information:
kent@newpeonyfarm.com

Van Bourgondien
P.O. Box 1000
Babylon, New York 11702
800-327-4268
www.dutchbulbs.com

Wayside Gardens
1 Garden Lane
Hodges, SC 29695
800-213-0379
www.waysidegardens.com

White Flower Farm
P.O. Box 50, Route 63
Litchfield, CT 06759
800-503-9624
www.whiteflowerfarm.com

*Willowglen Nursery
512 Lost Mile Road
Decorah IA 52101-7746
319-735-5570

*Visit in person; does not do mail order, but worth the trip.

Destinations for Gardeners

Kansas

Botanica, The Wichita Gardens
701 Amidon
Wichita, KS 67203
316-264-0448
www.botanica.org/
Contact Pat for talk: 312-264-0448

City Park Rose Garden
Poyntz Avenue & 11th Streets
1101 Poyntz Avenue
Manhattan, KS 66502
785-587-2489

Dyck Arboretum of the Plains
Hesston College
177 West Hickory Street
Hesston, KS 67062
620-327-8127
www.dyckarboretum.org

International Forest of Friendship Trail
Rt. 59, Warnock Lake
Atchison, KS 66002
913-367-2427
www.ninety-nines.org/fof3.html

Johnson County Community College
12345 College Boulevard
Overland Park, KS 66210
913-469-8500 x4536
web.jccc.net/academic/science/greenhouse/
    greenhs.htmcontact

Kansas State University Gardens
2021 Throckmorton Plant Sciences Center
Manhattan, KS 66506
785-532-6170
www.ksu.edu/gardens/

Konza Prairie Research Natural Area
McDowell Creek Road
232 Ackert Hall
Manhattan, KS 66506-0112
785-587-0441
www.ksu.edu/biology/bio/major/konza.html

Municipal Rose Garden
Huron Park, between 6th & 7th
Parks & Recreation, 3488 W. Drive
Kansas City, KS 96109
913-596-7077

Overland Park Arboretum & Botanical Gardens
179th & Antioch
8500 Santa Fe Drive
Overland Park, KS 66212
913-685-3604
www.opprf.org/arboretum.htm

Parsons Arboretum
2100 Wilson
Parsons, KS 67357
316-421-5677
www.parsonsks.com/arbor.htm

Riggs Arboretum
Waterloo, Kansas
785-227-3858
ome.earthlink.net/~bragan78/
    StJohnTreeBoard/riggs1.htm

Smith Municipal Rose Garden
Loose Park, 51st & Wornall
5200 Pennsylvania
Kansas City, KS 64112
913-784-5300

Iowa

Bentonsport Gardens
Bentonsport, IA
www.netins.net/showcase/rosegarden/

Better Homes and Gardens Test Garden
(Open Fridays from Noon to 2 pm only from
    May to October)
1716 Locust Street
Des Moines, IA 50309-3023
515-284-3994
http://www.bhg.com

Bickelhaupt Arboretum
340 S. 14th Street
Clinton, IA 52732-5432
563-242-4771
www.bickarb.org

Brenton Arboretum
2629 Palo Circle
Dallas Center, IA 50063
515-992-4211
www.brentonarboretum.com

Brucemore
2160 Linden Drive SE
Cedar Rapids, IA 52403-1748
319-362-7375
www.brucemore.org/

Cedar Valley Arboretum & Botanic Gardens
1927 East Orange Road
Waterloo, IA 50701
319-226-4966
www.cedarnet.org/gardens

Crapo and Dankwardt Parks
Burlington, IA
www.visit.burlington.ia.us/parks.html

Des Moines Botanical Center
909 East River Drive
Des Moines, IA 50316
515-323-8900
www.botanicalcenter.com

Dubuque Arboretum & Botanical Gardens
3800 Arboretum Drive
Dubuque, IA 52001
563-556-2100
www.dubuquearboretum.com

Earl May Nursery and Garden Center,
Trial Gardens
Highway 59 S
Shenandoah, IA 51601
712-246-2780
www.earlmay.com

Iowa Arboretum
1875 Peach Avenue
Madrid, IA 50156
515-795-3216
www.iowaarboretum.com

Prairie Pedlar
1677 270th Street
Odebolt, IA 51458-7555
712-668-4840
showcase.netins.net/web/ppgarden/

Reiman Gardens
Iowa State University
1407 Elwood Drive
Ames, IA 50011
515-294-2710
www.reimangardens.iastate.edu

Vander Veer Botanical Park
214 West Central Park
Davenport, IA 24803
563-326-7318
davenportmon.homestead.com/VanderVeerPark.
html

Nebraska
Alice Abel Arboretum, Nebraska Wesleyan
University
5000 St. Paul Avenue
Lincoln, NE 68504
402-465-2374
arboretum.unl.edu/poppages/affiliates.html

All America Selection Garden at Fort Omaha
30th & Fort
Omaha, NE 68104
402-556-7028
arboretum.unl.edu/poppages/affiliates.htm

Arboretum at University of Nebraska, Kearney
905 W. 25th Street
Kearney, NE 68847-4238
308-865-8883
arboretum.unl.edu/affiliate.html

Bellevue College Arboretum
Galvin Road
Bellevue, NE 68005
402-291-8100

Blair Community Arboretum
1129 Still Meadow Circle
Blair, NE 68008
402-426-4644
arboretum.unl.edu/poppages/affiliates.html

Chautauqua Park Arboretum
205 N. 4th Street
Beatrice, NE 69310
402-228-5248
arboretum.unl.edu/affiliate.html

Doane College Arboretum
1014 Boswell Avenue
Crete, NE 68333-2497
402-826-2161
arboretum.unl.edu/affiliate.html

Fontenelle Forest Nature Center
1111 Bellevue Boulevard N.
Bellevue, NE 68005-4000
402-731-3140
www.fontenelleforest.org/come.html

Governor Furnas Arboretum
3419 S. 42nd Street
Lincoln, NE 68506
402-489-6333
www.visitnemahacounty.org/nature/furnas.htm

J. Norman Walburn Memorial Arboretum
Cambridge City Park
Cambridge, NE 69022
308-697-3317
arboretum.unl.edu/poppages/affiliates.htm

John G. Neihardt State Historic Site
Elm & Washington Streets
Bancroft, NE 68004-0344
402-648-3388
www.nebraskahistory.org/sites/neihardt/

Joshua Turner Arboretum, Union College
3800 S. 48th Street
Lincoln, NE 68506-4300
402-488-2331
www.ilovegardens.com/Nebraska_Gardens/
    nebraska_gardens.htm

Lauritzen Gardens, Omaha's Botanical Center
100 Bancroft Street
Omaha, NE 68108
402-346-4002
www.omahabotanicalgardens.org

Metropolitan Community College Arboretum
30th & Fort Streets
Omaha, NE 68111
402-449-8400
arboretum.unl.edu/affiliate.html

Midland Lutheran College Heritage Arboretum
900 N Clarkson
Fremont, NE 68025
402-941-6328
www.mlc.edu/studentlife/arboretum/

**Nebraska College of Technical Agriculture
    Arboretum**
404 E 7th Street
Curtis, NE 69025
308-367-4124
arboretum.unl.edu/affiliate.html

Nebraska State Fair Park Arboretum
1800 State Fair Park Drive
Lincoln, NE 68508
402-474-5371
www.statefair.org

Nebraska Statewide Arboretum
University of Nebraska
206 Biochemistry Hall
Lincoln, NE 68583-0715
402-472-2971
www.arboretum.unl.edu

Nine-Mile Prairie
Lincoln, NE
402-472-2715
http://www.snrs.unl.edu/wedin/nefieldsites/
    NineMile/nine_mile_prairie.htm

Pheasant Point Arboretum
Lower Republican NRD
PO Box 618
Alma, NE 68920
308-928-2182
arboretum.unl.edu/poppages/affiliates.htm

Prairie Pines Arboretum
112th & Adams Street
Forestry, Fisheries & Wildlife,
    UNL-101 Plant Indu
Lincoln, NE 68583-0814
402-466-2491
snrs.unl.edu/wedin/nefieldsites/Prairie%20Pines/
    prairie_pines.htm

Sallows Arboretum and Conservatory
324 Laramie Avenue
Alliance, NE 69301
308-762-7422
www.westnebraska.com/SallowsSunkenGard.htm

University of Nebraska-Lincoln Botanical
    Garden & Arboretum
38th & Holdrege
P.O. Box 880609
Lincoln, NE 68508-0609
402-472-2679
www.unl.edu/unlbga/

West Pawnee Park Arboretum
2122 14th Street
Columbus, NE 68601
arboretum.unl.edu/affiliate.html

North Dakota
Gunlogson Arboretum Nature Preserve
Icelandic State Park, Star Route 1, Box 64A
Cavalier, ND 58220
701-265-4561

International Peace Garden
RR 1 Box 116 (at U.S./Canadian border)
Dunseith, ND 58329-9761
701-263-4390
www.peacegarden.com

Red River Zoo
4220 21st Avenue S.
Fargo, ND 58104-8603
701-277-9240
www.redriverzoo.org

South Dakota
Journey Museum
222 New York Street
Rapid City, SD 57701
605-394-6923
www.journeymuseum.org

Kuhnert Arboretum
E. Melgaard Road
Aberdeen, SD 57401
605-626-7015
www.aberdeen.sd.us/parks/park_tbl.pdf

McCrory Gardens
6th St. & 22nd Avenue
SD State Univ. Horticulture Dept.
Brookings, SD 57007
605-688-5137
martin_maca@sdstate.edu

McKennon Park
600 E. 7th Street
Dept. of Parks & Recreation, City of Sioux Falls
Sioux Falls, SD 57102-0406
605-367-7060

Sioux Prairie
Wentworth, SD
712-258-0838
www.avalon.net/~yiams/scprairie.html

Plans For My Garden

Garden Notes

Garden Notes

Garden Notes

Garden Notes

Garden Notes

Garden Notes

Garden Notes

Garden Notes

Garden Notes

Bibliography

Bailey, L. H. *How Plants Get Their Names*. New York, New York: Dover Publications, Inc., 1963.

Bailey, Liberty Hyde Hortorium. *Hortus Third*. New York, New York: Macmillan Publishing Company, 1976.

Ball, Liz. *Step-by-Step Garden Basics*. Des Moines, Iowa: Better Homes and Gardens® Books, 2000.

___. *Step-by-Step Yard Care*. Des Moines, Iowa: Better Homes and Gardens® Books, 2000.

Barash, Cathy Wilkinson. *Choosing Plant Combinations*. Des Moines, Iowa: Better Homes and Gardens® Books, 1999.

___. *Edible Flowers from Garden to Palate*. Golden, Colorado: Fulcrum Publishing, 1993.

___. *Evening Gardens*. Shelburne, Vermont: Chapters Publishing Ltd., 1993

___. *The Climbing Garden*. New York, New York: Friedman Fairfax Publishers, 2000.

Beales, Peter. *Roses*. New York, New York: Henry Holt and Company, 1992.

Beaubaire, Nancy, editor. *Native Perennials*. Brooklyn, New York: the Brooklyn Botanic Garden, Inc., 1996.

Bennett, Jennifer, editor. *Groundcovers*. Camden East, Ontario, Canada: Camden House, 1987.

Binetti, Marianne. *Tips for Carefree Landscapes*. Pownal, Vermont: Storey Communications, Inc., 1990.

Brickell, Christopher and Zuk, Judith D, editors-in-chief. *The American Horticultural Society A-Z Encyclopedia of Garden Plants*. New York, New York: DK Publishing, 1996.

Burrell, C. Colston. *Perennials for Today's Gardens*. Des Moines, Iowa: Better Homes and Gardens® Books, 2000.

Coughlin, Roberta M., *The Gardener's Companion – a Book of Lists and Lore*. New York, New York: HarperPerennial, 1991.

Cutler, Karan Davis, editor. *Flowering Vines*. Brooklyn, New York: the Brooklyn Botanic Garden, Inc., 1999.

Cutler, Karan Davis, editor. *Starting from Seed*. Brooklyn, New York: the Brooklyn Botanic Garden, Inc., 1998

Dirr, Michael. *Manual of Woody Landscape Plants - Their Identification, Ornamental Characteristics, Culture, Propagation and Use*. Champaign, Illinois: Stipes Publishing Company, 1990.

DiSabato-Aust, Tracy. *The Well-Tended Perennial Garden*. Portland, Oregon: Timber Press, 1998.

Druse, Ken with Roach Margaret. *The Natural Habitat Garden*. New York, New York: Clarkson Potter Publishers, 1994.

Dunn, Dawn. *Growing Herbs*. London, England: Cassell Publishers Limited, 1997.

Editors of Sunset books and Sunset Magazine. *Herbs, An Illustrated Guide*. Menlo Park, California, Sunset Publishing Corporation, 1993.

Ellefson, Connie, Stephens, Tom, and Welsh, Doug. *Xeriscape Gardening – Water Conservation for the American Landscape*. New York, New York: Macmillan Publishers, 1992.

Frieze, Charlotte M. *The Zone Garden 3-4-5*. New York, New York. Fireside, Simon & Schuster, 1997.

Gershuny, Grace. *Start with the Soil*. Emmaus, Pennsylvania: Rodale Press, 1993.

Griffiths, Mark. *Index of Garden Plants*. Portland, Oregon: Timber Press, 1994.

Halpin, Anne. *Horticulture Gardener's Desk Reference*. New York, New York: Macmillan, 1996.

Halpin, Anne Moyer and the editors of Rodale Press. *Foolproof Planting*. Emmaus, Pennsylvania: Rodale Press, 1990

Heger, Mike & Whitman, John. *Growing Perennials in Cold Climates*. Lincolnwood (Chicago), Illinois: Contemporary Books, *1998*

Hogan, Sean. *Flora, A Gardener's Encyclopedia*. Portland, Oregon: Timber Press, 2003

Hyland, Bob, editor. *Shrubs, The New Glamour Plants*. Brooklyn, New York: the Brooklyn Botanic Garden, Inc., 1994,

Jason, Dan. *Greening the Garden – A Guide to Sustainable Growing*. Philadelphia, Pennsylvania: New Society Publishers, 1991

Lanza, Patricia. *Lasagna Gardening*. Emmaus, Pennsylvania: Rodale Press, 1998.

Loewer, Peter. *Tough Plants for Tough Places*. Emmaus, Pennsylvania: Rodale Press, 1992.

Marinelli, Janet, editor. *Going Native*. Brooklyn, New York: the Brooklyn Botanic Garden, Inc., 1994,

Neal, Bill. *Gardener's Latin*. Chapel Hill, North Carolina: Algonquin books of Chapel Hill, 1992.

Ottesen, Carole. *The Native Plant Primer*. New York, New York: Harmony Books, 1995.

Philbrick, Helen and John. *The Bug Book–Harmless Insect Control*. Pownal, Vermont: Storey Communications, Inc., 1986.

Phillips, Ellen & Burrell, C. Colston. *Rodale's Illustrated Encyclopedia of Perennials*. Emmaus, Pennsylvania: Rodale Press, 1993

Proctor, Rob. Annuals, *A Gardener's Guide*. Brooklyn, New York: the Brooklyn Botanic Garden, Inc., 1992,

Ruggiero, Michael. *Perennial Gardening*. New York, New York: Pantheon Books, 1994.

Scanniello, Stephen, editor. *Easy-Care Roses*. Brooklyn, New York: the Brooklyn Botanic Garden, Inc., 1995.

Schultz, Warren, editor. *Natural Insect Control*. Brooklyn, New York: the Brooklyn Botanic Garden, Inc., 1994.

Sternberg, Guy and Wilson, Jim. *Landscaping with Native Trees*. Shelburne, Vermont: Chapters Publishing, Ltd., 1995.

Wallheim, Lance. *The Natural Rose Gardener*. Tucson, Arizona: Ironwood Press, 1994

Weiner, Michael A. *Earth Medicine Earth Food*. New York, New York: Fawcett Columbine, 1972

Wolfe, Pamela. *Midwest Gardens*. Chicago, Illinois: Chicago Review Press, Incorporated, 1991.

Photography Credits

William Adams: pages 112, 217, 218

Liz Ball and Rick Ray: pages 22, 26, 46, 52, 58, 59, 70, 81, 96, 122, 126, 127, 130, 168, 175, 176, 184, 186, 188, 193, 197, 205, 206, 214, 216

Cathy Wilkinson Barash: pages 30, 35, 37, 61, 62, 63, 67, 83, 131, 140, 142, 160, 161, 164

Rob Cardillo: front cover

Laura Coit: pages 159, 169

Mike Dirr: page 200

Thomas Eltzroth: pages 14, 20, 21, 24, 27, 28, 31, 32, 33, 34, 38, 40, 41, 43, 50, 53, 55, 56, 60, 64, 66, 68, 71, 73, 75, 80, 82, 85, 86, 87, 90, 92, 93, 94, 95, 97, 98, 99, 100, 101, 102, 103, 107, 109, 119, 120, 123, 129, 132, 134, 135, 136, 137, 138, 139, 144, 147, 148, 149, 150, 151, 152, 154, 156, 157, 163, 166, 172, 174, 178, 181, 183, 187, 190, 192, 194, 195, 196, 198, 201, 202, 207, 212, 219, back cover: 3rd photo

Pamela Harper: pages 74, 111, 153, 173

Dency Kane: pages 29, 143

Dave Mackenzie: pages 105, 113

Charles Mann: pages 42, 171, 180, 185

Jerry Pavia: pages 13, 25, 36, 39, 45, 49, 76, 77, 79, 106, 108, 110, 115, 116, 117, 118, 124, 128, 133, 141, 145, 146, 155, 165, 167, 177, 179, 199, 203, 204, 208, back cover: 1st, 2nd, and 4th photos

Felder Rushing: pages 17, 44, 72, 114, 125, 211

Ralph Snodsmith: pages 54, 182

Neil Soderstrom: page 162

Greg Speichert: page 215

Mark Turner: pages 51, 57, 65, 213

Andre Viette: pages 23, 78, 121, 170

David Winger: page 10

Plant Index by Botanical Name

Plant Index by Common Name

Featured plant selections are indicated in **boldface**.

Meet the Author

Cathy Wilkinson Barash

Cathy Wilkinson Barash is a life-long organic gardener. She has been active in the Garden Writers Association (a group of over 1800 professional garden communicators) since 1988. She is currently Garden Writers Association President.

From childhood, Cathy has held a firm belief in economy of space and time in the garden by planting edibles ("beautiful and tasty") among ornamentals. A garden designer whose designs have been published nationally, Cathy specializes in low-maintenance and edible landscapes. Anne Raver of *The New York Times* was the first to give her the appellation "gourmet horticulturist."

Cathy is author of nine books, and is a successful photographer, nationally acclaimed speaker, and avid cat lover. She is best known as the author of *Edible Flowers from Garden to Palate*, which Martha Stewart described on her television show as "very excellent." The book, published in 1993 and celebrating its 10th year in distribution was nominated for a Julia Child Cookbook Award and garnered an Award of Excellence from the Garden Writers Association of America.

Cathy's other books include *The Climbing Garden, Choosing Plant Combinations, Taylor's Weekend Guide: Kitchen Gardens, Edible Flowers: Desserts & Drinks, Vines & Climbers, Evening Gardens, Roses,* and *The Cultivated Gardener,* co-authored with Jim Wilson. Her writing and photographs have appeared in hundreds of books, calendars, magazines, and newspapers, including *The New York Times, Christian Science Monitor, Horticulture, Woman's Day*, and *Home.*

A life-long New Yorker (Long Islander), she moved to Des Moines in 1997. After moving to her second Des Moines home, she transformed a front lawn into a showplace garden in four months. Her garden combines edible landscaping with container plantings, and innumerable Prairie Lands plants. Of her gardening experience in Des Moines, she says, "It was like learning to garden all over again." She is continuing to learn and grow, while in awe of the Prairie Lands plants and gardens.